MY
GENEALOGY

14 generations – 16383 ancestors

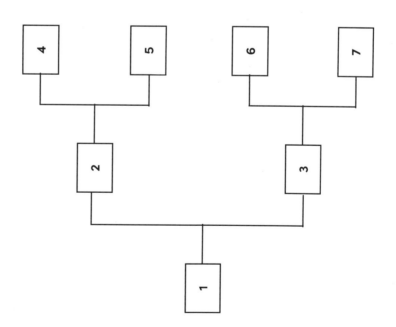

Olivier Léonard

Summary

Index

Individuals sheets

Extensions

This book belongs to:

....

Search Start Date :

....

ASCENDANTS INDEX

Several genealogical numbering systems have been widely adopted for presenting family trees and pedigree charts in text format.

Sosa-Stradonitz Method also known as Ahnentafel, the Eytzinger Method, allows for the numbering of ancestors beginning with a descendant. This system allows one to derive an ancestor's number without compiling the complete list, and allows one to derive an ancestor's relationship based on their number. The number of a person's father is twice their own number, and the number of a person's mother is twice their own, plus one. For instance, if John Smith is 10, his father is 20, and his mother is 21.

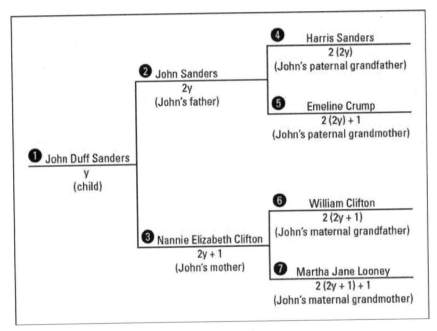

Below you will find the ancestry of each grandparent so that you can locate each of your ancestors in relation to you (sosa 1) until generation 14.

To better visualize the progress of your research, color the boxes of the ancestors that have been found (in green for example).

Index: Ancestors of the paternal grandfather (sosa 4)

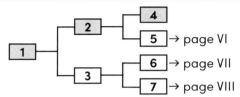

→ page VI
→ page VII
→ page VIII

→ To better visualize the progress of your research, color the boxes of the ancestors that have been found (in green for example).
→ The numbers of peer sosas are men.

Generation III	Generation IV	Generation V	Generation VI	Generation VII	Generation VIII	Generations IX to XIV

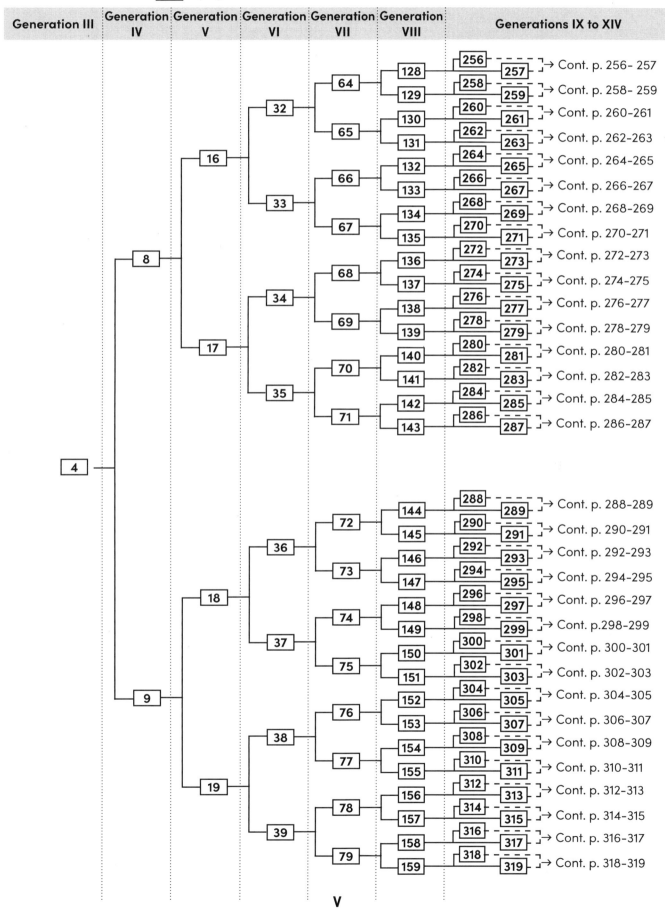

→ Cont. p. 256-257
→ Cont. p. 258-259
→ Cont. p. 260-261
→ Cont. p. 262-263
→ Cont. p. 264-265
→ Cont. p. 266-267
→ Cont. p. 268-269
→ Cont. p. 270-271
→ Cont. p. 272-273
→ Cont. p. 274-275
→ Cont. p. 276-277
→ Cont. p. 278-279
→ Cont. p. 280-281
→ Cont. p. 282-283
→ Cont. p. 284-285
→ Cont. p. 286-287
→ Cont. p. 288-289
→ Cont. p. 290-291
→ Cont. p. 292-293
→ Cont. p. 294-295
→ Cont. p. 296-297
→ Cont. p.298-299
→ Cont. p. 300-301
→ Cont. p. 302-303
→ Cont. p. 304-305
→ Cont. p. 306-307
→ Cont. p. 308-309
→ Cont. p. 310-311
→ Cont. p. 312-313
→ Cont. p. 314-315
→ Cont. p. 316-317
→ Cont. p. 318-319

V

Index: Ancestors of the paternal grandmother (sosa 5)

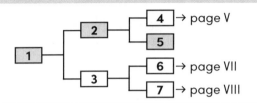

→ To better visualize the progress of your research, color the boxes of the ancestors that have been found (in green for example).
→ The numbers of peer sosas are men.

Generation III	Generation IV	Generation V	Generation VI	Generation VII	Generation VIII	Generations IX to XIV

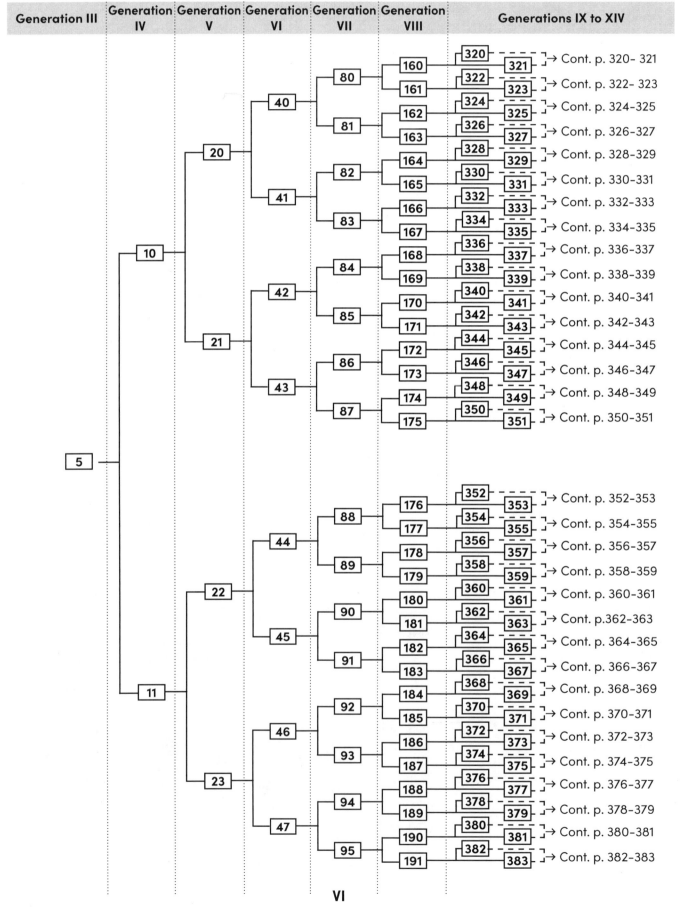

→ Cont. p. 320- 321
→ Cont. p. 322- 323
→ Cont. p. 324-325
→ Cont. p. 326-327
→ Cont. p. 328-329
→ Cont. p. 330-331
→ Cont. p. 332-333
→ Cont. p. 334-335
→ Cont. p. 336-337
→ Cont. p. 338-339
→ Cont. p. 340-341
→ Cont. p. 342-343
→ Cont. p. 344-345
→ Cont. p. 346-347
→ Cont. p. 348-349
→ Cont. p. 350-351
→ Cont. p. 352-353
→ Cont. p. 354-355
→ Cont. p. 356-357
→ Cont. p. 358-359
→ Cont. p. 360-361
→ Cont. p.362-363
→ Cont. p. 364-365
→ Cont. p. 366-367
→ Cont. p. 368-369
→ Cont. p. 370-371
→ Cont. p. 372-373
→ Cont. p. 374-375
→ Cont. p. 376-377
→ Cont. p. 378-379
→ Cont. p. 380-381
→ Cont. p. 382-383

Index: Ancestors of the maternal grandfather (sosa 6)

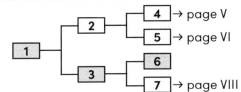

→ page V
→ page VI

→ page VIII

→ To better visualize the progress of your research, color the boxes of the ancestors that have been found (in green for example).
→ The numbers of peer sosas are men.

Generation III	Generation IV	Generation V	Generation VI	Generation VII	Generation VIII	Generations IX to XIV

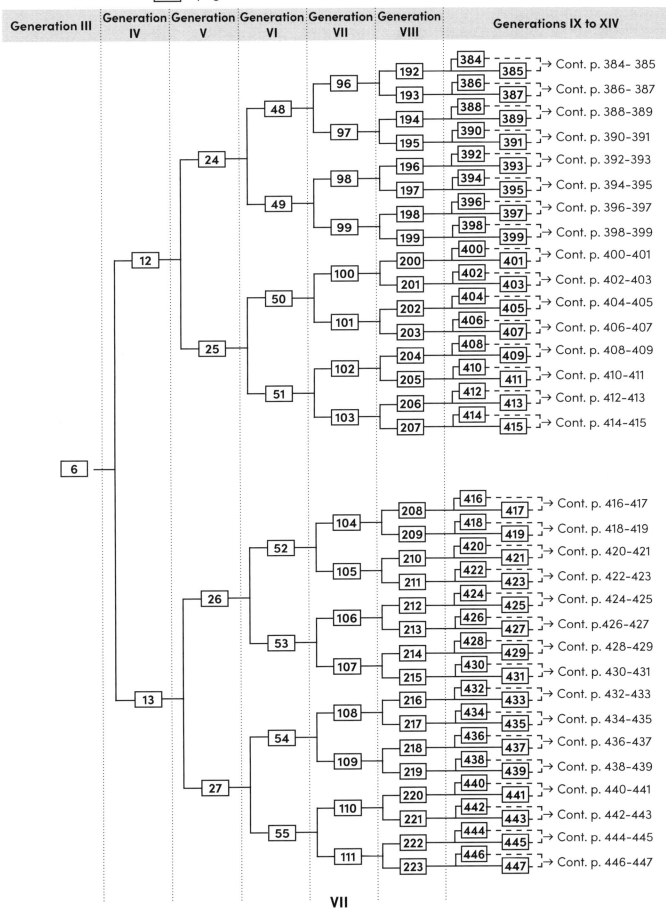

→ Cont. p. 384- 385
→ Cont. p. 386- 387
→ Cont. p. 388-389
→ Cont. p. 390-391
→ Cont. p. 392-393
→ Cont. p. 394-395
→ Cont. p. 396-397
→ Cont. p. 398-399
→ Cont. p. 400-401
→ Cont. p. 402-403
→ Cont. p. 404-405
→ Cont. p. 406-407
→ Cont. p. 408-409
→ Cont. p. 410-411
→ Cont. p. 412-413
→ Cont. p. 414-415
→ Cont. p. 416-417
→ Cont. p. 418-419
→ Cont. p. 420-421
→ Cont. p. 422-423
→ Cont. p. 424-425
→ Cont. p.426-427
→ Cont. p. 428-429
→ Cont. p. 430-431
→ Cont. p. 432-433
→ Cont. p. 434-435
→ Cont. p. 436-437
→ Cont. p. 438-439
→ Cont. p. 440-441
→ Cont. p. 442-443
→ Cont. p. 444-445
→ Cont. p. 446-447

VII

Index: Ancestors of the maternal grandmother (sosa 7)

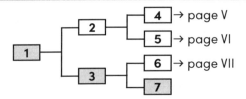

1
2
4 → page V
5 → page VI
3
6 → page VII
7

→ To better visualize the progress of your research, color the boxes of the ancestors that have been found (in green for example).
→ The numbers of peer sosas are men.

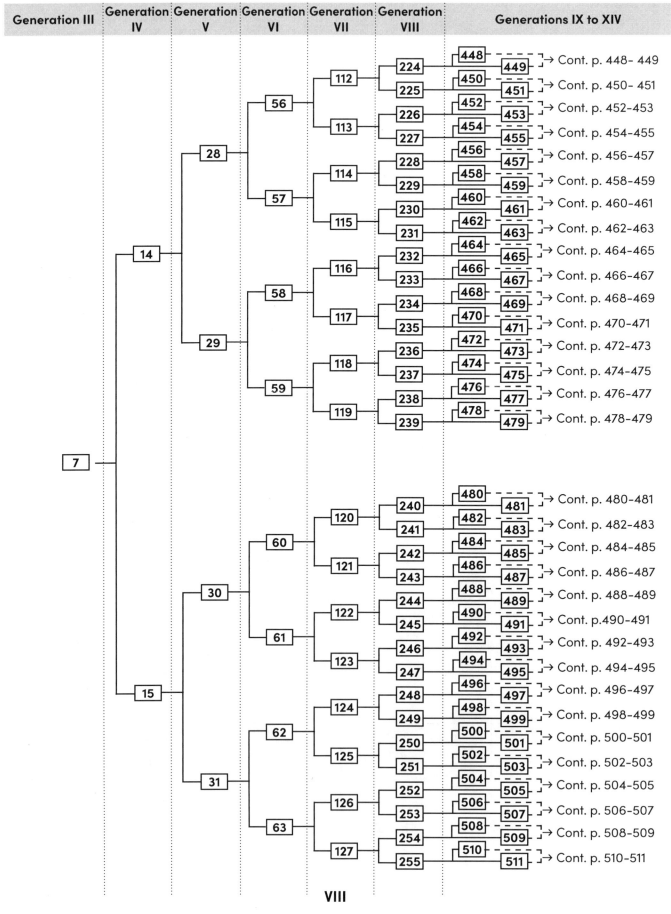

Generation III	Generation IV	Generation V	Generation VI	Generation VII	Generation VIII	Generations IX to XIV

→ Cont. p. 448- 449
→ Cont. p. 450- 451
→ Cont. p. 452-453
→ Cont. p. 454-455
→ Cont. p. 456-457
→ Cont. p. 458-459
→ Cont. p. 460-461
→ Cont. p. 462-463
→ Cont. p. 464-465
→ Cont. p. 466-467
→ Cont. p. 468-469
→ Cont. p. 470-471
→ Cont. p. 472-473
→ Cont. p. 474-475
→ Cont. p. 476-477
→ Cont. p. 478-479
→ Cont. p. 480-481
→ Cont. p. 482-483
→ Cont. p. 484-485
→ Cont. p. 486-487
→ Cont. p. 488-489
→ Cont. p.490-491
→ Cont. p. 492-493
→ Cont. p. 494-495
→ Cont. p. 496-497
→ Cont. p. 498-499
→ Cont. p. 500-501
→ Cont. p. 502-503
→ Cont. p. 504-505
→ Cont. p. 506-507
→ Cont. p. 508-509
→ Cont. p. 510-511

VIII

Surname : ....First name : ....

▶Generation 1 – *Origin*

□ *Implex*   Child : □ *Legitimate* □ *Natural* □ *Adopted* □ *Found* □ *Recognized* □ *Adulterated*

Born : ....in...

Baptized : ....in...

Godfather : ....Godmother : ....

Son/Daughter of : ....and: ....

Nationality : ....Religion : ....Studies: ....

Occupation(s) : ....

Deceased : ....in...............................Cause:...............................

□ *Buried* □*Cremated* □ *Disappeared* on : ....in :........................

💍 **MARITAL STATUS**   □ *Civil Marriage*   □ *Religious Marriage*   □ *Free Union*

Date : ....in.. □ *Marriage contract*

With : ....□ *Separation* □ *Divorce* □ *Widowhood* Date :........................

Notes : ....

👪 **CHILDREN** ♂ .... ♀ ....

	Gen.	° Birth	† Death	Spouse
....	......	....	....	....
....	......	....	....	....
....	......	....	....	....
....	......	....	....	....
....	......	....	....	....
....	......	....	....	....

💍 **OTHER UNION(S)/** 👪 **CHILDREN** ....

....

....

....

👪 **SIBLINGS**   ♂ .... ♀ ....   1..

2...3...4...

5...6...7...

8...9...10..

👤 **INDIVIDUAL EVENTS** ....

....

....

....

....

....

....

📑 **NOTES** ....

....

....

....

4	5	6	7
	2		3
		1	

Surname: .... First name : .... ♂

Child : □ *Legitimate* □ *Natural* □ *Adopted* □ *Found* □ *Recognized* □ *Adulterated* □ *Implex*

Born : ....in..

Baptized : ....in..

Godfather: ....Godmother : ....

Son of : ....and:...

Nationality : ....Religion : ....Studies: ....

Occupation(s) : ....

Deceased : ....in.............................Cause:..........................

□ *Buried* □ *Cremated* □ *Disappeared* on : ....in :....................

⚭ MARITAL STATUS   □ *Civil Marriage* □ *Religious Marriage* □ *Free Union*

Date : ....in.. □ *Marriage contract*

Witnesses : ....

....

□ *Separation* □ *Divorce* □ *Widowhood of the groom/bride* Date : ....

👪 FAMILY EVENTS ....

....

....

....

....

....

⚭ OTHER UNION(S)/👪 CHILDREN ....

....

....

....

👪 SIBLINGS ▶ *Details page 5* ♂ .... ♀ .... 1.....................................

2..3...4...............................

5..6...7...............................

8..9...10.............................

👤 INDIVIDUAL EVENTS ....

....

....

....

⛑ MILITARY LIFE Assignment(s) : ....

Campaign(s): ....

Medal(s) : ....□ *Died in combat* □ *Injured on* : ....

....

8	9	10	11
4		5	
2			
1			

📑 NOTES ....

....

....

....

....

♀ Surname : .... First name : ....

▶ Generation 2 – *ascendant*

□ *Implex*　　Child : □ *Legitimate* □ *Natural* □ *Adopted* □ *Found* □ *Recognized* □ *Adulterated*

Born : ....in..

Baptized : ....in..

Godfather: ....Godmother : ....

Daughter of : ....and: ....

Nationality : ....Religion : ....Studies: ....

Occupation(s) : ....

Deceased : ....in.............................Cause:..........................

□ *Buried* □ *Cremated* □ *Disappeared* on : ....in :.............................

👫 CHILDREN ♂ .... ♀ ....

	Gen.	° Birth	† Death	Spouse
....	......	....	....	....
....	......	....	....	....
....	......	....	....	....
....	......	....	....	....
....	......	....	....	....
....	......	....	....	....
....	......	....	....	....
....	......	....	....	....
....	......	....	....	....
....	......	....	....	....

💍 OTHER UNION(S)/ 👫 CHILDREN ....

....

....

👫 SIBLINGS ▶ *Details page 7* ♂ .... ♀ .... 1...

2... 3... 4...

5... 6... 7...

8... 9... 10...

👤 INDIVIDUAL EVENTS ....

....

....

....

....

....

....

📝 NOTES ....

....

....

....

....

12	13	14	15

| 6 | | 7 |

3

1

Surname: ....First name : .... ♂

Child : □ *Legitimate* □ *Natural* □ *Adopted* □ *Found* □ *Recognized* □ *Adulterated*   □ *Implex*

Born : ....in...

Baptized : ....in...

Godfather: ....Godmother : ....

Son of : ....and: ....

Nationality : ....Religion : ....Studies: ....

Occupation(s) : ....

Deceased : ....in...Cause:........................

□ *Buried* □ *Cremated* □ *Disappeared* on : ....in : ....

⚭ MARITAL STATUS   □ *Civil Marriage* □ *Religious Marriage* □ *Free Union*

Date : ....in...   □ *Marriage contract*

Witnesses : ....

....

□ *Separation* □ *Divorce* □ *Widowhood of the groom/bride* Date : ....

👫 FAMILY EVENTS ....

....
....
....
....
....

⚭ OTHER UNION(S)/ 👫 CHILDREN ....

....
....
....
....

👫 SIBLINGS   ▶ *Details page 9*   ♂ ....   ♀ ....   1................................

2................................   3................................   4................................

5................................   6................................   7................................

8................................   9................................   10................................

👤 INDIVIDUAL EVENTS ....

....
....
....

⛑ MILITARY LIFE   Assignment(s) : ....

Campaign(s): ....

Medal(s) : ....□ *Died in combat* □ *Injured on* : ....

....

16	17	18	19

8		9

4

2

📑 NOTES ....
....
....
....
....

♀ Surname : ....First name : ....

▶ Generation 3 – *paternal ascendant*

☐ *Implex*   Child : ☐ *Legitimate* ☐ *Natural* ☐ *Adopted* ☐ *Found* ☐ *Recognized* ☐ *Adulterated*

Born : ....in..

Baptized : ....in..

Godfather: ....Godmother : ....

Daughter of : ....and: ....

Nationality : ....Religion : ....Studies: ....

Occupation(s) : ....

Deceased : ....in........................Cause:...............

☐ *Buried* ☐ *Cremated* ☐ *Disappeared* on : ....in :....................

👪 CHILDREN ♂ .... ♀	Gen.	° Birth	† Death	Spouse
....	.....	....	....	....
....	.....	....	....	....
....	.....	....	....	....
....	.....	....	....	....
....	.....	....	....	....
....	.....	....	....	....
....	.....	....	....	....
....	.....	....	....	....
....	.....	....	....	....
....	.....	....	....	....
....	.....	....	....	....

💍 OTHER UNION(S)/ 👪 CHILDREN ....

....

....

....

👪 SIBLINGS   ▶ *Details page 11*   ♂ .... ♀ ....   1.................................

2..............................3..............................4..............................

5..............................6..............................7..............................

8..............................9..............................10.............................

👤 INDIVIDUAL EVENTS ....

....

....

....

....

....

📝 NOTES ....

....

....

....

....

20	21	22	23

10	11

5

2

Surname: .... First name : .... ♂

Child : ☐ *Legitimate* ☐ *Natural* ☐ *Adopted* ☐ *Found* ☐ *Recognized* ☐ *Adulterated*   ☐ *Implex*

Born : ....in...

Baptized : ....in...

Godfather: ....Godmother : ....

Son of : ....and:..

Nationality : ....Religion : ....Studies: ....

Occupation(s) : ....

Deceased : ....in.................................Cause:..........................

☐ *Buried* ☐ *Cremated* ☐ *Disappeared* on : ....in :....................

⚭ MARITAL STATUS   ☐ *Civil Marriage* ☐ *Religious Marriage* ☐ *Free Union*

Date : ....in.. ☐ *Marriage contract*

Witnesses : ....

....

☐ *Separation* ☐ *Divorce* ☐ *Widowhood of the groom/bride* Date : ....

👫 FAMILY EVENTS ....

....
....
....
....
....

⚭ OTHER UNION(S)/👫 CHILDREN ....

....
....
....

👫 SIBLINGS   ▶ *Details page 13*   ♂ .... ♀ ....   1................................
2......................................3.................................4...............................
5......................................6.................................7...............................
8......................................9.................................10..............................

👤 INDIVIDUAL EVENTS ....

....
....

⛑ MILITARY LIFE Assignment(s) : ....

Campaign(s): ....

Medal(s) : ....☐ *Died in combat* ☐ *Injured on* : ....

24	25	26	27

12		13

6

3

📄 NOTES ....

....
....
....

♀ Surname : ....First name : ....

▶ Generation 3 - *maternal ascendant*

□ *Implex*   Child : □ *Legitimate* □ *Natural* □ *Adopted* □ *Found* □ *Recognized* □ *Adulterated*

Born : ....in..

Baptized : ....in..

Godfather: ....Godmother : ....

Daughter of : ....and: ....

Nationality : ....Religion : ....Studies: ....

Occupation(s) : ....

Deceased : ....in..Cause:..........................

□ *Buried* □ *Cremated* □ *Disappeared* on : ....in :..........................

👫 CHILDREN ♂ .... ♀ ....

	Gen.	° Birth	† Death	Spouse
....	......	....	....	....
....	......	....	....	....
....	......	....	....	....
....	......	....	....	....
....	......	....	....	....
....	......	....	....	....
....	......	....	....	....
....	......	....	....	....
....	......	....	....	....

💍 OTHER UNION(S)/ 👫 CHILDREN ....

....

....

....

👫 SIBLINGS   ▶ *Details page 15*   ♂ .... ♀ ....   1...............................

2............................... 3............................... 4...............................

5............................... 6............................... 7...............................

8............................... 9............................... 10...............................

👤 INDIVIDUAL EVENTS ....

....

....

....

....

....

....

📝 NOTES ....

....

....

....

....

28	29	30	31
	14		15
		7	
		3	

Surname: ....First name : .... ♂

▶ Generation4 – *paternal ascendant*

Child : ☐ *Legitimate* ☐ *Natural* ☐ *Adopted* ☐ *Found* ☐ *Recognized* ☐ *Adulterated*   ☐ *Implex*

Born : ....in...

Baptized : ....in...

Godfather: ....Godmother : ....

Son of : ....and:..

Nationality : ....Religion : ....Studies: ....

Occupation(s) : ....

Deceased : ....in...Cause:...........................

☐ *Buried* ☐ *Cremated* ☐ *Disappeared* on : ....in :.............................

⚭ MARITAL STATUS   ☐ *Civil Marriage*   ☐ *Religious Marriage*   ☐ *Free Union*

Date : ....in.. ☐ *Marriage contract*

Witnesses : ....

....

☐ *Separation* ☐ *Divorce* ☐ *Widowhood of the groom/bride* Date : ....

👪 FAMILY EVENTS ....

....

....

....

....

....

⚭ OTHER UNION(S)/👪 CHILDREN ....

....

....

....

👫 SIBLINGS   ▶ *Details page 17*   ♂ ....   ♀ ....   1...

2..3..4...

5..6..7...

8..9..10...

👤 INDIVIDUAL EVENTS ....

....

....

....

⛑ MILITARY LIFE Assignment(s) : ....

Campaign(s): ....

Medal(s) : ....☐ *Died in combat* ☐ *Injured on* : ....

32	33	34	35

16	17

8

4

📑 NOTES ....

....

....

....

....

♀ Surname : ....First name : ....

Sosa
9

▶ Generation 4 - *paternal ascendant*

☐ *Implex* Child : ☐ *Legitimate* ☐ *Natural* ☐ *Adopted* ☐ *Found* ☐ *Recognized* ☐ *Adulterated*

Born : ....in..
Baptized : ....in..
Godfather: ....Godmother : ....
Daughter of : ....and: ....
Nationality : ....Religion : ....Studies: ....
Occupation(s) : ....
Deceased : ....in.........................Cause:..........................
☐ *Buried* ☐ *Cremated* ☐ *Disappeared* on : ....in :.............................

👫 CHILDREN ♂ .... ♀ ....

	Gen.	° Birth	† Death	Spouse
....	....	....	....	....
....	....	....	....	....
....	....	....	....	....
....	....	....	....	....
....	....	....	....	....
....	....	....	....	....
....	....	....	....	....
....	....	....	....	....
....	....	....	....	....
....	....	....	....	....

💍 OTHER UNION(S)/ 👫 CHILDREN ....
....
....
....

👫 SIBLINGS ▶ *Details page 19* ♂ .... ♀ .... 1..................................
2..3..4.............................
5..6..7.............................
8..9..10...........................

👤 INDIVIDUAL EVENTS ....
....
....
....
....
....
....

📝 NOTES ....
....
....
....
....

36	37	38	39
18		19	
9			
4			

Surname: ....First name : .... ♂

▶ Generation4 - *paternal ascendant*

Child : □ *Legitimate* □ *Natural* □ *Adopted* □ *Found* □ *Recognized* □ *Adulterated*   □ *Implex*

Born : ....in..

Baptized : ....in..

Godfather: ....Godmother : ....

Son of : ....and: ....

Nationality : ....Religion : ....Studies: ....

Occupation(s) : ....

Deceased : ....in...................................Cause:........................

□ *Buried* □ *Cremated* □ *Disappeared* on : ....in : ....

⚭ MARITAL STATUS   □ *Civil Marriage*   □ *Religious Marriage*   □ *Free Union*

Date : ....in.. □ *Marriage contract*

Witnesses : ....
....

□ *Separation* □ *Divorce*   □ *Widowhood of the groom/bride*   Date : ....

👪 FAMILY EVENTS   ....
....
....
....
....
....

⚭ OTHER UNION(S)/👪 CHILDREN   ....
....
....
....

👪 SIBLINGS   ▶ *Details page 21*   ♂ ....   ♀ ....   1. ....
2. ....   3. ....   4. ....
5. ....   6. ....   7. ....
8. ....   9. ....   10. ....

👤 INDIVIDUAL EVENTS   ....
....
....

⛑ MILITARY LIFE   Assignment(s) : ....

Campaign(s): ....

Medal(s) : ....□ *Died in combat* □ *Injured on* : ....

....

40	41	42	43

| 20 | | 21 |

| 10 |

| 5 |

📝 NOTES   ....
....
....
....
....

♀ Surname : ....First name : ....

▶ Generation 4 - *paternal ascendant*

☐ *Implex*   Child : ☐ *Legitimate* ☐ *Natural* ☐ *Adopted* ☐ *Found* ☐ *Recognized* ☐ *Adulterated*

Born : ....in...

Baptized : ....in...

Godfather: ....Godmother : ....

Daughter of : ....and: ....

Nationality : ....Religion : ....Studies: ....

Occupation(s) : ....

Deceased : ....in...........................Cause:......................

☐ *Buried* ☐ *Cremated* ☐ *Disappeared* on : ....in : ....

👫 CHILDREN ♂ .... ♀ ....

	Gen.	° Birth	† Death	Spouse
....	......	....	....	....
....	......	....	....	....
....	......	....	....	....
....	......	....	....	....
....	......	....	....	....
....	......	....	....	....
....	......	....	....	....
....	......	....	....	....
....	......	....	....	....
....	......	....	....	....

💍 OTHER UNION(S)/ 👫 CHILDREN ....

....

....

👫 SIBLINGS   ▶ *Details page 23*   ♂ .... ♀ ....   1..

2......................................3......................................4......................................

5......................................6......................................7......................................

8......................................9......................................10....................................

👤 INDIVIDUAL EVENTS ....

....

....

....

....

....

....

📑 NOTES ....

....

....

....

44	45	46	47
22		23	
	11		
	5		

11

Surname: .... First name : .... ♂

▶ Generation4 – *maternal ascendant*

Child : ☐ *Legitimate* ☐ *Natural* ☐ *Adopted* ☐ *Found* ☐ *Recognized* ☐ *Adulterated*   ☐ *Implex*

Born : ....in..

Baptized : ....in..

Godfather: ....Godmother : ....

Son of : ....and:..

Nationality : ....Religion : ....Studies: ....

Occupation(s) : ....

Deceased : ....in..................................Cause:..........................

☐ *Buried* ☐ *Cremated* ☐ *Disappeared* on : ....in :..............................

⚭ MARITAL STATUS   ☐ *Civil Marriage* ☐ *Religious Marriage* ☐ *Free Union*

Date : ....in.. ☐ *Marriage contract*

Witnesses : ....

....

☐ *Separation* ☐ *Divorce* ☐ *Widowhood of the groom/bride*   Date : ....

👫 FAMILY EVENTS ....

....

....

....

....

....

⚭ OTHER UNION(S)/ 👫 CHILDREN ....

....

....

....

....

👫 SIBLINGS   ▶ *Details page 25*   ♂ .... ♀ ....   1...........................

2.. 3.. 4..........................

5.. 6.. 7..........................

8.. 9.. 10.........................

👤 INDIVIDUAL EVENTS ....

....

....

....

⛑ MILITARY LIFE   Assignment(s) : ....

Campaign(s): ....

Medal(s) : .... ☐ *Died in combat* ☐ *Injured on* : ....

....

48	49	50	51

24		25

12

6

📑 NOTES ....

....

....

....

....

♀ Surname : ....First name : ....

▶ Generation 4 - *maternal ascendant*

□ *Implex*   Child : □ *Legitimate* □ *Natural* □ *Adopted* □ *Found* □ *Recognized* □ *Adulterated*

Born : ....in...

Baptized : ....in...

Godfather: ....Godmother : ....

Daughter of : ....and: ....

Nationality : ....Religion : ....Studies: ....

Occupation(s) : ....

Deceased : ....in.........................Cause:.......................

□ *Buried* □ *Cremated* □ *Disappeared* on : ....in :.......................

👫 CHILDREN ♂ .... ♀	Gen.	° Birth	† Death	Spouse
....	......	....	....	....
....	......	....	....	....
....	......	....	....	....
....	......	....	....	....
....	......	....	....	....
....	......	....	....	....
....	......	....	....	....
....	......	....	....	....
....	......	....	....	....
....	......	....	....	....

💍 OTHER UNION(S)/ 👫 CHILDREN ....

....

....

....

👫 SIBLINGS ▶ *Details page 27*   ♂ .... ♀ ....   1...

2...3...4...

5...6...7...

8...9...10...

👤 INDIVIDUAL EVENTS ....

....

....

....

....

....

....

📄 NOTES ....

....

....

....

52	53	54	55

26		27

13

6

Surname: ....First name : .... ♂

▶ Generation4 – *maternal ascendant*

Child : ☐ *Legitimate* ☐ *Natural* ☐ *Adopted* ☐ *Found* ☐ *Recognized* ☐ *Adulterated*   ☐ *Implex*

Born : ....in..

Baptized : ....in..

Godfather: ....Godmother : ....

Son of : ....and: ....

Nationality : ....Religion : ....Studies: ....

Occupation(s) : ....

Deceased : ....in................................Cause: ....

☐ *Buried* ☐ *Cremated* ☐ *Disappeared* on : ....in : ....

⚭ MARITAL STATUS   ☐ *Civil Marriage* ☐ *Religious Marriage* ☐ *Free Union*

Date : ....in................................ ☐ *Marriage contract*

Witnesses : ....

....

☐ *Separation* ☐ *Divorce* ☐ *Widowhood of the groom/bride* Date : ....

👪 FAMILY EVENTS ....

....

....

....

....

⚭ OTHER UNION(S)/ 👪 CHILDREN ....

....

....

....

👫 SIBLINGS   ▶ *Details page 29*   ♂ .... ♀ ....   1................................

2................................ 3................................ 4................................

5................................ 6................................ 7................................

8................................ 9................................ 10................................

👤 INDIVIDUAL EVENTS ....

....

....

....

⛑ MILITARY LIFE Assignment(s) : ....

Campaign(s): ....

Medal(s) : ....☐ *Died in combat* ☐ *Injured on* : ....

56	57	58	59
28		29	
	14		
	7		

📑 NOTES ....

....

....

....

♀ Surname : ....First name : ....

▶ Generation 4 – *maternal ascendant*

□ *Implex*　　Child : □ *Legitimate* □ *Natural* □ *Adopted* □ *Found* □ *Recognized* □ *Adulterated*

Born : ....in...

Baptized : ....in...

Godfather: ....Godmother : ....

Daughter of : ....and: ....

Nationality : ....Religion : ....Studies: ....

Occupation(s) : ....

Deceased : ....in...........................Cause:...........................

□ *Buried* □ *Cremated* □ *Disappeared* on : ....in : ....

👫 CHILDREN ♂ .... ♀	Gen.	° Birth	† Death	Spouse
....	......	....	....	....
....	......	....	....	....
....	......	....	....	....
....	......	....	....	....
....	......	....	....	....
....	......	....	....	....
....	......	....	....	....
....	......	....	....	....
....	......	....	....	....

💍 OTHER UNION(S)/ 👫 CHILDREN ....

....

....

....

👫 SIBLINGS　▶ *Details page 31*　♂ .... ♀ ..... 　1...

2...3................................4...

5...6................................7...

8...9................................10.......................................

👤 INDIVIDUAL EVENTS ....

....

....

....

....

....

....

📝 NOTES ....

....

....

....

....

60	61	62	63
	30	31	
		15	
		7	

Surname: .... First name : .... ♂

▶ Generation5 – *paternal ascendant*

Child : ☐ *Legitimate* ☐ *Natural* ☐ *Adopted* ☐ *Found* ☐ *Recognized* ☐ *Adulterated*   ☐ *Implex*

Born : ....in..

Baptized : ....in..

Godfather: ....Godmother : ....

Son of : ....and:..

Nationality : ....Religion : ....Studies: ....

Occupation(s) : ....

Deceased : ....in..........................Cause:.........................

☐ *Buried* ☐ *Cremated* ☐ *Disappeared* on : ....in :.........................

◎ **MARITAL STATUS**   ☐ *Civil Marriage* ☐ *Religious Marriage* ☐ *Free Union*

Date : ....in... ☐ *Marriage contract*

Witnesses : ....

....

☐ *Separation* ☐ *Divorce* ☐ *Widowhood of the groom/bride* Date : ....

FAMILY EVENTS ....

....

....

....

....

....

◎ **OTHER UNION(S)/ CHILDREN** ....

....

....

....

SIBLINGS   ▶ *Details page 33*   ♂ .... ♀ ....   1...........................

2...3..4.............................

5...6..7.............................

8...9..10...........................

INDIVIDUAL EVENTS ....

....

....

....

MILITARY LIFE Assignment(s) : ....

Campaign(s): ....

Medal(s) : ....☐ *Died in combat* ☐ *Injured on* : ....

....

| 64 | 65 | 66 | 67 |

NOTES ....

| 32 | | 33 |

....

16

....

| 8 |

....

....

♀ Surname : ....First name : ....

▶ Generation 5 - *paternal ascendant*

□ *Implex*   Child : □ *Legitimate* □ *Natural* □ *Adopted* □ *Found* □ *Recognized* □ *Adulterated*

Born : ....in..

Baptized : ....in..

Godfather: ....Godmother : ....

Daughter of : ....and: ....

Nationality : ....Religion : ....Studies: ....

Occupation(s) : ....

Deceased : ....in..........................Cause:..........................

□ *Buried* □ *Cremated* □ *Disappeared* on : ....in : ....

👫 CHILDREN ♂ .... ♀	Gen.	° Birth	† Death	Spouse
....	......	....	....	....
....	......	....	....	....
....	......	....	....	....
....	......	....	....	....
....	......	....	....	....
....	......	....	....	....
....	......	....	....	....
....	......	....	....	....
....	......	....	....	....
....	......	....	....	....

💍 OTHER UNION(S)/ 👫 CHILDREN ....

....

....

👫 SIBLINGS   ▶ *Details page 35*   ♂ .... ♀ ....   1..

2..   3..   4..

5..   6..   7..

8..   9..   10..

👤 INDIVIDUAL EVENTS ....

....

....

....

....

....

📝 NOTES ....

....

....

....

68	69	70	71

34	35

17

8

Surname: .... First name : .... ♂

Child : □ *Legitimate* □ *Natural* □ *Adopted* □ *Found* □ *Recognized* □ *Adulterated*   □ *Implex*

Born : ....in..

Baptized : ....in..

Godfather: ....Godmother : ....

Son of : ....and:..

Nationality : ....Religion : ....Studies:........................

Occupation(s) : ....

Deceased : ....in................................Cause:.........................

□ *Buried* □ *Cremated* □ *Disappeared* on : ....in :........................

⚭ MARITAL STATUS   □ *Civil Marriage* □ *Religious Marriage* □ *Free Union*

Date : ....in.. □ *Marriage contract*

Witnesses : ....

....

□ *Separation* □ *Divorce* □ *Widowhood of the groom/bride* Date : ....

👪 FAMILY EVENTS ....

....
....
....
....
....

⚭ OTHER UNION(S)/ 👫 CHILDREN ....

....
....
....
....

👫 SIBLINGS   ▶ *Details page 37*   ♂ ....   ♀ ....   1...

2...3...4...

5...6...7...

8...9...10...

👤 INDIVIDUAL EVENTS ....

....
....
....

⛑ MILITARY LIFE Assignment(s) : ....

Campaign(s): ....

Medal(s) : ....□ *Died in combat* □ *Injured on* : ....

| 72 | 73 | 74 | 75 |

| 36 | | 37 |

18

9

📑 NOTES ....

....
....
....
....

♀ Surname : .... First name : ....

▶ Generation 5 - *paternal ascendant*

□ *Implex*　　Child : □ *Legitimate* □ *Natural* □ *Adopted* □ *Found* □ *Recognized* □ *Adulterated*

Born : ....in..

Baptized : ....in..

Godfather: ....Godmother : ....

Daughter of : ....and: ....

Nationality : ....Religion : ....Studies: ....

Occupation(s) : ....

Deceased : ....in.........................Cause:.........................

□ *Buried* □ *Cremated* □ *Disappeared* on : ....in : ....

👫 CHILDREN ♂ .... ♀ ....

	Gen.	° Birth	† Death	Spouse

💍 OTHER UNION(S)/ 👫 CHILDREN

....

....

....

👫 SIBLINGS　▶ *Details page 39*　♂ ....　♀ ....　1..

2.. 3.. 4..

5.. 6.. 7..

8.. 9.. 10..

👤 INDIVIDUAL EVENTS ....

....

....

....

....

....

....

📑 NOTES ....

....

....

....

....

76	77	78	79
38		39	
	19		
	9		

Sosa 20

Surname: .... First name : .... ♂

Child : □ *Legitimate* □ *Natural* □ *Adopted* □ *Found* □ *Recognized* □ *Adulterated*   □ *Implex*

Born : ....in..

Baptized : ....in..

Godfather: ....Godmother : ....

Son of : ....and: ....

Nationality : ....Religion : ....Studies: ....

Occupation(s) : ....

Deceased : ....in.......................................Cause:........................

□ *Buried* □ *Cremated* □ *Disappeared* on : ....in :..............................

⚭ MARITAL STATUS   □ *Civil Marriage* □ *Religious Marriage* □ *Free Union*

Date : ....in.. □ *Marriage contract*

Witnesses : ....
....

□ *Separation* □ *Divorce* □ *Widowhood of the groom/bride* Date : ....

👫 FAMILY EVENTS   ....
....
....
....
....
....

⚭ OTHER UNION(S)/ 👫 CHILDREN   ....
....
....
....

👫 SIBLINGS   ▶ *Details page 41*   ♂ ....   ♀ ....   1..

2...3...4.....................................

5...6...7.....................................

8...9...10...................................

👤 INDIVIDUAL EVENTS   ....
....
....

⛑ MILITARY LIFE   Assignment(s) : ....

Campaign(s): ....

Medal(s) : ....□ *Died in combat* □ *Injured on* : ....
....

80	81	82	83

40		41

20

10

📑 NOTES   ....
....
....
....
....

♀ Surname : ....First name : ....

▶ Generation 5 – *paternal ascendant*

□ *Implex* Child : □ *Legitimate* □ *Natural* □ *Adopted* □ *Found* □ *Recognized* □ *Adulterated*

Born : ....in...

Baptized : ....in...

Godfather: ....Godmother : ....

Daughter of : ....and: ....

Nationality : ....Religion : ....Studies: ....

Occupation(s) : ....

Deceased : ....in...........................Cause:...................

□ *Buried* □ *Cremated* □ *Disappeared* on : ....in :......................

👪 CHILDREN ♂ .... ♀	Gen.	° Birth	† Death	Spouse
....	......	....	....	....
....	......	....	....	....
....	......	....	....	....
....	......	....	....	....
....	......	....	....	....
....	......	....	....	....
....	......	....	....	....
....	......	....	....	....
....	......	....	....	....
....	......	....	....	....

💍 OTHER UNION(S)/ 👪 CHILDREN ....
....
....
....

👪 SIBLINGS ▶ *Details page 43* ♂ .... ♀ .... 1...

2...3...4...

5...6...7...

8...9...10...

👤 INDIVIDUAL EVENTS ....
....
....
....
....
....
....
....

📑 NOTES ....
....
....
....
....

84	85	86	87
42		43	
21			
10			

Surname: ....First name : .... ♂

Child : □ *Legitimate* □ *Natural* □ *Adopted* □ *Found* □ *Recognized* □ *Adulterated*   □ *Implex*

Born : ....in...

Baptized : ....in...

Godfather: ....Godmother : ....

Son of : ....and: ....

Nationality : ....Religion : ....Studies: ....

Occupation(s) : ....

Deceased : ....in.............................Cause:...................................

□ *Buried* □ *Cremated* □ *Disappeared* on : ....in : ....

⊚ MARITAL STATUS   □ *Civil Marriage*   □ *Religious Marriage*   □ *Free Union*

Date : ....in... □ *Marriage contract*

Witnesses : ....

....

□ *Separation* □ *Divorce* □ *Widowhood of the groom/bride* Date : ....

👪 FAMILY EVENTS   ....

....

....

....

....

....

⊚ OTHER UNION(S)/ 👪 CHILDREN ....

....

....

....

👪 SIBLINGS   ▶ *Details page 45*   ♂ .... ♀ ....   1...

2..3...4.......................................

5..6...7.......................................

8..9...10.....................................

👤 INDIVIDUAL EVENTS ....

....

....

....

⛑ MILITARY LIFE Assignment(s) : ....

Campaign(s): ....

Medal(s) : ....□ *Died in combat* □ *Injured on* : ....

88	89	90	91

| 44 | | 45 |

| 22 |

| 11 |

🗐 NOTES ....

....

....

....

♀ Surname : ....First name : ....

▶ Generation 5 - *paternal ascendant*

□ *Implex*   Child : □ *Legitimate* □ *Natural* □ *Adopted* □ *Found* □ *Recognized* □ *Adulterated*

Born : ....in...

Baptized : ....in...

Godfather: ....Godmother : ....

Daughter of : ....and: ....

Nationality : ....Religion : ....Studies: ....

Occupation(s) : ....

Deceased : ....in...........................Cause:.....................

□ *Buried* □ *Cremated* □ *Disappeared* on : ....in :..................

👪 CHILDREN ♂ .... ♀ ....

	Gen.	° Birth	† Death	Spouse

💍 OTHER UNION(S)/ 👪 CHILDREN ....

....
....
....

👪 SIBLINGS   ▶ *Details page 47*   ♂ .... ♀ ....   1...............................

2... 3... 4.....................................

5... 6... 7.....................................

8... 9... 10...................................

👤 INDIVIDUAL EVENTS ....

....
....
....
....
....
....
....

📝 NOTES ....

....
....
....
....

92	93	94	95
46		47	
	23		
	11		

Surname: .... First name : .... ♂

▶ Generation5 - *maternal ascendant*

Child : ☐ *Legitimate* ☐ *Natural* ☐ *Adopted* ☐ *Found* ☐ *Recognized* ☐ *Adulterated*   ☐ *Implex*

Born : ....in...

Baptized : ....in...

Godfather: ....Godmother : ....

Son of : ....and:...

Nationality : ....Religion : ....Studies: ....

Occupation(s) : ....

Deceased : ....in...........................Cause:........................

☐ *Buried* ☐ *Cremated* ☐ *Disappeared* on : ....in :.................

⚭ MARITAL STATUS   ☐ *Civil Marriage*   ☐ *Religious Marriage*   ☐ *Free Union*

Date : ....in.. ☐ *Marriage contract*

Witnesses : ....

....

☐ *Separation* ☐ *Divorce* ☐ *Widowhood of the groom/bride* Date : ....

👪 FAMILY EVENTS ....

....
....
....
....
....

⚭ OTHER UNION(S)/👪 CHILDREN ....

....
....
....

👪 SIBLINGS   ▶ *Details page 49*   ♂ ....   ♀ ....   1.................................

2.............................3.............................4.............................

5.............................6.............................7.............................

8.............................9.............................10...........................

👤 INDIVIDUAL EVENTS ....

....
....

⛑ MILITARY LIFE   Assignment(s) : ....

Campaign(s): ....

Medal(s) : .... ☐ *Died in combat* ☐ *Injured on* : ....

96	97	98	99

📋 **NOTES** ....

48		49

....

	24	

....

	12	

....

♀ Surname : ....First name : ....

Sosa
25

☐ *Implex*   Child : ☐ *Legitimate* ☐ *Natural* ☐ *Adopted* ☐ *Found* ☐ *Recognized* ☐ *Adulterated*

Born : ....in...

Baptized : ....in...

Godfather: ....Godmother : ....

Daughter of : ....and:...

Nationality : ....Religion : ....Studies: ....

Occupation(s) : ....

Deceased : ....in.........................Cause:.......................

☐ *Buried* ☐ *Cremated* ☐ *Disappeared* on : ....in :...........................

👪 CHILDREN ♂ .... ♀	Gen.	° Birth	† Death	Spouse
....	......	....	....	....
....	......	....	....	....
....	......	....	....	....
....	......	....	....	....
....	......	....	....	....
....	......	....	....	....
....	......	....	....	....
....	......	....	....	....
....	......	....	....	....
....	......	....	....	....

💍 OTHER UNION(S)/ 👪 CHILDREN ....

....

....

....

👪 SIBLINGS ▶ *Details page 51*   ♂ .... ♀ ....   1.......................................

2.............................. 3.............................. 4..............................

5.............................. 6.............................. 7..............................

8.............................. 9.............................. 10..............................

👤 INDIVIDUAL EVENTS ....

....

....

....

....

....

....

📑 NOTES ....

....

....

....

100	101	102	103

| 50 | 51 |

25

12

Surname: ....First name : .... ♂

▶ Generation5 – *maternal ascendant*

Child : ☐ *Legitimate* ☐ *Natural* ☐ *Adopted* ☐ *Found* ☐ *Recognized* ☐ *Adulterated*   ☐ *Implex*

Born : ....in..

Baptized : ....in..

Godfather: ....Godmother : ....

Son of : ....and: ....

Nationality : ....Religion : ....Studies: ....

Occupation(s) : ....

Deceased : ....in...Cause:.........................

☐ *Buried* ☐ *Cremated* ☐ *Disappeared* on : ....in : ....

⭘⭘ MARITAL STATUS   ☐ *Civil Marriage* ☐ *Religious Marriage* ☐ *Free Union*

Date : ....in..   ☐ *Marriage contract*

Witnesses : ....

....

☐ *Separation* ☐ *Divorce* ☐ *Widowhood of the groom/bride* Date : ....

👫 FAMILY EVENTS

....

....

....

....

....

⭘⭘ OTHER UNION(S)/ 👫 CHILDREN ....

....

....

....

👫 SIBLINGS   ▶ *Details page 53*   ♂ .... ♀ ....   1. ....

2. ....   3. ....   4. ....

5. ....   6. ....   7. ....

8. ....   9. ....   10. ....

👤 INDIVIDUAL EVENTS ....

....

....

....

⛑ MILITARY LIFE Assignment(s) : ....

Campaign(s): ....

Medal(s) : ....☐ *Died in combat* ☐ *Injured on* : ....

104	105	106	107

52		53

26

13

📑 NOTES ....

....

....

....

....

26

♀ Surname : ....First name : ....

Sosa
27

□ *Implex*

Child : □ *Legitimate* □ *Natural* □ *Adopted* □ *Found* □ *Recognized* □ *Adulterated*

Born : ....in...

Baptized : ....in...

Godfather: ....Godmother : ....

Daughter of : ....and: ....

Nationality : ....Religion : ....Studies: ....

Occupation(s) : ....

Deceased : ....in..................Cause:................

□ *Buried* □ *Cremated* □ *Disappeared* on : ....in : ....

👫 CHILDREN ♂ .... ♀ ....

	Gen.	° Birth	† Death	Spouse
....	......	....	....	....
....	......	....	....	....
....	......	....	....	....
....	......	....	....	....
....	......	....	....	....
....	......	....	....	....
....	......	....	....	....
....	......	....	....	....
....	......	....	....	....
....	......	....	....	....

💍 OTHER UNION(S)/ 👫 CHILDREN ....

....

....

....

👫 SIBLINGS ▶ *Details page 55* ♂ .... ♀ .... 1.................

2..................................3..................................4.................

5..................................6..................................7.................

8..................................9..................................10................

👤 INDIVIDUAL EVENTS ....

....

....

....

....

....

....

📑 NOTES ....

....

....

....

....

108	109	110	111

54	55

27

13

Surname: ....First name : .... ♂

Child : □ *Legitimate* □ *Natural* □ *Adopted* □ *Found* □ *Recognized* □ *Adulterated*   □ *Implex*

Born : ....in...

Baptized : ....in...

Godfather: ....Godmother : ....

Son of : ....and: ....

Nationality : ....Religion : ....Studies: ....

Occupation(s) : ....

Deceased : ....in.............................Cause:.......................

□ *Buried* □ *Cremated* □ *Disappeared* on : ....in : ....

⚭ MARITAL STATUS   □ *Civil Marriage* □ *Religious Marriage* □ *Free Union*

Date : ....in... □ *Marriage contract*

Witnesses : ....

....

□ *Separation* □ *Divorce* □ *Widowhood of the groom/bride* Date : ....

👫 FAMILY EVENTS ....

....

....

....

....

....

⚭ OTHER UNION(S)/ 👫 CHILDREN ....

....

....

....

👫 SIBLINGS   ▶ *Details page 57*   ♂ .... ♀ ....   1...........................

2...........................   3...........................   4...........................

5...........................   6...........................   7...........................

8...........................   9...........................   10..........................

👤 INDIVIDUAL EVENTS ....

....

....

....

⛑ MILITARY LIFE Assignment(s) : ....

Campaign(s): ....

Medal(s) : ....□ *Died in combat* □ *Injured on* : ....

112	113	114	115
56		57	
	28		
	14		

📑 NOTES ....

....

....

....

....

♀ Surname : .... First name : ....

▶ Generation 5 - *maternal ascendant*

□ *Implex*   Child : □ *Legitimate* □ *Natural* □ *Adopted* □ *Found* □ *Recognized* □ *Adulterated*

Born : ....in...

Baptized : ....in...

Godfather: ....Godmother : ....

Daughter of : ....and: ....

Nationality : ....Religion : ....Studies: ....

Occupation(s) : ....

Deceased : ....in..........................Cause:...........................

□ *Buried* □ *Cremated* □ *Disappeared* on : ....in :...........................

👫 CHILDREN ♂ .... ♀	Gen.	° Birth	† Death	Spouse
....	......	....	....	....
....	......	....	....	....
....	......	....	....	....
....	......	....	....	....
....	......	....	....	....
....	......	....	....	....
....	......	....	....	....
....	......	....	....	....
....	......	....	....	....
....	......	....	....	....
....	......	....	....	....

💍 OTHER UNION(S)/ 👫 CHILDREN ....

....

....

....

👫 SIBLINGS   ▶ *Details page 59*   ♂ .... ♀ ....   1..

2... 3... 4...

5... 6... 7...

8... 9... 10..

👤 INDIVIDUAL EVENTS ....

....

....

....

....

....

....

📝 NOTES ....

....

....

....

116	117	118	119
58		59	
	29		
	14		

Surname: .... First name : .... ♂

Child : □ *Legitimate* □ *Natural* □ *Adopted* □ *Found* □ *Recognized* □ *Adulterated*   □ *Implex*

Born : ....in...

Baptized : ....in...

Godfather: ....Godmother : ....

Son of : ....and: ....

Nationality : ....Religion : ....Studies: ....

Occupation(s) : ....

Deceased : ....in..Cause:............................

□ *Buried* □ *Cremated* □ *Disappeared* on : ....in :.........................

💍 MARITAL STATUS   □ *Civil Marriage* □ *Religious Marriage* □ *Free Union*

Date : ....in.. □ *Marriage contract*

Witnesses : ....

....

□ *Separation* □ *Divorce* □ *Widowhood of the groom/bride* Date : ....

👫 FAMILY EVENTS ....

....

....

....

....

....

💍 OTHER UNION(S)/👫 CHILDREN ....

....

....

....

👫 SIBLINGS   ▶ *Details page 61*   ♂ .... ♀ ....   1..................................

2...3..4..............................

5...6..7..............................

8...9..10............................

👤 INDIVIDUAL EVENTS ....

....

....

....

⛑ MILITARY LIFE   Assignment(s) : ....

Campaign(s): ....

Medal(s) : ....□ *Died in combat* □ *Injured on* : ....

120	121	122	123

60		61

30

15

📑 NOTES ....

....

....

....

....

♀ Surname : ....First name : ....

▶ Generation 5 - *maternal ascendant*

□ *Implex* Child : □ *Legitimate* □ *Natural* □ *Adopted* □ *Found* □ *Recognized* □ *Adulterated*

Born : ....in...

Baptized : ....in...

Godfather: ....Godmother : ....

Daughter of : ....and: ....

Nationality : ....Religion : ....Studies: ....

Occupation(s) : ....

Deceased : ....in.......................Cause: ....

□ *Buried* □ *Cremated* □ *Disappeared* on : ....in : ....

👪 CHILDREN ♂ .... ♀ ....

	Gen.	° Birth	† Death	Spouse
....	......	....	....	....
....	......	....	....	....
....	......	....	....	....
....	......	....	....	....
....	......	....	....	....
....	......	....	....	....
....	......	....	....	....
....	......	....	....	....
....	......	....	....	....
....	......	....	....	....
....	......	....	....	....

💍 OTHER UNION(S)/ 👪 CHILDREN ....

....

....

....

👪 SIBLINGS ▶ *Details page 63* ♂ .... ♀ .... 1.....................................

2.................................3.................................4.................................

5.................................6.................................7.................................

8.................................9.................................10.................................

👤 INDIVIDUAL EVENTS ....

....

....

....

....

....

....

📑 NOTES ....

124	125	126	127
62		63	
	31		
	15		

Surname: .... First name : .... ♂

▶ Generation6 – *paternal ascendant*

Child : □ *Legitimate* □ *Natural* □ *Adopted* □ *Found* □ *Recognized* □ *Adulterated*   □ *Implex*

Born : ....in...

Baptized : ....in...

Godfather: ....Godmother : ....

Son of : ....and:..

Nationality : ....Religion : ....Studies: ....

Occupation(s) : ....

Deceased : ....in..............................Cause:..................................

□ *Buried* □ *Cremated* □ *Disappeared* on : ....in :...............................

(⊚) **MARITAL STATUS**   □ *Civil Marriage* □ *Religious Marriage* □ *Free Union*

Date : ....in.. □ *Marriage contract*

Witnesses : ....

....

□ *Separation* □ *Divorce* □ *Widowhood of the groom/bride* Date : ....

FAMILY EVENTS ....

....

....

....

....

....

(⊚) **OTHER UNION(S)/ CHILDREN** ....

....

....

....

SIBLINGS   ▶ *Details page 65*   ♂ ....   ♀ ....   1................................

2..3..4..

5..6..7..

8..9..10...

INDIVIDUAL EVENTS ....

....

....

....

MILITARY LIFE   Assignment(s) : ....

Campaign(s): ....

Medal(s) : ....□ *Died in combat* □ *Injured on* : ....

....

128	129	130	131

NOTES ....

64   65

....

32

....

16

....

♀ Surname : .... First name : ....

▶ Generation 6 - *paternal ascendant*

□ *Implex*   Child : □ *Legitimate* □ *Natural* □ *Adopted* □ *Found* □ *Recognized* □ *Adulterated*

Born : ....in..

Baptized : ....in..

Godfather: ....Godmother : ....

Daughter of : ....and: ....

Nationality : ....Religion : ....Studies: ....

Occupation(s) : ....

Deceased : ....in....................................Cause: ....

□ *Buried* □ *Cremated* □ *Disappeared* on : ....in : ....

👫 CHILDREN ♂ .... **♀** ....

Gen.	° Birth	† Death	Spouse
......	....	....	....
......	....	....	....
	....	....	....
	....	....	....
	....	....	....
	....	....	....
	....	....	....
	....	....	....
	....	....	....
	....	....	....

💍 OTHER UNION(S)/ 👫 CHILDREN ....
....
....
....

👫 SIBLINGS   ▶ *Details page 67*   ♂ ....   ♀ ....   1...

2..................................... 3..................................... 4.....................................

5..................................... 6..................................... 7.....................................

8..................................... 9..................................... 10....................................

👤 INDIVIDUAL EVENTS ....
....
....
....
....
....
....

📝 NOTES ....
....
....
....

132	133	134	135

66	67

33

16

33

Surname: ....First name : .... ♂

▶ Generation6 - *paternal ascendant*

Child : □ *Legitimate* □ *Natural* □ *Adopted* □ *Found* □ *Recognized* □ *Adulterated*   □ *Implex*

Born : ....in..

Baptized : ....in..

Godfather: ....Godmother : ....

Son of : ....and:..

Nationality : ....Religion : ....Studies:....................

Occupation(s) : ....

Deceased : ....in..Cause:............................

□ *Buried* □ *Cremated* □ *Disappeared* on : ....in :............................

🔗 MARITAL STATUS   □ *Civil Marriage*   □ *Religious Marriage*   □ *Free Union*

Date : ....in.. □ *Marriage contract*

Witnesses : ....
....

□ *Separation* □ *Divorce* □ *Widowhood of the groom/bride* Date : ....

👪 FAMILY EVENTS ....
....
....
....
....
....

🔗 OTHER UNION(S)/ 👪 CHILDREN ....
....
....
....
....

👫 SIBLINGS   ▶ *Details page 69*   ♂ ....   ♀ ....   1..

2...3...4..

5...6...7..

8...9...10.......................................

👤 INDIVIDUAL EVENTS ....
....
....
....

⛑ MILITARY LIFE   Assignment(s) : ....

Campaign(s): ....

Medal(s) : ....□ *Died in combat* □ *Injured on* :....................
....

136	137	138	139

68   69

34

17

📑 NOTES ....
....
....
....
....

♀ Surname : .... First name : ....

▶ Generation 6 – *paternal ascendant*

☐ *Implex*   Child : ☐ *Legitimate* ☐ *Natural* ☐ *Adopted* ☐ *Found* ☐ *Recognized* ☐ *Adulterated*

Born : .... in ....

Baptized : .... in ....

Godfather: ....Godmother : ....

Daughter of : ....and: ....

Nationality : ....Religion : ....Studies: ....

Occupation(s) : ....

Deceased : ....in ....Cause:...............................

☐ *Buried* ☐ *Cremated* ☐ *Disappeared* on : ....in : ....

👫 CHILDREN ♂ .... ♀	Gen.	° Birth	† Death	Spouse
....	......	....	....	....
....	......	....	....	....
....	......	....	....	....
....	......	....	....	....
....	......	....	....	....
....	......	....	....	....
....	......	....	....	....
....	......	....	....	....
....	......	....	....	....
....	......	....	....	....

💍 OTHER UNION(S)/ 👫 CHILDREN ....
....
....
....

👫 SIBLINGS   ▶ *Details page 71*   ♂ .... ♀ ....   1. ....
2. ....   3. ....   4. ....
5. ....   6. ....   7. ....
8. ....   9. ....   10. ....

👤 INDIVIDUAL EVENTS ....
....
....
....
....
....
....
....

📝 NOTES ....
....
....
....

140	141	142	143

70	71

35

17

Surname: .... First name : .... ♂

Child : □ *Legitimate* □ *Natural* □ *Adopted* □ *Found* □ *Recognized* □ *Adulterated*   □ *Implex*

Born : ....in..

Baptized : ....in...

Godfather: ....Godmother : ....

Son of : ....and: ....

Nationality : ....Religion : ....Studies: ....

Occupation(s) : ....

Deceased : ....in...............................Cause:...........................

□ *Buried* □ *Cremated* □ *Disappeared* on : ....in : ....

⚭ MARITAL STATUS   □ *Civil Marriage*   □ *Religious Marriage*   □ *Free Union*

Date : ....in... □ *Marriage contract*

Witnesses : ....

....

□ *Separation* □ *Divorce* □ *Widowhood of the groom/bride*   Date : ....

👪 FAMILY EVENTS   ....

....

....

....

....

....

⚭ OTHER UNION(S)/ 👪 CHILDREN ....

....

....

....

👫 SIBLINGS   ▶ *Details page 73*   ♂ ....   ♀ ....   1............................

2...3...4.........................

5...6...7.........................

8...9...10........................

👤 INDIVIDUAL EVENTS   ....

....

....

⛑ MILITARY LIFE   Assignment(s) : ....

Campaign(s): ....

Medal(s) : ....□ *Died in combat* □ *Injured on* : ....

....

144	145	146	147

| 72 | | 73 |

| 36 |

| 18 |

📄 NOTES ....

....

....

....

....

♀ Surname : .... First name : ....

▶ Generation 6 - *paternal ascendant*

☐ *Implex*   Child : ☐ *Legitimate* ☐ *Natural* ☐ *Adopted* ☐ *Found* ☐ *Recognized* ☐ *Adulterated*

Born : ....in..

Baptized : ....in...

Godfather: ....Godmother : ....

Daughter of : ....and: ....

Nationality : ....Religion : ....Studies: ....

Occupation(s) : ....

Deceased : ....in..........................Cause:.......................

☐ *Buried* ☐ *Cremated* ☐ *Disappeared* on : ....in : ....

👫 CHILDREN ♂ .... ♀	Gen.	° Birth	† Death	Spouse
....	....	....	....	....
....	....	....	....	....
....	....	....	....	....
....	....	....	....	....
....	....	....	....	....
....	....	....	....	....
....	....	....	....	....
....	....	....	....	....
....	....	....	....	....
....	....	....	....	....
....	....	....	....	....

💍 OTHER UNION(S)/ 👫 CHILDREN ....

....

....

👫 SIBLINGS ▶ *Details page 75* ♂ .... ♀ .... 1.................................

2.................................... 3.................................... 4....................................

5.................................... 6.................................... 7....................................

8.................................... 9.................................... 10....................................

👤 INDIVIDUAL EVENTS ....

....

....

....

....

....

....

📝 NOTES ....

....

....

148	149	150	151

74	75

37

18

Sosa 38

Surname: .... First name : .... ♂

Child : ☐ *Legitimate* ☐ *Natural* ☐ *Adopted* ☐ *Found* ☐ *Recognized* ☐ *Adulterated*   ☐ *Implex*

Born : ....in ....

Baptized : ....in ....

Godfather: ....Godmother : ....

Son of : ....and: ....

Nationality : ....Religion : ....Studies: ....

Occupation(s) : ....

Deceased : ....in ....Cause:..................

☐ *Buried* ☐ *Cremated* ☐ *Disappeared* on : ....in : ....

⚭ MARITAL STATUS   ☐ *Civil Marriage* ☐ *Religious Marriage* ☐ *Free Union*

Date : ....in..☐ *Marriage contract*

Witnesses : ....

....

☐ *Separation* ☐ *Divorce* ☐ *Widowhood of the groom/bride* Date : ....

👫 FAMILY EVENTS   ....

....

....

....

....

....

⚭ OTHER UNION(S)/ 👫 CHILDREN ....

....

....

....

👫 SIBLINGS   ▶ *Details page 77*   ♂ .... ♀ ....   1.......................................

2.......................................3.......................................4.......................................

5.......................................6.......................................7.......................................

8.......................................9.......................................10......................................

👤 INDIVIDUAL EVENTS   ....

....

....

....

⛑ MILITARY LIFE   Assignment(s) : ....

Campaign(s): ....

Medal(s) : ....☐ *Died in combat* ☐ *Injured on* : ....

....

152	153	154	155
76		77	
	38		
	19		

📋 NOTES   ....

....

....

....

....

♀ Surname : .... First name : ....

Sosa
39

□ *Implex* Child : □ *Legitimate* □ *Natural* □ *Adopted* □ *Found* □ *Recognized* □ *Adulterated*

Born : ....in..

Baptized : ....in..

Godfather: ....Godmother : ....

Daughter of : ....and: ....

Nationality : ....Religion : ....Studies: ....

Occupation(s) : ....

Deceased : ....in..Cause:........................

□ *Buried* □ *Cremated* □ *Disappeared* on : ....in :........................

👫 CHILDREN ♂ .... ♀	Gen.	° Birth	† Death	Spouse
....	......	....	....	....
....	......	....	....	....
....	......	....	....	....
....	......	....	....	....
....	......	....	....	....
....	......	....	....	....
....	......	....	....	....
....	......	....	....	....
....	......	....	....	....
....	......	....	....	....

💍 OTHER UNION(S)/ 👫 CHILDREN ....

....

....

👫 SIBLINGS ▶ *Details page 79*   ♂ .... ♀ .... 1.................................

2.....................................3.....................................4.....................................

5.....................................6.....................................7.....................................

8.....................................9.....................................10...................................

👤 INDIVIDUAL EVENTS ....

....

....

....

....

....

....

📑 NOTES ....

....

....

....

156	157	158	159

78	79

39

19

Surname: .... First name : .... ♂

► Generation6 - *paternal ascendant*

Child : □ *Legitimate* □ *Natural* □ *Adopted* □ *Found* □ *Recognized* □ *Adulterated*   □ *Implex*

Born : ....in...

Baptized : ....in...

Godfather: ....Godmother : ....

Son of : ....and:...

Nationality : ....Religion : ....Studies: ....

Occupation(s) : ....

Deceased : ....in...............................Cause:...............................

□ *Buried* □ *Cremated* □ *Disappeared* on : ....in : ....

⦾ MARITAL STATUS   □ *Civil Marriage*   □ *Religious Marriage*   □ *Free Union*

Date : ....in.. □ *Marriage contract*

Witnesses : ....
....

□ *Separation* □ *Divorce* □ *Widowhood of the groom/bride* Date : ....

👪 FAMILY EVENTS   ....
....
....
....
....
....

⦾ OTHER UNION(S)/👪 CHILDREN ....
....
....
....

👪 SIBLINGS   ► *Details page 81*   ♂ .... ♀ ....   1...

2.. 3... 4...

5.. 6... 7...

8.. 9... 10.......................................

👤 INDIVIDUAL EVENTS ....
....
....

⛑ MILITARY LIFE   Assignment(s) : ....

Campaign(s): ....

Medal(s) : ....□ *Died in combat* □ *Injured on* : ....
....

160	161	162	163
80		81	
	40		
	20		

🗒 NOTES ....
....
....
....
....

♀ Surname : ....First name : ....

▶ Generation 6 – *paternal ascendant*

□ *Implex* Child : □ *Legitimate* □ *Natural* □ *Adopted* □ *Found* □ *Recognized* □ *Adulterated*

Born : ....in...

Baptized : ....in...

Godfather: ....Godmother : ....

Daughter of : ....and: ....

Nationality : ....Religion : ....Studies: ....

Occupation(s) : ....

Deceased : ....in...............................Cause:......................................

□ *Buried* □ *Cremated* □ *Disappeared* on : ....in : ....

👫 CHILDREN ♂ .... ♀	Gen.	° Birth	† Death	Spouse
....	......	....	....	....
....	......	....	....	....
....	......	....	....	....
....	......	....	....	....
....	......	....	....	....
....	......	....	....	....
....	......	....	....	....
....	......	....	....	....
....	......	....	....	....
....	......	....	....	....

💍 OTHER UNION(S)/ 👫 CHILDREN ....

....

....

....

👫 SIBLINGS ▶ *Details page 83* ♂ .... ♀ .... 1...

2... 3................................. 4.................................

5... 6................................. 7.................................

8... 9................................. 10................................

👤 INDIVIDUAL EVENTS ....

....

....

....

....

....

....

📑 NOTES ....

....

....

....

164	165	166	167

82	83

41

20

41

Surname: ....First name : .... ♂

▶ Generation6 – *paternal ascendant*

Child : ☐ *Legitimate* ☐ *Natural* ☐ *Adopted* ☐ *Found* ☐ *Recognized* ☐ *Adulterated*   ☐ *Implex*

Born : ....in..

Baptized : ....in..

Godfather: ....Godmother : ....

Son of : ....and: ....

Nationality : ....Religion : ....Studies: ....

Occupation(s) : ....

Deceased : ....in................................Cause:........................

☐ *Buried* ☐ *Cremated* ☐ *Disappeared* on : ....in : ....

⚭ MARITAL STATUS   ☐ *Civil Marriage*   ☐ *Religious Marriage*   ☐ *Free Union*

Date : ....in.. ☐ *Marriage contract*

Witnesses : ....
....

☐ *Separation* ☐ *Divorce* ☐ *Widowhood of the groom/bride*   Date : ....

👫 FAMILY EVENTS ....
....
....
....
....
....

⚭ OTHER UNION(S)/ 👫 CHILDREN ....
....
....
....

👫 SIBLINGS ▶ *Details page 85*   ♂ ....   ♀ ....   1...

2... 3... 4...

5... 6... 7...

8... 9... 10..

👤 INDIVIDUAL EVENTS ....
....
....

⛑ MILITARY LIFE   Assignment(s) : ....

Campaign(s): ....

Medal(s) : ....☐ *Died in combat* ☐ *Injured on* : ....

168	169	170	171
84		85	

42

21

📄 NOTES ....
....
....
....
....

♀ Surname : ....First name : ....

□ *Implex*   Child : □ *Legitimate* □ *Natural* □ *Adopted* □ *Found* □ *Recognized* □ *Adulterated*

Born : ....in...

Baptized : ....in...

Godfather: ....Godmother : ....

Daughter of : ....and: ....

Nationality : ....Religion : ....Studies: ....

Occupation(s) : ....

Deceased : ....in...Cause:...

□ *Buried* □ *Cremated* □ *Disappeared* on : ....in : ....

👫 CHILDREN ♂ .... ♀	Gen.	° Birth	† Death	Spouse
....	......	....	....	....
....	......	....	....	....
....	......	....	....	....
....	......	....	....	....
....	......	....	....	....
....	......	....	....	....
....	......	....	....	....
....	......	....	....	....
....	......	....	....	....

💍 OTHER UNION(S)/ 👫 CHILDREN ....

....

....

👫 SIBLINGS   ▶ *Details page 87*   ♂ .... ♀ ....   1..

2....................................3....................................4....................................

5....................................6....................................7....................................

8....................................9....................................10....................................

👤 INDIVIDUAL EVENTS ....

....

....

....

....

....

....

📝 NOTES ....

....

....

....

172	173	174	175

86	87

43

21

Sosa 44

Surname: ....First name : .... ♂

Child : ☐ *Legitimate* ☐ *Natural* ☐ *Adopted* ☐ *Found* ☐ *Recognized* ☐ *Adulterated*   ☐ *Implex*

Born : ....in..

Baptized : ....in..

Godfather: ....Godmother : ....

Son of : ....and:...

Nationality : ....Religion : ....Studies: ....

Occupation(s) : ....

Deceased : ....in........................Cause:.....................................

☐ *Buried* ☐ *Cremated* ☐ *Disappeared* on : ....in : ....

⚭ MARITAL STATUS   ☐ *Civil Marriage* ☐ *Religious Marriage* ☐ *Free Union*

Date : ....in.. ☐ *Marriage contract*

Witnesses : ....
....

☐ *Separation* ☐ *Divorce* ☐ *Widowhood of the groom/bride* Date : ....

👫 FAMILY EVENTS   ....
....
....
....
....
....
....

⚭ OTHER UNION(S)/ 👫 CHILDREN ....
....
....
....

👫 SIBLINGS   ▶ *Details page 89*   ♂ .... ♀ ....   1...................................
2...3...................................4..
5...6...................................7..
8...9...................................10......................................

👤 INDIVIDUAL EVENTS ....
....
....

⛑ MILITARY LIFE   Assignment(s) : ....

Campaign(s): ....

Medal(s) : ....☐ *Died in combat* ☐ *Injured on* : ....
....

176	177	178	179

📄 NOTES ....

```
   88        89
       44
       22
```

....
....
....
....

♀ Surname : ....First name : ....

▶ Generation 6 - *paternal ascendant*

☐ *Implex*   Child : ☐ *Legitimate* ☐ *Natural* ☐ *Adopted* ☐ *Found* ☐ *Recognized* ☐ *Adulterated*

Born : ....in...

Baptized : ....in...

Godfather: ....Godmother : ....

Daughter of : ....and:..

Nationality : ....Religion : ....Studies: ....

Occupation(s) : ....

Deceased : ....in.........................Cause:......................

☐ *Buried* ☐ *Cremated* ☐ *Disappeared* on : ....in :...................

👫 CHILDREN ♂ .... ♀	Gen.	° Birth	† Death	Spouse
....	......	....	....	....
....	......	....	....	....
....	......	....	....	....
....	......	....	....	....
....	......	....	....	....
....	......	....	....	....
....	......	....	....	....
....	......	....	....	....
....	......	....	....	....
....	......	....	....	....

💍 OTHER UNION(S)/ 👫 CHILDREN ....

....

....

👫 SIBLINGS ▶ *Details page 91*   ♂ .... ♀ .... 1..

2..................................3...............................4...............................

5..................................6...............................7...............................

8..................................9...............................10..............................

👤 INDIVIDUAL EVENTS ....

....

....

....

....

....

....

📝 NOTES ....

....

| 180 | 181 | 182 | 183 |

| 90 | 91 |

| **45** |

| 22 |

Surname: .... First name : .... ♂

Child : □ *Legitimate* □ *Natural* □ *Adopted* □ *Found* □ *Recognized* □ *Adulterated*　　□ *Implex*

Born : ....in..

Baptized : ....in...

Godfather: ....Godmother : ....

Son of : ....and: ....

Nationality : ....Religion : ....Studies: ....

Occupation(s) : ....

Deceased : ....in.......................................Cause:.................

□ *Buried* □ *Cremated* □ *Disappeared* on : ....in : ....

⚭ MARITAL STATUS　　□ *Civil Marriage* □ *Religious Marriage* □ *Free Union*

Date : ....in... □ *Marriage contract*

Witnesses : ....

....

□ *Separation* □ *Divorce* □ *Widowhood of the groom/bride* Date : ....

👫 FAMILY EVENTS ....

....
....
....
....
....
....

⚭ OTHER UNION(S)/👫 CHILDREN ....

....
....
....

👫 SIBLINGS　▶ *Details page 93*　♂ ....　♀ ....　1.............................

2...3...4.............................

5...6...7.............................

8...9...10...........................

👤 INDIVIDUAL EVENTS ....

....
....
....

⛑ MILITARY LIFE　Assignment(s) : ....

Campaign(s): ....

Medal(s) : ....□ *Died in combat* □ *Injured on* : ....

....

184	185	186	187

92	93

46

23

📑 NOTES ....
....
....
....
....
....

♀ Surname : ....First name : ....

▶ Generation 6 – *paternal ascendant*

□ *Implex* Child : □ *Legitimate* □ *Natural* □ *Adopted* □ *Found* □ *Recognized* □ *Adulterated*

Born : ....in...

Baptized : ....in...

Godfather: ....Godmother : ....

Daughter of : ....and: ....

Nationality : ....Religion : ....Studies: ....

Occupation(s) : ....

Deceased : ....in.........................Cause:...................

□ *Buried* □ *Cremated* □ *Disappeared* on : ....in : ....

👫 CHILDREN ♂ .... ♀	Gen.	° Birth	† Death	Spouse
....	......	....	....	....
....	......	....	....	....
....	......	....	....	....
....	......	....	....	....
....	......	....	....	....
....	......	....	....	....
....	......	....	....	....
....	......	....	....	....
....	......	....	....	....
....	......	....	....	....
....	......	....	....	....

💍 OTHER UNION(S)/ 👫 CHILDREN ....

....

....

....

👫 SIBLINGS ▶ *Details page 95* ♂ .... ♀ .... 1................................

2...3...4...

5...6...7...

8...9...10...

👤 INDIVIDUAL EVENTS ....

....

....

....

....

....

....

....

📝 NOTES ....

....

....

....

....

188	189	190	191
94		95	

47

23

Surname: .... First name : .... ♂

Child : □ *Legitimate* □ *Natural* □ *Adopted* □ *Found* □ *Recognized* □ *Adulterated*   □ *Implex*

Born : ....in...

Baptized : ....in...

Godfather: ....Godmother : ....

Son of : ....and:...

Nationality : ....Religion : ....Studies: ....

Occupation(s) : ....

Deceased : ....in.........................Cause:...............................

□ *Buried* □ *Cremated* □ *Disappeared* on : ....in : ....

🔘 MARITAL STATUS   □ *Civil Marriage* □ *Religious Marriage* □ *Free Union*

Date : ....in... □ *Marriage contract*

Witnesses : ....

....

□ *Separation* □ *Divorce* □ *Widowhood of the groom/bride* Date : ....

👫 FAMILY EVENTS   ....

....

....

....

....

....

🔘 OTHER UNION(S)/ 👫 CHILDREN   ....

....

....

....

👫 SIBLINGS   ▶ *Details page 97*   ♂ .... ♀ ....   1............................

2... 3... 4...............................

5... 6... 7...............................

8... 9... 10..............................

👤 INDIVIDUAL EVENTS   ....

....

....

....

⛑ MILITARY LIFE   Assignment(s) : ....

Campaign(s): ....

Medal(s) : ....□ *Died in combat* □ *Injured on* : ....

....

```
┌────┬────┬────┬────┐
│192 │193 │194 │195 │
└────┴────┴────┴────┘
  ┌────┐   ┌────┐
  │ 96 │   │ 97 │
  └────┘   └────┘
     ┌────┐
     │ 48 │
     └────┘
     ┌────┐
     │ 24 │
     └────┘
```

📋 NOTES   ....

....

....

....

....

♀ Surname : ....First name : ....

▶ Generation 6 - *maternal ascendant*

□ *Implex*   Child : □ *Legitimate* □ *Natural* □ *Adopted* □ *Found* □ *Recognized* □ *Adulterated*

Born : ....in...

Baptized : ....in..

Godfather: ....Godmother : ....

Daughter of : ....and: ....

Nationality : ....Religion : ....Studies: ....

Occupation(s) : ....

Deceased : ....in...........................Cause:...................

□ *Buried* □ *Cremated* □ *Disappeared* on : ....in : ....

👫 CHILDREN ♂ .... ♀	Gen.	° Birth	† Death	Spouse
....	....	....	....	....
....	....	....	....	....
....	....	....	....	....
....	....	....	....	....
....	....	....	....	....
....	....	....	....	....
....	....	....	....	....
....	....	....	....	....
....	....	....	....	....
....	....	....	....	....

💍 OTHER UNION(S)/ 👫 CHILDREN ....
....
....

👫 SIBLINGS   ▶ *Details page 99*   ♂ .... ♀ ....   1...
2...................................3...................................4...................................
5...................................6...................................7...................................
8...................................9...................................10.................................

👤 INDIVIDUAL EVENTS ....
....
....
....
....
....
....
....

📑 NOTES ....

196	197	198	199

98		99

49

24

....
....
....

Surname: .... First name : .... ♂

▶ Generation6 – *maternal ascendant*

Child : ☐ *Legitimate* ☐ *Natural* ☐ *Adopted* ☐ *Found* ☐ *Recognized* ☐ *Adulterated*   ☐ *Implex*

Born : ....in..

Baptized : ....in...

Godfather: .... Godmother : ....

Son of : .... and: ....

Nationality : .... Religion : .... Studies: ....

Occupation(s) : ....

Deceased : ....in............................ Cause:...............................

☐ *Buried* ☐ *Cremated* ☐ *Disappeared* on : ....in :.....................

⚭ MARITAL STATUS   ☐ *Civil Marriage* ☐ *Religious Marriage* ☐ *Free Union*

Date : ....in.. ☐ *Marriage contract*

Witnesses : ....

....

☐ *Separation* ☐ *Divorce* ☐ *Widowhood of the groom/bride* Date : ....

👪 FAMILY EVENTS   ....

....
....
....
....
....

⚭ OTHER UNION(S)/ 👪 CHILDREN   ....

....
....
....

👫 SIBLINGS   ▶ *Details page 101*   ♂ .... ♀ ....   1.................................

2.. 3.. 4..............................
5.. 6.. 7..............................
8.. 9.. 10............................

👤 INDIVIDUAL EVENTS   ....

....
....
....

⛑ MILITARY LIFE   Assignment(s) : ....

Campaign(s): ....

Medal(s) : ....☐ *Died in combat* ☐ *Injured on* : ....

200	201	202	203

100   101

50

25

📑 NOTES ....

....
....
....
....

♀ Surname : ....First name : ....

▶ Generation 6 – *maternal ascendant*

☐ *Implex*   Child : ☐ *Legitimate* ☐ *Natural* ☐ *Adopted* ☐ *Found* ☐ *Recognized* ☐ *Adulterated*

Born : ....in..

Baptized : ....in..

Godfather: ....Godmother : ....

Daughter of : ....and: ....

Nationality : ....Religion : ....Studies: ....

Occupation(s) : ....

Deceased : ....in........................Cause:....................

☐ *Buried* ☐ *Cremated* ☐ *Disappeared* on : ....in : ....

👫 CHILDREN ♂ .... ♀ ....

	Gen.	° Birth	† Death	Spouse
....	......	....	....	....
....	......	....	....	....
....	......	....	....	....
....	......	....	....	....
....	......	....	....	....
....	......	....	....	....
....	......	....	....	....
....	......	....	....	....
....	......	....	....	....
....	......	....	....	....

💍 OTHER UNION(S)/ 👫 CHILDREN ....

....

....

....

👫 SIBLINGS ▶ *Details page 103* ♂ .... ♀ .... 1..................................

2..................................3..................................4..................................

5..................................6..................................7..................................

8..................................9..................................10.................................

👤 INDIVIDUAL EVENTS ....

....

....

....

....

....

📋 NOTES ....

....

....

....

204	205	206	207

102		103

51

25

Surname: .... First name : .... ♂

▶ Generation6 – *maternal ascendant*

Child : ☐ *Legitimate* ☐ *Natural* ☐ *Adopted* ☐ *Found* ☐ *Recognized* ☐ *Adulterated*   ☐ *Implex*

Born : ....in..

Baptized : ....in...

Godfather: ....Godmother : ....

Son of : ....and: ....

Nationality : ....Religion : ....Studies: ....

Occupation(s) : ....

Deceased : ....in.........................Cause:.............................

☐ *Buried* ☐ *Cremated* ☐ *Disappeared* on : ....in :.............................

⚭ MARITAL STATUS   ☐ *Civil Marriage*   ☐ *Religious Marriage*   ☐ *Free Union*

Date : ....in.. ☐ *Marriage contract*

Witnesses : ....

....

☐ *Separation* ☐ *Divorce* ☐ *Widowhood of the groom/bride* Date : ....

👪 FAMILY EVENTS   ....

....

....

....

....

....

⚭ OTHER UNION(S)/ 👪 CHILDREN   ....

....

....

....

👫 SIBLINGS   ▶ *Details page 105*   ♂ .... ♀ ....   1..

2.. 3.. 4..

5.. 6.. 7..

8.. 9.. 10..

👤 INDIVIDUAL EVENTS   ....

....

....

....

⛑ MILITARY LIFE   Assignment(s) : ....

Campaign(s): ....

Medal(s) : ....☐ *Died in combat* ☐ *Injured on* : ....

....

208	209	210	211
104		105	
	52		
	26		

📝 NOTES   ....

....

....

....

....

♀ Surname : ....First name : ....

▶ Generation 6 - *maternal ascendant*

□ *Implex* Child : □ *Legitimate* □ *Natural* □ *Adopted* □ *Found* □ *Recognized* □ *Adulterated*

Born : ....in...

Baptized : ....in...

Godfather: ....Godmother : ....

Daughter of : ....and: ....

Nationality : ....Religion : ....Studies: ....

Occupation(s) : ....

Deceased : ....in.................................Cause:............................

□ *Buried* □ *Cremated* □ *Disappeared* on : ....in : ....

👫 CHILDREN ♂ .... ♀	Gen.	° Birth	† Death	Spouse
....	......	....	....	....
....	......	....	....	....
....	......	....	....	....
....	......	....	....	....
....	......	....	....	....
....	......	....	....	....
....	......	....	....	....
....	......	....	....	....
....	......	....	....	....
....	......	....	....	....

💍 OTHER UNION(S)/👫 CHILDREN ....

....

....

👫 SIBLINGS ▶ *Details page 107* ♂ .... ♀ .... 1..

2... 3............................. 4...

5... 6............................. 7...

8... 9............................. 10...

👤 INDIVIDUAL EVENTS ....

....

....

....

....

....

....

📝 NOTES ....

....

....

....

212	213	214	215
106		107	
53			
26			

Surname: .... First name : .... ♂

Child : □ *Legitimate* □ *Natural* □ *Adopted* □ *Found* □ *Recognized* □ *Adulterated*   □ *Implex*

Born : ....in..

Baptized : ....in...

Godfather: ....Godmother : ....

Son of : ....and: ....

Nationality : ....Religion : ....Studies: ....

Occupation(s) : ....

Deceased : ....in..........................Cause:...........................

□ *Buried* □ *Cremated* □ *Disappeared* on : ....in : ....

⛉ MARITAL STATUS   □ *Civil Marriage* □ *Religious Marriage* □ *Free Union*

Date : ....in... □ *Marriage contract*

Witnesses : ....

....

□ *Separation* □ *Divorce* □ *Widowhood of the groom/bride* Date : ....

👫 FAMILY EVENTS ....

....
....
....
....
....
....

⛉ OTHER UNION(S)/👫 CHILDREN ....

....
....
....

👫 SIBLINGS   ▶ *Details page 109*   ♂ .... ♀ .... 1.............................

2..3..4..

5..6..7..

8..9..10..

👤 INDIVIDUAL EVENTS ....

....
....
....

⛑ MILITARY LIFE   Assignment(s) : ....

Campaign(s): ....

Medal(s) : ....□ *Died in combat* □ *Injured on* : ....

....

216	217	218	219
108		109	
	54		
	27		

🗒 NOTES ....

....
....
....
....

♀ Surname : ....First name : ....

▶ Generation 6 - *maternal ascendant*

☐ *Implex*　　　Child : ☐ *Legitimate* ☐ *Natural* ☐ *Adopted* ☐ *Found* ☐ *Recognized* ☐ *Adulterated*

Born : ....in...

Baptized : ....in...

Godfather: ....Godmother : ....

Daughter of : ....and: ....

Nationality : ....Religion : ....Studies: ....

Occupation(s) : ....

Deceased : ....in.......................Cause:.......................

☐ *Buried* ☐ *Cremated* ☐ *Disappeared* on : ....in : ....

👫 CHILDREN ♂ .... ♀	Gen.	° Birth	† Death	Spouse
....	......	....	....	....
....	......	....	....	....
....	......	....	....	....
....	......	....	....	....
....	......	....	....	....
....	......	....	....	....
....	......	....	....	....
....	......	....	....	....
....	......	....	....	....
....	......	....	....	....

💍 OTHER UNION(S)/ 👫 CHILDREN ....

....

....

👫 SIBLINGS　▶ *Details page 111*　　♂ .... ♀ ....　1...

2...3...4...

5...6...7...

8...9...10...

👤 INDIVIDUAL EVENTS ....

....

....

....

....

....

....

📑 NOTES ....

....

....

....

....

220	221	222	223
	110		111
		55	
		27	

Surname: .... First name : .... ♂

Child : □ *Legitimate* □ *Natural* □ *Adopted* □ *Found* □ *Recognized* □ *Adulterated*   □ *Implex*

Born : ....in...

Baptized : ....in...

Godfather: ....Godmother : ....

Son of : ....and: ....

Nationality : ....Religion : ....Studies: ....

Occupation(s) : ....

Deceased : ....in...................................Cause:..................................

□ *Buried* □ *Cremated* □ *Disappeared* on : ....in : ....

⚭ MARITAL STATUS   □ *Civil Marriage* □ *Religious Marriage* □ *Free Union*

Date : ....in.. □ *Marriage contract*

Witnesses : ....

....

□ *Separation* □ *Divorce* □ *Widowhood of the groom/bride* Date : ....

👪 FAMILY EVENTS   ....

....

....

....

....

....

⚭ OTHER UNION(S)/ 👪 CHILDREN   ....

....

....

....

👫 SIBLINGS   ▶ *Details page 113*   ♂ .... ♀ ....   1..

2.. 3... 4..

5.. 6... 7..

8.. 9... 10...

👤 INDIVIDUAL EVENTS   ....

....

....

....

⛑ MILITARY LIFE   Assignment(s) : ....

Campaign(s): ....

Medal(s) : ....□ *Died in combat* □ *Injured on* : ....

....

224	225	226	227
112		113	
	56		
	28		

📑 NOTES ....

....

....

....

....

♀ Surname : ....First name : ....

▶ Generation 6 – *maternal ascendant*

☐ *Implex* Child : ☐ *Legitimate* ☐ *Natural* ☐ *Adopted* ☐ *Found* ☐ *Recognized* ☐ *Adulterated*

Born : ....in...
Baptized : ....in...........................
Godfather: ....Godmother : ....
Daughter of : ....and: ....
Nationality : ....Religion : ....Studies: ....
Occupation(s) : ....
Deceased : ....in...Cause:.................................
☐ *Buried* ☐ *Cremated* ☐ *Disappeared* on : ....in : ....

👪 CHILDREN ♂ .... ♀	Gen.	° Birth	† Death	Spouse
....	......	....	....	....
....	......	....	....	....
....	......	....	....	....
....	......	....	....	....
....	......	....	....	....
....	......	....	....	....
....	......	....	....	....
....	......	....	....	....
....	......	....	....	....
....	......	....	....	....

💍 OTHER UNION(S)/👪 CHILDREN ....

....
....

👪 SIBLINGS ▶ *Details page 115* ♂ .... ♀ .... 1..
2.. 3.. 4..
5.. 6.. 7..
8.. 9.. 10..

👤 INDIVIDUAL EVENTS ....

....
....
....
....
....
....

📝 NOTES ....

....
....
....

228	229	230	231
	114		115
		57	
		28	

Sosa 58

Surname: .... First name : .... ♂

Child : ☐ *Legitimate* ☐ *Natural* ☐ *Adopted* ☐ *Found* ☐ *Recognized* ☐ *Adulterated*　　　☐ *Implex*

Born : .... in ....

Baptized : .... in ....

Godfather: .... Godmother : ....

Son of : .... and: ....

Nationality : .... Religion : .... Studies: ....

Occupation(s) : ....

Deceased : .... in .... Cause: ....

☐ *Buried* ☐ *Cremated* ☐ *Disappeared* on : .... in : ....

💍 MARITAL STATUS　　　☐ *Civil Marriage* ☐ *Religious Marriage* ☐ *Free Union*

Date : .... in .... ☐ *Marriage contract*

Witnesses : ....

☐ *Separation* ☐ *Divorce* ☐ *Widowhood of the groom/bride* Date : ....

👫 FAMILY EVENTS ....

....
....
....
....
....

💍 OTHER UNION(S)/ 👫 CHILDREN ....

....
....
....

👫 SIBLINGS ▶ *Details page 117* ♂ .... ♀ .... 1. ....

2. .... 3. .... 4. ....
5. .... 6. .... 7. ....
8. .... 9. .... 10. ....

👤 INDIVIDUAL EVENTS ....

....
....
....

⛑ MILITARY LIFE Assignment(s) : ....

Campaign(s): ....

Medal(s) : .... ☐ *Died in combat* ☐ *Injured on* : ....

....

232	233	234	235

📝 NOTES ....

....
....
....
....
....

116　117
58
29

♀ Surname : ....First name : ....

▶ Generation 6 - *maternal ascendant*

☐ *Implex*   Child : ☐ *Legitimate* ☐ *Natural* ☐ *Adopted* ☐ *Found* ☐ *Recognized* ☐ *Adulterated*

Born : ....in..

Baptized : ....in..

Godfather: ....Godmother : ....

Daughter of : ....and:....................................

Nationality : ....Religion : ....Studies:...................

Occupation(s) : ....

Deceased : ....in................................Cause:......................

☐ *Buried* ☐ *Cremated* ☐ *Disappeared* on : ....in :...................

👫 CHILDREN ♂ .... ♀	Gen.	° Birth	† Death	Spouse
....	......	....	....	....
....	......	....	....	....
....	......	....	....	....
....	......	....	....	....
....	......	....	....	....
....	......	....	....	....
....	......	....	....	....
....	......	....	....	....
....	......	....	....	....
....	......	....	....	....

💍 OTHER UNION(S)/ 👫 CHILDREN ....

....

....

👫 SIBLINGS ▶ *Details page 119*   ♂ .... ♀ ....   1..

2...3.....................................4....................................

5...6.....................................7....................................

8...9.....................................10..................................

👤 INDIVIDUAL EVENTS ....

....

....

....

....

....

....

📑 NOTES ....

....

....

....

236	237	238	239

| 118 | | 119 |

| 59 |

| 29 |

Surname: .... First name : .... ♂

Child : □ *Legitimate* □ *Natural* □ *Adopted* □ *Found* □ *Recognized* □ *Adulterated*   □ *Implex*

Born : ....in...

Baptized : ....in...

Godfather: ....Godmother : ....

Son of : ....and: ....

Nationality : ....Religion : ....Studies: ....

Occupation(s) : ....

Deceased : ....in...Cause:...............................

□ *Buried* □ *Cremated* □ *Disappeared* on : ....in : ....

⊙⊙ MARITAL STATUS   □ *Civil Marriage*   □ *Religious Marriage*   □ *Free Union*

Date : ....in...   □ *Marriage contract*

Witnesses : ....

....

□ *Separation* □ *Divorce* □ *Widowhood of the groom/bride*   Date : ....

👪 FAMILY EVENTS ....

....
....
....
....
....

⊙⊙ OTHER UNION(S)/👪 CHILDREN ....

....
....
....

👫 SIBLINGS   ▶ *Details page 121*   ♂ .... ♀ ....   1..

2.. 3.. 4..

5.. 6.. 7..

8.. 9.. 10..

👤 INDIVIDUAL EVENTS ....

....
....
....

⛑ MILITARY LIFE   Assignment(s) : ....

Campaign(s): ....

Medal(s) : ....□ *Died in combat* □ *Injured on* : ....

....

240	241	242	243

120		121

60
30

📝 NOTES ....

....
....
....
....

♀ Surname : ....First name : ....

▶ Generation 6 – *maternal ascendant*

☐ *Implex*   Child : ☐ *Legitimate* ☐ *Natural* ☐ *Adopted* ☐ *Found* ☐ *Recognized* ☐ *Adulterated*

Born : ....in..

Baptized : ....in..

Godfather: ....Godmother : ....

Daughter of : ....and:..

Nationality : ....Religion : ....Studies:.................................

Occupation(s) : ....

Deceased : ....in..........................Cause:..........................

☐ *Buried* ☐ *Cremated* ☐ *Disappeared* on : ....in : ....

👪 CHILDREN ♂ .... ♀	Gen.	° Birth	† Death	Spouse
....	......	....	....	....
....	......	....	....	....
....	......	....	....	....
....	......	....	....	....
....	......	....	....	....
....	......	....	....	....
....	......	....	....	....
....	......	....	....	....
....	......	....	....	....

💍 OTHER UNION(S)/ 👪 CHILDREN ....
....
....

👪 SIBLINGS ▶ *Details page 123*   ♂ .... ♀ ....   1..................................

2................................3................................4................................

5................................6................................7................................

8................................9................................10................................

👤 INDIVIDUAL EVENTS ....
....
....
....
....
....
....

📝 NOTES ....
....
....
....

244	245	246	247
122		123	

61

30

Sosa 62

Surname: .... First name : .... ♂

Child : □ *Legitimate* □ *Natural* □ *Adopted* □ *Found* □ *Recognized* □ *Adulterated*   □ *Implex*

Born : .... in ....

Baptized : .... in ....

Godfather: .... Godmother : ....

Son of : .... and: ....

Nationality : .... Religion : .... Studies: ....

Occupation(s) : ....

Deceased : .... in .... Cause:.............................

□ *Buried* □ *Cremated* □ *Disappeared* on : .... in : ....

⚭ MARITAL STATUS   □ *Civil Marriage* □ *Religious Marriage* □ *Free Union*

Date : .... in .... □ *Marriage contract*

Witnesses : ....

....

□ *Separation* □ *Divorce* □ *Widowhood of the groom/bride* Date : ....

👫 FAMILY EVENTS   ....

....

....

....

....

....

⚭ OTHER UNION(S)/ 👫 CHILDREN   ....

....

....

....

👫 SIBLINGS   ▶ *Details page 125*   ♂ .... ♀ .... 1................................

2................................ 3................................ 4................................

5................................ 6................................ 7................................

8................................ 9................................ 10...............................

👤 INDIVIDUAL EVENTS   ....

....

....

....

⛑ MILITARY LIFE   Assignment(s) : ....

Campaign(s): ....

Medal(s) : .... □ *Died in combat* □ *Injured on* : ....

....

248	249	250	251
124		125	
	62		
	31		

🗒 NOTES   ....

....

....

....

....

♀ Surname : ....First name : ....

▶ Generation 6 – *maternal ascendant*

☐ *Implex*   Child : ☐ *Legitimate* ☐ *Natural* ☐ *Adopted* ☐ *Found* ☐ *Recognized* ☐ *Adulterated*

Born : ....in..

Baptized : ....in..

Godfather: ....Godmother : ....

Daughter of : ....and:...

Nationality : ....Religion : ....Studies:...............................

Occupation(s) : ....

Deceased : ....in.........................Cause:...........................

☐ *Buried* ☐ *Cremated* ☐ *Disappeared* on : ....in :................

👫 CHILDREN ♂ .... ♀	Gen.	° Birth	† Death	Spouse
....	......	....	....	....
....	......	....	....	....
....	......	....	....	....
....	......	....	....	....
....	......	....	....	....
....	......	....	....	....
....	......	....	....	....
....	......	....	....	....
....	......	....	....	....
....	......	....	....	....

⚭ OTHER UNION(S)/ 👫 CHILDREN ....
....
....

👫 SIBLINGS   ▶ *Details page 127*   ♂ .... ♀ ....   1...
2...3...4...
5...6...7...
8...9...10...

👤 INDIVIDUAL EVENTS ....
....
....
....
....
....
....

📑 NOTES ....
....
....
....
....

252	253	254	255

126		127

63

31

Surname: .... First name : .... ♂

▶ Generation7 – *paternal ascendant*

Child : ☐ *Legitimate* ☐ *Natural* ☐ *Adopted* ☐ *Found* ☐ *Recognized* ☐ *Adulterated*   ☐ *Implex*

Born : ....in ....

Baptized : ....in ....

Godfather: ....Godmother : ....

Son of : ....and: ....

Nationality : ....Religion : ....Studies: ....

Occupation(s) : ....

Deceased : ....in ....Cause:.............................

☐ *Buried* ☐ *Cremated* ☐ *Disappeared* on : ....in : ....

⚭ MARITAL STATUS   ☐ *Civil Marriage*   ☐ *Religious Marriage*   ☐ *Free Union*

Date : ....in... ☐ *Marriage contract*

Witnesses : ....

....

☐ *Separation* ☐ *Divorce* ☐ *Widowhood of the groom/bride* Date : ....

👪 FAMILY EVENTS   ....

....
....
....
....
....
....

⚭ OTHER UNION(S)/ 👪 CHILDREN   ....

....
....
....

👫 SIBLINGS   ▶ *Details page 129*   ♂ .... ♀ ....   1.....................................

2...3.................................4.....................................

5...6.................................7.....................................

8...9.................................10....................................

👤 INDIVIDUAL EVENTS   ....

....
....
....

⛑ MILITARY LIFE   Assignment(s) : ....

Campaign(s): ....

Medal(s) : ....☐ *Died in combat* ☐ *Injured on* : ....

256	257	258	259

| 128 | | 129 |

64

32

🗒 NOTES   ....

....
....
....
....

♀ Surname : .... First name : ....

□ *Implex*   Child : □ *Legitimate* □ *Natural* □ *Adopted* □ *Found* □ *Recognized* □ *Adulterated*

Born : ....in...

Baptized : ....in...

Godfather: ....Godmother : ....

Daughter of : ....and: ....

Nationality : ....Religion : ....Studies: ....

Occupation(s) : ....

Deceased : ....in.......................Cause:...........................

□ *Buried* □ *Cremated* □ *Disappeared* on : ....in : ....

👫 CHILDREN ♂ .... ♀	Gen.	° Birth	† Death	Spouse
....	......	....	....	....
....	......	....	....	....
....	......	....	....	....
....	......	....	....	....
....	......	....	....	....
....	......	....	....	....
....	......	....	....	....
....	......	....	....	....
....	......	....	....	....
....	......	....	....	....

💍 OTHER UNION(S)/ 👫 CHILDREN ....

....

....

👫 SIBLINGS   ▶ *Details page 131*   ♂ .... ♀ ....   1...

2..3..4...............................

5..6..7...............................

8..9..10..............................

👤 INDIVIDUAL EVENTS ....

....

....

....

....

....

....

📑 NOTES ....

....

....

....

....

260	261	262	263
130		131	
	65		
	32		

Sosa 65

Surname: .... First name : .... ♂

▶ Generation7 – *paternal ascendant*

Child : □ *Legitimate* □ *Natural* □ *Adopted* □ *Found* □ *Recognized* □ *Adulterated*   □ *Implex*

Born : ....in ....

Baptized : ....in ....

Godfather: ....Godmother : ....

Son of : ....and: ....

Nationality : ....Religion : ....Studies: ....

Occupation(s) : ....

Deceased : ....in ....Cause:...............................

□ *Buried* □ *Cremated* □ *Disappeared* on : ....in : ....

ⓐ MARITAL STATUS   □ *Civil Marriage* □ *Religious Marriage* □ *Free Union*

Date : ....in ....   □ *Marriage contract*

Witnesses : ....

....

□ *Separation* □ *Divorce* □ *Widowhood of the groom/bride* Date : ....

👫 FAMILY EVENTS   ....

....

....

....

....

....

ⓐ OTHER UNION(S)/ 👫 CHILDREN   ....

....

....

....

👫 SIBLINGS   ▶ *Details page 133*   ♂ .... ♀ .... 1..

2.. 3.. 4..

5.. 6.. 7..

8.. 9.. 10...

👤 INDIVIDUAL EVENTS   ....

....

....

⛑ MILITARY LIFE   Assignment(s) : ....

Campaign(s): ....

Medal(s) : ....□ *Died in combat* □ *Injured on* : ....

....

264	265	266	267

| 132 | | 133 |

66

33

📄 NOTES   ....

....

....

....

....

....

♀ Surname : .... First name : ....

Sosa
67

▶ Generation 7 – *paternal ascendant*

☐ *Implex*   Child : ☐ *Legitimate* ☐ *Natural* ☐ *Adopted* ☐ *Found* ☐ *Recognized* ☐ *Adulterated*

Born : ....in...

Baptized : ....in...

Godfather: ....Godmother : ....

Daughter of : ....and:.............................

Nationality : ....Religion : ....Studies: ....

Occupation(s) : ....

Deceased : ....in.........................Cause:.....................

☐ *Buried* ☐ *Cremated* ☐ *Disappeared* on : ....in : ....

👫 CHILDREN ♂ .... ♀ ....

	Gen.	° Birth	† Death	Spouse
....	......	....	....	....
....	......	....	....	....
....	......	....	....	....
....	......	....	....	....
....	......	....	....	....
....	......	....	....	....
....	......	....	....	....
....	......	....	....	....
....	......	....	....	....
....	......	....	....	....

💍 OTHER UNION(S)/ 👫 CHILDREN ....

....
....
....

👫 SIBLINGS   ▶ *Details page 135*   ♂ .... ♀ ....   1............................

2............................ 3............................ 4............................
5............................ 6............................ 7............................
8............................ 9............................ 10...........................

👤 INDIVIDUAL EVENTS ....

....
....
....
....
....
....

📑 NOTES ....

| 268 | 269 | 270 | 271 |

| 134 | | 135 |

67

33

....

67

Sosa 68 ♂

Surname: .... **First name :** ....

Child : □ *Legitimate* □ *Natural* □ *Adopted* □ *Found* □ *Recognized* □ *Adulterated*   □ *Implex*

Born : ....in......................................

Baptized : ....in...............................

Godfather: ....Godmother : ....

Son of : ....and: ....

Nationality : ....Religion : ....Studies: ....

Occupation(s) : ....

Deceased : ....in................................Cause:.........................

□ *Buried* □ *Cremated* □ *Disappeared* on : ....in :.....................

🔗 MARITAL STATUS   □ *Civil Marriage*   □ *Religious Marriage*   □ *Free Union*

Date : ....in... □ *Marriage contract*

Witnesses : ....

....

□ *Separation* □ *Divorce* □ *Widowhood of the groom/bride*   Date : ....

👫 FAMILY EVENTS ....

....
....
....
....
....

🔗 OTHER UNION(S)/ 👫 CHILDREN ....

....
....
....

👫 SIBLINGS   ▶ *Details page 137*   ♂ .... ♀ ....   1..................

2................................ 3................................ 4................................

5................................ 6................................ 7................................

8................................ 9................................ 10................................

👤 INDIVIDUAL EVENTS ....

....
....

⛑ MILITARY LIFE   Assignment(s) : ....

Campaign(s): ....

Medal(s) : ....□ *Died in combat* □ *Injured on* : ....

....

| 272 | 273 | 274 | 275 |

| 136 | 137 |

| 68 |

| 34 |

📝 NOTES ....

....
....
....
....

68

♀ Surname : ....First name : ....

▶ Generation 7 - *paternal ascendant*

□ *Implex*   Child : □ *Legitimate* □ *Natural* □ *Adopted* □ *Found* □ *Recognized* □ *Adulterated*

Born : ....in..

Baptized : ....in...

Godfather: ....Godmother : ....

Daughter of : ....and:...

Nationality : ....Religion : ....Studies: ....

Occupation(s) : ....

Deceased : ....in.......................Cause:..........................

□ *Buried* □ *Cremated* □ *Disappeared* on : ....in : ....

👫 CHILDREN ♂ .... ♀	Gen.	° Birth	† Death	Spouse
....	......	....	....	....
....	......	....	....	....
....	......	....	....	....
....	......	....	....	....
....	......	....	....	....
....	......	....	....	....
....	......	....	....	....
....	......	....	....	....
....	......	....	....	....
....	......	....	....	....
....	......	....	....	....

💍 OTHER UNION(S)/ 👫 CHILDREN ....

....

....

👫 SIBLINGS   ▶ *Details page 139*   ♂ .... ♀ ....   1.....................................

2.................................... 3.................................... 4.....................................

5.................................... 6.................................... 7.....................................

8.................................... 9.................................... 10....................................

👤 INDIVIDUAL EVENTS ....

....

....

....

....

....

....

📝 NOTES ....

....

....

....

276	277	278	279

138		139

69

34

Surname: .... First name : .... ♂

▶ Generation7 – *paternal ascendant*

Child : ☐ *Legitimate* ☐ *Natural* ☐ *Adopted* ☐ *Found* ☐ *Recognized* ☐ *Adulterated*   ☐ *Implex*

Born : ....in ....

Baptized : ....in ....

Godfather: ....Godmother : ....

Son of : ....and: ....

Nationality : ....Religion : ....Studies: ....

Occupation(s) : ....

Deceased : ....in................................Cause:..........................

☐ *Buried* ☐ *Cremated* ☐ *Disappeared* on : ....in : ....

⚭ MARITAL STATUS   ☐ *Civil Marriage*   ☐ *Religious Marriage*   ☐ *Free Union*

Date : ....in... ☐ *Marriage contract*

Witnesses : ....

....

☐ *Separation* ☐ *Divorce* ☐ *Widowhood of the groom/bride*   Date : ....

👫 FAMILY EVENTS   ....

....
....
....
....
....

⚭ OTHER UNION(S)/👫 CHILDREN ....

....
....
....

👫 SIBLINGS   ▶ *Details page 141*   ♂ .... ♀ .... 1.................................

2.. 3............................... 4.................................

5.. 6............................... 7.................................

8.. 9............................... 10................................

👤 INDIVIDUAL EVENTS ....

....
....
....

⛑ MILITARY LIFE   Assignment(s) : ....

Campaign(s): ....

Medal(s) : ....☐ *Died in combat* ☐ *Injured on* : ....

....

280	281	282	283

| 140 | | 141 |

| 70 |

| 35 |

📑 NOTES ....

....
....
....
....

♀ Surname : .... First name : ....

▶ Generation 7 – *paternal ascendant*

☐ *Implex*   Child : ☐ *Legitimate* ☐ *Natural* ☐ *Adopted* ☐ *Found* ☐ *Recognized* ☐ *Adulterated*

Born : ....in...

Baptized : ....in...

Godfather: ....Godmother : ....

Daughter of : ....and:...

Nationality : ....Religion : ....Studies: ....

Occupation(s) : ....

Deceased : ....in...........................Cause:.......................

☐ *Buried* ☐ *Cremated* ☐ *Disappeared* on : ....in : ....

👫 CHILDREN ♂ .... ♀	Gen.	° Birth	† Death	Spouse
....	......	....	....	....
....	......	....	....	....
....	......	....	....	....
....	......	....	....	....
....	......	....	....	....
....	......	....	....	....
....	......	....	....	....
....	......	....	....	....
....	......	....	....	....
....	......	....	....	....

💍 OTHER UNION(S)/ 👫 CHILDREN ....

....

....

....

👫 SIBLINGS   ▶ *Details page 143*   ♂ .... ♀ .... 1..

2.. 3............................ 4..

5.. 6............................ 7..

8.. 9............................ 10..

👤 INDIVIDUAL EVENTS ....

....

....

....

....

....

....

📝 NOTES ....

....

....

....

284	285	286	287
142		143	
71			
35			

Surname: .... First name : .... ♂

Child : □ *Legitimate* □ *Natural* □ *Adopted* □ *Found* □ *Recognized* □ *Adulterated*   □ *Implex*

Born : ....in...

Baptized : ....in...

Godfather: ....Godmother : ....

Son of : ....and:...

Nationality : ....Religion : ....Studies: ....

Occupation(s) : ....

Deceased : ....in...........................Cause:..............................

□ *Buried* □ *Cremated* □ *Disappeared* on : ....in :.........................

⚭ MARITAL STATUS   □ *Civil Marriage* □ *Religious Marriage* □ *Free Union*

Date : ....in.......................................   □ *Marriage contract*

Witnesses : ....
....

□ *Separation* □ *Divorce* □ *Widowhood of the groom/bride* Date : ....

👪 FAMILY EVENTS ....
....
....
....
....
....

⚭ OTHER UNION(S)/ 👫 CHILDREN ....
....
....
....

👫 SIBLINGS   ▶ *Details page 145*   ♂ .... ♀ ....   1................................

2.................................... 3.................................... 4....................................

5.................................... 6.................................... 7....................................

8.................................... 9.................................... 10...................................

👤 INDIVIDUAL EVENTS ....
....
....

⛑ MILITARY LIFE Assignment(s) : ....

Campaign(s): ....

Medal(s) : ....□ *Died in combat* □ *Injured on :* ....

288	289	290	291
144		145	
	72		
	36		

🗐 NOTES ....
....
....
....

♀ Surname : ....First name : ....

▶ Generation 7 – *paternal ascendant*

☐ *Implex*   Child : ☐ *Legitimate* ☐ *Natural* ☐ *Adopted* ☐ *Found* ☐ *Recognized* ☐ *Adulterated*

Born : ....in...

Baptized : ....in...

Godfather: ....Godmother : ....

Daughter of : ....and:..

Nationality : ....Religion : ....Studies: ....

Occupation(s) : ....

Deceased : ....in.........................Cause:.....................

☐ *Buried* ☐ *Cremated* ☐ *Disappeared* on : ....in :..................

👫 CHILDREN ♂ .... ♀	Gen.	° Birth	† Death	Spouse
....	......	....	....	....
....	......	....	....	....
....	......	....	....	....
....	......	....	....	....
....	......	....	....	....
....	......	....	....	....
....	......	....	....	....
....	......	....	....	....
....	......	....	....	....
....	......	....	....	....

💍 OTHER UNION(S)/ 👫 CHILDREN ....

....

....

👫 SIBLINGS ▶ *Details page 147* ♂ .... ♀ .... **1.**..

2.......................................**3.**......................................**4.**......................................

5.......................................**6.**......................................**7.**......................................

8.......................................**9.**......................................**10.**....................................

👤 INDIVIDUAL EVENTS ....

....

....

....

....

....

....

📝 NOTES ....

....

....

....

292	293	294	295

146	147

73

36

Surname: .... First name : .... ♂

Child : ☐ *Legitimate* ☐ *Natural* ☐ *Adopted* ☐ *Found* ☐ *Recognized* ☐ *Adulterated*   ☐ *Implex*

Born : ....in...

Baptized : ....in...

Godfather: ....Godmother : ....

Son of : ....and: ....

Nationality : ....Religion : ....Studies: ....

Occupation(s) : ....

Deceased : ....in.......................Cause:...........................

☐ *Buried* ☐ *Cremated* ☐ *Disappeared* on : ....in : ....

⚭ MARITAL STATUS   ☐ *Civil Marriage* ☐ *Religious Marriage* ☐ *Free Union*

Date : ....in...

☐ *Marriage contract*

Witnesses : ....

....

☐ *Separation* ☐ *Divorce* ☐ *Widowhood of the groom/bride* Date : ....

👫 FAMILY EVENTS   ....

....

....

....

....

....

⚭ OTHER UNION(S)/ 👫 CHILDREN   ....

....

....

....

👫 SIBLINGS   ▶ *Details page 149*   ♂ ....   ♀ ....   1. ....

2. ....3. ....4. ....

5. ....6. ....7. ....

8. ....9. ....10. ....

👤 INDIVIDUAL EVENTS   ....

....

....

....

⛑ MILITARY LIFE   Assignment(s) : ....

Campaign(s): ....

Medal(s) : ....☐ *Died in combat* ☐ *Injured on :* ....

296	297	298	299

| 148 | | 149 |

| 74 |

| 37 |

📑 NOTES   ....

....

....

....

....

♀ Surname : ....First name : ....

▶ Generation 7 – *paternal ascendant*

□ *Implex*   Child : □ *Legitimate* □ *Natural* □ *Adopted* □ *Found* □ *Recognized* □ *Adulterated*

Born : ....in...

Baptized : ....in...

Godfather: ....Godmother : ....

Daughter of : ....and: ....

Nationality : ....Religion : ....Studies: ....

Occupation(s) : ....

Deceased : ....in...................Cause:........................

□ *Buried* □ *Cremated* □ *Disappeared* on : ....in : ....

👫 CHILDREN ♂ .... ♀	Gen.	° Birth	† Death	Spouse
....	......	....	....	....
....	......	....	....	....
....	......	....	....	....
....	......	....	....	....
....	......	....	....	....
....	......	....	....	....
....	......	....	....	....
....	......	....	....	....
....	......	....	....	....
....	......	....	....	....

💍 **OTHER UNION(S)/** 👫 **CHILDREN** ....

....

....

👫 **SIBLINGS** ▶ *Details page 151*   ♂ .... ♀ .... 1...

2..3..4...

5..6..7...

8..9..10..

👤 **INDIVIDUAL EVENTS** ....

....

....

....

....

....

....

📝 **NOTES** ....

....

....

....

300	301	302	303

| 150 | | 151 |

75

| 37 |

Surname: .... First name : .... ♂

Child : □ *Legitimate* □ *Natural* □ *Adopted* □ *Found* □ *Recognized* □ *Adulterated*   □ *Implex*

Born : ....in ....

Baptized : ....in ....

Godfather: ....Godmother : ....

Son of : ....and: ....

Nationality : ....Religion : ....Studies: ....

Occupation(s) : ....

Deceased : ....in..................................Cause:..............................

□ *Buried* □ *Cremated* □ *Disappeared* on : ....in : ....

💍 MARITAL STATUS   □ *Civil Marriage*   □ *Religious Marriage*   □ *Free Union*

Date : ....in..................................   □ *Marriage contract*

Witnesses : ....

....

□ *Separation* □ *Divorce* □ *Widowhood of the groom/bride* Date : ....

👫 FAMILY EVENTS   ....

....
....
....
....
....
....

💍 OTHER UNION(S)/👫 CHILDREN ....

....
....
....

👫 SIBLINGS   ▶ *Details page 153*   ♂ ....   ♀ ....   1.............................

2..3..4..............................

5..6..7..............................

8..9..10..............................

👤 INDIVIDUAL EVENTS   ....

....
....
....

⛑ MILITARY LIFE   Assignment(s) : ....

Campaign(s): ....

Medal(s) : ....□ *Died in combat* □ *Injured on* : ....

....

304	305	306	307

📑 NOTES ....

....
....
....
....
....

152 ... 153 ... 76 ... 38

♀ Surname : ....First name : ....

▶ Generation 7 – *paternal ascendant*

□ *Implex*   Child : □ *Legitimate* □ *Natural* □ *Adopted* □ *Found* □ *Recognized* □ *Adulterated*

Born : ....in..

Baptized : ....in..

Godfather: ....Godmother : ....

Daughter of : ....and: ....

Nationality : ....Religion : ....Studies: ....

Occupation(s) : ....

Deceased : ....in..Cause:....................

□ *Buried* □ *Cremated* □ *Disappeared* on : ....in : ....

👫 CHILDREN ♂ .... ♀ ....

	Gen.	° Birth	† Death	Spouse
....	......	....	....	....
....	......	....	....	....
....	......	....	....	....
....	......	....	....	....
....	......	....	....	....
....	......	....	....	....
....	......	....	....	....
....	......	....	....	....
....	......	....	....	....
....	......	....	....	....

💍 OTHER UNION(S)/ 👫 CHILDREN ....

....

....

👫 SIBLINGS   ▶ *Details page 155*   ♂ .... ♀ ....   1. ....

2. .... 3. .... 4. ....

5. .... 6. .... 7. ....

8. .... 9. .... 10. ....

👤 INDIVIDUAL EVENTS ....

....

....

....

....

....

📝 NOTES ....

....

....

....

....

308	309	310	311

| 154 | | 155 |

77

38

Surname: .... First name : .... ♂

► Generation7 – *paternal ascendant*

Child : ☐ *Legitimate* ☐ *Natural* ☐ *Adopted* ☐ *Found* ☐ *Recognized* ☐ *Adulterated*   ☐ *Implex*

Born : ....in...

Baptized : ....in...

Godfather: ....Godmother : ....

Son of : ....and:...

Nationality : ....Religion : ....Studies: ....

Occupation(s) : ....

Deceased : ....in............................Cause:........................

☐ *Buried* ☐ *Cremated* ☐ *Disappeared* on : ....in : ....

💍 MARITAL STATUS   ☐ *Civil Marriage*   ☐ *Religious Marriage*   ☐ *Free Union*

Date : ....in... ☐ *Marriage contract*

Witnesses : ....
....

☐ *Separation* ☐ *Divorce* ☐ *Widowhood of the groom/bride* Date : ....

👫 FAMILY EVENTS   ....
....
....
....
....
....
....

💍 OTHER UNION(S)/ 👫 CHILDREN ....
....
....
....

👫 SIBLINGS   ► *Details page 157*   ♂ .... ♀ ....   1.....................................
2.....................................3.....................................4.....................................
5.....................................6.....................................7.....................................
8.....................................9.....................................10....................................

👤 INDIVIDUAL EVENTS ....
....
....

⛑ MILITARY LIFE   Assignment(s) : ....
Campaign(s): ....
Medal(s) : ....☐ *Died in combat* ☐ *Injured on* : ....
....

312	313	314	315

156   157

78

39

📝 NOTES ....
....
....
....
....

♀ Surname : ....First name : ....

▶ Generation 7 – paternal ascendant

☐ *Implex*   Child : ☐ *Legitimate* ☐ *Natural* ☐ *Adopted* ☐ *Found* ☐ *Recognized* ☐ *Adulterated*

Born : ....in..

Baptized : ....in.......................................

Godfather: ....Godmother : ....

Daughter of : ....and: ....

Nationality : ....Religion : ....Studies:...............

Occupation(s) : ....

Deceased : ....in...............................Cause:...............

☐ *Buried* ☐ *Cremated* ☐ *Disappeared* on : ....in : ....

👫 CHILDREN ♂ .... ♀	Gen.	° Birth	† Death	Spouse
....	......	....	....	....
....	......	....	....	....
....	......	....	....	....
....	......	....	....	....
....	......	....	....	....
....	......	....	....	....
....	......	....	....	....
....	......	....	....	....
....	......	....	....	....
....	......	....	....	....

💍 OTHER UNION(S)/ 👫 CHILDREN ....

....

....

....

👫 SIBLINGS ▶ *Details page 159*   ♂ .... ♀ ....   1.........................

2............................3............................4............................

5............................6............................7............................

8............................9............................10...........................

👤 INDIVIDUAL EVENTS ....

....

....

....

....

....

....

📑 NOTES ....

....

....

....

....

316	317	318	319
158		159	
79			
39			

Surname: .... First name : .... ♂

Child : □ *Legitimate* □ *Natural* □ *Adopted* □ *Found* □ *Recognized* □ *Adulterated*　　□ *Implex*

Born : ....in..

Baptized : ....in..

Godfather: ....Godmother : ....

Son of : ....and: ....

Nationality : ....Religion : ....Studies: ....

Occupation(s) : ....

Deceased : ....in...................Cause:...............................

□ *Buried* □ *Cremated* □ *Disappeared* on : ....in : ....

🪐 MARITAL STATUS　　　□ *Civil Marriage* □ *Religious Marriage* □ *Free Union*

Date : ....in..□ *Marriage contract*

Witnesses : ....

....

□ *Separation* □ *Divorce* □ *Widowhood of the groom/bride* Date : ....

🧑‍🧒 FAMILY EVENTS ....

....

....

....

....

....

💍 OTHER UNION(S)/ 🧑‍🧒 CHILDREN ....

....

....

....

👫 SIBLINGS　▶ *Details page 161*　♂ .... ♀ ....　1..............................

2.................................... 3.................................... 4....................................

5.................................... 6.................................... 7....................................

8.................................... 9.................................... 10...................................

👤 INDIVIDUAL EVENTS ....

....

....

⛑ MILITARY LIFE　Assignment(s) : ....

Campaign(s): ....

Medal(s) : ....□ *Died in combat* □ *Injured on* : ....

....

| 320 | 321 | 322 | 323 |

| 160 | | 161 |

| 80 |

| 40 |

📝 NOTES ....

....

....

....

....

♀ Surname : ....First name : ....

▶ Generation 7 – *paternal ascendant*

□ *Implex*   Child : □ *Legitimate* □ *Natural* □ *Adopted* □ *Found* □ *Recognized* □ *Adulterated*

Born : ....in...

Baptized : ....in...

Godfather: ....Godmother : ....

Daughter of : ....and:...

Nationality : ....Religion : ....Studies:..................

Occupation(s) : ....

Deceased : ....in.........................Cause:...................

□ *Buried* □ *Cremated* □ *Disappeared* on : ....in : ....

👫 CHILDREN ♂ .... ♀	Gen.	° Birth	† Death	Spouse
....	......	....	....	....
....	......	....	....	....
....	......	....	....	....
....	......	....	....	....
....	......	....	....	....
....	......	....	....	....
....	......	....	....	....
....	......	....	....	....
....	......	....	....	....
....	......	....	....	....

💍 OTHER UNION(S)/ 👫 CHILDREN ....

....

....

👫 SIBLINGS   ▶ *Details page 163*   ♂ .... ♀ ....   1..................................

2...3...4..................................

5...6...7..................................

8...9...10.................................

👤 INDIVIDUAL EVENTS ....

....

....

....

....

....

....

📑 NOTES ....

....

....

....

324	325	326	327
	162	163	
		81	
		40	

Surname: ....First name : .... ♂

Child : ☐ *Legitimate* ☐ *Natural* ☐ *Adopted* ☐ *Found* ☐ *Recognized* ☐ *Adulterated*   ☐ *Implex*

Born : ....in...

Baptized : ....in...

Godfather: ....Godmother : ....

Son of : ....and: ....

Nationality : ....Religion : ....Studies: ....

Occupation(s) : ....

Deceased : ....in...........................Cause:...........................

☐ *Buried* ☐ *Cremated* ☐ *Disappeared* on : ....in : ....

⊙ MARITAL STATUS   ☐ *Civil Marriage*   ☐ *Religious Marriage*   ☐ *Free Union*

Date : ....in..☐ *Marriage contract*

Witnesses : ....

....

☐ *Separation* ☐ *Divorce* ☐ *Widowhood of the groom/bride*   Date : ....

👪 FAMILY EVENTS   ....

....

....

....

....

....

....

⊙ OTHER UNION(S)/👪 CHILDREN ....

....

....

....

👫 SIBLINGS   ▶ *Details page 165*   ♂ ....   ♀ ....   1............................

2..3..4..........................

5..6..7..........................

8..9..10........................

👤 INDIVIDUAL EVENTS   ....

....

....

....

⛑ MILITARY LIFE   Assignment(s) : ....

Campaign(s): ....

Medal(s) : ....☐ *Died in combat* ☐ *Injured on* : ....

....

328	329	330	331

164		165

82

41

🗒 NOTES ....

....

....

....

....

♀ Surname : ....First name : ....

▶ Generation 7 – *paternal ascendant*

□ *Implex*   Child : □ *Legitimate* □ *Natural* □ *Adopted* □ *Found* □ *Recognized* □ *Adulterated*

Born : ....in...

Baptized : ....in...

Godfather: ....Godmother : ....

Daughter of : ....and: ....

Nationality : ....Religion : ....Studies: ....

Occupation(s) : ....

Deceased : ....in.................................Cause:.................................

□ *Buried* □ *Cremated* □ *Disappeared* on : ....in : ....

👫 CHILDREN ♂ .... ♀ ....

	Gen.	° Birth	† Death	Spouse
....	......	....	....	....
....	......	....	....	....
....	......	....	....	....
....	......	....	....	....
....	......	....	....	....
....	......	....	....	....
....	......	....	....	....
....	......	....	....	....
....	......	....	....	....
....	......	....	....	....

💍 OTHER UNION(S)/ 👫 CHILDREN ....

....

....

....

👫 SIBLINGS ▶ *Details page 167* ♂ .... ♀ .... 1. ....

2. .... 3. .... 4. ....

5. .... 6. .... 7. ....

8. .... 9. .... 10. ....

👤 INDIVIDUAL EVENTS ....

....

....

....

....

....

....

📝 NOTES ....

332	333	334	335
	166		167
		83	
		41	

....

....

....

Surname: .... First name : .... ♂

▶ Generation7 – *paternal ascendant*

Child : ☐ *Legitimate* ☐ *Natural* ☐ *Adopted* ☐ *Found* ☐ *Recognized* ☐ *Adulterated*   ☐ *Implex*

Born : ....in...............

Baptized : ....in...............

Godfather: ....Godmother : ....

Son of : ....and:.....................

Nationality : ....Religion : ....Studies: ....

Occupation(s) : ....

Deceased : ....in......................Cause:.............................

☐ *Buried* ☐ *Cremated* ☐ *Disappeared* on : ....in :.............................

💍 MARITAL STATUS   ☐ *Civil Marriage* ☐ *Religious Marriage* ☐ *Free Union*

Date : ....in...☐ *Marriage contract*

Witnesses : ....

....

☐ *Separation* ☐ *Divorce* ☐ *Widowhood of the groom/bride* Date : ....

👪 FAMILY EVENTS

....
....
....
....
....

💍 OTHER UNION(S)/👪 CHILDREN

....
....
....

👫 SIBLINGS ▶ *Details page 169* ♂ .... ♀ .... 1..............................

2................................3................................4...............................

5................................6................................7...............................

8................................9................................10..............................

👤 INDIVIDUAL EVENTS

....
....

⛑ MILITARY LIFE Assignment(s) : ....

Campaign(s): ....

Medal(s) : ....☐ *Died in combat* ☐ *Injured on* : ....

336	337	338	339

168		169

84

42

📑 NOTES ....

....
....
....
....

♀ Surname : .... First name : ....

Sosa 85

▶ Generation 7 – *paternal ascendant*

□ *Implex*   Child : □ *Legitimate* □ *Natural* □ *Adopted* □ *Found* □ *Recognized* □ *Adulterated*

Born : ....in..

Baptized : ....in..

Godfather: ....Godmother : ....

Daughter of : ....and:...

Nationality : ....Religion : ....Studies:...

Occupation(s) : ....

Deceased : ....in..............................Cause:.......................................

□ *Buried* □ *Cremated* □ *Disappeared* on : ....in :.............................

👫 CHILDREN ♂ .... ♀ ....

	Gen.	° Birth	† Death	Spouse

💍 OTHER UNION(S)/ 👫 CHILDREN ....

....

....

....

👫 SIBLINGS   ▶ *Details page 171*   ♂ .... ♀ ....   1..

2..3...4...

5..6...7...

8..9...10...

👤 INDIVIDUAL EVENTS ....

....

....

....

....

....

....

📝 NOTES ....

....

....

....

340	341	342	343
170		171	
85			
42			

Surname: .... First name : .... ♂

Child : ☐ *Legitimate* ☐ *Natural* ☐ *Adopted* ☐ *Found* ☐ *Recognized* ☐ *Adulterated*   ☐ *Implex*

Born : ....in..

Baptized : ....in...

Godfather: ....Godmother : ....

Son of : ....and:...

Nationality : ....Religion : ....Studies: ....

Occupation(s) : ....

Deceased : ....in...........................Cause:..............................

☐ *Buried* ☐ *Cremated* ☐ *Disappeared* on : ....in : ....

⚭ MARITAL STATUS   ☐ *Civil Marriage* ☐ *Religious Marriage* ☐ *Free Union*

Date : ....in.. ☐ *Marriage contract*

Witnesses : ....

....

☐ *Separation* ☐ *Divorce* ☐ *Widowhood of the groom/bride*   Date : ....

👪 FAMILY EVENTS ....

....

....

....

....

....

⚭ OTHER UNION(S)/ 👪 CHILDREN ....

....

....

....

👫 SIBLINGS   ▶ *Details page 173*   ♂ .... ♀ ....   1...

2...3...4...

5...6...7...

8...9...10.......................................

👤 INDIVIDUAL EVENTS ....

....

....

....

⛑ MILITARY LIFE   Assignment(s) : ....

Campaign(s): ....

Medal(s) : ....☐ *Died in combat* ☐ *Injured on* : ....

....

344	345	346	347

172   173

86

43

🗐 NOTES ....

....

....

....

♀ Surname : ....First name : ....

▶ Generation 7 – *paternal ascendant*

☐ *Implex* Child : ☐ *Legitimate* ☐ *Natural* ☐ *Adopted* ☐ *Found* ☐ *Recognized* ☐ *Adulterated*

Born : ....in...

Baptized : ....in...

Godfather: ....Godmother : ....

Daughter of : ....and: ....

Nationality : ....Religion : ....Studies: ....

Occupation(s) : ....

Deceased : ....in.........................Cause:.....................

☐ *Buried* ☐ *Cremated* ☐ *Disappeared* on : ....in :.....................

👫 CHILDREN ♂ .... ♀ ....

	Gen.	° Birth	† Death	Spouse
....	......	....	....	....
....	......	....	....	....
....	......	....	....	....
....	......	....	....	....
....	......	....	....	....
....	......	....	....	....
....	......	....	....	....
....	......	....	....	....
....	......	....	....	....
....	......	....	....	....
....	......	....	....	....

💍 OTHER UNION(S)/ 👫 CHILDREN ....

....

....

....

👫 SIBLINGS ▶ *Details page 175* ♂ .... ♀ .... 1.................................

2.................................... 3.................................... 4....................................

5.................................... 6.................................... 7....................................

8.................................... 9.................................... 10....................................

👤 INDIVIDUAL EVENTS ....

....

....

....

....

....

....

📑 NOTES ....

....

....

....

....

348	349	350	351
	174	175	

87

43

Surname: ....First name : .... ♂

▶ Generation7 – *paternal ascendant*

Child : □ *Legitimate* □ *Natural* □ *Adopted* □ *Found* □ *Recognized* □ *Adulterated*   □ *Implex*

Born : ....in...

Baptized : ....in...............................

Godfather: ....Godmother : ....

Son of : ....and: ....

Nationality : ....Religion : ....Studies: ....

Occupation(s) : ....

Deceased : ....in...............................Cause:...............................

□ *Buried* □ *Cremated* □ *Disappeared* on : ....in : ....

⚭ MARITAL STATUS   □ *Civil Marriage*   □ *Religious Marriage*   □ *Free Union*

Date : ....in...............................   □ *Marriage contract*

Witnesses : ....

....

□ *Separation* □ *Divorce* □ *Widowhood of the groom/bride*   Date : ....

👫 FAMILY EVENTS ....

....

....

....

....

⚭ OTHER UNION(S)/ 👫 CHILDREN ....

....

....

....

👫 SIBLINGS   ▶ *Details page 177*   ♂ .... ♀ .... 1................................

2................................ 3................................ 4................................

5................................ 6................................ 7................................

8................................ 9................................ 10................................

👤 INDIVIDUAL EVENTS

....

....

⛑ MILITARY LIFE   Assignment(s) : ....

Campaign(s): ....

Medal(s) : ....□ *Died in combat* □ *Injured on* : ....

....

352	353	354	355

```
  176        177
       88
       44
```

📋 NOTES ....

....

....

....

....

♀ Surname : ....First name : ....

▶ Generation 7 – *paternal ascendant*

□ *Implex*   Child : □ *Legitimate* □ *Natural* □ *Adopted* □ *Found* □ *Recognized* □ *Adulterated*

Born : ....in...

Baptized : ....in...

Godfather: ....Godmother : ....

Daughter of : ....and: ....

Nationality : ....Religion : ....Studies: ....

Occupation(s) : ....

Deceased : ....in...............................Cause:........................

□ *Buried* □ *Cremated* □ *Disappeared* on : ....in : ....

👫 CHILDREN ♂ .... ♀	Gen.	° Birth	† Death	Spouse
....	......	....	....	....
....	......	....	....	....
....	......	....	....	....
....	......	....	....	....
....	......	....	....	....
....	......	....	....	....
....	......	....	....	....
....	......	....	....	....
....	......	....	....	....
....	......	....	....	....

💍 OTHER UNION(S)/ 👫 CHILDREN ....
....
....

👫 SIBLINGS ▶ *Details page 179*   ♂ .... ♀ ....   1...

2.....................................3.....................................4.....................................

5.....................................6.....................................7.....................................

8.....................................9.....................................10....................................

👤 INDIVIDUAL EVENTS ....
....
....
....
....
....
....

📝 NOTES ....

| 356 | 357 | 358 | 359 |

| 178 | 179 |

89

44

....
....
....
....

90

Surname: .... First name : .... ♂

Child : ☐ *Legitimate* ☐ *Natural* ☐ *Adopted* ☐ *Found* ☐ *Recognized* ☐ *Adulterated*   ☐ *Implex*

Born : ....in...................................

Baptized : ....in...................................

Godfather: ....Godmother : ....

Son of : ....and:...................................

Nationality : ....Religion : ....Studies: ....

Occupation(s) : ....

Deceased : ....in.......................Cause:......................

☐ *Buried* ☐ *Cremated* ☐ *Disappeared* on : ....in : ....

⊚ MARITAL STATUS   ☐ *Civil Marriage* ☐ *Religious Marriage* ☐ *Free Union*

Date : ....in.............................. ☐ *Marriage contract*

Witnesses : ....

....

☐ *Separation* ☐ *Divorce* ☐ *Widowhood of the groom/bride* Date : ....

👪 FAMILY EVENTS ....

....
....
....
....
....

⊚ OTHER UNION(S)/👪 CHILDREN ....

....
....
....

👫 SIBLINGS ▶ *Details page 181* ♂ .... ♀ .... 1.................................

2..................................... 3..................................... 4.................................

5..................................... 6..................................... 7.................................

8..................................... 9..................................... 10................................

👤 INDIVIDUAL EVENTS ....

....
....

⛑ MILITARY LIFE Assignment(s) : ....

Campaign(s): ....

Medal(s) : ....☐ *Died in combat* ☐ *Injured on* : ....

....

360	361	362	363
180		181	
	90		
	45		

📰 NOTES ....

....
....
....
....

♀ Surname : ....First name : ....

□ *Implex*　　　Child : □ *Legitimate* □ *Natural* □ *Adopted* □ *Found* □ *Recognized* □ *Adulterated*

Born : ....in...

Baptized : ....in..

Godfather: ....Godmother : ....

Daughter of : ....and: ....

Nationality : ....Religion : ....Studies: ....

Occupation(s) : ....

Deceased : ....in.............................Cause:...........................

□ *Buried* □ *Cremated* □ *Disappeared* on : ....in : ....

👪 CHILDREN ♂ .... ♀ ....

	Gen.	° Birth	† Death	Spouse
....	......	....	....	....
....	......	....	....	....
....	......	....	....	....
....	......	....	....	....
....	......	....	....	....
....	......	....	....	....
....	......	....	....	....
....	......	....	....	....
....	......	....	....	....
....	......	....	....	....

💍 OTHER UNION(S)/ 👪 CHILDREN ....

....

....

....

👪 SIBLINGS ▶ *Details page 183* ♂ .... ♀ .... 1...

2...3...4................................

5...6...7................................

8...9...10..............................

👤 INDIVIDUAL EVENTS ....

....

....

....

....

....

....

....

📝 NOTES ....

....

....

....

364	365	366	367
	182		183
		91	
		45	

Surname: ....First name : .... ♂

Child : □ *Legitimate* □ *Natural* □ *Adopted* □ *Found* □ *Recognized* □ *Adulterated*   □ *Implex*

Born : ....in ....

Baptized : ....in ....

Godfather: ....Godmother : ....

Son of : ....and: ....

Nationality : ....Religion : ....Studies: ....

Occupation(s) : ....

Deceased : ....in...........................Cause:........................

□ *Buried* □ *Cremated* □ *Disappeared* on : ....in : ....

⚭ MARITAL STATUS   □ *Civil Marriage* □ *Religious Marriage* □ *Free Union*

Date : ....in.. □ *Marriage contract*

Witnesses : ....

....

□ *Separation* □ *Divorce* □ *Widowhood of the groom/bride* Date : ....

👪 FAMILY EVENTS ....

....

....

....

....

....

⚭ OTHER UNION(S)/ 👪 CHILDREN ....

....

....

....

👫 SIBLINGS   ▶ *Details page 185*   ♂ .... ♀ ....   1................................

2...................................... 3................................... 4.................................

5...................................... 6................................... 7.................................

8...................................... 9................................... 10................................

👤 INDIVIDUAL EVENTS ....

....

....

....

⛑ MILITARY LIFE   Assignment(s) : ....

Campaign(s): ....

Medal(s) : ....□ *Died in combat* □ *Injured on* : ....

....

368	369	370	371
184		185	
	92		
	46		

📑 NOTES ....

....

....

....

....

♀ Surname : .... First name : ....

▶ Generation 7 – *paternal ascendant*

☐ *Implex*

Child : ☐ *Legitimate* ☐ *Natural* ☐ *Adopted* ☐ *Found* ☐ *Recognized* ☐ *Adulterated*

Born : ....in..

Baptized : ....in..

Godfather: ....Godmother : ....

Daughter of : ....and: ....

Nationality : ....Religion : ....Studies: ....

Occupation(s) : ....

Deceased : ....in.....................Cause:................

☐ *Buried* ☐ *Cremated* ☐ *Disappeared* on : ....in : ....

👫 CHILDREN ♂ .... ♀ ....

	Gen.	° Birth	† Death	Spouse

💍 OTHER UNION(S)/ 👫 CHILDREN ....

....
....

👫 SIBLINGS ▶ *Details page 187* ♂ .... ♀ .... 1............

2............................. 3............................. 4.............................
5............................. 6............................. 7.............................
8............................. 9............................. 10............................

👤 INDIVIDUAL EVENTS ....

....
....
....
....
....
....
....

📑 NOTES ....

....
....
....
....

372	373	374	375
186		187	
	93		
	46		

Surname: .... First name : .... ♂

▶ Generation7 – *paternal ascendant*

Child : □ *Legitimate* □ *Natural* □ *Adopted* □ *Found* □ *Recognized* □ *Adulterated*   □ *Implex*

Born : ....in ....

Baptized : ....in ....

Godfather: ....Godmother : ....

Son of : ....and: ....

Nationality : ....Religion : ....Studies: ....

Occupation(s) : ....

Deceased : ....in..........................Cause:........................

□ *Buried* □ *Cremated* □ *Disappeared* on : ....in :..........................

💍 MARITAL STATUS   □ *Civil Marriage* □ *Religious Marriage* □ *Free Union*

Date : ....in.. □ *Marriage contract*

Witnesses : ....
....

□ *Separation* □ *Divorce* □ *Widowhood of the groom/bride* Date : ....

👫 FAMILY EVENTS   ....
....
....
....
....
....

💍 OTHER UNION(S)/👫 CHILDREN   ....
....
....
....

👫 SIBLINGS   ▶ *Details page 189*   ♂ .... ♀ .... 1.............................

2.. 3.............................. 4..............................

5.. 6.............................. 7..............................

8.. 9.............................. 10.............................

👤 INDIVIDUAL EVENTS   ....
....
....
....

⛑ MILITARY LIFE   Assignment(s) : ....

Campaign(s): ....

Medal(s) : ....□ *Died in combat* □ *Injured on* : ....

376	377	378	379
188		189	
	94		
	47		

📑 NOTES ....
....
....
....
....

♀ Surname : .... First name : ....

▶ Generation 7 – *paternal ascendant*

☐ *Implex*   Child : ☐ *Legitimate* ☐ *Natural* ☐ *Adopted* ☐ *Found* ☐ *Recognized* ☐ *Adulterated*

Born : .... .in..

Baptized : .... .in..

Godfather: ....Godmother : ....

Daughter of : ....and: ....

Nationality : ....Religion : ....Studies: ....

Occupation(s) : ....

Deceased : ....in............................Cause:..................

☐ *Buried* ☐ *Cremated* ☐ *Disappeared* on : ....in : ....

👪 CHILDREN ♂ .... ♀	Gen.	° Birth	† Death	Spouse
....	......	....	....	....
....	......	....	....	....
....	......	....	....	....
....	......	....	....	....
....	......	....	....	....
....	......	....	....	....
....	......	....	....	....
....	......	....	....	....
....	......	....	....	....
....	......	....	....	....

💍 OTHER UNION(S)/ 👪 CHILDREN ....

....

....

👪 SIBLINGS ▶ *Details page 191* ♂ .... ♀ .... 1. ....

2. .... 3. .... 4. ....

5. .... 6. .... 7. ....

8. .... 9. .... 10. ....

👤 INDIVIDUAL EVENTS ....

....

....

....

....

....

....

📑 NOTES ....

....

....

....

380	381	382	383
190		191	
95			
47			

Surname: .... First name : .... ♂

Child : ☐ *Legitimate* ☐ *Natural* ☐ *Adopted* ☐ *Found* ☐ *Recognized* ☐ *Adulterated*   ☐ *Implex*

Born : ....in.....................................

Baptized : ....in.....................................

Godfather: ....Godmother : ....

Son of : ....and: ....

Nationality : ....Religion : ....Studies: ....

Occupation(s) : ....

Deceased : ....in.....................Cause:.....................

☐ *Buried* ☐ *Cremated* ☐ *Disappeared* on : ....in : ....

ⓞ MARITAL STATUS   ☐ *Civil Marriage* ☐ *Religious Marriage* ☐ *Free Union*

Date : ....in.....................................   ☐ *Marriage contract*

Witnesses : ....

....

☐ *Separation* ☐ *Divorce* ☐ *Widowhood of the groom/bride* Date : ....

👪 FAMILY EVENTS ....

....
....
....
....
....

ⓞ OTHER UNION(S)/ 👪 CHILDREN ....

....
....
....

👪 SIBLINGS ▶ *Details page 193* ♂ .... ♀ .... 1.....................................

2..................................... 3..................................... 4.....................................

5..................................... 6..................................... 7.....................................

8..................................... 9..................................... 10.....................................

👤 INDIVIDUAL EVENTS ....

....
....
....

⛑ MILITARY LIFE Assignment(s) : ....

Campaign(s): ....

Medal(s) : ....☐ *Died in combat* ☐ *Injured on* : ....

384	385	386	387

192   193

96

48

📝 NOTES ....

....
....
....
....

♀ Surname : .... First name : ....

▶ Generation 7 – *maternal ascendant*

☐ *Implex*   Child : ☐ *Legitimate* ☐ *Natural* ☐ *Adopted* ☐ *Found* ☐ *Recognized* ☐ *Adulterated*

Born : .... in ....

Baptized : .... in ....

Godfather: .... Godmother : ....

Daughter of : .... and: ....

Nationality : .... Religion : .... Studies: ....

Occupation(s) : ....

Deceased : .... in .... Cause:......................

☐ *Buried* ☐ *Cremated* ☐ *Disappeared* on : .... in : ....

👫 CHILDREN ♂ .... ♀	Gen.	° Birth	† Death	Spouse
....	......	....	....	....
....	......	....	....	....
....	......	....	....	....
....	......	....	....	....
....	......	....	....	....
....	......	....	....	....
....	......	....	....	....
....	......	....	....	....
....	......	....	....	....
....	......	....	....	....

💍 OTHER UNION(S)/👫 CHILDREN ....

....

....

👫 SIBLINGS   ▶ *Details page 195*   ♂ ....   ♀ ....   1...

2.................................. 3.................................. 4..................................

5.................................. 6.................................. 7..................................

8.................................. 9.................................. 10..................................

👤 INDIVIDUAL EVENTS ....

....

....

....

....

....

....

📑 NOTES ....

....

....

....

....

388	389	390	391
194		195	
	97		
	48		

Sosa 98

Surname: .... First name : .... ♂

Child : □ *Legitimate* □ *Natural* □ *Adopted* □ *Found* □ *Recognized* □ *Adulterated*   □ *Implex*

Born : .... in ....

Baptized : .... in ....

Godfather: .... Godmother : ....

Son of : .... and: ....

Nationality : .... Religion : .... Studies: ....

Occupation(s) : ....

Deceased : .... in .... Cause: ....

□ *Buried* □ *Cremated* □ *Disappeared* on : .... in : ....

⚭ MARITAL STATUS   □ *Civil Marriage* □ *Religious Marriage* □ *Free Union*

Date : .... in ....   □ *Marriage contract*

Witnesses : ....

....

□ *Separation* □ *Divorce* □ *Widowhood of the groom/bride*   Date : ....

👪 FAMILY EVENTS ....

....

....

....

....

....

⚭ OTHER UNION(S)/ 👪 CHILDREN ....

....

....

....

👫 SIBLINGS   ▶ *Details page 197*   ♂ .... ♀ ....   1. ....

2. .... 3. .... 4. ....

5. .... 6. .... 7. ....

8. .... 9. .... 10. ....

👤 INDIVIDUAL EVENTS ....

....

....

....

⛑ MILITARY LIFE   Assignment(s) : ....

Campaign(s): ....

Medal(s) : .... □ *Died in combat* □ *Injured on* : ....

....

392	393	394	395

```
  ┌─────┬─────┐
 196       197
    └──┬──┘
      98
      49
```

🗒 NOTES ....

....

....

....

....

♀ Surname : .... First name : ....

▶ Generation 7 – *maternal ascendant*

☐ *Implex*　　Child : ☐ *Legitimate* ☐ *Natural* ☐ *Adopted* ☐ *Found* ☐ *Recognized* ☐ *Adulterated*

Born : ....in...

Baptized : ....in..

Godfather: ....Godmother : ....

Daughter of : ....and: ....

Nationality : ....Religion : ....Studies: ....

Occupation(s) : ....

Deceased : ....in....................Cause:........................

☐ *Buried* ☐ *Cremated* ☐ *Disappeared* on : ....in : ....

👫 CHILDREN ♂ .... ♀	Gen.	° Birth	† Death	Spouse
....	......	....	....	....
....	......	....	....	....
....	......	....	....	....
....	......	....	....	....
....	......	....	....	....
....	......	....	....	....
....	......	....	....	....
....	......	....	....	....
....	......	....	....	....
....	......	....	....	....

💍 OTHER UNION(S)/ 👫 CHILDREN ....

....

....

....

👫 SIBLINGS ▶ *Details page 199* ♂ .... ♀ .... 1....................................

2............................... 3............................... 4...............................

5............................... 6............................... 7...............................

8............................... 9............................... 10..............................

👤 INDIVIDUAL EVENTS ....

....

....

....

....

....

....

📝 NOTES ....

....

....

....

396	397	398	399
198		199	
	99		
	49		

Surname: .... First name : .... ♂

▶ Generation7 – *maternal ascendant*

Child : □ *Legitimate* □ *Natural* □ *Adopted* □ *Found* □ *Recognized* □ *Adulterated*   □ *Implex*

Born : ....in...

Baptized : ....in...

Godfather: ....Godmother : ....

Son of : ....and: ....

Nationality : ....Religion : ....Studies: ....

Occupation(s) : ....

Deceased : ....in...........................Cause:..........................

□ *Buried* □ *Cremated* □ *Disappeared* on : ....in :..........................

🔗 MARITAL STATUS   □ *Civil Marriage* □ *Religious Marriage* □ *Free Union*

Date : ....in...□ *Marriage contract*

Witnesses : ....

....

□ *Separation* □ *Divorce* □ *Widowhood of the groom/bride* Date : ....

👪 FAMILY EVENTS   ....

....
....
....
....
....
....

🔗 OTHER UNION(S)/👪 CHILDREN   ....

....
....
....

👫 SIBLINGS   ▶ *Details page 201*   ♂ .... ♀ ....   1............................
2..3..4............................
5..6..7............................
8..9..10............................

👤 INDIVIDUAL EVENTS   ....

....
....
....

⛑ MILITARY LIFE   Assignment(s) : ....

Campaign(s): ....

Medal(s) : ....□ *Died in combat* □ *Injured on* : ....

....

400	401	402	403

📑 NOTES ....

```
400  401  402  403
  200      201
     100
      50
```

....
....
....
....

♀ Surname : .... First name : ....

▶ Generation 7 – *maternal ascendant*

□ *Implex*   Child : □ *Legitimate* □ *Natural* □ *Adopted* □ *Found* □ *Recognized* □ *Adulterated*

Born : ....in..

Baptized : ....in..

Godfather: ....Godmother : ....

Daughter of : ....and: ....

Nationality : ....Religion : ....Studies: ....

Occupation(s) : ....

Deceased : ....in.................................Cause:.............

□ *Buried* □ *Cremated* □ *Disappeared* on : ....in : ....

👫 CHILDREN ♂ .... ♀	Gen.	° Birth	† Death	Spouse
....	.....	....	....	....
....	.....	....	....	....
....	.....	....	....	....
....	.....	....	....	....
....	.....	....	....	....
....	.....	....	....	....
....	.....	....	....	....
....	.....	....	....	....
....	.....	....	....	....
....	.....	....	....	....
....	.....	....	....	....

💍 OTHER UNION(S)/ 👫 CHILDREN ....

....

....

....

👫 SIBLINGS   ▶ *Details page 203*   ♂ .... ♀ .... 1..

2..3..4..

5..6..7..

8..9..10..

👤 INDIVIDUAL EVENTS ....

....

....

....

....

....

....

📑 NOTES ....

....

....

....

....

404	405	406	407
	202		203
		101	
		50	

Surname: .... First name : .... ♂

Child : ☐ *Legitimate* ☐ *Natural* ☐ *Adopted* ☐ *Found* ☐ *Recognized* ☐ *Adulterated*   ☐ *Implex*

Born : ....in...

Baptized : ....in..

Godfather: ....Godmother : ....

Son of : ....and: ....

Nationality : ....Religion : ....Studies: ....

Occupation(s) : ....

Deceased : ....in...........................Cause:......................................

☐ *Buried* ☐ *Cremated* ☐ *Disappeared* on : ....in : ....

⚭ MARITAL STATUS   ☐ *Civil Marriage* ☐ *Religious Marriage* ☐ *Free Union*

Date : ....in..............................☐ *Marriage contract*

Witnesses : ....
....

☐ *Separation* ☐ *Divorce* ☐ *Widowhood of the groom/bride* Date : ....

👫 FAMILY EVENTS ....
....
....
....
....
....

⚭ OTHER UNION(S)/👫 CHILDREN ....
....
....
....

👫 SIBLINGS   ▶ *Details page 205*   ♂ .... ♀ ....   1.....................................
2.. 3.............................. 4....................................
5.. 6.............................. 7....................................
8.. 9.............................. 10..................................

👤 INDIVIDUAL EVENTS ....
....
....

⛑ MILITARY LIFE Assignment(s) : ....

Campaign(s): ....

Medal(s) : ....☐ *Died in combat* ☐ *Injured on* : ....
....

408	409	410	411

| 204 | | 205 |

102

51

📑 NOTES ....
....
....
....
....

♀ Surname : ....First name : ....

■ Sosa 103

▶ Generation 7 - *maternal ascendant*

☐ *Implex* Child : ☐ *Legitimate* ☐ *Natural* ☐ *Adopted* ☐ *Found* ☐ *Recognized* ☐ *Adulterated*

Born : ....in..

Baptized : ....in..

Godfather: ....Godmother : ....

Daughter of : ....and: ....

Nationality : ....Religion : ....Studies: ....

Occupation(s) : ....

Deceased : ....in..Cause:....................

☐ *Buried* ☐ *Cremated* ☐ *Disappeared* on : ....in : ....

👫 CHILDREN ♂ .... ♀ ......

	Gen.	° Birth	† Death	Spouse
....	......	....	....	....
....	......	....	....	....
....	......	....	....	....
....	......	....	....	....
....	......	....	....	....
....	......	....	....	....
....	......	....	....	....
....	......	....	....	....
....	......	....	....	....
....	......	....	....	....

💍 OTHER UNION(S)/ 👫 CHILDREN ....

....

....

....

👫 SIBLINGS ▶ *Details page 207* ♂ .... ♀ .... 1...

2............................. 3............................. 4.............................

5............................. 6............................. 7.............................

8............................. 9............................. 10............................

👤 INDIVIDUAL EVENTS ....

....

....

....

....

....

....

📑 NOTES ....

....

....

....

412	413	414	415

206   207

103

51

Surname: .... First name : .... ♂

▶ Generation7 – maternal ascendant

Child : ☐ Legitimate ☐ Natural ☐ Adopted ☐ Found ☐ Recognized ☐ Adulterated   ☐ Implex

Born : ....in..

Baptized : ....in..

Godfather: ....Godmother : ....

Son of : ....and:..

Nationality : ....Religion : ....Studies:...

Occupation(s) : ....

Deceased : ....in...Cause:...............................

☐ Buried ☐ Cremated ☐ Disappeared on : ....in :.......................................

💍 MARITAL STATUS   ☐ Civil Marriage   ☐ Religious Marriage   ☐ Free Union

Date : ....in...☐ Marriage contract

Witnesses : ....

....

☐ Separation ☐ Divorce ☐ Widowhood of the groom/bride Date : ....

👪 FAMILY EVENTS   ....

....

....

....

....

....

💍 OTHER UNION(S)/ 👪 CHILDREN   ....

....

....

....

👪 SIBLINGS   ▶ Details page 209   ♂ .... ♀ ....   1...

2... 3... 4...

5... 6... 7...

8... 9... 10...

👤 INDIVIDUAL EVENTS   ....

....

....

⛑ MILITARY LIFE   Assignment(s) : ....

Campaign(s): ....

Medal(s) : ....☐ Died in combat ☐ Injured on : ....

....

| 416 | 417 | 418 | 419 |

| 208 | | 209 |

| 104 |

| 52 |

📑 NOTES ....

....

....

....

....

♀ Surname : ....First name : ....

▶ Generation 7 – *maternal ascendant*

☐ *Implex* Child : ☐ *Legitimate* ☐ *Natural* ☐ *Adopted* ☐ *Found* ☐ *Recognized* ☐ *Adulterated*

Born : ....in..

Baptized : ....in..

Godfather: ....Godmother : ....

Daughter of : ....and: ....

Nationality : ....Religion : ....Studies: ....

Occupation(s) : ....

Deceased : ....in........................Cause:.................................

☐ *Buried* ☐ *Cremated* ☐ *Disappeared* on : ....in : ....

👪 CHILDREN ♂ .... ♀ ....

	Gen.	° Birth	† Death	Spouse
....	......	....	....	....
....	......	....	....	....
....	......	....	....	....
....	......	....	....	....
....	......	....	....	....
....	......	....	....	....
....	......	....	....	....
....	......	....	....	....
....	......	....	....	....
....	......	....	....	....

💍 OTHER UNION(S)/ 👪 CHILDREN ....

....

....

....

👪 SIBLINGS ▶ *Details page 211* ♂ .... ♀ ....

1. ....
2. ....3. ....4. ....
5. ....6. ....7. ....
8. ....9. ....10. ....

👤 INDIVIDUAL EVENTS ....

....

....

....

....

....

....

📝 NOTES ....

....

....

....

420	421	422	423
210		211	
	105		
	52		

Surname: .... First name : .... ♂

Child : ☐ *Legitimate* ☐ *Natural* ☐ *Adopted* ☐ *Found* ☐ *Recognized* ☐ *Adulterated*   ☐ *Implex*

Born : ....in...

Baptized : ....in..

Godfather: ....Godmother : ....

Son of : ....and:...

Nationality : ....Religion : ....Studies: ....

Occupation(s) : ....

Deceased : ....in.......................Cause:.........................

☐ *Buried* ☐ *Cremated* ☐ *Disappeared* on : ....in : ....

💍 MARITAL STATUS   ☐ *Civil Marriage* ☐ *Religious Marriage* ☐ *Free Union*

Date : ....in...☐ *Marriage contract*

Witnesses : ....

....

☐ *Separation* ☐ *Divorce* ☐ *Widowhood of the groom/bride* Date : ....

👪 FAMILY EVENTS ....

....

....

....

....

....

💍 OTHER UNION(S)/ 👪 CHILDREN ....

....

....

....

👫 SIBLINGS   ▶ *Details page 213*   ♂ .... ♀ ....   1....................................
2.......................................3...4............................
5.......................................6...7............................
8.......................................9...10..........................

👤 INDIVIDUAL EVENTS ....

....

....

....

⛑ MILITARY LIFE   Assignment(s) : ....

Campaign(s): ....

Medal(s) : ....☐ *Died in combat* ☐ *Injured on* : ....

....

424	425	426	427

```
  ┌212┐   ┌213┐
     ┌106┐
      53
```

📝 NOTES ....

....

....

....

....

♀ Surname : .... First name : ....

▶ Generation 7 – *maternal ascendant*

□ *Implex*   Child : □ *Legitimate* □ *Natural* □ *Adopted* □ *Found* □ *Recognized* □ *Adulterated*

Born : ....in..

Baptized : ....in..

Godfather: ....Godmother : ....

Daughter of : ....and: ....

Nationality : ....Religion : ....Studies: ....

Occupation(s) : ....

Deceased : ....in......................Cause:...........................

□ *Buried* □ *Cremated* □ *Disappeared* on : ....in : ....

👫 CHILDREN ♂ .... ♀	Gen.	° Birth	† Death	Spouse
....	......	....	....	....
....	......	....	....	....
....	......	....	....	....
....	......	....	....	....
....	......	....	....	....
....	......	....	....	....
....	......	....	....	....
....	......	....	....	....
....	......	....	....	....
....	......	....	....	....
....	......	....	....	....

💍 OTHER UNION(S)/ 👫 CHILDREN ....

....

....

👫 SIBLINGS   ▶ *Details page 215*   ♂ .... ♀ .... 1...

2...3...4...

5...6...7...

8...9...10.......................................

👤 INDIVIDUAL EVENTS ....

....

....

....

....

....

....

📑 NOTES ....

....

....

....

428	429	430	431

| 214 | | 215 |

107

| 53 |

Surname: .... First name : .... ♂

Child : ☐ *Legitimate* ☐ *Natural* ☐ *Adopted* ☐ *Found* ☐ *Recognized* ☐ *Adulterated* ☐ *Implex*

Born : ....in...

Baptized : ....in...

Godfather: ....Godmother : ....

Son of : ....and: ....

Nationality : ....Religion : ....Studies: ....

Occupation(s) : ....

Deceased : ....in...........................Cause:...........................

☐ *Buried* ☐ *Cremated* ☐ *Disappeared* on : ....in : ....

(⊙) MARITAL STATUS ☐ *Civil Marriage* ☐ *Religious Marriage* ☐ *Free Union*

Date : ....in........................... ☐ *Marriage contract*

Witnesses : ....

....

☐ *Separation* ☐ *Divorce* ☐ *Widowhood of the groom/bride* Date : ....

👫 FAMILY EVENTS ....

....
....
....
....
....
....

(⊙) OTHER UNION(S)/ 👫 CHILDREN ....

....
....
....

👫 SIBLINGS ▶ *Details page 217* ♂ .... ♀ .... 1............................

2............................ 3............................ 4............................

5............................ 6............................ 7............................

8............................ 9............................ 10............................

👤 INDIVIDUAL EVENTS ....

....
....

⛑ MILITARY LIFE Assignment(s) : ....

Campaign(s): ....

Medal(s) : ....☐ *Died in combat* ☐ *Injured on* : ....

432	433	434	435

216   217

108

54

📇 NOTES ....

....
....
....

♀ Surname : .... First name : ....

▶ Generation 7 – *maternal ascendant*

☐ *Implex* Child : ☐ *Legitimate* ☐ *Natural* ☐ *Adopted* ☐ *Found* ☐ *Recognized* ☐ *Adulterated*

Born : ....in...

Baptized : ....in...

Godfather: ....Godmother : ....

Daughter of : ....and: ....

Nationality : ....Religion : ....Studies: ....

Occupation(s) : ....

Deceased : ....in...........................Cause:...........................

☐ *Buried* ☐ *Cremated* ☐ *Disappeared* on : ....in : ....

👫 CHILDREN ♂ .... ♀ ....

	Gen.	° Birth	† Death	Spouse

💍 OTHER UNION(S)/ 👫 CHILDREN ....

....

....

....

👫 SIBLINGS ▶ *Details page 219* ♂ .... ♀ .... 1...

2.. 3.. 4.....................................

5.. 6.. 7.....................................

8.. 9.. 10...................................

👤 INDIVIDUAL EVENTS ....

....

....

....

....

....

....

....

📝 NOTES ....

....

....

....

436	437	438	439

218		219

109

54

Surname: .... First name : .... ♂

Child : ☐ *Legitimate* ☐ *Natural* ☐ *Adopted* ☐ *Found* ☐ *Recognized* ☐ *Adulterated*   ☐ *Implex*

Born : ....in...

Baptized : ....in.........................

Godfather: ....Godmother : ....

Son of : ....and: ....

Nationality : ....Religion : ....Studies: ....

Occupation(s) : ....

Deceased : ....in...................Cause:...........................

☐ *Buried* ☐ *Cremated* ☐ *Disappeared* on : ....in : ....

💍 MARITAL STATUS   ☐ *Civil Marriage*   ☐ *Religious Marriage*   ☐ *Free Union*

Date : ....in... ☐ *Marriage contract*

Witnesses : ....

....

☐ *Separation* ☐ *Divorce* ☐ *Widowhood of the groom/bride*   Date : ....

👫 FAMILY EVENTS ....

....
....
....
....
....

💍 OTHER UNION(S)/ 👫 CHILDREN ....

....
....
....

👫 SIBLINGS   ▶ *Details page 221*   ♂ .... ♀ ....   1.................................
2.................................. 3.................................. 4..................................
5.................................. 6.................................. 7..................................
8.................................. 9.................................. 10.................................

👤 INDIVIDUAL EVENTS

....
....
....

⛑ MILITARY LIFE   Assignment(s) : ....

Campaign(s): ....

Medal(s) : ....☐ *Died in combat* ☐ *Injured on* : ....

....

| 440 | 441 | 442 | 443 |

| 220 | | 221 |

| 110 |

| 55 |

📑 NOTES ....

....
....
....
....

♀ Surname : .... First name : ....

▶ Generation *7 – maternal ascendant*

☐ *Implex*   Child : ☐ *Legitimate* ☐ *Natural* ☐ *Adopted* ☐ *Found* ☐ *Recognized* ☐ *Adulterated*

Born : ....in.......................................

Baptized : ....in.......................................

Godfather: ....Godmother : ....

Daughter of : ....and: ....

Nationality : ....Religion : ....Studies: ....

Occupation(s) : ....

Deceased : ....in...................Cause:...............

☐ *Buried* ☐ *Cremated* ☐ *Disappeared* on : ....in : ....

👫 CHILDREN ♂ .... ♀	Gen.	° Birth	† Death	Spouse
....	......	....	....	....
....	......	....	....	....
....	......	....	....	....
....	......	....	....	....
....	......	....	....	....
....	......	....	....	....
....	......	....	....	....
....	......	....	....	....
....	......	....	....	....
....	......	....	....	....

💍 OTHER UNION(S)/ 👫 CHILDREN ....
....
....

👫 SIBLINGS   ▶ *Details page 223*   ♂ .... ♀ .... 1..........................
2.......................... 3.......................... 4..........................
5.......................... 6.......................... 7..........................
8.......................... 9.......................... 10..........................

👤 INDIVIDUAL EVENTS ....
....
....
....
....
....
....

📝 NOTES ....
....
....
....

444	445	446	447
222		223	
111			
55			

Sosa 112 ♂

Surname: .... **First name :** .... ♂

Child : □ *Legitimate* □ *Natural* □ *Adopted* □ *Found* □ *Recognized* □ *Adulterated*   □ *Implex*

Born : ....in...

Baptized : ....in..

Godfather: ....Godmother : ....

Son of : ....and: ....

Nationality : ....Religion : ....Studies: ....

Occupation(s) : ....

Deceased : ....in........................Cause:................................

□ *Buried* □ *Cremated* □ *Disappeared* on : ....in : ....

⚭ MARITAL STATUS   □ *Civil Marriage* □ *Religious Marriage* □ *Free Union*

Date : ....in.. □ *Marriage contract*

Witnesses : ....

....

□ *Separation* □ *Divorce* □ *Widowhood of the groom/bride*   Date : ....

👫 FAMILY EVENTS ....

....

....

....

....

....

....

⚭ OTHER UNION(S)/👫 CHILDREN ....

....

....

....

👫 SIBLINGS   ► *Details page 225*   ♂ .... ♀ ....   1................................

2.. 3.. 4..............................

5.. 6.. 7..............................

8.. 9.. 10.............................

👤 INDIVIDUAL EVENTS ....

....

....

⛑ MILITARY LIFE   Assignment(s) : ....

Campaign(s): ....

Medal(s) : ....□ *Died in combat* □ *Injured on :* ....

....

448	449	450	451

```
448 449 450 451
  224      225
     112
      56
```

📑 NOTES ....

....

....

....

....

♀ Surname : ....First name : ....

Sosa
113

▶ Generation 7 – *maternal ascendant*

☐ *Implex*   Child : ☐ *Legitimate* ☐ *Natural* ☐ *Adopted* ☐ *Found* ☐ *Recognized* ☐ *Adulterated*

Born : ....in ....

Baptized : ....in ....

Godfather: ....Godmother : ....

Daughter of : ....and: ....

Nationality : ....Religion : ....Studies: ....

Occupation(s) : ....

Deceased : ....in ....Cause:.......................

☐ *Buried* ☐ *Cremated* ☐ *Disappeared* on : ....in : ....

👫 CHILDREN ♂ .... ♀	Gen.	° Birth	† Death	Spouse
....	....	....	....	....
....	....	....	....	....
....	....	....	....	....
....	....	....	....	....
....	....	....	....	....
....	....	....	....	....
....	....	....	....	....
....	....	....	....	....
....	....	....	....	....
....	....	....	....	....

💍 OTHER UNION(S)/ 👫 CHILDREN ....
....
....
....

👫 SIBLINGS   ▶ *Details page 227*   ♂ .... ♀ ....   1..
2...................................... 3...................................... 4..................................
5...................................... 6...................................... 7..................................
8...................................... 9...................................... 10.................................

👤 INDIVIDUAL EVENTS ....
....
....
....
....
....
....

📝 NOTES ....

| 452 | 453 | 454 | 455 |

| 226 | 227 |

113

| 56 |

....
....
....

113

Surname: .... First name : .... ♂

▶ Generation7 – *maternal ascendant*

Child : ☐ *Legitimate* ☐ *Natural* ☐ *Adopted* ☐ *Found* ☐ *Recognized* ☐ *Adulterated*　　☐ *Implex*

Born : ....in..

Baptized : ....in..

Godfather: ....Godmother : ....

Son of : ....and: ....

Nationality : ....Religion : ....Studies: ....

Occupation(s) : ....

Deceased : ....in.......................................Cause:...............................

☐ *Buried* ☐ *Cremated* ☐ *Disappeared* on : ....in : ....

⚭ MARITAL STATUS　　　　☐ *Civil Marriage* ☐ *Religious Marriage* ☐ *Free Union*

Date : ....in..

☐ *Marriage contract*

Witnesses : ....

....

☐ *Separation* ☐ *Divorce* ☐ *Widowhood of the groom/bride*　Date : ....

👫 FAMILY EVENTS ....

....

....

....

....

....

⚭ OTHER UNION(S)/👫 CHILDREN ....

....

....

....

👫 SIBLINGS　▶ *Details page 229*　♂ ....　♀ ....　1.....................................
2..3.....................................4.......................................
5..6.....................................7.......................................
8..9.....................................10.....................................

👤 INDIVIDUAL EVENTS

....

....

....

⛑ MILITARY LIFE　Assignment(s) : ....

Campaign(s): ....

Medal(s) : ....☐ *Died in combat* ☐ *Injured on* : ....

....

456	457	458	459

228		229

114

57

📝 NOTES ....

....

....

....

....

♀ Surname : .... First name : ....

▶ Generation 7 – *maternal ascendant*

☐ *Implex* Child : ☐ *Legitimate* ☐ *Natural* ☐ *Adopted* ☐ *Found* ☐ *Recognized* ☐ *Adulterated*

Born : ....in...

Baptized : ....in...

Godfather: ....Godmother : ....

Daughter of : ....and: ....

Nationality : ....Religion : ....Studies: ....

Occupation(s) : ....

Deceased : ....in...............................Cause:...............

☐ *Buried* ☐ *Cremated* ☐ *Disappeared* on : ....in : ....

👫 **CHILDREN** ♂ .... ♀ ....

	Gen.	° Birth	† Death	Spouse

💍 **OTHER UNION(S)/** 👫 **CHILDREN** ....

....

....

👫 **SIBLINGS** ▶ *Details page 231* ♂ .... ♀ .... 1................................

2................................ 3................................ 4................................

5................................ 6................................ 7................................

8................................ 9................................ 10...............................

👤 **INDIVIDUAL EVENTS** ....

....

....

....

....

📑 **NOTES** ....

....

460	461	462	463
230		231	
115			
57			

Sosa 116 ♂

Surname: .... First name : ....

Child : ☐ *Legitimate* ☐ *Natural* ☐ *Adopted* ☐ *Found* ☐ *Recognized* ☐ *Adulterated*   ☐ *Implex*

Born : ....in ....

Baptized : ....in ....

Godfather: ....Godmother : ....

Son of : ....and: ....

Nationality : ....Religion : ....Studies: ....

Occupation(s) : ....

Deceased : ....in ....Cause:.......................

☐ *Buried* ☐ *Cremated* ☐ *Disappeared* on : ....in : ....

⚭ MARITAL STATUS   ☐ *Civil Marriage* ☐ *Religious Marriage* ☐ *Free Union*

Date : ....in.............................. ☐ *Marriage contract*

Witnesses : ....

....

☐ *Separation* ☐ *Divorce* ☐ *Widowhood of the groom/bride* Date : ....

👫 FAMILY EVENTS ....

....
....
....
....
....

⚭ OTHER UNION(S)/ 👫 CHILDREN ....

....
....
....

👫 SIBLINGS   ▶ *Details page 233*   ♂ .... ♀ ....   1.......................

2.....................................3.............................4.............................

5.....................................6.............................7.............................

8.....................................9.............................10.............................

👤 INDIVIDUAL EVENTS ....

....
....
....

⛑ MILITARY LIFE   Assignment(s) : ....

Campaign(s): ....

Medal(s) : ....☐ *Died in combat* ☐ *Injured on* : ....

| 464 | 465 | 466 | 467 |

| 232 | | 233 | |

116

58

📑 NOTES ....

....
....
....

♀ Surname : ....First name : ....

▶ Generation 7 – *maternal ascendant*

☐ *Implex*   Child : ☐ *Legitimate* ☐ *Natural* ☐ *Adopted* ☐ *Found* ☐ *Recognized* ☐ *Adulterated*

Born : ....in..

Baptized : ....in...

Godfather: ....Godmother : ....

Daughter of : ....and: ....

Nationality : ....Religion : ....Studies: ....

Occupation(s) : ....

Deceased : ....in...........................Cause:.....................................

☐ *Buried* ☐ *Cremated* ☐ *Disappeared* on : ....in : ....

👫 CHILDREN ♂ .... ♀	Gen.	° Birth	† Death	Spouse
....	....	....	....	....
....	....	....	....	....
....	....	....	....	....
....	....	....	....	....
....	....	....	....	....
....	....	....	....	....
....	....	....	....	....
....	....	....	....	....
....	....	....	....	....
....	....	....	....	....

💍 OTHER UNION(S)/ 👫 CHILDREN ....
....
....
....

👫 SIBLINGS ▶ *Details page 235*   ♂ .... ♀ .... 1.....................................

2...3..4..

5...6..7..

8...9..10..

👤 INDIVIDUAL EVENTS ....
....
....
....
....
....
....

📑 NOTES ....
....
....
....

468	469	470	471

234		235

117

58

Surname: .... First name : .... ♂

▶ Generation7 - *maternal ascendant*

Child : ☐ *Legitimate* ☐ *Natural* ☐ *Adopted* ☐ *Found* ☐ *Recognized* ☐ *Adulterated*   ☐ *Implex*

Born : ....in...

Baptized : ....in...

Godfather: ....Godmother : ....

Son of : ....and:...

Nationality : ....Religion : ....Studies: ....

Occupation(s) : ....

Deceased : ....in...........................Cause:.........................

☐ *Buried* ☐ *Cremated* ☐ *Disappeared* on : ....in :.........

⚭ MARITAL STATUS   ☐ *Civil Marriage* ☐ *Religious Marriage* ☐ *Free Union*

Date : ....in... ☐ *Marriage contract*

Witnesses : ....

....

☐ *Separation* ☐ *Divorce* ☐ *Widowhood of the groom/bride* Date : ....

👪 FAMILY EVENTS   ....

....
....
....
....
....

⚭ OTHER UNION(S)/ 👪 CHILDREN ....

....
....
....

👫 SIBLINGS   ▶ *Details page 237*   ♂ ....   ♀ ....   1.................................

2..3...4...

5..6...7...

8..9...10..

👤 INDIVIDUAL EVENTS   ....

....
....
....

⛑ MILITARY LIFE   Assignment(s) : ....

Campaign(s): ....

Medal(s) : ....☐ *Died in combat* ☐ *Injured on* : ....

....

472	473	474	475

📋 NOTES ....

236   237

....

118

....

59

....

♀ Surname : .... First name : ....

▶ Generation 7 – *maternal ascendant*

☐ *Implex*   Child : ☐ *Legitimate* ☐ *Natural* ☐ *Adopted* ☐ *Found* ☐ *Recognized* ☐ *Adulterated*

Born : .... in ....

Baptized : .... in ....

Godfather: .... Godmother : ....

Daughter of : .... and: ....

Nationality : .... Religion : .... Studies: ....

Occupation(s) : ....

Deceased : .... in .... Cause: ....

☐ *Buried* ☐ *Cremated* ☐ *Disappeared* on : .... in : ....

👫 CHILDREN ♂ .... ♀ ....

	Gen.	° Birth	† Death	Spouse
....	....	....	....	....
....	....	....	....	....
....	....	....	....	....
....	....	....	....	....
....	....	....	....	....
....	....	....	....	....
....	....	....	....	....
....	....	....	....	....
....	....	....	....	....
....	....	....	....	....

💍 OTHER UNION(S)/ 👫 CHILDREN ....

....

....

👫 SIBLINGS   ▶ *Details page 239*   ♂ .... ♀ ....   1. ....

2. .... 3. .... 4. ....

5. .... 6. .... 7. ....

8. .... 9. .... 10. ....

👤 INDIVIDUAL EVENTS ....

....

....

....

....

....

....

📝 NOTES ....

....

....

....

....

476	477	478	479
238		239	
	119		
	59		

Surname: .... First name : .... ♂

▶ Generation7 – *maternal ascendant*

Child : ☐ *Legitimate* ☐ *Natural* ☐ *Adopted* ☐ *Found* ☐ *Recognized* ☐ *Adulterated*   ☐ *Implex*

Born : ....in...

Baptized : ....in.............................

Godfather: ....Godmother : ....

Son of : ....and: ....

Nationality : ....Religion : ....Studies: ....

Occupation(s) : ....

Deceased : ....in............................Cause:.......................

☐ *Buried* ☐ *Cremated* ☐ *Disappeared* on : ....in :..................

💍 MARITAL STATUS   ☐ *Civil Marriage* ☐ *Religious Marriage* ☐ *Free Union*

Date : ....in...   ☐ *Marriage contract*

Witnesses : ....

....

☐ *Separation* ☐ *Divorce* ☐ *Widowhood of the groom/bride* Date : ....

👪 FAMILY EVENTS ....

....

....

....

....

....

💍 OTHER UNION(S)/ 👫 CHILDREN ....

....

....

....

👫 SIBLINGS   ▶ *Details page 241*   ♂ .... ♀ ....   1.................................

2.................................3.................................4.................................

5.................................6.................................7.................................

8.................................9.................................10.................................

👤 INDIVIDUAL EVENTS ....

....

....

⛑ MILITARY LIFE   Assignment(s) : ....

Campaign(s): ....

Medal(s) : ....☐ *Died in combat* ☐ *Injured on* : ....

480	481	482	483
240		241	
	120		
	60		

📑 NOTES ....

....

....

....

....

♀ Surname : .... First name : ....

□ *Implex*　Child : □ *Legitimate* □ *Natural* □ *Adopted* □ *Found* □ *Recognized* □ *Adulterated*

Born : ....in...

Baptized : ....in...

Godfather: ....Godmother : ....

Daughter of : ....and: ....

Nationality : ....Religion : ....Studies: ....

Occupation(s) : ....

Deceased : ....in..........................Cause:..........................

□ *Buried* □ *Cremated* □ *Disappeared* on : ....in : ....

👫 CHILDREN ♂ .... ♀ ....

	Gen.	° Birth	† Death	Spouse

⚭ OTHER UNION(S)/ 👫 CHILDREN ....

....

....

....

👫 SIBLINGS ▶ *Details page 243* ♂ .... ♀ .... 1...........................

2.................................3.........................4..............................

5.................................6.........................7..............................

8.................................9.........................10.............................

👤 INDIVIDUAL EVENTS ....

....

....

....

....

....

....

📑 NOTES ....

....

....

....

484	485	486	487
242		243	
121			
60			

Surname: .... First name : .... ♂

▶ Generation7 – *maternal ascendant*

Child : □ *Legitimate* □ *Natural* □ *Adopted* □ *Found* □ *Recognized* □ *Adulterated*   □ *Implex*

Born : ....in...

Baptized : ....in...

Godfather: ....Godmother : ....

Son of : ....and: ....

Nationality : ....Religion : ....Studies: ....

Occupation(s) : ....

Deceased : ....in.......................Cause:...................

□ *Buried* □ *Cremated* □ *Disappeared* on : ....in : ....

🔗 MARITAL STATUS   □ *Civil Marriage* □ *Religious Marriage* □ *Free Union*

Date : ....in...................................... □ *Marriage contract*

Witnesses : ....

....

□ *Separation* □ *Divorce* □ *Widowhood of the groom/bride* Date : ....

👪 FAMILY EVENTS ....

....

....

....

....

....

🔗 OTHER UNION(S)/👪 CHILDREN ....

....

....

....

👫 SIBLINGS ▶ *Details page 245* ♂ .... ♀ .... 1..................................

2......................................3......................................4......................................

5......................................6......................................7......................................

8......................................9......................................10......................................

👤 INDIVIDUAL EVENTS ....

....

....

⛑ MILITARY LIFE Assignment(s) : ....

Campaign(s): ....

Medal(s) : ....□ *Died in combat* □ *Injured on* : ....

....

488	489	490	491
244		245	
	122		
	61		

📑 NOTES ....

....

....

....

....

♀ Surname : .... First name : ....

□ *Implex*   Child : □ *Legitimate* □ *Natural* □ *Adopted* □ *Found* □ *Recognized* □ *Adulterated*

Born : ....in ....

Baptized : ....in ....

Godfather: ....Godmother : ....

Daughter of : ....and: ....

Nationality : ....Religion : ....Studies: ....

Occupation(s) : ....

Deceased : ....in ....Cause:..............................

□ *Buried* □ *Cremated* □ *Disappeared* on : ....in : ....

👫 CHILDREN ♂ .... ♀ ....

	Gen.	° Birth	† Death	Spouse
....	.....	....	....	....
....	.....	....	....	....
....	.....	....	....	....
....	.....	....	....	....
....	.....	....	....	....
....	.....	....	....	....
....	.....	....	....	....
....	.....	....	....	....
....	.....	....	....	....
....	.....	....	....	....

💍 OTHER UNION(S)/ 👫 CHILDREN ....

....

....

👫 SIBLINGS   ▶ *Details page 247*   ♂ .... ♀ ....   1. ....

2. ....3. ....4. ....

5. ....6. ....7. ....

8. ....9. ....10. ....

👤 INDIVIDUAL EVENTS ....

....

....

....

....

....

....

📝 NOTES ....

....

....

....

....

492	493	494	495
246		247	
	123		
	61		

Surname: .... First name : .... ♂

▶ Generation7 – *maternal ascendant*

Child : □ *Legitimate* □ *Natural* □ *Adopted* □ *Found* □ *Recognized* □ *Adulterated*   □ *Implex*

Born : ....in ....

Baptized : ....in ....

Godfather: ....Godmother : ....

Son of : ....and: ....

Nationality : ....Religion : ....Studies: ....

Occupation(s) : ....

Deceased : ....in ....Cause:.............................

□ *Buried* □ *Cremated* □ *Disappeared* on : ....in : ....

⚭ MARITAL STATUS   □ *Civil Marriage* □ *Religious Marriage* □ *Free Union*

Date : ....in...□ *Marriage contract*

Witnesses : ....

....

□ *Separation* □ *Divorce* □ *Widowhood of the groom/bride* Date : ....

👫 FAMILY EVENTS   ....

....
....
....
....
....

⚭ OTHER UNION(S)/ 👫 CHILDREN   ....

....
....
....

👫 SIBLINGS   ▶ *Details page 249*   ♂ .... ♀ ....   1. ....

2. ....3. ....4. ....

5. ....6. ....7. ....

8. ....9. ....10. ....

👤 INDIVIDUAL EVENTS   ....

....
....

⛑ MILITARY LIFE   Assignment(s) : ....

Campaign(s): ....

Medal(s) : ....□ *Died in combat* □ *Injured on* : ....

....

496	497	498	499

| 248 | | 249 |

| 124 |

| 62 |

📝 NOTES   ....

....
....
....
....

♀ Surname : .... First name : ....

▶ Generation 7 – *maternal ascendant*

□ *Implex*   Child : □ *Legitimate* □ *Natural* □ *Adopted* □ *Found* □ *Recognized* □ *Adulterated*

Born : ....in...

Baptized : ....in...

Godfather: ....Godmother : ....

Daughter of : ....and: ....

Nationality : ....Religion : ....Studies: ....

Occupation(s) : ....

Deceased : ....in...Cause:.....................

□ *Buried* □ *Cremated* □ *Disappeared* on : ....in : ....

👫 CHILDREN ♂ .... ♀ ....

	Gen.	° Birth	† Death	Spouse

💍 OTHER UNION(S)/ 👫 CHILDREN ....

....

....

....

👫 SIBLINGS   ▶ *Details page 251*   ♂ ....   ♀ ....   1...

2... 3... 4...

5... 6... 7...

8... 9... 10...

👤 INDIVIDUAL EVENTS ....

....

....

....

....

....

....

📑 NOTES ....

....

....

....

500	501	502	503
	250		251
		125	
		62	

Surname: .... First name : .... ♂

▶ Generation7 – *maternal ascendant*

Child : ☐ *Legitimate* ☐ *Natural* ☐ *Adopted* ☐ *Found* ☐ *Recognized* ☐ *Adulterated*   ☐ *Implex*

Born : .... in ....

Baptized : .... in ....

Godfather: .... Godmother : ....

Son of : .... and: ....

Nationality : .... Religion : .... Studies: ....

Occupation(s) : ....

Deceased : .... in .... Cause: ....

☐ *Buried* ☐ *Cremated* ☐ *Disappeared* on : .... in : ....

(◯) MARITAL STATUS   ☐ *Civil Marriage* ☐ *Religious Marriage* ☐ *Free Union*

Date : .... in ....   ☐ *Marriage contract*

Witnesses : ....

....

☐ *Separation* ☐ *Divorce* ☐ *Widowhood of the groom/bride* Date : ....

👪 FAMILY EVENTS ....

....

....

....

....

....

(◯) OTHER UNION(S)/👪 CHILDREN ....

....

....

....

👫 SIBLINGS ▶ *Details page 253* ♂ .... ♀ .... 1. ....

2. .... 3. .... 4. ....

5. .... 6. .... 7. ....

8. .... 9. .... 10. ....

👤 INDIVIDUAL EVENTS ....

....

....

⛑ MILITARY LIFE Assignment(s) : ....

Campaign(s): ....

Medal(s) : .... ☐ *Died in combat* ☐ *Injured on* : ....

....

504	505	506	507

| 252 | | 253 |

126

63

📇 NOTES ....

....

....

....

....

♀ Surname : .... First name : ....

▶ Generation 7 – *maternal ascendant*

□ *Implex*　　　Child : □ *Legitimate* □ *Natural* □ *Adopted* □ *Found* □ *Recognized* □ *Adulterated*

Born : ....in...

Baptized : ....in..

Godfather: ....Godmother : ....

Daughter of : ....and: ....

Nationality : ....Religion : ....Studies: ....

Occupation(s) : ....

Deceased : ....in..........................Cause:................................

□ *Buried* □ *Cremated* □ *Disappeared* on : ....in :..............................

👫 CHILDREN ♂ .... ♀ ....

	Gen.	° Birth	† Death	Spouse
....	......	....	....	....
....	......	....	....	....
....	......	....	....	....
....	......	....	....	....
....	......	....	....	....
....	......	....	....	....
....	......	....	....	....
....	......	....	....	....
....	......	....	....	....
....	......	....	....	....

💍 OTHER UNION(S)/ 👫 CHILDREN ....

....

....

....

👫 SIBLINGS ▶ *Details page 255* ♂ .... ♀ .... 1.......................

2...3...4..............................

5...6...7..............................

8...9...10.............................

👤 INDIVIDUAL EVENTS ....

....

....

....

....

....

....

📑 NOTES ....

....

....

....

....

508	509	510	511

254　　255

127

63

Surname: .... First name : .... ♂

Child : ☐ *Legitimate* ☐ *Natural* ☐ *Adopted* ☐ *Found* ☐ *Recognized* ☐ *Adulterated*   ☐ *Implex*

Born : ....in ....

Baptized : ....in ....

Godfather: ....Godmother : ....

Son of : ....and: ....

Nationality : ....Religion : ....Studies: ....

Occupation(s) : ....

Deceased : ....in...............................Cause:...............................

☐ *Buried* ☐ *Cremated* ☐ *Disappeared* on : ....in : ....

⚭ MARITAL STATUS   ☐ *Civil Marriage*   ☐ *Religious Marriage*   ☐ *Free Union*

Date : ....in...............................   ☐ *Marriage contract*

Witnesses : ....

....

☐ *Separation* ☐ *Divorce* ☐ *Widowhood of the groom/bride*   Date : ....

👫 FAMILY EVENTS ....

....

....

....

....

....

⚭ OTHER UNION(S)/👫 CHILDREN ....

....

....

👫 SIBLINGS   ▶ *Details page 257*   ♂ ....   ♀ ....   1..................................

2.................................... 3.................................... 4....................................

5.................................... 6.................................... 7....................................

8.................................... 9.................................... 10....................................

👤 INDIVIDUAL EVENTS ....

....

....

⛑ MILITARY LIFE   Assignment(s) : ....

Campaign(s): ....

Medal(s) : ....☐ *Died in combat* ☐ *Injured on* : ....

| 512 | 513 | 514 | 515 |

256   257

128

64

📑 NOTES ....

....

....

....

♀ Surname : .... First name : ....

▶ Generation 8 - *paternal ascendant*

☐ *Implex* Child : ☐ *Legitimate* ☐ *Natural* ☐ *Adopted* ☐ *Found* ☐ *Recognized* ☐ *Adulterated*

Born : ....in..

Baptized : ....in..

Godfather: ....Godmother : ....

Daughter of : ....and: ....

Nationality : ....Religion : ....Studies: ....

Occupation(s) : ....

Deceased : ....in......................Cause:....................................

☐ *Buried* ☐ *Cremated* ☐ *Disappeared* on : ....in : ....

👪 CHILDREN ♂ .... ♀ ....

	Gen.	° Birth	† Death	Spouse
....	......	....	....	....
....	......	....	....	....
....	......	....	....	....
....	......	....	....	....
....	......	....	....	....
....	......	....	....	....
....	......	....	....	....
....	......	....	....	....
....	......	....	....	....
....	......	....	....	....

💍 OTHER UNION(S)/ 👪 CHILDREN ....

....

....

....

👫 SIBLINGS ▶ *Details page 259* ♂ .... ♀ .... 1..................................

2....................................... 3....................................... 4...................................

5....................................... 6....................................... 7...................................

8....................................... 9....................................... 10.................................

👤 INDIVIDUAL EVENTS ....

....

....

....

....

....

....

📝 NOTES ....

....

....

....

516	517	518	519
258		259	
129			
64			

129

130

Surname: .... First name : .... ♂

▶ Generation8 – *paternal ascendant*

Child : ☐ *Legitimate* ☐ *Natural* ☐ *Adopted* ☐ *Found* ☐ *Recognized* ☐ *Adulterated*　　　☐ *Implex*

Born : ....in...

Baptized : ....in...

Godfather: ....Godmother : ....

Son of : ....and: ....

Nationality : ....Religion : ....Studies: ....

Occupation(s) : ....

Deceased : ....in.........................Cause:...............................

☐ *Buried* ☐ *Cremated* ☐ *Disappeared* on : ....in :...............................

⚭ MARITAL STATUS　　　☐ *Civil Marriage* ☐ *Religious Marriage* ☐ *Free Union*

Date : ....in...☐ *Marriage contract*

Witnesses : ....

....

☐ *Separation* ☐ *Divorce* ☐ *Widowhood of the groom/bride* Date : ....

👫 FAMILY EVENTS ....

....
....
....
....
....

⚭ OTHER UNION(S)/👫 CHILDREN ....

....
....
....

👫 SIBLINGS　▶ *Details page 261*　♂ ....　♀ ....　1................................

2................................ 3................................ 4................................

5................................ 6................................ 7................................

8................................ 9................................ 10...............................

👤 INDIVIDUAL EVENTS ....

....
....

⛑ MILITARY LIFE　Assignment(s) : ....

Campaign(s): ....

Medal(s) : ....☐ *Died in combat* ☐ *Injured on* : ....

....

520	521	522	523

260　　261

130

65

📑 NOTES ....

....
....
....
....

♀ Surname : ....First name : ....

▶ Generation 8 – *paternal ascendant*

☐ *Implex*   Child : ☐ *Legitimate* ☐ *Natural* ☐ *Adopted* ☐ *Found* ☐ *Recognized* ☐ *Adulterated*

Born : ....in...

Baptized : ....in...

Godfather: ....Godmother : ....

Daughter of : ....and: ....

Nationality : ....Religion : ....Studies: ....

Occupation(s) : ....

Deceased : ....in........................Cause:........................

☐ *Buried* ☐ *Cremated* ☐ *Disappeared* on : ....in :........................

👫 CHILDREN ♂ .... ♀ ....

	Gen.	° Birth	† Death	Spouse
....	......	....	....	....
....	......	....	....	....
....	......	....	....	....
....	......	....	....	....
....	......	....	....	....
....	......	....	....	....
....	......	....	....	....
....	......	....	....	....
....	......	....	....	....
....	......	....	....	....

💍 OTHER UNION(S)/ 👫 CHILDREN ....

....

....

👫 SIBLINGS ▶ *Details page 263* ♂ .... ♀ .... 1...

2.................................3.................................4.................................

5.................................6.................................7.................................

8.................................9.................................10.................................

👤 INDIVIDUAL EVENTS ....

....

....

....

....

....

....

📑 NOTES ....

524	525	526	527
	262		263
		131	
		65	

Surname: .... First name : .... ♂

Child : ☐ *Legitimate* ☐ *Natural* ☐ *Adopted* ☐ *Found* ☐ *Recognized* ☐ *Adulterated*   ☐ *Implex*

Born : ....in ....

Baptized : ....in ....

Godfather: ....Godmother : ....

Son of : ....and: ....

Nationality : ....Religion : ....Studies: ....

Occupation(s) : ....

Deceased : ....in ....Cause:.................................

☐ *Buried* ☐ *Cremated* ☐ *Disappeared* on : ....in : ....

⚭ MARITAL STATUS   ☐ *Civil Marriage* ☐ *Religious Marriage* ☐ *Free Union*

Date : ....in .... ☐ *Marriage contract*

Witnesses : ....

....

☐ *Separation* ☐ *Divorce* ☐ *Widowhood of the groom/bride* Date : ....

👪 FAMILY EVENTS   ....

....

....

....

....

....

⚭ OTHER UNION(S)/ 👪 CHILDREN ....

....

....

....

👫 SIBLINGS   ▶ *Details page 265*   ♂ .... ♀ ....   1.......................................

2.................................... 3.................................... 4....................................

5.................................... 6.................................... 7....................................

8.................................... 9.................................... 10....................................

👤 INDIVIDUAL EVENTS ....

....

....

....

⛑ MILITARY LIFE   Assignment(s) : ....

Campaign(s): ....

Medal(s) : ....☐ *Died in combat* ☐ *Injured on* : ....

....

528	529	530	531

📑 NOTES ....

264   265

132

66

....

....

....

....

♀ Surname : ....First name : ....

▶ Generation 8 – *paternal ascendant*

☐ *Implex*   Child : ☐ *Legitimate* ☐ *Natural* ☐ *Adopted* ☐ *Found* ☐ *Recognized* ☐ *Adulterated*

Born : ....in ....

Baptized : ....in ....

Godfather: ....Godmother : ....

Daughter of : ....and: ....

Nationality : ....Religion : ....Studies: ....

Occupation(s) : ....

Deceased : ....in ....Cause: ....

☐ *Buried* ☐ *Cremated* ☐ *Disappeared* on : ....in : ....

👫 CHILDREN ♂ .... ♀	Gen.	° Birth	† Death	Spouse
....	......	....	....	....
....	......	....	....	....
....	......	....	....	....
....	......	....	....	....
....	......	....	....	....
....	......	....	....	....
....	......	....	....	....
....	......	....	....	....
....	......	....	....	....
....	......	....	....	....

💍 OTHER UNION(S)/ 👫 CHILDREN ....
....
....
....

👫 SIBLINGS ▶ *Details page 267* ♂ .... ♀ .... 1..

2.......................................3.............................4...

5.......................................6.............................7...

8.......................................9.............................10...

👤 INDIVIDUAL EVENTS ....
....
....
....
....
....
....
....

📝 NOTES ....

532	533	534	535

266	267

133

66

Surname: .... First name : .... ♂

Child : ☐ *Legitimate* ☐ *Natural* ☐ *Adopted* ☐ *Found* ☐ *Recognized* ☐ *Adulterated*   ☐ *Implex*

Born : ....in ....

Baptized : ....in ....

Godfather: ....Godmother : ....

Son of : ....and: ....

Nationality : ....Religion : ....Studies: ....

Occupation(s) : ....

Deceased : ....in ....Cause:........................

☐ *Buried* ☐ *Cremated* ☐ *Disappeared* on : ....in : ....

⚭ MARITAL STATUS   ☐ *Civil Marriage* ☐ *Religious Marriage* ☐ *Free Union*

Date : ....in...................................... ☐ *Marriage contract*

Witnesses : ....

....

☐ *Separation* ☐ *Divorce* ☐ *Widowhood of the groom/bride* Date : ....

👫 FAMILY EVENTS ....

....

....

....

....

....

⚭ OTHER UNION(S)/ 👪 CHILDREN ....

....

....

....

👫 SIBLINGS ▶ *Details page 269*   ♂ .... ♀ ....   1. ....

2. ....3. ....4. ....

5. ....6. ....7. ....

8. ....9. ....10. ....

👤 INDIVIDUAL EVENTS ....

....

....

⛑ MILITARY LIFE Assignment(s) : ....

Campaign(s): ....

Medal(s) : ....☐ *Died in combat* ☐ *Injured on* : ....

```
536  537  538  539
  268      269
     134
      67
```

📝 NOTES ....

....

....

....

....

♀ Surname : ....First name : ....

Sosa **135**

▶ Generation 8 - *paternal ascendant*

□ *Implex*　　Child : □ *Legitimate* □ *Natural* □ *Adopted* □ *Found* □ *Recognized* □ *Adulterated*

Born : ....in...

Baptized : ....in...

Godfather: ....Godmother : ....

Daughter of : ....and: ....

Nationality : ....Religion : ....Studies: ....

Occupation(s) : ....

Deceased : ....in...........................Cause:....................

□ *Buried* □ *Cremated* □ *Disappeared* on : ....in : ....

👫 CHILDREN ♂ .... ♀ ....

	Gen.	° Birth	† Death	Spouse
....	......	....	....	....
....	......	....	....	....
....	......	....	....	....
....	......	....	....	....
....	......	....	....	....
....	......	....	....	....
....	......	....	....	....
....	......	....	....	....
....	......	....	....	....
....	......	....	....	....

💍 OTHER UNION(S)/ 👫 CHILDREN ....

....
....
....

👫 SIBLINGS ▶ *Details page 271* ♂ .... ♀ .... 1..............................

2..3..4..

5..6..7..

8..9..10..

👤 INDIVIDUAL EVENTS ....

....
....
....
....
....
....
....

📝 NOTES ....

....

....

....

540	541	542	543

270		271

135

67

135

Sosa 136

Surname: .... First name : .... ♂

Child : □ *Legitimate* □ *Natural* □ *Adopted* □ *Found* □ *Recognized* □ *Adulterated*   □ *Implex*

Born : ....in...

Baptized : ....in...

Godfather: ....Godmother : ....

Son of : ....and: ....

Nationality : ....Religion : ....Studies: ....

Occupation(s) : ....

Deceased : ....in...........................Cause:...

□ *Buried* □ *Cremated* □ *Disappeared* on : ....in : ....

⌀ MARITAL STATUS   □ *Civil Marriage* □ *Religious Marriage* □ *Free Union*

Date : ....in.. □ *Marriage contract*

Witnesses : ....

....

□ *Separation* □ *Divorce* □ *Widowhood of the groom/bride* Date : ....

👪 FAMILY EVENTS   ....

....
....
....
....
....

⌀ OTHER UNION(S)/ 👪 CHILDREN   ....

....
....
....

👪 SIBLINGS   ▶ *Details page 273*   ♂ ....   ♀ ....   1...

2.. 3.................................... 4...................................

5.. 6.................................... 7...................................

8.. 9.................................... 10..................................

👤 INDIVIDUAL EVENTS

....
....
....

⛑ MILITARY LIFE   Assignment(s) : ....

Campaign(s): ....

Medal(s) : ....□ *Died in combat* □ *Injured on* : ....

544	545	546	547

272		273

136

68

📑 NOTES ....

....
....
....
....

♀ Surname : ....First name : ....

▶ Generation 8 - *paternal ascendant*

☐ *Implex*   Child : ☐ *Legitimate* ☐ *Natural* ☐ *Adopted* ☐ *Found* ☐ *Recognized* ☐ *Adulterated*

Born : ....in...

Baptized : ....in...

Godfather: ....Godmother : ....

Daughter of : ....and: ....

Nationality : ....Religion : ....Studies: ....

Occupation(s) : ....

Deceased : ....in...............................Cause:..................

☐ *Buried* ☐ *Cremated* ☐ *Disappeared* on : ....in : ....

👫 CHILDREN ♂ .... ♀	Gen.	° Birth	† Death	Spouse
....	......	....	....	....
....	......	....	....	....
....	......	....	....	....
....	......	....	....	....
....	......	....	....	....
....	......	....	....	....
....	......	....	....	....
....	......	....	....	....
....	......	....	....	....
....	......	....	....	....

💍 OTHER UNION(S)/ 👫 CHILDREN ....
....
....
....

👫 SIBLINGS   ▶ *Details page 275*   ♂ .... ♀ ....   1.......................................
2...3...4.............................
5...6...7.............................
8...9...10...........................

🧍 INDIVIDUAL EVENTS ....
....
....
....
....
....
....

📝 NOTES ....

548	549	550	551

274		275

137

68

Surname: .... First name : .... ♂

▶ Generation8 – *paternal ascendant*

Child : □ *Legitimate* □ *Natural* □ *Adopted* □ *Found* □ *Recognized* □ *Adulterated*   □ *Implex*

Born : ....in...

Baptized : ....in...

Godfather: ....Godmother : ....

Son of : ....and: ....

Nationality : ....Religion : ....Studies: ....

Occupation(s) : ....

Deceased : ....in.........................Cause:.......................

□ *Buried* □ *Cremated* □ *Disappeared* on : ....in :.........................

⚭ MARITAL STATUS   □ *Civil Marriage*   □ *Religious Marriage*   □ *Free Union*

Date : ....in... □ *Marriage contract*

Witnesses : ....

....

□ *Separation* □ *Divorce* □ *Widowhood of the groom/bride*   Date : ....

👪 FAMILY EVENTS   ....

....
....
....
....
....

⚭ OTHER UNION(S)/ 👪 CHILDREN   ....

....
....
....

👪 SIBLINGS   ▶ *Details page 277*   ♂ .... ♀ ....   1.............................

2...3..............................4........................

5...6..............................7........................

8...9..............................10.......................

👤 INDIVIDUAL EVENTS   ....

....
....
....

⛑ MILITARY LIFE   Assignment(s) : ....

Campaign(s): ....

Medal(s) : ....□ *Died in combat* □ *Injured on* : ....

....

552	553	554	555

276   277

138

69

📑 NOTES   ....

....
....
....
....

♀ Surname : .... First name : ....

Sosa

▶ Generation 8 - *paternal ascendant*

□ *Implex*   Child : □ *Legitimate* □ *Natural* □ *Adopted* □ *Found* □ *Recognized* □ *Adulterated*

Born : ....in..

Baptized : ....in..

Godfather: ....Godmother : ....

Daughter of : ....and: ....

Nationality : ....Religion : ....Studies: ....

Occupation(s) : ....

Deceased : ....in...............................Cause:.................

□ *Buried* □ *Cremated* □ *Disappeared* on : ....in : ....

👫 CHILDREN ♂ .... ♀	Gen.	° Birth	† Death	Spouse
....	......	....	....	....
....	......	....	....	....
....	......	....	....	....
....	......	....	....	....
....	......	....	....	....
....	......	....	....	....
....	......	....	....	....
....	......	....	....	....
....	......	....	....	....
....	......	....	....	....

💍 OTHER UNION(S)/ 👫 CHILDREN ....

....

....

👫 SIBLINGS   ▶ *Details page 279*   ♂ .... ♀ ....   1.......................................

2... 3............................. 4.............................

5... 6............................. 7.............................

8... 9............................. 10...........................

👤 INDIVIDUAL EVENTS ....

....

....

....

....

....

....

📝 NOTES ....

....

....

....

556	557	558	559

278	279

139

69

Surname: .... First name : .... ♂

Child : ☐ *Legitimate* ☐ *Natural* ☐ *Adopted* ☐ *Found* ☐ *Recognized* ☐ *Adulterated*   ☐ *Implex*

Born : ....in..

Baptized : ....in..

Godfather: ....Godmother : ....

Son of : ....and:..

Nationality : ....Religion : ....Studies: ....

Occupation(s) : ....

Deceased : ....in...............................Cause:..

☐ *Buried* ☐ *Cremated* ☐ *Disappeared* on : ....in : ....

⚭ MARITAL STATUS   ☐ *Civil Marriage* ☐ *Religious Marriage* ☐ *Free Union*

Date : ....in.. ☐ *Marriage contract*

Witnesses : ....

....

☐ *Separation* ☐ *Divorce* ☐ *Widowhood of the groom/bride* Date : ....

👪 FAMILY EVENTS   ....

....

....

....

....

....

⚭ OTHER UNION(S)/ 👪 CHILDREN   ....

....

....

....

👫 SIBLINGS   ▶ *Details page 281*   ♂ .... ♀ ....   1..................................

2..   3..   4...

5..   6..   7...

8..   9..   10...

👤 INDIVIDUAL EVENTS   ....

....

....

....

⛑ MILITARY LIFE   Assignment(s) : ....

Campaign(s): ....

Medal(s) : ....☐ *Died in combat* ☐ *Injured on* : ....

560	561	562	563

| 280 | | 281 |

| 140 |

| 70 |

📑 NOTES   ....

....

....

....

♀ Surname : .... First name : ....

▶ Generation 8 – *paternal ascendant*

☐ *Implex*　　Child : ☐ *Legitimate* ☐ *Natural* ☐ *Adopted* ☐ *Found* ☐ *Recognized* ☐ *Adulterated*

Born : ....in ....

Baptized : ....in ....

Godfather: ....Godmother : ....

Daughter of : ....and: ....

Nationality : ....Religion : ....Studies: ....

Occupation(s) : ....

Deceased : ....in ....Cause:...............................

☐ *Buried* ☐ *Cremated* ☐ *Disappeared* on : ....in : ....

👫 CHILDREN ♂ .... ♀	Gen.	° Birth	† Death	Spouse
....	......	....	....	....
....	......	....	....	....
....	......	....	....	....
....	......	....	....	....
....	......	....	....	....
....	......	....	....	....
....	......	....	....	....
....	......	....	....	....
....	......	....	....	....
....	......	....	....	....

💍 OTHER UNION(S)/ 👫 CHILDREN ....

....

....

👫 SIBLINGS　▶ *Details page 283*　　♂ .... ♀ ....　　1. ....

2. ....　3. ....　4. ....

5. ....　6. ....　7. ....

8. ....　9. ....　10. ....

👤 INDIVIDUAL EVENTS ....

....

....

....

....

....

....

📑 NOTES ....

....

....

....

564	565	566	567
282		283	
141			
70			

Surname: .... First name : .... ♂

Child : ☐ *Legitimate* ☐ *Natural* ☐ *Adopted* ☐ *Found* ☐ *Recognized* ☐ *Adulterated*   ☐ *Implex*

Born : ....in...................................

Baptized : ....in...............................

Godfather: ....Godmother : ....

Son of : ....and: ....

Nationality : ....Religion : ....Studies: ....

Occupation(s) : ....

Deceased : ....in...Cause:................................

☐ *Buried* ☐ *Cremated* ☐ *Disappeared* on : ....in :...............................

⚭ MARITAL STATUS   ☐ *Civil Marriage* ☐ *Religious Marriage* ☐ *Free Union*

Date : ....in...☐ *Marriage contract*

Witnesses : ....

....

☐ *Separation* ☐ *Divorce* ☐ *Widowhood of the groom/bride*   Date : ....

👪 FAMILY EVENTS ....

....

....

....

....

....

⚭ OTHER UNION(S)/👪 CHILDREN ....

....

....

....

👪 SIBLINGS   ▶ *Details page 285*   ♂ .... ♀ ....   1..............................

2.. 3................................ 4................................

5.. 6................................ 7................................

8.. 9................................ 10..............................

👤 INDIVIDUAL EVENTS ....

....

....

⛑ MILITARY LIFE   Assignment(s) : ....

Campaign(s): ....

Medal(s) : ....☐ *Died in combat* ☐ *Injured on* : ....

568	569	570	571

284		285

142

71

📑 NOTES ....

....

....

....

....

♀ Surname : .... First name : ....

▶ Generation 8 – *paternal ascendant*

☐ *Implex*   Child : ☐ *Legitimate* ☐ *Natural* ☐ *Adopted* ☐ *Found* ☐ *Recognized* ☐ *Adulterated*

Born : ....in...

Baptized : ....in...

Godfather: ....Godmother : ....

Daughter of : ....and: ....

Nationality : ....Religion : ....Studies: ....

Occupation(s) : ....

Deceased : ....in.................................Cause:.................................

☐ *Buried* ☐ *Cremated* ☐ *Disappeared* on : ....in : ....

👫 CHILDREN ♂ .... ♀	Gen.	° Birth	† Death	Spouse
....	......	....	....	....
....	......	....	....	....
....	......	....	....	....
....	......	....	....	....
....	......	....	....	....
....	......	....	....	....
....	......	....	....	....
....	......	....	....	....
....	......	....	....	....
....	......	....	....	....

💍 OTHER UNION(S)/ 👫 CHILDREN ....
....
....
....

👫 SIBLINGS ▶ *Details page 287* ♂ .... ♀ .... 1...

2...3...4...

5...6...7...

8...9...10...

👤 INDIVIDUAL EVENTS ....
....
....
....
....
....
....

📝 NOTES ....
....
....
....

572	573	574	575
286		287	
	143		
	71		

Surname: .... First name : .... ♂

Child : □ *Legitimate* □ *Natural* □ *Adopted* □ *Found* □ *Recognized* □ *Adulterated*   □ *Implex*

Born : ....in...

Baptized : ....in..

Godfather: ....Godmother : ....

Son of : ....and: ....

Nationality : ....Religion : ....Studies: ....

Occupation(s) : ....

Deceased : ....in...........................Cause:............................

□ *Buried* □ *Cremated* □ *Disappeared* on : ....in : ....

⚭ MARITAL STATUS   □ *Civil Marriage* □ *Religious Marriage* □ *Free Union*

Date : ....in.. □ *Marriage contract*

Witnesses : ....

....

□ *Separation* □ *Divorce* □ *Widowhood of the groom/bride* Date : ....

👫 FAMILY EVENTS ....

....
....
....
....
....

⚭ OTHER UNION(S)/ 👫 CHILDREN ....

....
....
....

👫 SIBLINGS   ▶ *Details page 289*   ♂ .... ♀ ....   1...........................

2..3..4...............................

5..6..7...............................

8..9..10.............................

👤 INDIVIDUAL EVENTS ....

....
....
....

⛑ MILITARY LIFE   Assignment(s) : ....

Campaign(s): ....

Medal(s) : ....□ *Died in combat* □ *Injured on* : ....

....

576	577	578	579
288		289	

144
72

📝 NOTES ....

....
....
....
....

♀ Surname : ....First name : ....

▶ Generation 8 – *paternal ascendant*

☐ *Implex*   Child : ☐ *Legitimate* ☐ *Natural* ☐ *Adopted* ☐ *Found* ☐ *Recognized* ☐ *Adulterated*

Born : ....in..

Baptized : ....in...

Godfather: ....Godmother : ....

Daughter of : ....and: ....

Nationality : ....Religion : ....Studies: ....

Occupation(s) : ....

Deceased : ....in..........................Cause:...................

☐ *Buried* ☐ *Cremated* ☐ *Disappeared* on : ....in :.................

👫 CHILDREN ♂ .... ♀	Gen.	° Birth	† Death	Spouse
....	......	....	....	....
....	......	....	....	....
....	......	....	....	....
....	......	....	....	....
....	......	....	....	....
....	......	....	....	....
....	......	....	....	....
....	......	....	....	....
....	......	....	....	....
....	......	....	....	....

💍 OTHER UNION(S)/👫 CHILDREN ....
....
....

👫 SIBLINGS ▶ *Details page 291*   ♂ .... ♀ .... 1...

2.................................. 3.................................. 4..................................

5.................................. 6.................................. 7..................................

8.................................. 9.................................. 10.................................

👤 INDIVIDUAL EVENTS ....
....
....
....
....
....
....

📝 NOTES ....
....
....
....
....

580	581	582	583
290		291	
	145		
	72		

Surname: .... First name : .... ♂

Child : ☐ *Legitimate* ☐ *Natural* ☐ *Adopted* ☐ *Found* ☐ *Recognized* ☐ *Adulterated* ☐ *Implex*

Born : ....in...

Baptized : ....in...

Godfather: ....Godmother : ....

Son of : ....and: ....

Nationality : ....Religion : ....Studies: ....

Occupation(s) : ....

Deceased : ....in...........................Cause:....................................

☐ *Buried* ☐ *Cremated* ☐ *Disappeared* on : ....in : ....

⚭ MARITAL STATUS   ☐ *Civil Marriage* ☐ *Religious Marriage* ☐ *Free Union*

Date : ....in...☐ *Marriage contract*

Witnesses : ....

....

☐ *Separation* ☐ *Divorce* ☐ *Widowhood of the groom/bride* Date : ....

👫 FAMILY EVENTS ....

....
....
....
....
....

⚭ OTHER UNION(S)/👫 CHILDREN ....

....
....
....

👫 SIBLINGS ▶ *Details page 293*   ♂ .... ♀ ....   1.......................................

2..3..4....................................

5..6..7....................................

8..9..10..................................

👤 INDIVIDUAL EVENTS ....

....
....
....

⛑ MILITARY LIFE Assignment(s) : ....

Campaign(s): ....

Medal(s) : ....☐ *Died in combat* ☐ *Injured on* : ....

584	585	586	587

| 292 | | 293 |

| 146 |

| 73 |

📄 NOTES ....

....
....
....

▶ Generation 8 – *paternal ascendant*

☐ *Implex*　　Child : ☐ *Legitimate* ☐ *Natural* ☐ *Adopted* ☐ *Found* ☐ *Recognized* ☐ *Adulterated*

Born : ....in...

Baptized : ....in...

Godfather: ....Godmother : ....

Daughter of : ....and: ....

Nationality : ....Religion : ....Studies: ....

Occupation(s) : ....

Deceased : ....in...Cause:...........................

☐ *Buried* ☐ *Cremated* ☐ *Disappeared* on : ....in : ....

👫 CHILDREN ♂ .... ♀ ....

	Gen.	° Birth	† Death	Spouse
....	......	....	....	....
....	......	....	....	....
....	......	....	....	....
....	......	....	....	....
....	......	....	....	....
....	......	....	....	....
....	......	....	....	....
....	......	....	....	....
....	......	....	....	....
....	......	....	....	....

💍 OTHER UNION(S)/ 👫 CHILDREN ....

....

....

....

👫 SIBLINGS ▶ *Details page 295* ♂ .... ♀ ....

1. ....
2. .... 3. .... 4. ....
5. .... 6. .... 7. ....
8. .... 9. .... 10. ....

👤 INDIVIDUAL EVENTS ....

....

....

....

....

....

....

📑 NOTES ....

....

....

....

....

588	589	590	591
294		295	
147			
73			

Surname: .... First name : .... ♂

Child : ☐ *Legitimate* ☐ *Natural* ☐ *Adopted* ☐ *Found* ☐ *Recognized* ☐ *Adulterated*   ☐ *Implex*

Born : ....in...

Baptized : ....in...

Godfather: ....Godmother : ....

Son of : ....and: ....

Nationality : ....Religion : ....Studies: ....

Occupation(s) : ....

Deceased : ....in...........................Cause:........................

☐ *Buried* ☐ *Cremated* ☐ *Disappeared* on : ....in :..................

⚭ MARITAL STATUS   ☐ *Civil Marriage* ☐ *Religious Marriage* ☐ *Free Union*

Date : ....in... ☐ *Marriage contract*

Witnesses : ....

....

☐ *Separation* ☐ *Divorce* ☐ *Widowhood of the groom/bride* Date : ....

👪 FAMILY EVENTS ....

....
....
....
....
....
....

⚭ OTHER UNION(S)/ 👫 CHILDREN ....

....
....
....

👫 SIBLINGS   ▶ *Details page 297*   ♂ ....   ♀ ....   1...

2..3...4...

5..6...7...

8..9...10...

👤 INDIVIDUAL EVENTS

....
....
....

⛑ MILITARY LIFE   Assignment(s) : ....

Campaign(s): ....

Medal(s) : ....☐ *Died in combat* ☐ *Injured on* : ....

592	593	594	595

296   297

148

74

📋 NOTES ....

....
....
....
....

♀ Surname : ....First name : ....

▶ Generation 8 – *paternal ascendant*

☐ *Implex*   Child : ☐ *Legitimate* ☐ *Natural* ☐ *Adopted* ☐ *Found* ☐ *Recognized* ☐ *Adulterated*

Born : ....in..

Baptized : ....in..

Godfather: ....Godmother : ....

Daughter of : ....and: ....

Nationality : ....Religion : ....Studies: ....

Occupation(s) : ....

Deceased : ....in.............................Cause:............................

☐ *Buried* ☐ *Cremated* ☐ *Disappeared* on : ....in : ....

👪 CHILDREN ♂ .... ♀	Gen.	° Birth	† Death	Spouse
....	....	....	....	....
....	....	....	....	....
....	....	....	....	....
....	....	....	....	....
....	....	....	....	....
....	....	....	....	....
....	....	....	....	....
....	....	....	....	....
....	....	....	....	....
....	....	....	....	....

💍 OTHER UNION(S)/ 👪 CHILDREN ....

....
....
....

👪 SIBLINGS   ▶ *Details page 299*   ♂ .... ♀ ....   1...

2..3..4...

5..6..7...

8..9..10..

👤 INDIVIDUAL EVENTS ....

....
....
....
....
....
....
....

📝 NOTES ....

....

....

....

....

596	597	598	599
298		299	
149			
74			

Surname: .... First name : .... ♂

▶ Generation8 – *paternal ascendant*

Child : □ *Legitimate* □ *Natural* □ *Adopted* □ *Found* □ *Recognized* □ *Adulterated*   □ *Implex*

Born : ....in...

Baptized : ....in...

Godfather: ....Godmother : ....

Son of : ....and: ....

Nationality : ....Religion : ....Studies: ....

Occupation(s) : ....

Deceased : ....in...Cause:........................

□ *Buried* □ *Cremated* □ *Disappeared* on : ....in :...........................

⌾ MARITAL STATUS   □ *Civil Marriage*   □ *Religious Marriage*   □ *Free Union*

Date : ....in.. □ *Marriage contract*

Witnesses : ....

....

□ *Separation* □ *Divorce* □ *Widowhood of the groom/bride* Date : ....

👪 FAMILY EVENTS   ....

....

....

....

....

⌾ OTHER UNION(S)/ 👪 CHILDREN ....

....

....

....

👪 SIBLINGS   ▶ *Details page 301*   ♂ .... ♀ ....   1..

2....................................... 3....................................... 4.......................................

5....................................... 6....................................... 7.......................................

8....................................... 9....................................... 10......................................

👤 INDIVIDUAL EVENTS ....

....

....

⛑ MILITARY LIFE Assignment(s) : ....

Campaign(s): ....

Medal(s) : ....□ *Died in combat* □ *Injured on :* ....

....

| 600 | 601 | 602 | 603 |

| 300 | 301 |

| 150 |

| 75 |

🗒 NOTES ....

....

....

....

....

♀ Surname : ....First name : ....

▶ Generation 8 – *paternal ascendant*

☐ *Implex*   Child : ☐ *Legitimate* ☐ *Natural* ☐ *Adopted* ☐ *Found* ☐ *Recognized* ☐ *Adulterated*

Born : ....in...

Baptized : ....in...

Godfather: ....Godmother : ....

Daughter of : ....and:...

Nationality : ....Religion : ....Studies: ....

Occupation(s) : ....

Deceased : ....in...Cause:.........................

☐ *Buried* ☐ *Cremated* ☐ *Disappeared* on : ....in :.........................

👫 CHILDREN ♂ .... ♀	Gen.	° Birth	† Death	Spouse

💍 OTHER UNION(S)/ 👫 CHILDREN ....

....

....

👫 SIBLINGS ▶ *Details page 303* ♂ .... ♀ .... 1...

2...3...4...

5...6...7...

8...9...10...

👤 INDIVIDUAL EVENTS ....

....

....

....

....

....

....

📑 NOTES ....

....

....

....

604	605	606	607

| 302 | | 303 |

151

75

Surname: .... First name : .... ♂

Child : ☐ *Legitimate* ☐ *Natural* ☐ *Adopted* ☐ *Found* ☐ *Recognized* ☐ *Adulterated*　　☐ *Implex*

Born : ....in..

Baptized : ....in..

Godfather: ....Godmother : ....

Son of : ....and: ....

Nationality : ....Religion : ....Studies: ....

Occupation(s) : ....

Deceased : ....in...Cause:............................

☐ *Buried* ☐ *Cremated* ☐ *Disappeared* on : ....in : ....

⚭ MARITAL STATUS　　　☐ *Civil Marriage* ☐ *Religious Marriage* ☐ *Free Union*

Date : ....in...☐ *Marriage contract*

Witnesses : ....

....

☐ *Separation* ☐ *Divorce* ☐ *Widowhood of the groom/bride* Date : ....

👫 FAMILY EVENTS ....

....

....

....

....

....

⚭ OTHER UNION(S)/ 👫 CHILDREN ....

....

....

....

👫 SIBLINGS　▶ *Details page 305*　♂ .... ♀ .... 1.....................................

2...3...4...

5...6...7...

8...9...10...

👤 INDIVIDUAL EVENTS ....

....

....

⛑ MILITARY LIFE　Assignment(s) : ....

Campaign(s): ....

Medal(s) : ....☐ *Died in combat* ☐ *Injured on* : ....

608	609	610	611

304　　305

152

76

📑 NOTES ....

....

....

....

....

♀ Surname : ....First name : ....

Sosa
153

▶ Generation 8 – *paternal ascendant*

☐ *Implex*   Child : ☐ *Legitimate* ☐ *Natural* ☐ *Adopted* ☐ *Found* ☐ *Recognized* ☐ *Adulterated*

Born : ....in...

Baptized : ....in...

Godfather: ....Godmother : ....

Daughter of : ....and: ....

Nationality : ....Religion : ....Studies: ....

Occupation(s) : ....

Deceased : ....in...Cause: ....

☐ *Buried* ☐ *Cremated* ☐ *Disappeared* on : ....in : ....

👫 CHILDREN ♂ .... ♀	Gen.	° Birth	† Death	Spouse
....	......	....	....	....
....	......	....	....	....
....	......	....	....	....
....	......	....	....	....
....	......	....	....	....
....	......	....	....	....
....	......	....	....	....
....	......	....	....	....
....	......	....	....	....
....	......	....	....	....

💍 OTHER UNION(S)/ 👫 CHILDREN ....

....
....
....

👫 SIBLINGS ▶ *Details page 307* ♂ .... ♀ .... 1...

2...3...4...

5...6...7...

8...9...10...

👤 INDIVIDUAL EVENTS ....

....
....
....
....
....
....
....

📝 NOTES ....

....
....
....

612	613		614	615
	306		307	
		153		
		76		

153

Sosa
154

Surname: ....First name : .... ♂

▶ Generation8 – *paternal ascendant*

Child : ☐ *Legitimate* ☐ *Natural* ☐ *Adopted* ☐ *Found* ☐ *Recognized* ☐ *Adulterated*   ☐ *Implex*

Born : ....in ....

Baptized : ....in ....

Godfather: ....Godmother : ....

Son of : ....and: ....

Nationality : ....Religion : ....Studies: ....

Occupation(s) : ....

Deceased : ....in.............................Cause:......................................

☐ *Buried* ☐ *Cremated* ☐ *Disappeared* on : ....in :........................

⚭ MARITAL STATUS   ☐ *Civil Marriage* ☐ *Religious Marriage* ☐ *Free Union*

Date : ....in... ☐ *Marriage contract*

Witnesses : ....

....

☐ *Separation* ☐ *Divorce* ☐ *Widowhood of the groom/bride* Date : ....

👫 FAMILY EVENTS ....

....

....

....

....

....

⚭ OTHER UNION(S)/ 👫 CHILDREN ....

....

....

....

👫 SIBLINGS   ▶ *Details page 309*   ♂ .... ♀ ....   1.................................

2..3..4..

5..6..7..

8..9..10..

👤 INDIVIDUAL EVENTS ....

....

....

🪖 MILITARY LIFE   Assignment(s) : ....

Campaign(s): ....

Medal(s) : ....☐ *Died in combat* ☐ *Injured on* : ....

....

| 616 | 617 | 618 | 619 |

| 308 | | 309 |

| 154 |

| 77 |

📝 NOTES ....

....

....

....

....

154

Sosa
155

▶ Generation 8 - *paternal ascendant*

□ *Implex*   Child : □ *Legitimate* □ *Natural* □ *Adopted* □ *Found* □ *Recognized* □ *Adulterated*

Born : ....in...

Baptized : ....in...

Godfather: ....Godmother : ....

Daughter of : ....and:...

Nationality : ....Religion : ....Studies: ....

Occupation(s) : ....

Deceased : ....in..........................Cause:.................................

□ *Buried* □ *Cremated* □ *Disappeared* on : ....in :.................................

👫 CHILDREN ♂ .... ♀	Gen.	° Birth	† Death	Spouse
....	......	....	....	....
....	......	....	....	....
....	......	....	....	....
....	......	....	....	....
....	......	....	....	....
....	......	....	....	....
....	......	....	....	....
....	......	....	....	....
....	......	....	....	....
....	......	....	....	....

💍 OTHER UNION(S)/ 👫 CHILDREN ....

....

....

....

👫 SIBLINGS   ▶ *Details page 311*   ♂ .... ♀ ....   1..

2.. 3.................................... 4....................................

5.. 6.................................... 7....................................

8.. 9.................................... 10...................................

👤 INDIVIDUAL EVENTS ....

....

....

....

....

....

....

📑 NOTES ....

....

....

....

620	621	622	623

310	311

155

77

Surname: .... First name : .... ♂

Child : ☐ *Legitimate* ☐ *Natural* ☐ *Adopted* ☐ *Found* ☐ *Recognized* ☐ *Adulterated*   ☐ *Implex*

Born : ....in...

Baptized : ....in...

Godfather: ....Godmother : ....

Son of : ....and: ....

Nationality : ....Religion : ....Studies: ....

Occupation(s) : ....

Deceased : ....in..........................Cause:...........................

☐ *Buried* ☐ *Cremated* ☐ *Disappeared* on : ....in : ....

⚭ MARITAL STATUS   ☐ *Civil Marriage*   ☐ *Religious Marriage*   ☐ *Free Union*

Date : ....in... ☐ *Marriage contract*

Witnesses : ....
....

☐ *Separation* ☐ *Divorce* ☐ *Widowhood of the groom/bride*   Date : ....

👫 FAMILY EVENTS ....
....
....
....
....
....

⚭ OTHER UNION(S)/👫 CHILDREN ....
....
....
....

👫 SIBLINGS   ▶ *Details page 313*   ♂ .... ♀ ....   1..

2..3..4..

5..6..7..

8..9..10..

👤 INDIVIDUAL EVENTS ....
....
....
....

⛑ MILITARY LIFE   Assignment(s) : ....

Campaign(s): ....

Medal(s) : ....☐ *Died in combat* ☐ *Injured on* : ....

624	625	626	627
312		313	
	156		
	78		

📑 NOTES ....
....
....
....
....

♀ Surname : ....First name : ....

▶ Generation 8 – *paternal ascendant*

☐ *Implex*   Child : ☐ *Legitimate* ☐ *Natural* ☐ *Adopted* ☐ *Found* ☐ *Recognized* ☐ *Adulterated*

Born : ....in...

Baptized : ....in...

Godfather: ....Godmother : ....

Daughter of : ....and: ....

Nationality : ....Religion : ....Studies: ....

Occupation(s) : ....

Deceased : ....in.........................Cause:.............................

☐ *Buried* ☐ *Cremated* ☐ *Disappeared* on : ....in : ....

👫 CHILDREN ♂ .... ♀	Gen.	° Birth	† Death	Spouse
....	......	....	....	....
....	......	....	....	....
....	......	....	....	....
....	......	....	....	....
....	......	....	....	....
....	......	....	....	....
....	......	....	....	....
....	......	....	....	....
....	......	....	....	....
....	......	....	....	....

💍 OTHER UNION(S)/ 👫 CHILDREN ....

....

....

....

👫 SIBLINGS ▶ *Details page 315*   ♂ .... ♀ ....   1..

2...3...............................4..

5...6...............................7..

8...9...............................10..

👤 INDIVIDUAL EVENTS ....

....

....

....

....

....

....

📓 NOTES ....

....

....

....

628	629	630	631

314   315

157

78

Surname: .... First name : .... ♂

▶ Generation8 – *paternal ascendant*

Child : ☐ *Legitimate* ☐ *Natural* ☐ *Adopted* ☐ *Found* ☐ *Recognized* ☐ *Adulterated*   ☐ *Implex*

Born : ....in ....

Baptized : ....in ....

Godfather: .... Godmother : ....

Son of : .... and: ....

Nationality : .... Religion : .... Studies: ....

Occupation(s) : ....

Deceased : ....in..................................Cause:..................

☐ *Buried* ☐ *Cremated* ☐ *Disappeared* on : ....in : ....

⚭ MARITAL STATUS   ☐ *Civil Marriage*   ☐ *Religious Marriage*   ☐ *Free Union*

Date : ....in....................................... ☐ *Marriage contract*

Witnesses : ....
....

☐ *Separation* ☐ *Divorce* ☐ *Widowhood of the groom/bride*   Date : ....

👫 FAMILY EVENTS ....
....
....
....
....
....
....

⚭ OTHER UNION(S)/ 👫 CHILDREN ....
....
....
....

👫 SIBLINGS   ▶ *Details page 317*   ♂ .... ♀ ....   1...........................
2.. 3.. 4........................
5.. 6.. 7........................
8.. 9.. 10.......................

👤 INDIVIDUAL EVENTS ....
....
....

⛑ MILITARY LIFE   Assignment(s) : ....
Campaign(s): ....
Medal(s) : .... ☐ *Died in combat* ☐ *Injured on* : ....

632	633	634	635

316		317

158

79

📑 NOTES ....
....
....
....
....

♀ Surname : .... First name : ....

▶ Generation 8 – *paternal ascendant*

☐ *Implex*   Child : ☐ *Legitimate* ☐ *Natural* ☐ *Adopted* ☐ *Found* ☐ *Recognized* ☐ *Adulterated*

Born : ....in...

Baptized : ....in...

Godfather: ....Godmother : ....

Daughter of : ....and: ....

Nationality : ....Religion : ....Studies: ....

Occupation(s) : ....

Deceased : ....in..Cause:........................

☐ *Buried* ☐ *Cremated* ☐ *Disappeared* on : ....in : ....

👪 CHILDREN ♂ .... ♀ ....

	Gen.	° Birth	† Death	Spouse
....	....	....	....	....
....	....	....	....	....
....	....	....	....	....
....	....	....	....	....
....	....	....	....	....
....	....	....	....	....
....	....	....	....	....
....	....	....	....	....
....	....	....	....	....
....	....	....	....	....

💍 OTHER UNION(S)/ 👪 CHILDREN ....

....

....

....

👫 SIBLINGS ▶ *Details page 319* ♂ .... ♀ .... 1..

2.. 3.. 4..

5.. 6.. 7..

8.. 9.. 10..

👤 INDIVIDUAL EVENTS ....

....

....

....

....

....

📑 NOTES ....

....

....

....

636	637	638	639
318		319	
159			
79			

Surname: .... First name : .... ♂

▶ Generation8 – *paternal ascendant*

Child : □ *Legitimate* □ *Natural* □ *Adopted* □ *Found* □ *Recognized* □ *Adulterated*   □ *Implex*

Born : ....in...

Baptized : ....in...

Godfather: ....Godmother : ....

Son of : ....and: ....

Nationality : ....Religion : ....Studies: ....

Occupation(s) : ....

Deceased : ....in.........................Cause:...............................

□ *Buried* □ *Cremated* □ *Disappeared* on : ....in : ....

⊚ MARITAL STATUS   □ *Civil Marriage* □ *Religious Marriage* □ *Free Union*

Date : ....in..□ *Marriage contract*

Witnesses : ....

....

□ *Separation* □ *Divorce* □ *Widowhood of the groom/bride* Date : ....

👪 FAMILY EVENTS ....

....

....

....

....

⊚ OTHER UNION(S)/👪 CHILDREN ....

....

....

....

👪 SIBLINGS   ▶ *Details page 321*   ♂ .... ♀ ....   1................................
2.. 3............................... 4...............................
5.. 6............................... 7...............................
8.. 9............................... 10.............................

👤 INDIVIDUAL EVENTS ....

....

....

⛑ MILITARY LIFE Assignment(s) : ....

Campaign(s): ....

Medal(s) : ....□ *Died in combat* □ *Injured on :* ....

....

640	641	642	643

```
   320         321
        160
        80
```

📑 NOTES ....

....

....

....

♀ Surname : ....First name : ....

▶ Generation 8 – *paternal ascendant*

☐ *Implex* Child : ☐ *Legitimate* ☐ *Natural* ☐ *Adopted* ☐ *Found* ☐ *Recognized* ☐ *Adulterated*

Born : ....in ....

Baptized : ....in ....

Godfather: ....Godmother : ....

Daughter of : ....and: ....

Nationality : ....Religion : ....Studies: ....

Occupation(s) : ....

Deceased : ....in ....Cause:..

☐ *Buried* ☐ *Cremated* ☐ *Disappeared* on : ....in : ....

👫 CHILDREN ♂ .... ♀ ....

	Gen.	° Birth	† Death	Spouse

💍 OTHER UNION(S)/ 👫 CHILDREN ....

....

....

👫 SIBLINGS ▶ *Details page 323* ♂ .... ♀ ....

1. ....
2. .... 3. .... 4. ....
5. .... 6. .... 7. ....
8. .... 9. .... 10. ....

👤 INDIVIDUAL EVENTS ....

....

....

....

....

....

....

📑 NOTES ....

....

....

....

644	645	646	647
322		323	
161			
80			

Surname: .... First name : .... ♂

Child : □ *Legitimate* □ *Natural* □ *Adopted* □ *Found* □ *Recognized* □ *Adulterated*   □ *Implex*

Born : ....in..

Baptized : ....in..

Godfather: ....Godmother : ....

Son of : ....and: ....

Nationality : ....Religion : ....Studies: ....

Occupation(s) : ....

Deceased : ....in..............................Cause:..............................

□ *Buried* □ *Cremated* □ *Disappeared* on : ....in : ....

⚭ MARITAL STATUS   □ *Civil Marriage* □ *Religious Marriage* □ *Free Union*

Date : ....in....................................... □ *Marriage contract*

Witnesses : ....

....

□ *Separation* □ *Divorce* □ *Widowhood of the groom/bride* Date : ....

👪 FAMILY EVENTS   ....

....
....
....
....
....

⚭ OTHER UNION(S)/👪 CHILDREN ....

....
....
....

👪 SIBLINGS ▶ *Details page 325* ♂ .... ♀ .... 1..............................

2.. 3.. 4..............................

5.. 6.. 7..............................

8.. 9.. 10............................

👤 INDIVIDUAL EVENTS ....

....
....

⛑ MILITARY LIFE Assignment(s) : ....

Campaign(s): ....

Medal(s) : ....□ *Died in combat* □ *Injured on* : ....

648	649	650	651

324   325

162

81

📑 NOTES ....

....
....
....
....

♀ Surname : .... First name : ....

▶ Generation 8 - *paternal ascendant*

☐ *Implex*   Child : ☐ *Legitimate* ☐ *Natural* ☐ *Adopted* ☐ *Found* ☐ *Recognized* ☐ *Adulterated*

Born : ....in..

Baptized : ....in..

Godfather: ....Godmother : ....

Daughter of : ....and: ....

Nationality : ....Religion : ....Studies: ....

Occupation(s) : ....

Deceased : ....in..Cause:..................................

☐ *Buried* ☐ *Cremated* ☐ *Disappeared* on : ....in : ....

👫 CHILDREN ♂ .... ♀ ....

	Gen.	° Birth	† Death	Spouse

💍 OTHER UNION(S)/ 👫 CHILDREN ....

....

....

👫 SIBLINGS ▶ *Details page 327* ♂ .... ♀ .... 1..................................

2.................................. 3.................................. 4..................................

5.................................. 6.................................. 7..................................

8.................................. 9.................................. 10..................................

👤 INDIVIDUAL EVENTS ....

....

....

....

....

....

....

📝 NOTES ....

....

....

....

652	653	654	655

326   327

163

81

163

164

Surname: .... First name : .... ♂

Child : □ *Legitimate* □ *Natural* □ *Adopted* □ *Found* □ *Recognized* □ *Adulterated*   □ *Implex*

Born : ....in...

Baptized : ....in...

Godfather: ....Godmother : ....

Son of : ....and:..

Nationality : ....Religion : ....Studies: ....

Occupation(s) : ....

Deceased : ....in..............................Cause:....................................

□ *Buried* □ *Cremated* □ *Disappeared* on : ....in :.............................

💍 MARITAL STATUS   □ *Civil Marriage*   □ *Religious Marriage*   □ *Free Union*

Date : ....in...

□ *Marriage contract*

Witnesses : ....

....

□ *Separation* □ *Divorce* □ *Widowhood of the groom/bride*   Date : ....

👫 FAMILY EVENTS ....

....

....

....

....

....

💍 OTHER UNION(S)/ 👫 CHILDREN ....

....

....

....

👫 SIBLINGS   ▶ *Details page 329*   ♂ ....   ♀ ....   1.....................................

2.. 3.............................. 4......................................

5.. 6.............................. 7......................................

8.. 9.............................. 10....................................

👤 INDIVIDUAL EVENTS ....

....

....

⛑ MILITARY LIFE   Assignment(s) : ....

Campaign(s): ....

Medal(s) : ....□ *Died in combat* □ *Injured on :* ....

....

```
┌──────┬──────┬──────┬──────┐
│ 656  │ 657  │ 658  │ 659  │
└──┬───┴──┬───┴──┬───┴──┬───┘
   └─ 328 ─┘      └─ 329 ─┘
        └──── 164 ────┘
             └─ 82 ─┘
```

📑 NOTES ....

....

....

....

....

♀ Surname : ....First name : ....

☐ *Implex*   Child : ☐ *Legitimate* ☐ *Natural* ☐ *Adopted* ☐ *Found* ☐ *Recognized* ☐ *Adulterated*

Born : ....in...

Baptized : ....in...

Godfather: ....Godmother : ....

Daughter of : ....and:...

Nationality : ....Religion : ....Studies:...........................

Occupation(s) : ....

Deceased : ....in..........................Cause:.........................

☐ *Buried* ☐ *Cremated* ☐ *Disappeared* on : ....in : ....

👫 CHILDREN ♂ .... ♀	Gen.	° Birth	† Death	Spouse
....	......	....	....	....
....	......	....	....	....
....	......	....	....	....
....	......	....	....	....
....	......	....	....	....
....	......	....	....	....
....	......	....	....	....
....	......	....	....	....
....	......	....	....	....
....	......	....	....	....

💍 OTHER UNION(S)/👫 CHILDREN ....

....

....

👫 SIBLINGS   ▶ *Details page 331*   ♂ .... ♀ ....   1...........................

2............................   3............................   4............................

5............................   6............................   7............................

8............................   9............................   10...........................

👤 INDIVIDUAL EVENTS ....

....

....

....

....

....

....

📑 NOTES ....

....

....

....

660	661	662	663

| 330 | | 331 |

165

| 82 |

Surname: .... First name : .... ♂

Child : ☐ *Legitimate* ☐ *Natural* ☐ *Adopted* ☐ *Found* ☐ *Recognized* ☐ *Adulterated*   ☐ *Implex*

Born : ....in..

Baptized : ....in...

Godfather: ....Godmother : ....

Son of : ....and: ....

Nationality : ....Religion : ....Studies: ....

Occupation(s) : ....

Deceased : ....in....................Cause:..............................

☐ *Buried* ☐ *Cremated* ☐ *Disappeared* on : ....in : ....

⓪ MARITAL STATUS   ☐ *Civil Marriage*   ☐ *Religious Marriage*   ☐ *Free Union*

Date : ....in.. ☐ *Marriage contract*

Witnesses : ....

....

☐ *Separation* ☐ *Divorce* ☐ *Widowhood of the groom/bride*   Date : ....

👫 FAMILY EVENTS ....

....

....

....

....

⓪ OTHER UNION(S)/ 👫 CHILDREN ....

....

....

👫 SIBLINGS   ▶ *Details page 333*   ♂ ....   ♀ ....   1..............................

2..3..4.............................

5..6..7.............................

8..9..10...........................

👤 INDIVIDUAL EVENTS ....

....

....

⛑ MILITARY LIFE   Assignment(s) : ....

Campaign(s): ....

Medal(s) : ....☐ *Died in combat* ☐ *Injured on* : ....

664	665	666	667

📑 NOTES ....

332   333

166

83

....

....

....

....

♀ Surname : .... First name : ....

▶ Generation 8 – *paternal ascendant*

☐ *Implex*   Child : ☐ *Legitimate* ☐ *Natural* ☐ *Adopted* ☐ *Found* ☐ *Recognized* ☐ *Adulterated*

Born : ....in...

Baptized : ....in...

Godfather: ....Godmother : ....

Daughter of : ....and: ....

Nationality : ....Religion : ....Studies: ....

Occupation(s) : ....

Deceased : ....in....................................Cause:........................

☐ *Buried* ☐ *Cremated* ☐ *Disappeared* on : ....in : ....

👫 CHILDREN ♂ .... ♀	Gen.	° Birth	† Death	Spouse
....	......	....	....	....
....	......	....	....	....
....	......	....	....	....
....	......	....	....	....
....	......	....	....	....
....	......	....	....	....
....	......	....	....	....
....	......	....	....	....
....	......	....	....	....
....	......	....	....	....

💍 OTHER UNION(S)/ 👫 CHILDREN ....
....
....
....

👫 SIBLINGS ▶ *Details page 335*   ♂ .... ♀ ....   1..................................
2...3..................................4.................................
5...6..................................7.................................
8...9..................................10................................

👤 INDIVIDUAL EVENTS ....
....
....
....
....
....
....

📑 NOTES ....
....
....
....

668	669	670	671
334		335	
	167		
	83		

Sosa 168

Surname: .... First name : .... ♂

Child : □ *Legitimate* □ *Natural* □ *Adopted* □ *Found* □ *Recognized* □ *Adulterated*　　　□ *Implex*

Born : ....in...

Baptized : ....in...

Godfather: ....Godmother : ....

Son of : ....and: ....

Nationality : ....Religion : ....Studies: ....

Occupation(s) : ....

Deceased : ....in....................Cause:...............................

□ *Buried* □ *Cremated* □ *Disappeared* on : ....in : ....

◎ MARITAL STATUS　　　□ *Civil Marriage* □ *Religious Marriage* □ *Free Union*

Date : ....in... □ *Marriage contract*

Witnesses : ....

....

□ *Separation* □ *Divorce* □ *Widowhood of the groom/bride* Date : ....

👪 FAMILY EVENTS　...

....

....

....

....

....

◎ OTHER UNION(S)/👪 CHILDREN　...

....

....

....

👫 SIBLINGS　▶ *Details page 337*　♂ ....　♀ ....　1.............................

2...3................................4...............................

5...6................................7...............................

8...9................................10.............................

👤 INDIVIDUAL EVENTS　..

....

....

....

⛑ MILITARY LIFE　Assignment(s) : ....

Campaign(s): ....

Medal(s) : ....□ *Died in combat* □ *Injured on* : ....

672	673	674	675

📑 NOTES　..

336　　337

168

84

....

....

....

....

♀ Surname : .... First name : ....

Sosa
169

▶ Generation 8 – *paternal ascendant*

□ *Implex*　　Child : □ *Legitimate* □ *Natural* □ *Adopted* □ *Found* □ *Recognized* □ *Adulterated*

Born : ....in ....

Baptized : ....in ....

Godfather: ....Godmother : ....

Daughter of : ....and: ....

Nationality : ....Religion : ....Studies: ....

Occupation(s) : ....

Deceased : ....in ....Cause: ....

□ *Buried* □ *Cremated* □ *Disappeared* on : ....in : ....

👫 CHILDREN ♂ .... ♀ ....

	Gen.	° Birth	† Death	Spouse

💍 OTHER UNION(S)/ 👫 CHILDREN ....

....

....

👫 SIBLINGS ▶ *Details page 339* ♂ .... ♀ .... 1...

2...3...4...

5...6...7...

8...9...10...

👤 INDIVIDUAL EVENTS ....

....

....

....

....

....

📝 NOTES ....

....

....

....

676	677	678	679
338		339	
	169		
	84		

169

Surname: .... First name : .... ♂

▶ Generation8 – *paternal ascendant*

Child : □ *Legitimate* □ *Natural* □ *Adopted* □ *Found* □ *Recognized* □ *Adulterated*   □ *Implex*

Born : ....in...

Baptized : ....in...

Godfather: ....Godmother : ....

Son of : ....and:..

Nationality : ....Religion : ....Studies: ....

Occupation(s) : ....

Deceased : ....in.......................Cause:...............................

□ *Buried* □ *Cremated* □ *Disappeared* on : ....in :..........................

⚭ MARITAL STATUS   □ *Civil Marriage*   □ *Religious Marriage*   □ *Free Union*

Date : ....in.. □ *Marriage contract*

Witnesses : ....
....

□ *Separation* □ *Divorce* □ *Widowhood of the groom/bride*   Date : ....

👫 FAMILY EVENTS ....

⚭ OTHER UNION(S)/ 👫 CHILDREN ....
....
....

👫 SIBLINGS   ▶ *Details page 341*   ♂ ....   ♀ ....   1.............................

2.................................... 3.................................... 4.............................

5.................................... 6.................................... 7.............................

8.................................... 9.................................... 10...........................

👤 INDIVIDUAL EVENTS ....

⛑ MILITARY LIFE   Assignment(s) : ....

Campaign(s): ....

Medal(s) : ....□ *Died in combat* □ *Injured on* : ....

680	681	682	683

📑 NOTES ....
340   341   ....
170   ....
85   ....

♀ Surname : .... First name : ....

▶ Generation 8 - *paternal ascendant*

☐ *Implex*   Child : ☐ *Legitimate* ☐ *Natural* ☐ *Adopted* ☐ *Found* ☐ *Recognized* ☐ *Adulterated*

Born : .... in ....

Baptized : .... in ....

Godfather: .... Godmother : ....

Daughter of : .... and: ....

Nationality : .... Religion : .... Studies: ....

Occupation(s) : ....

Deceased : .... in .... Cause:...........................

☐ *Buried* ☐ *Cremated* ☐ *Disappeared* on : .... in : ....

👫 CHILDREN ♂ .... ♀	Gen.	° Birth	† Death	Spouse
....	......	....	....	....
....	......	....	....	....
....	......	....	....	....
....	......	....	....	....
....	......	....	....	....
....	......	....	....	....
....	......	....	....	....
....	......	....	....	....
....	......	....	....	....
....	......	....	....	....
....	......	....	....	....

💍 OTHER UNION(S)/ 👫 CHILDREN ....

....

....

....

👫 SIBLINGS   ▶ *Details page 343*   ♂ .... ♀ ....   1.......................................

2.. 3............................ 4...................................

5.. 6............................ 7...................................

8.. 9............................ 10..................................

👤 INDIVIDUAL EVENTS ....

....

....

....

....

....

....

📑 NOTES ....

....

....

....

684	685	686	687
342		343	
171			
85			

Surname: .... First name : .... ♂

Child : □ *Legitimate* □ *Natural* □ *Adopted* □ *Found* □ *Recognized* □ *Adulterated*   □ *Implex*

Born : ....in..

Baptized : ....in..

Godfather: ....Godmother : ....

Son of : ....and: ....

Nationality : ....Religion : ....Studies: ....

Occupation(s) : ....

Deceased : ....in..Cause:..........................

□ *Buried* □ *Cremated* □ *Disappeared* on : ....in :..........................

⊚ MARITAL STATUS   □ *Civil Marriage* □ *Religious Marriage* □ *Free Union*

Date : ....in.. □ *Marriage contract*

Witnesses : ....

....

□ *Separation* □ *Divorce* □ *Widowhood of the groom/bride* Date : ....

👫 FAMILY EVENTS   ....

....
....
....
....
....

⊚ OTHER UNION(S)/ 👫 CHILDREN   ....

....
....
....

👫 SIBLINGS   ▶ *Details page 345*   ♂ .... ♀ ....   1..

2.. 3.. 4..
5.. 6.. 7..
8.. 9.. 10..

👤 INDIVIDUAL EVENTS   ....

....
....

⛑ MILITARY LIFE   Assignment(s) : ....

Campaign(s): ....

Medal(s) : ....□ *Died in combat* □ *Injured on :* ....

688	689	690	691

344   345

172

86

🗒 NOTES   ....

....
....
....
....

♀ Surname : .... First name : ....

▶ Generation 8 – *paternal ascendant*

☐ *Implex*   Child : ☐ *Legitimate* ☐ *Natural* ☐ *Adopted* ☐ *Found* ☐ *Recognized* ☐ *Adulterated*

Born : .... in ....

Baptized : .... in ....

Godfather: .... Godmother : ....

Daughter of : .... and: ....

Nationality : .... Religion : .... Studies: ....

Occupation(s) : ....

Deceased : .... in .... Cause: ....

☐ *Buried* ☐ *Cremated* ☐ *Disappeared* on : .... in : ....

👫 CHILDREN ♂ .... ♀ ....

	Gen.	° Birth	† Death	Spouse

💍 OTHER UNION(S)/ 👫 CHILDREN ....

....

....

👫 SIBLINGS   ▶ *Details page 347*   ♂ .... ♀ ....   1.................................

2................................. 3................................. 4.................................

5................................. 6................................. 7.................................

8................................. 9................................. 10................................

👤 INDIVIDUAL EVENTS ....

....

....

....

....

....

....

📝 NOTES ....

....

....

....

692	693	694	695
346		347	
	173		
	86		

Surname: .... First name : .... ♂

Child : ☐ *Legitimate* ☐ *Natural* ☐ *Adopted* ☐ *Found* ☐ *Recognized* ☐ *Adulterated*   ☐ *Implex*

Born : ....in ....

Baptized : ....in ....

Godfather: ....Godmother : ....

Son of : ....and: ....

Nationality : ....Religion : ....Studies: ....

Occupation(s) : ....

Deceased : ....in...Cause:.............................

☐ *Buried* ☐ *Cremated* ☐ *Disappeared* on : ....in : ....

⚭ MARITAL STATUS   ☐ *Civil Marriage* ☐ *Religious Marriage* ☐ *Free Union*

Date : ....in... ☐ *Marriage contract*

Witnesses : ....

....

☐ *Separation* ☐ *Divorce* ☐ *Widowhood of the groom/bride* Date : ....

👪 FAMILY EVENTS ....

....

....

....

....

....

⚭ OTHER UNION(S)/ 👪 CHILDREN ....

....

....

....

👫 SIBLINGS   ▶ *Details page 349*   ♂ .... ♀ ....   1...............................

2... 3.. 4...............................

5... 6.. 7...............................

8... 9.. 10.............................

👤 INDIVIDUAL EVENTS ....

....

....

⛑ MILITARY LIFE Assignment(s) : ....

Campaign(s): ....

Medal(s) : ....☐ *Died in combat* ☐ *Injured on* : ....

696	697	698	699

348		349

174

87

📑 NOTES ....

....

....

....

....

♀ Surname : .... First name : ....

▶ Generation 8 - *paternal ascendant*

□ *Implex*   Child : □ *Legitimate* □ *Natural* □ *Adopted* □ *Found* □ *Recognized* □ *Adulterated*

Born : ....in...

Baptized : ....in...

Godfather: ....Godmother : ....

Daughter of : ....and: ....

Nationality : ....Religion : ....Studies: ....

Occupation(s) : ....

Deceased : ....in.......................Cause:........................

□ *Buried* □ *Cremated* □ *Disappeared* on : ....in : ....

👫 CHILDREN ♂ .... ♀ ....

	Gen.	° Birth	† Death	Spouse
....	......	....	....	....
....	......	....	....	....
....	......	....	....	....
....	......	....	....	....
....	......	....	....	....
....	......	....	....	....
....	......	....	....	....
....	......	....	....	....
....	......	....	....	....
....	......	....	....	....

💍 OTHER UNION(S)/ 👫 CHILDREN ....

....

....

....

👫 SIBLINGS   ▶ *Details page 351*   ♂ .... ♀ ....   1..................................

2..3...............................4..................................

5..6...............................7..................................

8..9...............................10................................

👤 INDIVIDUAL EVENTS ....

....

....

....

....

....

....

....

📑 NOTES ....

....

....

....

700	701	702	703

| 350 | | 351 |

175

87

Surname: .... First name : .... ♂

Child : □ *Legitimate* □ *Natural* □ *Adopted* □ *Found* □ *Recognized* □ *Adulterated*   □ *Implex*

Born : ....in ....

Baptized : ....in ....

Godfather: ....Godmother : ....

Son of : ....and: ....

Nationality : ....Religion : ....Studies: ....

Occupation(s) : ....

Deceased : ....in ....Cause: ....

□ *Buried* □ *Cremated* □ *Disappeared* on : ....in : ....

⊚ MARITAL STATUS   □ *Civil Marriage* □ *Religious Marriage* □ *Free Union*

Date : ....in ....   □ *Marriage contract*

Witnesses : ....

....

□ *Separation* □ *Divorce* □ *Widowhood of the groom/bride* Date : ....

👫 FAMILY EVENTS ....

....
....
....
....
....

⊚ OTHER UNION(S)/ 👫 CHILDREN ....

....
....
....

👫 SIBLINGS   ▶ *Details page 353*   ♂ .... ♀ ....   1. ....
2. .... 3. .... 4. ....
5. .... 6. .... 7. ....
8. .... 9. .... 10. ....

👤 INDIVIDUAL EVENTS ....

....
....
....

⛑ MILITARY LIFE Assignment(s) : ....

Campaign(s): ....

Medal(s) : ....□ *Died in combat* □ *Injured on* : ....

....

704	705	706	707

352   353

176

88

📑 NOTES
....
....
....
....

♀ Surname : .... First name : ....

Sosa
177

▶ Generation 8 – *paternal ascendant*

☐ *Implex*   Child : ☐ *Legitimate* ☐ *Natural* ☐ *Adopted* ☐ *Found* ☐ *Recognized* ☐ *Adulterated*

Born : ....in..

Baptized : ....in..

Godfather: ....Godmother : ....

Daughter of : ....and: ....

Nationality : ....Religion : ....Studies: ....

Occupation(s) : ....

Deceased : ....in....................Cause:....................

☐ *Buried* ☐ *Cremated* ☐ *Disappeared* on : ....in : ....

👫 CHILDREN ♂ .... ♀	Gen.	° Birth	† Death	Spouse
....	......	....	....	....
....	......	....	....	....
....	......	....	....	....
....	......	....	....	....
....	......	....	....	....
....	......	....	....	....
....	......	....	....	....
....	......	....	....	....
....	......	....	....	....
....	......	....	....	....
....	......	....	....	....

💍 **OTHER UNION(S)/ 👫 CHILDREN** ....

....

....

👫 **SIBLINGS** ▶ *Details page 355* ♂ .... ♀ .... 1....................

2.................... 3.................... 4....................

5.................... 6.................... 7....................

8.................... 9.................... 10....................

👤 **INDIVIDUAL EVENTS** ....

....

....

....

....

....

....

📝 **NOTES** ....

....

....

....

708	709	710	711
354		355	
	177		
	88		

177

Surname: .... First name : .... ♂

▶ Generation8 – *paternal ascendant*

Child : ☐ *Legitimate* ☐ *Natural* ☐ *Adopted* ☐ *Found* ☐ *Recognized* ☐ *Adulterated*   ☐ *Implex*

Born : ....in...

Baptized : ....in..

Godfather: ....Godmother : ....

Son of : ....and:..

Nationality : ....Religion : ....Studies: ....

Occupation(s) : ....

Deceased : ....in..............................Cause:...........................

☐ *Buried* ☐ *Cremated* ☐ *Disappeared* on : ....in :......................

⚭ MARITAL STATUS   ☐ *Civil Marriage* ☐ *Religious Marriage* ☐ *Free Union*

Date : ....in..☐ *Marriage contract*

Witnesses : ....

....

☐ *Separation* ☐ *Divorce* ☐ *Widowhood of the groom/bride* Date : ....

👫 FAMILY EVENTS ....

....

....

....

....

....

⚭ OTHER UNION(S)/ 👫 CHILDREN ....

....

....

....

👫 SIBLINGS   ▶ *Details page 357*   ♂ .... ♀ ....   1...

2.. 3.. 4.............................

5.. 6.. 7.............................

8.. 9.. 10...........................

👤 INDIVIDUAL EVENTS ....

....

....

⛑ MILITARY LIFE   Assignment(s) : ....

Campaign(s): ....

Medal(s) : ....☐ *Died in combat* ☐ *Injured on* : ....

712	713	714	715

356   357

178

89

📑 NOTES ....

....

....

....

♀ Surname : ....First name : ....

▶ Generation 8 – *paternal ascendant*

☐ *Implex*   Child : ☐ *Legitimate* ☐ *Natural* ☐ *Adopted* ☐ *Found* ☐ *Recognized* ☐ *Adulterated*

Born : ....in...

Baptized : ....in...

Godfather: ....Godmother : ....

Daughter of : ....and: ....

Nationality : ....Religion : ....Studies: ....

Occupation(s) : ....

Deceased : ....in................................Cause:..........................

☐ *Buried* ☐ *Cremated* ☐ *Disappeared* on : ....in : ....

👫 CHILDREN ♂ .... ♀ ....

	Gen.	° Birth	† Death	Spouse
....	......	....	....	....
....	......	....	....	....
....	......	....	....	....
....	......	....	....	....
....	......	....	....	....
....	......	....	....	....
....	......	....	....	....
....	......	....	....	....
....	......	....	....	....
....	......	....	....	....

💍 OTHER UNION(S)/ 👫 CHILDREN ....

....

....

👫 SIBLINGS ▶ *Details page 359* ♂ .... ♀ .... 1...

2...3...4...

5...6...7...

8...9...10...

👤 INDIVIDUAL EVENTS ....

....

....

....

....

....

....

📝 NOTES ....

....

....

....

....

716	717	718	719
	358		359
		179	
		89	

Surname: .... First name : .... ♂

▶ Generation8 – *paternal ascendant*

Child : ☐ *Legitimate* ☐ *Natural* ☐ *Adopted* ☐ *Found* ☐ *Recognized* ☐ *Adulterated*   ☐ *Implex*

Born : ....in ....

Baptized : ....in ....

Godfather: ....Godmother : ....

Son of : ....and: ....

Nationality : ....Religion : ....Studies: ....

Occupation(s) : ....

Deceased : ....in...Cause:...................................

☐ *Buried* ☐ *Cremated* ☐ *Disappeared* on : ....in : ....

◎ MARITAL STATUS   ☐ *Civil Marriage*   ☐ *Religious Marriage*   ☐ *Free Union*

Date : ....in...   ☐ *Marriage contract*

Witnesses : ....

....

☐ *Separation* ☐ *Divorce* ☐ *Widowhood of the groom/bride*   Date : ....

◎◎ FAMILY EVENTS   ....

....

....

....

....

....

◎ OTHER UNION(S)/ ◎◎ CHILDREN   ....

....

....

....

◎◎ SIBLINGS   ▶ *Details page 361*   ♂ .... ♀ ....   1...

2.. 3... 4..

5.. 6... 7..

8.. 9... 10..

◎ INDIVIDUAL EVENTS   ....

....

....

◎ MILITARY LIFE   Assignment(s) : ....

Campaign(s): ....

Medal(s) : ....☐ *Died in combat* ☐ *Injured on :* ....

720	721	722	723

360		361

180

90

◎ NOTES ....

....

....

....

....

♀ Surname : ....First name : ....

▶ Generation 8 – *paternal ascendant*

☐ *Implex* Child : ☐ *Legitimate* ☐ *Natural* ☐ *Adopted* ☐ *Found* ☐ *Recognized* ☐ *Adulterated*

Born : ....in..

Baptized : ....in...

Godfather: ....Godmother : ....

Daughter of : ....and: ....

Nationality : ....Religion : ....Studies: ....

Occupation(s) : ....

Deceased : ....in.........................Cause:....................

☐ *Buried* ☐ *Cremated* ☐ *Disappeared* on : ....in : ....

👪 CHILDREN ♂ .... ♀	Gen.	° Birth	† Death	Spouse
....	......	....	....	....
....	......	....	....	....
....	......	....	....	....
....	......	....	....	....
....	......	....	....	....
....	......	....	....	....
....	......	....	....	....
....	......	....	....	....
....	......	....	....	....
....	......	....	....	....

💍 OTHER UNION(S)/ 👪 CHILDREN ....

....

....

👪 SIBLINGS ▶ *Details page 363* ♂ .... ♀ .... 1.......................

2.............................. 3.............................. 4..............................

5.............................. 6.............................. 7..............................

8.............................. 9.............................. 10.............................

👤 INDIVIDUAL EVENTS ....

....

....

....

....

....

....

📝 NOTES ....

....

....

....

724	725	726	727
362		363	
	181		
	90		

Surname: .... First name : .... ♂

Child : □ *Legitimate* □ *Natural* □ *Adopted* □ *Found* □ *Recognized* □ *Adulterated*   □ *Implex*

Born : ....in ....

Baptized : ....in ....

Godfather: ....Godmother : ....

Son of : ....and: ....

Nationality : ....Religion : ....Studies: ....

Occupation(s) : ....

Deceased : ....in.............................Cause:...................................

□ *Buried* □ *Cremated* □ *Disappeared* on : ....in : ....

🔗 MARITAL STATUS   □ *Civil Marriage*   □ *Religious Marriage*   □ *Free Union*

Date : ....in.. □ *Marriage contract*

Witnesses : ....

....

□ *Separation* □ *Divorce* □ *Widowhood of the groom/bride* Date : ....

👪 FAMILY EVENTS ....

....

....

....

....

....

🔗 OTHER UNION(S)/ 👪 CHILDREN ....

....

....

....

👫 SIBLINGS   ▶ *Details page 365*   ♂ ....   ♀ ....   1. ....

2. .... 3. .... 4. ....

5. .... 6. .... 7. ....

8. .... 9. .... 10. ....

👤 INDIVIDUAL EVENTS ....

....

....

....

⛑ MILITARY LIFE   Assignment(s) : ....

Campaign(s): ....

Medal(s) : ....□ *Died in combat* □ *Injured on* : ....

728	729	730	731

| 364 | | 365 |

| 182 |

| 91 |

📑 NOTES ....

....

....

....

♀ Surname : ....First name : ....

▶ Generation 8 - *paternal ascendant*

☐ *Implex*　　Child : ☐ *Legitimate* ☐ *Natural* ☐ *Adopted* ☐ *Found* ☐ *Recognized* ☐ *Adulterated*

Born : ....in...

Baptized : ....in...

Godfather: ....Godmother : ....

Daughter of : ....and:...

Nationality : ....Religion : ....Studies:.................................

Occupation(s) : ....

Deceased : ....in.........................Cause:..................

☐ *Buried* ☐ *Cremated* ☐ *Disappeared* on : ....in : ....

👫 CHILDREN ♂ .... ♀	Gen.	° Birth	† Death	Spouse
....	......	....	....	....
....	......	....	....	....
....	......	....	....	....
....	......	....	....	....
....	......	....	....	....
....	......	....	....	....
....	......	....	....	....
....	......	....	....	....
....	......	....	....	....
....	......	....	....	....

💍 **OTHER UNION(S)/** 👫 **CHILDREN** ....

....

....

....

👫 **SIBLINGS** ▶ *Details page 367* ♂ .... ♀ .... 1...

2...3...4.............................

5...6...7.............................

8...9...10...........................

👤 **INDIVIDUAL EVENTS** ....

....

....

....

....

....

....

📑 **NOTES** ....

....

....

....

732	733	734	735

366	367

183

91

Surname: .... First name : .... ♂

Child : ☐ *Legitimate* ☐ *Natural* ☐ *Adopted* ☐ *Found* ☐ *Recognized* ☐ *Adulterated*   ☐ *Implex*

Born : ....in...

Baptized : ....in..

Godfather: ....Godmother : ....

Son of : ....and:..

Nationality : ....Religion : ....Studies: ....

Occupation(s) : ....

Deceased : ....in.............................Cause:.......................

☐ *Buried* ☐ *Cremated* ☐ *Disappeared* on : ....in :.........................

⊚ MARITAL STATUS   ☐ *Civil Marriage*   ☐ *Religious Marriage*   ☐ *Free Union*

Date : ....in...☐ *Marriage contract*

Witnesses : ....

....

☐ *Separation* ☐ *Divorce* ☐ *Widowhood of the groom/bride* Date : ....

👫 FAMILY EVENTS ....

....

....

....

....

....

⊚ OTHER UNION(S)/ 👫 CHILDREN ....

....

....

....

👫 SIBLINGS   ▶ *Details page 369*   ♂ ....   ♀ ....   1...

2.. 3................................... 4.......................................

5.. 6................................... 7.......................................

8.. 9................................... 10......................................

👤 INDIVIDUAL EVENTS ....

....

....

....

⛑ MILITARY LIFE   Assignment(s) : ....

Campaign(s): ....

Medal(s) : ....☐ *Died in combat* ☐ *Injured on* : ....

....

| 736 | 737 | 738 | 739 |

| 368 | | 369 |

184

| 92 |

📋 NOTES ....

....

....

....

....

♀ Surname : .... First name : ....

Sosa **185**

▶ Generation 8 – *paternal ascendant*

□ *Implex*   Child : □ *Legitimate* □ *Natural* □ *Adopted* □ *Found* □ *Recognized* □ *Adulterated*

Born : ....in ....

Baptized : ....in ....

Godfather: ....Godmother : ....

Daughter of : ....and: ....

Nationality : ....Religion : ....Studies: ....

Occupation(s) : ....

Deceased : ....in ....Cause:.....................

□ *Buried* □ *Cremated* □ *Disappeared* on : ....in : ....

👪 CHILDREN ♂ .... **♀** .... | Gen. | ° Birth | † Death | Spouse

	Gen.	° Birth	† Death	Spouse

💍 OTHER UNION(S)/ 👪 CHILDREN ....
....
....
....

👪 SIBLINGS ▶ *Details page 371*   ♂ .... ♀ ....   1..
2...3...4..
5...6...7..
8...9...10...

👤 INDIVIDUAL EVENTS ....
....
....
....
....
....
....

📋 NOTES ....

| 740 | 741 | 742 | 743 |

| 370 | | 371 |

185

92

185

Surname: .... First name : .... ♂

Child : □ *Legitimate* □ *Natural* □ *Adopted* □ *Found* □ *Recognized* □ *Adulterated*   □ *Implex*

Born : ....in..

Baptized : ....in..

Godfather: ....Godmother : ....

Son of : ....and: ....

Nationality : ....Religion : ....Studies: ....

Occupation(s) : ....

Deceased : ....in........................Cause:........................

□ *Buried* □ *Cremated* □ *Disappeared* on : ....in :........................

⚭ MARITAL STATUS   □ *Civil Marriage* □ *Religious Marriage* □ *Free Union*

Date : ....in.. □ *Marriage contract*

Witnesses : ....

....

□ *Separation* □ *Divorce* □ *Widowhood of the groom/bride* Date : ....

👪 FAMILY EVENTS ....

....

....

....

....

⚭ OTHER UNION(S)/ 👪 CHILDREN ....

....

....

....

👪 SIBLINGS ▶ *Details page 373*   ♂ .... ♀ ....   1.....................

2.....................   3.....................   4.....................

5.....................   6.....................   7.....................

8.....................   9.....................   10....................

👤 INDIVIDUAL EVENTS ....

....

....

⛑ MILITARY LIFE   Assignment(s) : ....

Campaign(s): ....

Medal(s) : ....□ *Died in combat* □ *Injured on* : ....

....

744	745	746	747

372		373

186

93

📑 NOTES ....

....

....

....

....

♀ Surname : ....First name : ....

□ *Implex*   Child : □ *Legitimate* □ *Natural* □ *Adopted* □ *Found* □ *Recognized* □ *Adulterated*

Born : ....in..

Baptized : ....in..

Godfather: ....Godmother : ....

Daughter of : ....and: ....

Nationality : ....Religion : ....Studies: ....

Occupation(s) : ....

Deceased : ....in.........................Cause:................................

□ *Buried* □ *Cremated* □ *Disappeared* on : ....in :........................

👫 CHILDREN ♂ .... ♀ ....

	Gen.	° Birth	† Death	Spouse
....	.....	....	....	....
....	.....	....	....	....
....	.....	....	....	....
....	.....	....	....	....
....	.....	....	....	....
....	.....	....	....	....
....	.....	....	....	....
....	.....	....	....	....
....	.....	....	....	....
....	.....	....	....	....
....	.....	....	....	....

💍 OTHER UNION(S)/ 👫 CHILDREN ....

....

....

....

👫 SIBLINGS ▶ *Details page 375* ♂ .... ♀ .... 1.......................................

2...3...4.................................

5...6...7.................................

8...9...10................................

👤 INDIVIDUAL EVENTS ....

....

....

....

....

....

📑 NOTES ....

....

....

....

....

748	749	750	751
374		375	
187			
93			

Surname: .... First name : .... ♂

▶ Generation8 – *paternal ascendant*

Child : ☐ *Legitimate* ☐ *Natural* ☐ *Adopted* ☐ *Found* ☐ *Recognized* ☐ *Adulterated*   ☐ *Implex*

Born : ....in ....

Baptized : ....in ....

Godfather: ....Godmother : ....

Son of : ....and: ....

Nationality : ....Religion : ....Studies: ....

Occupation(s) : ....

Deceased : ....in...........................Cause:.......................

☐ *Buried* ☐ *Cremated* ☐ *Disappeared* on : ....in : ....

⊚ MARITAL STATUS   ☐ *Civil Marriage* ☐ *Religious Marriage* ☐ *Free Union*

Date : ....in...☐ *Marriage contract*

Witnesses : ....

....

☐ *Separation* ☐ *Divorce* ☐ *Widowhood of the groom/bride* Date : ....

👫 FAMILY EVENTS

....

....

....

....

....

⊚ OTHER UNION(S)/ 👫 CHILDREN ....

....

....

....

👫 SIBLINGS   ▶ *Details page 377*   ♂ .... ♀ ....   1..............................

2.. 3.. 4..

5.. 6.. 7..

8.. 9.. 10......................................

👤 INDIVIDUAL EVENTS ....

....

....

⛑ MILITARY LIFE Assignment(s) : ....

Campaign(s): ....

Medal(s) : ....☐ *Died in combat* ☐ *Injured on* : ....

752	753	754	755

| 376 | | 377 |

188

94

📑 NOTES ....

....

....

....

♀ Surname : ....First name : ....

▶ Generation 8 - *paternal ascendant*

☐ *Implex*   Child : ☐ *Legitimate* ☐ *Natural* ☐ *Adopted* ☐ *Found* ☐ *Recognized* ☐ *Adulterated*

Born : ....in...

Baptized : ....in...

Godfather: ....Godmother : ....

Daughter of : ....and: ....

Nationality : ....Religion : ....Studies: ....

Occupation(s) : ....

Deceased : ....in.............................Cause:.....................................

☐ *Buried* ☐ *Cremated* ☐ *Disappeared* on : ....in : ....

👫 CHILDREN ♂ .... ♀	Gen.	° Birth	† Death	Spouse
....	....	....	....	....
....	....	....	....	....
....	....	....	....	....
....	....	....	....	....
....	....	....	....	....
....	....	....	....	....
....	....	....	....	....
....	....	....	....	....
....	....	....	....	....
....	....	....	....	....

💍 OTHER UNION(S)/ 👫 CHILDREN ....

....

....

....

👫 SIBLINGS   ▶ *Details page 379*   ♂ .... ♀ ....   1..

2..3..4..

5..6..7..

8..9..10...

👤 INDIVIDUAL EVENTS ....

....

....

....

....

....

📑 NOTES ....

....

....

....

756	757	758	759
378		379	
189			
94			

Surname: .... First name : .... ♂

Child : ☐ *Legitimate* ☐ *Natural* ☐ *Adopted* ☐ *Found* ☐ *Recognized* ☐ *Adulterated*   ☐ *Implex*

Born : ....in...

Baptized : ....in...

Godfather: ....Godmother : ....

Son of : ....and: ....

Nationality : ....Religion : ....Studies: ....

Occupation(s) : ....

Deceased : ....in...........................Cause:...........................

☐ *Buried* ☐ *Cremated* ☐ *Disappeared* on : ....in : ....

ⓞ MARITAL STATUS   ☐ *Civil Marriage* ☐ *Religious Marriage* ☐ *Free Union*

Date : ....in... ☐ *Marriage contract*

Witnesses : ....
....

☐ *Separation* ☐ *Divorce* ☐ *Widowhood of the groom/bride* Date : ....

FAMILY EVENTS ....
....
....
....
....
....
....

ⓞ OTHER UNION(S)/ CHILDREN ....
....
....
....

SIBLINGS   ▶ *Details page 381*   ♂ .... ♀ .... 1...

2... 3... 4...

5... 6... 7...

8... 9... 10...

INDIVIDUAL EVENTS ....
....
....

MILITARY LIFE   Assignment(s) : ....

Campaign(s): ....

Medal(s) : ....☐ *Died in combat* ☐ *Injured on* : ....

760	761	762	763

380   381

190

95

NOTES ....
....
....
....
....

♀ Surname : ....First name : ....

▶ Generation 8 – *paternal ascendant*

□ *Implex*   Child : □ *Legitimate* □ *Natural* □ *Adopted* □ *Found* □ *Recognized* □ *Adulterated*

Born : ....in...

Baptized : ....in...

Godfather: ....Godmother : ....

Daughter of : ....and: ....

Nationality : ....Religion : ....Studies: ....

Occupation(s) : ....

Deceased : ....in..........................Cause:..............

□ *Buried* □ *Cremated* □ *Disappeared* on : ....in : ....

👫 CHILDREN ♂ .... ♀	Gen.	° Birth	† Death	Spouse
....	......	....	....	....
....	......	....	....	....
....	......	....	....	....
....	......	....	....	....
....	......	....	....	....
....	......	....	....	....
....	......	....	....	....
....	......	....	....	....
....	......	....	....	....
....	......	....	....	....
....	......	....	....	....

💍 OTHER UNION(S)/ 👫 CHILDREN ....

....

....

....

👫 SIBLINGS   ▶ *Details page 383*   ♂ .... ♀ ....   1................................

2..3..4.......................

5..6..7.......................

8..9..10......................

👤 INDIVIDUAL EVENTS ....

....

....

....

....

....

....

📑 NOTES ....

....

....

....

764	765	766	767
382		383	
191			
95			

Surname: .... First name : .... ♂

▶ Generation8 – *maternal ascendant*

Child : ☐ *Legitimate* ☐ *Natural* ☐ *Adopted* ☐ *Found* ☐ *Recognized* ☐ *Adulterated*   ☐ *Implex*

Born : ....in..

Baptized : ....in..

Godfather: ....Godmother : ....

Son of : ....and: ....

Nationality : ....Religion : ....Studies: ....

Occupation(s) : ....

Deceased : ....in.....................Cause:.......................

☐ *Buried* ☐ *Cremated* ☐ *Disappeared* on : ....in : ....

⊙ MARITAL STATUS   ☐ *Civil Marriage*   ☐ *Religious Marriage*   ☐ *Free Union*

Date : ....in... ☐ *Marriage contract*

Witnesses : ....

....

☐ *Separation* ☐ *Divorce* ☐ *Widowhood of the groom/bride* Date : ....

👪 FAMILY EVENTS   ....

....
....
....
....
....

⊙ OTHER UNION(S)/ 👪 CHILDREN   ....

....
....
....

👪 SIBLINGS   ▶ *Details page 385*   ♂ ....   ♀ ....   1..

2... 3... 4.....................................

5... 6... 7.....................................

8... 9... 10...................................

👤 INDIVIDUAL EVENTS   ....

....
....

⛑ MILITARY LIFE   Assignment(s) : ....

Campaign(s): ....

Medal(s) : ....☐ *Died in combat* ☐ *Injured on* : ....

....

768	769	770	771
384		385	
	192		
	96		

📋 NOTES   ....

....
....
....
....

♀ Surname : ....First name : ....

193

▶ Generation 8 - *maternal ascendant*

□ *Implex*   Child : □ *Legitimate* □ *Natural* □ *Adopted* □ *Found* □ *Recognized* □ *Adulterated*

Born : ....in...

Baptized : ....in...

Godfather: ....Godmother : ....

Daughter of : ....and: ....

Nationality : ....Religion : ....Studies: ....

Occupation(s) : ....

Deceased : ....in............................Cause:......................

□ *Buried* □ *Cremated* □ *Disappeared* on : ....in : ....

👫 CHILDREN ♂ .... ♀ ....

	Gen.	° Birth	† Death	Spouse

💍 OTHER UNION(S)/ 👫 CHILDREN ....

....
....
....

👫 SIBLINGS ▶ *Details page 387* ♂ .... ♀ .... 1.....................................

2...3.............................4.............................

5...6.............................7.............................

8...9.............................10.............................

👤 INDIVIDUAL EVENTS ....

....
....
....
....
....
....
....

🗒 NOTES ....

....

772	773	774	775
386		387	

193

96

Surname: .... First name : .... ♂

Child : □ *Legitimate* □ *Natural* □ *Adopted* □ *Found* □ *Recognized* □ *Adulterated*　　□ *Implex*

Born : ....in..

Baptized : ....in..

Godfather: ....Godmother : ....

Son of : ....and:..

Nationality : ....Religion : ....Studies: ....

Occupation(s) : ....

Deceased : ....in..............................Cause:..............................

□ *Buried* □ *Cremated* □ *Disappeared* on : ....in :..............................

⌾ MARITAL STATUS　　　□ *Civil Marriage* □ *Religious Marriage* □ *Free Union*

Date : ....in.. □ *Marriage contract*

Witnesses : ....

....

□ *Separation* □ *Divorce* □ *Widowhood of the groom/bride*　Date : ....

👪 FAMILY EVENTS ....

....
....
....
....
....
....

⌾ OTHER UNION(S)/👪 CHILDREN ....

....
....
....

👪 SIBLINGS　▶ *Details page 389*　♂ ....　♀ ....　1.................................

2.................................　3.................................　4.................................

5.................................　6.................................　7.................................

8.................................　9.................................　10.................................

👤 INDIVIDUAL EVENTS ....

....
....
....

⛑ MILITARY LIFE　Assignment(s) : ....

Campaign(s): ....

Medal(s) : ....□ *Died in combat* □ *Injured on* : ....

```
┌─────┬─────┬─────┬─────┐
│ 776 │ 777 │ 778 │ 779 │
└──┬──┴──┬──┴──┬──┴──┬──┘
   └─┬───┘     └─┬───┘
   ┌─┴─┐       ┌─┴─┐
   │388│       │389│
   └─┬─┘       └─┬─┘
     └─────┬─────┘
         ┌─┴─┐
         │194│
         └─┬─┘
         ┌─┴─┐
         │ 97│
         └───┘
```

🗐 NOTES ....

....
....
....
....

♀ Surname : ....First name : ....

▶ Generation 8 – *maternal ascendant*

☐ *Implex*   Child : ☐ *Legitimate* ☐ *Natural* ☐ *Adopted* ☐ *Found* ☐ *Recognized* ☐ *Adulterated*

Born : ....in..

Baptized : ....in...

Godfather: ....Godmother : ....

Daughter of : ....and: ....

Nationality : ....Religion : ....Studies: ....

Occupation(s) : ....

Deceased : ....in.........................Cause:............................

☐ *Buried* ☐ *Cremated* ☐ *Disappeared* on : ....in : ....

👪 CHILDREN ♂ .... ♀ ....

	Gen.	° Birth	† Death	Spouse
....	....	....	....	....
....	....	....	....	....
....	....	....	....	....
....	....	....	....	....
....	....	....	....	....
....	....	....	....	....
....	....	....	....	....
....	....	....	....	....
....	....	....	....	....
....	....	....	....	....
....	....	....	....	....

💍 OTHER UNION(S)/ 👪 CHILDREN ....

....

....

....

👪 SIBLINGS   ▶ *Details page 391*   ♂ .... ♀ ....   1.....................................

2..................................... 3..................................... 4.....................................

5..................................... 6..................................... 7.....................................

8..................................... 9..................................... 10...................................

👤 INDIVIDUAL EVENTS ....

....

....

....

....

....

....

🗒 NOTES ....

780	781	782	783

....

.... | 390 | | 391 |

.... | 195 |

.... | 97 |

Sosa
196

Surname: .... First name : .... ♂

Child : ☐ *Legitimate* ☐ *Natural* ☐ *Adopted* ☐ *Found* ☐ *Recognized* ☐ *Adulterated*   ☐ *Implex*

Born : ....in...

Baptized : ....in...

Godfather: ....Godmother : ....

Son of : ....and: ....

Nationality : ....Religion : ....Studies: ....

Occupation(s) : ....

Deceased : ....in............................Cause:...........................

☐ *Buried* ☐ *Cremated* ☐ *Disappeared* on : ....in : ....

⚭ MARITAL STATUS   ☐ *Civil Marriage*   ☐ *Religious Marriage*   ☐ *Free Union*

Date : ....in..☐ *Marriage contract*

Witnesses : ....

....

☐ *Separation* ☐ *Divorce* ☐ *Widowhood of the groom/bride* Date : ....

👪 FAMILY EVENTS

....

....

....

....

....

⚭ OTHER UNION(S)/👪 CHILDREN

....

....

....

👪 SIBLINGS   ▶ *Details page 393*   ♂ ....   ♀ ....   1...........................

2....................................... 3............................... 4...............................

5....................................... 6............................... 7...............................

8....................................... 9............................... 10..............................

👤 INDIVIDUAL EVENTS

....

....

....

⛑ MILITARY LIFE   Assignment(s) : ....

Campaign(s): ....

Medal(s) : ....☐ *Died in combat* ☐ *Injured on* : ....

....

784	785	786	787

392   393

196

98

📑 NOTES ....

....

....

....

♀ Surname : .... First name : ....

▶ Generation 8 – *maternal ascendant*

☐ *Implex*   Child : ☐ *Legitimate* ☐ *Natural* ☐ *Adopted* ☐ *Found* ☐ *Recognized* ☐ *Adulterated*

Born : ....in..

Baptized : ....in..

Godfather: ....Godmother : ....

Daughter of : ....and: ....

Nationality : ....Religion : ....Studies: ....

Occupation(s) : ....

Deceased : ....in.............................Cause:..................

☐ *Buried* ☐ *Cremated* ☐ *Disappeared* on : ....in : ....

👫 CHILDREN ♂ .... ♀	Gen.	° Birth	† Death	Spouse
....	......	....	....	....
....	......	....	....	....
....	......	....	....	....
....	......	....	....	....
....	......	....	....	....
....	......	....	....	....
....	......	....	....	....
....	......	....	....	....
....	......	....	....	....
....	......	....	....	....

💍 OTHER UNION(S)/ 👫 CHILDREN ....

....

....

....

👫 SIBLINGS   ▶ *Details page 395*   ♂ .... ♀ ....   1....................................

2...3.................................4..................................

5...6.................................7..................................

8...9.................................10.................................

👤 INDIVIDUAL EVENTS ....

....

....

....

....

....

....

📑 NOTES ....

....

....

....

788	789	790	791
394		395	
197			
98			

Generation 8 – maternal ascendant

Surname: .... First name : .... ♂

Child : ☐ *Legitimate* ☐ *Natural* ☐ *Adopted* ☐ *Found* ☐ *Recognized* ☐ *Adulterated*   ☐ *Implex*

Born : ....in..

Baptized : ....in................

Godfather: ....Godmother : ....

Son of : ....and: ....

Nationality : ....Religion : ....Studies: ....

Occupation(s) : ....

Deceased : ....in.................Cause:......................

☐ *Buried* ☐ *Cremated* ☐ *Disappeared* on : ....in : ....

⚭ MARITAL STATUS   ☐ *Civil Marriage* ☐ *Religious Marriage* ☐ *Free Union*

Date : ....in.. ☐ *Marriage contract*

Witnesses : ....

....

☐ *Separation* ☐ *Divorce* ☐ *Widowhood of the groom/bride*   Date : ....

👫 FAMILY EVENTS ....

....
....
....
....
....

⚭ OTHER UNION(S)/ 👫 CHILDREN ....

....
....
....

👫 SIBLINGS   ▶ *Details page 397*   ♂ .... ♀ ....   1.................................

2......................................3..4..............................

5......................................6..7..............................

8......................................9..10............................

👤 INDIVIDUAL EVENTS ....

....
....

⛑ MILITARY LIFE   Assignment(s) : ....

Campaign(s): ....

Medal(s) : ....☐ *Died in combat* ☐ *Injured on* : ....

792	793	794	795
396		397	
	198		
	99		

📑 NOTES ....

....
....
....
....

♀ Surname : .... First name : ....

Sosa
199

□ *Implex*   Child : □ *Legitimate* □ *Natural* □ *Adopted* □ *Found* □ *Recognized* □ *Adulterated*

Born : ....in...

Baptized : ....in...

Godfather: ....Godmother : ....

Daughter of : ....and: ....

Nationality : ....Religion : ....Studies: ....

Occupation(s) : ....

Deceased : ....in.................................Cause:...............................

□ *Buried* □ *Cremated* □ *Disappeared* on : ....in : ....

👫 CHILDREN ♂ .... ♀	Gen.	° Birth	† Death	Spouse
....	......	....	....	....
....	......	....	....	....
....	......	....	....	....
....	......	....	....	....
....	......	....	....	....
....	......	....	....	....
....	......	....	....	....
....	......	....	....	....
....	......	....	....	....
....	......	....	....	....
....	......	....	....	....

💍 OTHER UNION(S)/ 👫 CHILDREN ....

....

....

👫 **SIBLINGS** ► *Details page 399* ♂ .... ♀ .... 1...

2.. 3.. 4..

5.. 6.. 7..

8.. 9.. 10...

👤 **INDIVIDUAL EVENTS** ....

....

....

....

....

....

📑 **NOTES** ....

....

....

....

796	797	798	799

| 398 | | 399 |

199

99

Surname: .... First name : .... ♂

▶ Generation8 - *maternal ascendant*

Child : □ *Legitimate* □ *Natural* □ *Adopted* □ *Found* □ *Recognized* □ *Adulterated*   □ *Implex*

Born : ....in...

Baptized : ....in.............

Godfather: ....Godmother : ....

Son of : ....and: ....

Nationality : ....Religion : ....Studies: ....

Occupation(s) : ....

Deceased : ....in.............................Cause:...........................

□ *Buried* □ *Cremated* □ *Disappeared* on : ....in : ....

⊚ MARITAL STATUS   □ *Civil Marriage* □ *Religious Marriage* □ *Free Union*

Date : ....in.. □ *Marriage contract*

Witnesses : ....
....

□ *Separation* □ *Divorce* □ *Widowhood of the groom/bride* Date : ....

👪 FAMILY EVENTS   ....
....
....
....
....
....

⊚ OTHER UNION(S)/ 👪 CHILDREN   ....
....
....
....

👪 SIBLINGS   ▶ *Details page 401*   ♂ .... ♀ ....   1...

2... 3... 4...

5... 6... 7...

8... 9... 10...

👤 INDIVIDUAL EVENTS   ....
....
....
....

⛑ MILITARY LIFE   Assignment(s) : ....

Campaign(s): ....

Medal(s) : ....□ *Died in combat* □ *Injured on* : ....

800	801	802	803

400   401

200

100

🗒 NOTES   ....
....
....
....

♀ Surname : .... First name : ....

▶ Generation 8 – *maternal ascendant*

☐ *Implex*   Child : ☐ *Legitimate* ☐ *Natural* ☐ *Adopted* ☐ *Found* ☐ *Recognized* ☐ *Adulterated*

Born : ....in...

Baptized : ....in...

Godfather: ....Godmother : ....

Daughter of : ....and: ....

Nationality : ....Religion : ....Studies: ....

Occupation(s) : ....

Deceased : ....in.......................Cause:.......................

☐ *Buried* ☐ *Cremated* ☐ *Disappeared* on : ....in : ....

👫 CHILDREN ♂ .... ♀ ....

	Gen.	° Birth	† Death	Spouse
....	......	....	....	....
....	......	....	....	....
....	......	....	....	....
....	......	....	....	....
....	......	....	....	....
....	......	....	....	....
....	......	....	....	....
....	......	....	....	....
....	......	....	....	....
....	......	....	....	....

💍 OTHER UNION(S)/👫 CHILDREN ....
....
....

👫 SIBLINGS ▶ *Details page 403* ♂ .... ♀ .... 1..................................
2............................... 3............................... 4...............................
5............................... 6............................... 7...............................
8............................... 9............................... 10...............................

👤 INDIVIDUAL EVENTS ....
....
....
....
....
....
....

📝 NOTES ....

804	805	806	807

402		403

201

100

....
....
....
....

Surname: .... First name : .... ♂

Child : ☐ *Legitimate* ☐ *Natural* ☐ *Adopted* ☐ *Found* ☐ *Recognized* ☐ *Adulterated*   ☐ *Implex*

Born : ....in.......................

Baptized : ....in.......................

Godfather: ....Godmother : ....

Son of : ....and:..............................

Nationality : ....Religion : ....Studies: ....

Occupation(s) : ....

Deceased : ....in...................................Cause:.........................

☐ *Buried* ☐ *Cremated* ☐ *Disappeared* on : ....in :.........................

⚭ MARITAL STATUS   ☐ *Civil Marriage*   ☐ *Religious Marriage*   ☐ *Free Union*

Date : ....in...☐ *Marriage contract*

Witnesses : ....

....

☐ *Separation* ☐ *Divorce* ☐ *Widowhood of the groom/bride* Date : ....

👫 FAMILY EVENTS ....

....

....

....

....

....

⚭ OTHER UNION(S)/ 👫 CHILDREN ....

....

....

....

👫 SIBLINGS   ▶ *Details page 405*   ♂ ....   ♀ ....   1..............................

2............................. 3............................. 4.............................

5............................. 6............................. 7.............................

8............................. 9............................. 10.............................

👤 INDIVIDUAL EVENTS ....

....

....

⛑ MILITARY LIFE   Assignment(s) : ....

Campaign(s): ....

Medal(s) : ....☐ *Died in combat* ☐ *Injured on* : ....

808	809	810	811

404   405

202

101

📑 NOTES ....

....

....

....

....

♀ Surname : .... First name : ....

▶ Generation 8 - *maternal ascendant*

□ *Implex*   Child : □ *Legitimate* □ *Natural* □ *Adopted* □ *Found* □ *Recognized* □ *Adulterated*

Born : ....in...

Baptized : ....in...

Godfather: ....Godmother : ....

Daughter of : ....and: ....

Nationality : ....Religion : ....Studies: ....

Occupation(s) : ....

Deceased : ....in.......................Cause:...............

□ *Buried* □ *Cremated* □ *Disappeared* on : ....in : ....

👪 CHILDREN ♂ .... ♀ ....

	Gen.	° Birth	† Death	Spouse
....	......	....	....	....
....	......	....	....	....
....	......	....	....	....
....	......	....	....	....
....	......	....	....	....
....	......	....	....	....
....	......	....	....	....
....	......	....	....	....
....	......	....	....	....
....	......	....	....	....

💍 OTHER UNION(S)/ 👪 CHILDREN ....

....

....

👪 SIBLINGS ▶ *Details page 407* ♂ .... ♀ .... 1.................................

2.............................. 3.............................. 4..............................

5.............................. 6.............................. 7..............................

8.............................. 9.............................. 10.............................

👤 INDIVIDUAL EVENTS ....

....

....

....

....

....

📑 NOTES ....

812	813	814	815

| 406 | | 407 |

203

101

....

....

....

Surname: .... First name : .... ♂

Child : ☐ *Legitimate* ☐ *Natural* ☐ *Adopted* ☐ *Found* ☐ *Recognized* ☐ *Adulterated*   ☐ *Implex*

Born : ....in...

Baptized : ....in..

Godfather: ....Godmother : ....

Son of : ....and: ....

Nationality : ....Religion : ....Studies: ....

Occupation(s) : ....

Deceased : ....in...........................Cause:.............................

☐ *Buried* ☐ *Cremated* ☐ *Disappeared* on : ....in : ....

⚭ MARITAL STATUS   ☐ *Civil Marriage* ☐ *Religious Marriage* ☐ *Free Union*

Date : ....in...☐ *Marriage contract*

Witnesses : ....

....

☐ *Separation* ☐ *Divorce* ☐ *Widowhood of the groom/bride* Date : ....

👪 FAMILY EVENTS   ....

....

....

....

....

....

⚭ OTHER UNION(S)/ 👫 CHILDREN ....

....

....

....

👫 SIBLINGS   ▶ *Details page 409*   ♂ .... ♀ ....   1. ....

2. .... 3. .... 4. ....

5. .... 6. .... 7. ....

8. .... 9. .... 10. ....

👤 INDIVIDUAL EVENTS   ....

....

....

⛑ MILITARY LIFE   Assignment(s) : ....

Campaign(s): ....

Medal(s) : ....☐ *Died in combat* ☐ *Injured on* : ....

....

| 816 | 817 | 818 | 819 |

| 408 | | 409 |

| 204 |

| 102 |

📑 NOTES ....

....

....

....

....

♀ Surname : .... First name : ....

Sosa
205

▶ Generation 8 – *maternal ascendant*

☐ *Implex*   Child : ☐ *Legitimate* ☐ *Natural* ☐ *Adopted* ☐ *Found* ☐ *Recognized* ☐ *Adulterated*

Born : ....in...

Baptized : ....in...

Godfather: ....Godmother : ....

Daughter of : ....and: ....

Nationality : ....Religion : ....Studies: ....

Occupation(s) : ....

Deceased : ....in.............................Cause:....................

☐ *Buried* ☐ *Cremated* ☐ *Disappeared* on : ....in : ....

👨‍👧 CHILDREN ♂ .... ♀ ....

	Gen.	° Birth	† Death	Spouse

💍 OTHER UNION(S)/ 👨‍👧 CHILDREN ....

....

....

👨‍👧 SIBLINGS   ▶ *Details page 411*   ♂ .... ♀ ....   1...........................

2..3..4..

5..6..7..

8..9..10.......................................

👤 INDIVIDUAL EVENTS ....

....

....

....

....

....

📄 NOTES ....

| 820 | 821 | 822 | 823 |

410   411

205

102

205

Surname: .... First name : .... ♂

▶ Generation8 – *maternal ascendant*

Child : ☐ *Legitimate* ☐ *Natural* ☐ *Adopted* ☐ *Found* ☐ *Recognized* ☐ *Adulterated*   ☐ *Implex*

Born : ....in..

Baptized : ....in..

Godfather: ....Godmother : ....

Son of : ....and: ....

Nationality : ....Religion : ....Studies: ....

Occupation(s) : ....

Deceased : ....in...........................Cause:..............................

☐ *Buried* ☐ *Cremated* ☐ *Disappeared* on : ....in :.............................

⚭ MARITAL STATUS   ☐ *Civil Marriage* ☐ *Religious Marriage* ☐ *Free Union*

Date : ....in.. ☐ *Marriage contract*

Witnesses : ....

....

☐ *Separation* ☐ *Divorce* ☐ *Widowhood of the groom/bride* Date : ....

👫 FAMILY EVENTS ....

....

....

....

....

....

⚭ OTHER UNION(S)/ 👫 CHILDREN ....

....

....

👫 SIBLINGS ▶ *Details page 413*   ♂ .... ♀ ....   1...

2.. 3.. 4....................................

5.. 6.. 7....................................

8.. 9.. 10...................................

👤 INDIVIDUAL EVENTS ....

....

....

⛑ MILITARY LIFE Assignment(s) : ....

Campaign(s): ....

Medal(s) : ....☐ *Died in combat* ☐ *Injured on* : ....

824	825	826	827

412		413

206

103

📝 NOTES ....

....

....

....

....

♀ Surname : .... First name : ....

Sosa
207

▶ Generation 8 – *maternal ascendant*

☐ *Implex*   Child : ☐ *Legitimate* ☐ *Natural* ☐ *Adopted* ☐ *Found* ☐ *Recognized* ☐ *Adulterated*

Born : ....in...

Baptized : ....in...

Godfather: ....Godmother : ....

Daughter of : ....and: ....

Nationality : ....Religion : ....Studies: ....

Occupation(s) : ....

Deceased : ....in...............................Cause:...................

☐ *Buried* ☐ *Cremated* ☐ *Disappeared* on : ....in : ....

👪 CHILDREN ♂ .... ♀ ....

	Gen.	° Birth	† Death	Spouse

💍 OTHER UNION(S)/ 👪 CHILDREN ....

....

....

....

👪 SIBLINGS ▶ *Details page 415* ♂ .... ♀ .... 1...

2...3...4...

5...6...7...

8...9...10...

👤 INDIVIDUAL EVENTS ....

....

....

....

....

....

....

📝 NOTES ....

....

....

....

828	829	830	831
414		415	
207			
103			

207

Surname: .... First name : .... ♂

Child : □ *Legitimate* □ *Natural* □ *Adopted* □ *Found* □ *Recognized* □ *Adulterated*   □ *Implex*

Born : ....in...

Baptized : ....in...

Godfather: ....Godmother : ....

Son of : ....and:..

Nationality : ....Religion : ....Studies: ....

Occupation(s) : ....

Deceased : ....in.............................Cause:...........................

□ *Buried* □ *Cremated* □ *Disappeared* on : ....in :.........................

⊚ MARITAL STATUS   □ *Civil Marriage*   □ *Religious Marriage*   □ *Free Union*

Date : ....in... □ *Marriage contract*

Witnesses : ....

....

□ *Separation* □ *Divorce* □ *Widowhood of the groom/bride* Date : ....

👪 FAMILY EVENTS ....

....

....

....

....

....

⊚ OTHER UNION(S)/ 👪 CHILDREN ....

....

....

....

👪 SIBLINGS ▶ *Details page 417*   ♂ .... ♀ .... 1.......................................

2...3.............................4.............................

5...6.............................7.............................

8...9.............................10.............................

👤 INDIVIDUAL EVENTS ....

....

....

⛑ MILITARY LIFE Assignment(s) : ....

Campaign(s): ....

Medal(s) : ....□ *Died in combat* □ *Injured on* : ....

....

| 832 | 833 | 834 | 835 |

📋 NOTES ....

| 416 | | 417 |

....

| 208 |

....

| 104 |

....

♀ Surname : ....First name : ....

▶ Generation 8 – *maternal ascendant*

☐ *Implex*   Child : ☐ *Legitimate* ☐ *Natural* ☐ *Adopted* ☐ *Found* ☐ *Recognized* ☐ *Adulterated*

Born : ....in..

Baptized : ....in..

Godfather: ....Godmother : ....

Daughter of : ....and: ....

Nationality : ....Religion : ....Studies: ....

Occupation(s) : ....

Deceased : ....in.........................Cause:......................

☐ *Buried* ☐ *Cremated* ☐ *Disappeared* on : ....in : ....

👫 CHILDREN ♂ .... ♀ ....

	Gen.	° Birth	† Death	Spouse
....	......	....	....	....
....	......	....	....	....
....	......	....	....	....
....	......	....	....	....
....	......	....	....	....
....	......	....	....	....
....	......	....	....	....
....	......	....	....	....
....	......	....	....	....
....	......	....	....	....

💍 OTHER UNION(S)/ 👫 CHILDREN ....

....

....

👫 SIBLINGS ▶ *Details page 419* ♂ .... ♀ .... 1.........................

2..3..4..

5..6..7..

8..9..10.......................................

👤 INDIVIDUAL EVENTS ....

....

....

....

....

....

....

📝 NOTES ....

....

....

....

836	837	838	839

418	419

209

104

Surname: .... First name : .... ♂

Child : ☐ *Legitimate* ☐ *Natural* ☐ *Adopted* ☐ *Found* ☐ *Recognized* ☐ *Adulterated*   ☐ *Implex*

Born : ....in...

Baptized : ....in.................................

Godfather: ....Godmother : ....

Son of : ....and: ....

Nationality : ....Religion : ....Studies: ....

Occupation(s) : ....

Deceased : ....in.................................Cause:..............................

☐ *Buried* ☐ *Cremated* ☐ *Disappeared* on : ....in :...................

⚭ MARITAL STATUS   ☐ *Civil Marriage* ☐ *Religious Marriage* ☐ *Free Union*

Date : ....in... ☐ *Marriage contract*

Witnesses : ....

....

☐ *Separation* ☐ *Divorce* ☐ *Widowhood of the groom/bride* Date : ....

👪 FAMILY EVENTS   ....

....
....
....
....
....

⚭ OTHER UNION(S)/ 👪 CHILDREN   ....

....
....
....

👪 SIBLINGS   ▶ *Details page 421*   ♂ .... ♀ .... 1..

2.. 3.. 4..

5.. 6.. 7..

8.. 9.. 10..

👤 INDIVIDUAL EVENTS   ....

....
....
....

⛑ MILITARY LIFE   Assignment(s) : ....

Campaign(s): ....

Medal(s) : ....☐ *Died in combat* ☐ *Injured on* : ....

840	841	842	843

📝 NOTES ....

420 ... 421

210

105

....
....
....
....
....

♀ Surname : ....First name : ....

▶ Generation 8 – *maternal ascendant*

☐ *Implex*   Child : ☐ *Legitimate* ☐ *Natural* ☐ *Adopted* ☐ *Found* ☐ *Recognized* ☐ *Adulterated*

Born : ....in..

Baptized : ....in...

Godfather: ....Godmother : ....

Daughter of : ....and: ....

Nationality : ....Religion : ....Studies: ....

Occupation(s) : ....

Deceased : ....in......................Cause:...................

☐ *Buried* ☐ *Cremated* ☐ *Disappeared* on : ....in : ....

👫 CHILDREN ♂ .... ♀ ....

	Gen.	° Birth	† Death	Spouse

💍 OTHER UNION(S)/ 👫 CHILDREN ....

....

....

👫 SIBLINGS ▶ *Details page 423*   ♂ .... ♀ ....   1.................................

2..3..4..

5..6..7..

8..9..10..

👤 INDIVIDUAL EVENTS ....

....

....

....

....

....

....

📑 NOTES ....

844	845	846	847

.... | 422 | | 423 |

.... 211

.... 105

Sosa 212

Surname: .... First name : .... ♂

Child : ☐ *Legitimate* ☐ *Natural* ☐ *Adopted* ☐ *Found* ☐ *Recognized* ☐ *Adulterated*   ☐ *Implex*

Born : ....in...

Baptized : ....in...

Godfather: ....Godmother : ....

Son of : ....and:...

Nationality : ....Religion : ....Studies: ....

Occupation(s) : ....

Deceased : ....in...............................Cause:..............................

☐ *Buried* ☐ *Cremated* ☐ *Disappeared* on : ....in : ....

⚭ MARITAL STATUS   ☐ *Civil Marriage* ☐ *Religious Marriage* ☐ *Free Union*

Date : ....in...☐ *Marriage contract*

Witnesses : ....

....

☐ *Separation* ☐ *Divorce* ☐ *Widowhood of the groom/bride* Date : ....

👫 FAMILY EVENTS ....

....

....

....

....

....

⚭ OTHER UNION(S)/ 👫 CHILDREN ....

....

....

....

👫 SIBLINGS   ▶ *Details page 425*   ♂ .... ♀ ....   1..................................

2..3..4............................

5..6..7............................

8..9..10..........................

👤 INDIVIDUAL EVENTS ....

....

....

....

⛑ MILITARY LIFE   Assignment(s) : ....

Campaign(s): ....

Medal(s) : ....☐ *Died in combat* ☐ *Injured on :* ....

848	849	850	851

📑 NOTES ....

| 424 | | 425 |

....

| **212** |

....

| 106 |

....

213

♀ Surname : .... First name : ....

▶ Generation 8 - *maternal ascendant*

☐ *Implex* Child : ☐ *Legitimate* ☐ *Natural* ☐ *Adopted* ☐ *Found* ☐ *Recognized* ☐ *Adulterated*

Born : ....in...

Baptized : ....in...

Godfather: ....Godmother : ....

Daughter of : ....and: ....

Nationality : ....Religion : ....Studies: ....

Occupation(s) : ....

Deceased : ....in..................Cause:.................

☐ *Buried* ☐ *Cremated* ☐ *Disappeared* on : ....in : ....

👫 CHILDREN ♂ .... ♀ ....

	Gen.	° Birth	† Death	Spouse
....	......	....	....	....
....	......	....	....	....
....	......	....	....	....
....	......	....	....	....
....	......	....	....	....
....	......	....	....	....
....	......	....	....	....
....	......	....	....	....
....	......	....	....	....
....	......	....	....	....

💍 OTHER UNION(S)/ 👫 CHILDREN ....

....
....
....

👫 SIBLINGS ▶ *Details page 427* ♂ .... ♀ .... 1..............................
2............................... 3............................... 4...............................
5............................... 6............................... 7...............................
8............................... 9............................... 10..............................

👤 INDIVIDUAL EVENTS ....

....
....
....
....
....
....

📝 NOTES ....

852	853	854	855

| 426 | | 427 |

213

106

Surname: ....First name : .... ♂

Child : ☐ *Legitimate* ☐ *Natural* ☐ *Adopted* ☐ *Found* ☐ *Recognized* ☐ *Adulterated*   ☐ *Implex*

Born : ....in ....

Baptized : ....in ....

Godfather: ....Godmother : ....

Son of : ....and: ....

Nationality : ....Religion : ....Studies: ....

Occupation(s) : ....

Deceased : ....in...........................Cause:...............................

☐ *Buried* ☐ *Cremated* ☐ *Disappeared* on : ....in : ....

⊙ MARITAL STATUS   ☐ *Civil Marriage*   ☐ *Religious Marriage*   ☐ *Free Union*

Date : ....in... ☐ *Marriage contract*

Witnesses : ....

....

☐ *Separation* ☐ *Divorce* ☐ *Widowhood of the groom/bride*   Date : ....

👪 FAMILY EVENTS   ....

....
....
....
....
....

⊙ OTHER UNION(S)/👪 CHILDREN   ....

....
....
....

👪 SIBLINGS   ▶ *Details page 429*   ♂ ....   ♀ ....   1..............................
2.. 3.. 4..
5.. 6.. 7..
8.. 9.. 10..

👤 INDIVIDUAL EVENTS   ....

....
....
....

⛑ MILITARY LIFE   Assignment(s) : ....

Campaign(s): ....

Medal(s) : .... ☐ *Died in combat* ☐ *Injured on* : ....

856	857	858	859

428   429

214

107

🗒 NOTES   ....

....
....
....
....

♀ Surname : .... First name : ....

▶ Generation 8 – *maternal ascendant*

□ *Implex*   Child : □ *Legitimate* □ *Natural* □ *Adopted* □ *Found* □ *Recognized* □ *Adulterated*

Born : .... in ....

Baptized : .... in ....

Godfather: .... Godmother : ....

Daughter of : .... and: ....

Nationality : .... Religion : .... Studies: ....

Occupation(s) : ....

Deceased : .... in .... Cause:........................

□ *Buried* □ *Cremated* □ *Disappeared* on : .... in : ....

👪 CHILDREN ♂ .... ♀	Gen.	° Birth	† Death	Spouse
....	.....	....	....	....
....	.....	....	....	....
....	.....	....	....	....
....	.....	....	....	....
....	.....	....	....	....
....	.....	....	....	....
....	.....	....	....	....
....	.....	....	....	....
....	.....	....	....	....
....	.....	....	....	....
....	.....	....	....	....

💍 OTHER UNION(S)/ 👪 CHILDREN ....

....

....

....

👪 SIBLINGS   ▶ *Details page 431*   ♂ .... ♀ ......   1..

2.................................... 3.................................... 4....................................

5.................................... 6.................................... 7....................................

8.................................... 9.................................... 10...................................

👤 INDIVIDUAL EVENTS ....

....

....

....

....

....

📑 NOTES ....

860	861	862	863

....

430		431

....

215

....

107

215

Surname: .... First name : .... ♂

Child : □ *Legitimate* □ *Natural* □ *Adopted* □ *Found* □ *Recognized* □ *Adulterated*   □ *Implex*

Born : ....in...

Baptized : ....in..........................

Godfather: ....Godmother : ....

Son of : ....and: ....

Nationality : ....Religion : ....Studies: ....

Occupation(s) : ....

Deceased : ....in..............................Cause:.................................

□ *Buried* □ *Cremated* □ *Disappeared* on : ....in : ....

⊚ MARITAL STATUS   □ *Civil Marriage*   □ *Religious Marriage*   □ *Free Union*

Date : ....in.. □ *Marriage contract*

Witnesses : ....

....

□ *Separation* □ *Divorce* □ *Widowhood of the groom/bride* Date : ....

👫 FAMILY EVENTS

⊚ OTHER UNION(S)/👫 CHILDREN

👫 SIBLINGS   ▶ *Details page 433*   ♂ ....   ♀ ....   1..

2..3...4...

5..6...7...

8..9...10...

👤 INDIVIDUAL EVENTS

⛑ MILITARY LIFE   Assignment(s) : ....

Campaign(s): ....

Medal(s) : ....□ *Died in combat* □ *Injured on* : ....

```
┌─────┬─────┬─────┬─────┐
│ 864 │ 865 │ 866 │ 867 │
└──┬──┴──┬──┴──┬──┴──┬──┘
   └ 432 ┘     └ 433 ┘
      └──  216  ──┘
           108
```

📄 NOTES

♀ Surname : ....First name : ....

☐ *Implex* Child : ☐ *Legitimate* ☐ *Natural* ☐ *Adopted* ☐ *Found* ☐ *Recognized* ☐ *Adulterated*

Born : ....in..

Baptized : ....in..

Godfather: ....Godmother : ....

Daughter of : ....and: ....

Nationality : ....Religion : ....Studies: ....

Occupation(s) : ....

Deceased : ....in..................................Cause:..........................

☐ *Buried* ☐ *Cremated* ☐ *Disappeared* on : ....in : ....

👪 CHILDREN ♂ .... ♀	Gen.	° Birth	† Death	Spouse
....	......	....	....	....
....	......	....	....	....
....	......	....	....	....
....	......	....	....	....
....	......	....	....	....
....	......	....	....	....
....	......	....	....	....
....	......	....	....	....
....	......	....	....	....
....	......	....	....	....

💍 OTHER UNION(S)/ 👪 CHILDREN ....
....
....

👪 SIBLINGS ▶ *Details page 435* ♂ .... ♀ .... 1..
2...3...4.....................................
5...6...7.....................................
8...9...10...................................

👤 INDIVIDUAL EVENTS ....
....
....
....
....
....
....

📑 NOTES ....

868	869	870	871

434		435

217

108

Surname: .... First name : .... ♂

▶ Generation8 – *maternal ascendant*

Child : ☐ *Legitimate* ☐ *Natural* ☐ *Adopted* ☐ *Found* ☐ *Recognized* ☐ *Adulterated*　　☐ *Implex*

Born : ....in..

Baptized : ....in..

Godfather: ....Godmother : ....

Son of : ....and: ....

Nationality : ....Religion : ....Studies: ....

Occupation(s) : ....

Deceased : ....in............................Cause:........................

☐ *Buried* ☐ *Cremated* ☐ *Disappeared* on : ....in : ....

⚭ MARITAL STATUS　　　　☐ *Civil Marriage*　☐ *Religious Marriage*　☐ *Free Union*

Date : ....in.. ☐ *Marriage contract*

Witnesses : ....
....

☐ *Separation* ☐ *Divorce* ☐ *Widowhood of the groom/bride*　Date : ....

👪 FAMILY EVENTS ....

....
....
....
....
....

⚭ OTHER UNION(S)/👪 CHILDREN ....
....
....
....

👪 SIBLINGS　▶ *Details page 437*　　♂ ....　♀ ....　　1.................................

2.................................. 3.................................. 4..................................

5.................................. 6.................................. 7..................................

8.................................. 9.................................. 10.................................

👤 INDIVIDUAL EVENTS ....
....
....

⛑ MILITARY LIFE　Assignment(s) : ....

Campaign(s): ....

Medal(s) : ....☐ *Died in combat* ☐ *Injured on* : ....
....

872	873	874	875

436　　437

218

109

📋 NOTES ....
....
....
....
....

♀ Surname : .... First name : ....

▶ Generation 8 – *maternal ascendant*

☐ *Implex*   Child : ☐ *Legitimate* ☐ *Natural* ☐ *Adopted* ☐ *Found* ☐ *Recognized* ☐ *Adulterated*

Born : ....in...
Baptized : ....in...
Godfather: ....Godmother : ....
Daughter of : ....and:...
Nationality : ....Religion : ....Studies: ....
Occupation(s) : ....
Deceased : ....in............................Cause:.......................
☐ *Buried* ☐ *Cremated* ☐ *Disappeared* on : ....in :...................

👫 CHILDREN ♂ .... ♀	Gen.	° Birth	† Death	Spouse
....	......	....	....	....
....	......	....	....	....
....	......	....	....	....
....	......	....	....	....
....	......	....	....	....
....	......	....	....	....
....	......	....	....	....
....	......	....	....	....
....	......	....	....	....
....	......	....	....	....

💍 OTHER UNION(S)/ 👫 CHILDREN ....
....
....

👫 SIBLINGS   ▶ *Details page 439*   ♂ .... ♀ .... 1..
2.................................... 3.................................... 4....................................
5.................................... 6.................................... 7....................................
8.................................... 9.................................... 10...................................

👤 INDIVIDUAL EVENTS ....
....
....
....
....
....

📑 NOTES ....
....
....
....

876	877	878	879
438		439	
219			
109			

Surname: .... First name : .... ♂

Child : ☐ *Legitimate* ☐ *Natural* ☐ *Adopted* ☐ *Found* ☐ *Recognized* ☐ *Adulterated*   ☐ *Implex*

Born : ....in ....

Baptized : ....in ....

Godfather: ....Godmother : ....

Son of : ....and: ....

Nationality : ....Religion : ....Studies: ....

Occupation(s) : ....

Deceased : ....in...Cause:.............................

☐ *Buried* ☐ *Cremated* ☐ *Disappeared* on : ....in : ....

⌾ MARITAL STATUS   ☐ *Civil Marriage* ☐ *Religious Marriage* ☐ *Free Union*

Date : ....in...☐ *Marriage contract*

Witnesses : ....

....

☐ *Separation* ☐ *Divorce* ☐ *Widowhood of the groom/bride* Date : ....

👫 FAMILY EVENTS   ....

....

....

....

....

....

⌾ OTHER UNION(S)/👫 CHILDREN   ....

....

....

....

👫 SIBLINGS   ▶ *Details page 441*   ♂ .... ♀ ....   1..................................

2................................   3................................   4................................

5................................   6................................   7................................

8................................   9................................   10.................................

👤 INDIVIDUAL EVENTS   ....

....

....

⛑ MILITARY LIFE   Assignment(s) : ....

Campaign(s): ....

Medal(s) : ....☐ *Died in combat* ☐ *Injured on* : ....

....

| 880 | 881 | 882 | 883 |

440   441

220

110

📄 NOTES ....

....

....

....

....

....

♀ Surname : .... First name : ....

▶ Generation 8 – *maternal ascendant*

☐ *Implex*   Child : ☐ *Legitimate* ☐ *Natural* ☐ *Adopted* ☐ *Found* ☐ *Recognized* ☐ *Adulterated*

Born : ....in...

Baptized : ....in...

Godfather: ....Godmother : ....

Daughter of : ....and:...

Nationality : ....Religion : ....Studies: ....

Occupation(s) : ....

Deceased : ....in..............................Cause:......................

☐ *Buried* ☐ *Cremated* ☐ *Disappeared* on : ....in :....................

👫 CHILDREN ♂ .... ♀	Gen.	° Birth	† Death	Spouse
....	......	....	....	....
....	......	....	....	....
....	......	....	....	....
....	......	....	....	....
....	......	....	....	....
....	......	....	....	....
....	......	....	....	....
....	......	....	....	....
....	......	....	....	....
....	......	....	....	....

💍 OTHER UNION(S)/ 👫 CHILDREN ....
....
....
....

👫 SIBLINGS   ▶ *Details page 443*   ♂ .... ♀ .... 1.............................

2.. 3............................... 4...............................

5.. 6............................... 7...............................

8.. 9............................... 10.............................

👤 INDIVIDUAL EVENTS ....
....
....
....
....
....
....

📑 NOTES ....

884	885	886	887
	442		443
		221	
		110	

....
....
....

Surname: ....First name : .... ♂

▶ Generation8 – *maternal ascendant*

Child : ☐ *Legitimate* ☐ *Natural* ☐ *Adopted* ☐ *Found* ☐ *Recognized* ☐ *Adulterated*   ☐ *Implex*

Born : ....in ....

Baptized : ....in ....

Godfather: ....Godmother : ....

Son of : ....and: ....

Nationality : ....Religion : ....Studies: ....

Occupation(s) : ....

Deceased : ....in................................Cause:.............................

☐ *Buried* ☐ *Cremated* ☐ *Disappeared* on : ....in : ....

💍 MARITAL STATUS   ☐ *Civil Marriage*   ☐ *Religious Marriage*   ☐ *Free Union*

Date : ....in.. ☐ *Marriage contract*

Witnesses : ....
....

☐ *Separation* ☐ *Divorce* ☐ *Widowhood of the groom/bride*   Date : ....

👪 FAMILY EVENTS ....
....
....
....
....
....

💍 OTHER UNION(S)/👪 CHILDREN ....
....
....
....

👫 SIBLINGS   ▶ *Details page 445*   ♂ ....   ♀ ....   1.......................................
2.................................... 3.................................... 4....................................
5.................................... 6.................................... 7....................................
8.................................... 9.................................... 10....................................

👤 INDIVIDUAL EVENTS ....
....
....

⛑ MILITARY LIFE   Assignment(s) : ....
Campaign(s): ....
Medal(s) : ....☐ *Died in combat* ☐ *Injured on* : ....

888	889	890	891
444		445	
	222		
	111		

📑 NOTES ....
....
....
....
....

♀ Surname : ....First name : ....

▶ Generation 8 – *maternal ascendant*

□ *Implex*   Child : □ *Legitimate* □ *Natural* □ *Adopted* □ *Found* □ *Recognized* □ *Adulterated*

Born : ....in...

Baptized : ....in...

Godfather: ....Godmother : ....

Daughter of : ....and: ....

Nationality : ....Religion : ....Studies: ....

Occupation(s) : ....

Deceased : ....in...Cause:......................

□ *Buried* □ *Cremated* □ *Disappeared* on : ....in : ....

👪 CHILDREN ♂ .... ♀	Gen.	° Birth	† Death	Spouse
....	......	....	....	....
....	......	....	....	....
....	......	....	....	....
....	......	....	....	....
....	......	....	....	....
....	......	....	....	....
....	......	....	....	....
....	......	....	....	....
....	......	....	....	....
....	......	....	....	....

💍 OTHER UNION(S)/ 👪 CHILDREN ....

....

....

....

👪 SIBLINGS   ▶ *Details page 447*   ♂ .... ♀ ....   1.................................

2...3.................................4.................................

5...6.................................7.................................

8...9.................................10...............................

👤 INDIVIDUAL EVENTS ....

....

....

....

....

....

....

📑 NOTES ....

....

....

....

....

892	893	894	895

446   447

223

111

Sosa 224

Surname: .... First name : .... ♂

▶ Generation8 – *maternal ascendant*

Child : ☐ *Legitimate* ☐ *Natural* ☐ *Adopted* ☐ *Found* ☐ *Recognized* ☐ *Adulterated*   ☐ *Implex*

Born : ....in..

Baptized : ....in............................

Godfather: ....Godmother : ....

Son of : ....and: ....

Nationality : ....Religion : ....Studies: ....

Occupation(s) : ....

Deceased : ....in............................Cause:........................

☐ *Buried* ☐ *Cremated* ☐ *Disappeared* on : ....in : ....

💍 MARITAL STATUS   ☐ *Civil Marriage* ☐ *Religious Marriage* ☐ *Free Union*

Date : ....in.. ☐ *Marriage contract*

Witnesses : ....
....

☐ *Separation* ☐ *Divorce* ☐ *Widowhood of the groom/bride* Date : ....

👫 FAMILY EVENTS ....
....
....
....
....
....

💍 OTHER UNION(S)/ 👫 CHILDREN ....
....
....
....

👫 SIBLINGS ▶ *Details page 449*   ♂ .... ♀ ....   1........................
2..3..4........................
5..6..7........................
8..9..10........................

👤 INDIVIDUAL EVENTS ....
....
....

⛑ MILITARY LIFE Assignment(s) : ....
Campaign(s): ....
Medal(s) : .... ☐ *Died in combat* ☐ *Injured on* : ....
....

896	897	898	899

448   449

224

112

📋 NOTES ....
....
....
....
....

♀ Surname : .... First name : ....

▶ Generation 8 – *maternal ascendant*

☐ *Implex* Child : ☐ *Legitimate* ☐ *Natural* ☐ *Adopted* ☐ *Found* ☐ *Recognized* ☐ *Adulterated*

Born : ....in..

Baptized : ....in...

Godfather: ....Godmother : ....

Daughter of : ....and: ....

Nationality : ....Religion : ....Studies: ....

Occupation(s) : ....

Deceased : ....in..Cause:...........................

☐ *Buried* ☐ *Cremated* ☐ *Disappeared* on : ....in : ....

👫 CHILDREN ♂ .... ♀ ....

	Gen.	° Birth	† Death	Spouse
....	......	....	....	....
....	......	....	....	....
....	......	....	....	....
....	......	....	....	....
....	......	....	....	....
....	......	....	....	....
....	......	....	....	....
....	......	....	....	....
....	......	....	....	....
....	......	....	....	....

💍 OTHER UNION(S)/ 👫 CHILDREN ....

....

....

👫 SIBLINGS ▶ *Details page 451* ♂ .... ♀ .... 1...

2.. 3.............................. 4...

5.. 6.............................. 7...

8.. 9.............................. 10...

👤 INDIVIDUAL EVENTS ....

....

....

....

....

....

....

📝 NOTES ....

900	901	902	903

450	451

225

112

Surname: .... First name : .... ♂

Child : ☐ *Legitimate* ☐ *Natural* ☐ *Adopted* ☐ *Found* ☐ *Recognized* ☐ *Adulterated*   ☐ *Implex*

Born : ....in..

Baptized : ....in..

Godfather: ....Godmother : ....

Son of : ....and: ....

Nationality : ....Religion : ....Studies: ....

Occupation(s) : ....

Deceased : ....in.....................................Cause:...........................

☐ *Buried* ☐ *Cremated* ☐ *Disappeared* on : ....in :............................

⚭ MARITAL STATUS   ☐ *Civil Marriage*   ☐ *Religious Marriage*   ☐ *Free Union*

Date : ....in...☐ *Marriage contract*

Witnesses : ....

....

☐ *Separation* ☐ *Divorce* ☐ *Widowhood of the groom/bride* Date : ....

👫 FAMILY EVENTS ....

....

....

....

....

....

⚭ OTHER UNION(S)/ 👫 CHILDREN ....

....

....

....

👫 SIBLINGS   ▶ *Details page 453*   ♂ .... ♀ ....   1..

2.................................. 3.................................. 4..................................

5.................................. 6.................................. 7..................................

8.................................. 9.................................. 10..................................

👤 INDIVIDUAL EVENTS ....

....

....

⛑ MILITARY LIFE   Assignment(s) : ....

Campaign(s): ....

Medal(s) : ....☐ *Died in combat* ☐ *Injured on* : ....

904	905	906	907
452		453	
226			
113			

📑 NOTES ....

....

....

....

♀ Surname : ....First name : ....

▶ Generation 8 – *maternal ascendant*

☐ *Implex*   Child : ☐ *Legitimate* ☐ *Natural* ☐ *Adopted* ☐ *Found* ☐ *Recognized* ☐ *Adulterated*

Born : ....in...

Baptized : ....in...

Godfather: ....Godmother : ....

Daughter of : ....and: ....

Nationality : ....Religion : ....Studies: ....

Occupation(s) : ....

Deceased : ....in.............................Cause:.........................

☐ *Buried* ☐ *Cremated* ☐ *Disappeared* on : ....in :......................

👪 CHILDREN ♂ .... ♀	Gen.	° Birth	† Death	Spouse
....	......	....	....	....
....	......	....	....	....
....	......	....	....	....
....	......	....	....	....
....	......	....	....	....
....	......	....	....	....
....	......	....	....	....
....	......	....	....	....
....	......	....	....	....
....	......	....	....	....

💍 OTHER UNION(S)/ 👪 CHILDREN ....

....

....

👪 SIBLINGS   ▶ *Details page 455*   ♂ .... ♀ ....   1.................................

2..3..4...............................

5..6..7...............................

8..9..10.............................

👤 INDIVIDUAL EVENTS ....

....

....

....

....

....

....

📝 NOTES ....

....

....

....

....

908	909	910	911

454		455

227

113

Surname: .... First name : .... ♂

▶ Generation8 – *maternal ascendant*

Child : □ *Legitimate* □ *Natural* □ *Adopted* □ *Found* □ *Recognized* □ *Adulterated*   □ *Implex*

Born : ....in ....
Baptized : ....in ....
Godfather: ....Godmother : ....
Son of : ....and: ....
Nationality : ....Religion : ....Studies: ....
Occupation(s) : ....
Deceased : ....in ....Cause:........................
□ *Buried* □ *Cremated* □ *Disappeared* on : ....in : ....

⚭ MARITAL STATUS   □ *Civil Marriage* □ *Religious Marriage* □ *Free Union*

Date : ....in... □ *Marriage contract*
Witnesses : ....
....
□ *Separation* □ *Divorce* □ *Widowhood of the groom/bride* Date : ....

👫 FAMILY EVENTS ....
....
....
....
....
....

⚭ OTHER UNION(S)/👫 CHILDREN ....
....
....
....

👫 SIBLINGS   ▶ *Details page 457*   ♂ .... ♀ .... 1.....................
2.................................... 3.................................... 4....................................
5.................................... 6.................................... 7....................................
8.................................... 9.................................... 10...................................

👤 INDIVIDUAL EVENTS ....
....
....
....

⛑ MILITARY LIFE   Assignment(s) : ....
Campaign(s): ....
Medal(s) : ....□ *Died in combat* □ *Injured on* : ....
....

912	913	914	915
456		457	
	228		
	114		

📑 NOTES ....
....
....
....
....

♀ Surname : .... First name : ....

▶ Generation 8 – *maternal ascendant*

□ *Implex* Child : □ *Legitimate* □ *Natural* □ *Adopted* □ *Found* □ *Recognized* □ *Adulterated*

Born : ....in...

Baptized : ....in...

Godfather: ....Godmother : ....

Daughter of : ....and: ....

Nationality : ....Religion : ....Studies: ....

Occupation(s) : ....

Deceased : ....in...Cause:...

□ *Buried* □ *Cremated* □ *Disappeared* on : ....in : ....

👪 CHILDREN ♂ .... ♀ ....

	Gen.	° Birth	† Death	Spouse
....	.....	....	....	....
....	.....	....	....	....
....	.....	....	....	....
....	.....	....	....	....
....	.....	....	....	....
....	.....	....	....	....
....	.....	....	....	....
....	.....	....	....	....
....	.....	....	....	....
....	.....	....	....	....

💍 OTHER UNION(S)/ 👪 CHILDREN ....

....

....

👫 SIBLINGS ▶ *Details page 459* ♂ .... ♀ .... 1...

2... 3... 4...

5... 6... 7...

8... 9... 10...

👤 INDIVIDUAL EVENTS ....

....

....

....

....

....

📑 NOTES ....

....

....

....

916	917	918	919

458		459

229

114

Surname: .... First name : .... ♂

▶ Generation8 – *maternal ascendant*

Child : □ *Legitimate* □ *Natural* □ *Adopted* □ *Found* □ *Recognized* □ *Adulterated*   □ *Implex*

Born : ....in...

Baptized : ....in...

Godfather: ....Godmother : ....

Son of : ....and:..

Nationality : ....Religion : ....Studies: ....

Occupation(s) : ....

Deceased : ....in.......................................Cause:........................

□ *Buried* □ *Cremated* □ *Disappeared* on : ....in :.....................

⊚ MARITAL STATUS   □ *Civil Marriage* □ *Religious Marriage* □ *Free Union*

Date : ....in.......................................□ *Marriage contract*

Witnesses : ....

....

□ *Separation* □ *Divorce* □ *Widowhood of the groom/bride* Date : ....

👫 FAMILY EVENTS ....

....
....
....
....
....

⊚ OTHER UNION(S)/ 👫 CHILDREN ....

....
....
....

👫 SIBLINGS   ▶ *Details page 461*   ♂ .... ♀ ....   1.............................
2.............................. 3.............................. 4..............................
5.............................. 6.............................. 7..............................
8.............................. 9.............................. 10..............................

👤 INDIVIDUAL EVENTS ....

....
....

⛑ MILITARY LIFE Assignment(s) : ....

Campaign(s): ....

Medal(s) : ....□ *Died in combat* □ *Injured on* : ....

920	921	922	923

460   461

230

115

🗒 NOTES ....
....
....
....
....

► Generation 8 - *maternal ascendant*

□ *Implex*   Child : □ *Legitimate* □ *Natural* □ *Adopted* □ *Found* □ *Recognized* □ *Adulterated*

Born : ....in..
Baptized : ....in..
Godfather: ....Godmother : ....
Daughter of : ....and: ....
Nationality : ....Religion : ....Studies: ....
Occupation(s) : ....
Deceased : ....in..................................Cause:.............................
□ *Buried* □ *Cremated* □ *Disappeared* on : ....in : ....

👫 CHILDREN ♂ .... ♀	Gen.	° Birth	† Death	Spouse
....	......	....	....	....
....	......	....	....	....
....	......	....	....	....
....	......	....	....	....
....	......	....	....	....
....	......	....	....	....
....	......	....	....	....
....	......	....	....	....
....	......	....	....	....
....	......	....	....	....

💍 OTHER UNION(S)/ 👫 CHILDREN ....
....
....
....

👫 SIBLINGS   ► *Details page 463*   ♂ .... ♀ ....   1..
2............................   3............................   4............................
5............................   6............................   7............................
8............................   9............................   10............................

👤 INDIVIDUAL EVENTS ....
....
....
....
....
....
....

📑 NOTES ....
....
....
....

924	925	926	927
462		463	
231			
115			

Sosa 232

Surname: .... First name : .... ♂

Child : ☐ *Legitimate* ☐ *Natural* ☐ *Adopted* ☐ *Found* ☐ *Recognized* ☐ *Adulterated*   ☐ *Implex*

Born : ....in...

Baptized : ....in...

Godfather: ....Godmother : ....

Son of : ....and: ....

Nationality : ....Religion : ....Studies: ....

Occupation(s) : ....

Deceased : ....in....................Cause:...............................

☐ *Buried* ☐ *Cremated* ☐ *Disappeared* on : ....in : ....

⓪ MARITAL STATUS   ☐ *Civil Marriage* ☐ *Religious Marriage* ☐ *Free Union*

Date : ....in...☐ *Marriage contract*

Witnesses : ....

....

☐ *Separation* ☐ *Divorce* ☐ *Widowhood of the groom/bride* Date : ....

👪 FAMILY EVENTS ....

....

....

....

....

....

⓪ OTHER UNION(S)/ 👪 CHILDREN ....

....

....

....

👪 SIBLINGS   ▶ *Details page 465*   ♂ .... ♀ ....   1................................
2....................................3............................4................................
5....................................6............................7................................
8....................................9............................10...............................

👤 INDIVIDUAL EVENTS ....

....

....

....

⛑ MILITARY LIFE Assignment(s) : ....

Campaign(s): ....

Medal(s) : ....☐ *Died in combat* ☐ *Injured on* : ....

....

| 928 | 929 | 930 | 931 |

464   465

232

116

📋 NOTES ....

....

....

....

232

♀ Surname : ....First name : ....

▶ Generation 8 – *maternal ascendant*

☐ *Implex*　　Child : ☐ *Legitimate* ☐ *Natural* ☐ *Adopted* ☐ *Found* ☐ *Recognized* ☐ *Adulterated*

Born : ....in...

Baptized : ....in...

Godfather: ....Godmother : ....

Daughter of : ....and:...

Nationality : ....Religion : ....Studies: ....

Occupation(s) : ....

Deceased : ....in...........................Cause:.......................

☐ *Buried* ☐ *Cremated* ☐ *Disappeared* on : ....in : ....

👫 CHILDREN ♂ .... ♀	Gen.	° Birth	† Death	Spouse
....	....	....	....	....
....	....	....	....	....
....	....	....	....	....
....	....	....	....	....
....	....	....	....	....
....	....	....	....	....
....	....	....	....	....
....	....	....	....	....
....	....	....	....	....
....	....	....	....	....

💍 OTHER UNION(S)/ 👫 CHILDREN ....

....

....

👫 SIBLINGS　▶ *Details page 467*　　♂ .... ♀ ....　1...

2..3................................4...

5..6................................7...

8..9................................10...

👤 INDIVIDUAL EVENTS ....

....

....

....

....

....

....

....

📝 NOTES ....

932	933	934	935

....| 466 |　　| 467 |

....| 233 |

....| 116 |

233

Surname: .... First name : .... ♂

▶ Generation8 – *maternal ascendant*

Child : □ *Legitimate* □ *Natural* □ *Adopted* □ *Found* □ *Recognized* □ *Adulterated*   □ *Implex*

Born : ....in...

Baptized : ....in...

Godfather: ....Godmother : ....

Son of : ....and: ....

Nationality : ....Religion : ....Studies: ....

Occupation(s) : ....

Deceased : ....in...........................Cause:........................

□ *Buried* □ *Cremated* □ *Disappeared* on : ....in : ....

💍 MARITAL STATUS   □ *Civil Marriage*   □ *Religious Marriage*   □ *Free Union*

Date : ....in... □ *Marriage contract*

Witnesses : ....

....

□ *Separation* □ *Divorce* □ *Widowhood of the groom/bride*   Date : ....

👪 FAMILY EVENTS ....

....
....
....
....
....

💍 OTHER UNION(S)/👫 CHILDREN ....

....
....
....

👫 SIBLINGS   ▶ *Details page 469*   ♂ ....   ♀ ....   1..............................

2............................... 3............................... 4...............................

5............................... 6............................... 7...............................

8............................... 9............................... 10...............................

👤 INDIVIDUAL EVENTS ....

....
....

⛑ MILITARY LIFE   Assignment(s) : ....

Campaign(s): ....

Medal(s) : ....□ *Died in combat* □ *Injured on* : ....

936	937	938	939

468   469

234

117

🗒 NOTES ....

....
....
....
....

♀ Surname : ....First name : ....

▶ Generation 8 - *maternal ascendant*

☐ *Implex*   Child : ☐ *Legitimate* ☐ *Natural* ☐ *Adopted* ☐ *Found* ☐ *Recognized* ☐ *Adulterated*

Born : ....in...

Baptized : ....in...

Godfather: ....Godmother : ....

Daughter of : ....and: ....

Nationality : ....Religion : ....Studies: ....

Occupation(s) : ....

Deceased : ....in..............................Cause:....................

☐ *Buried* ☐ *Cremated* ☐ *Disappeared* on : ....in : ....

👫 CHILDREN ♂ .... ♀	Gen.	° Birth	† Death	Spouse
....	......	....	....	....
....	......	....	....	....
....	......	....	....	....
....	......	....	....	....
....	......	....	....	....
....	......	....	....	....
....	......	....	....	....
....	......	....	....	....
....	......	....	....	....
....	......	....	....	....

💍 OTHER UNION(S)/ 👫 CHILDREN ....

....

....

👫 SIBLINGS   ▶ *Details page 471*   ♂ .... ♀ ....   1.......................................

2.................................... 3.................................... 4....................................

5.................................... 6.................................... 7....................................

8.................................... 9.................................... 10...................................

👤 INDIVIDUAL EVENTS ....

....

....

....

....

....

....

📝 NOTES ....

....

....

....

940	941	942	943

470		471

235

117

Surname: .... First name : .... ♂

Child : □ Legitimate □ Natural □ Adopted □ Found □ Recognized □ Adulterated   □ Implex

Born : ....in...

Baptized : ....in...

Godfather: ....Godmother : ....

Son of : ....and: ....

Nationality : ....Religion : ....Studies: ....

Occupation(s) : ....

Deceased : ....in...............................Cause:........................

□ Buried □ Cremated □ Disappeared on : ....in :.......................

💍 MARITAL STATUS   □ Civil Marriage □ Religious Marriage □ Free Union

Date : ....in...□ Marriage contract

Witnesses : ....

....

□ Separation □ Divorce □ Widowhood of the groom/bride Date : ....

👫 FAMILY EVENTS   ....

....

....

....

....

💍 OTHER UNION(S)/ 👫 CHILDREN ....

....

....

....

👫 SIBLINGS   ▶ Details page 473   ♂ .... ♀ ....   1.....................................

2..................................... 3..................................... 4.....................................

5..................................... 6..................................... 7.....................................

8..................................... 9..................................... 10...................................

👤 INDIVIDUAL EVENTS ....

....

....

⛑ MILITARY LIFE   Assignment(s) : ....

Campaign(s): ....

Medal(s) : ....□ Died in combat □ Injured on : ....

944	945	946	947

| 472 | | 473 |

| 236 |

| 118 |

📑 NOTES ....

....

....

....

....

♀ Surname : .... First name : ....

▶ Generation 8 – *maternal ascendant*

☐ *Implex* Child : ☐ *Legitimate* ☐ *Natural* ☐ *Adopted* ☐ *Found* ☐ *Recognized* ☐ *Adulterated*

Born : ....in...

Baptized : ....in...

Godfather: ....Godmother : ....

Daughter of : ....and: ....

Nationality : ....Religion : ....Studies: ....

Occupation(s) : ....

Deceased : ....in...Cause:..................

☐ *Buried* ☐ *Cremated* ☐ *Disappeared* on : ....in : ....

👫 CHILDREN ♂ .... ♀	Gen.	° Birth	† Death	Spouse
....	......	....	....	....
....	......	....	....	....
....	......	....	....	....
....	......	....	....	....
....	......	....	....	....
....	......	....	....	....
....	......	....	....	....
....	......	....	....	....
....	......	....	....	....
....	......	....	....	....

💍 OTHER UNION(S)/ 👫 CHILDREN ....

....

....

....

👫 SIBLINGS ▶ *Details page 475* ♂ .... ♀ .... 1...

2...................................... 3.. 4..

5...................................... 6.. 7..

8...................................... 9.. 10.......................................

👤 INDIVIDUAL EVENTS ....

....

....

....

....

....

....

📝 NOTES ....

....

....

....

948	949	950	951
474		475	
237			
118			

Surname: .... First name : .... ♂

▶ Generation8 – *maternal ascendant*

Child : □ *Legitimate* □ *Natural* □ *Adopted* □ *Found* □ *Recognized* □ *Adulterated*   □ *Implex*

Born : ....in....................................

Baptized : ....in....................................

Godfather: ....Godmother : ....

Son of : ....and: ....

Nationality : ....Religion : ....Studies: ....

Occupation(s) : ....

Deceased : ....in....................................Cause:....................................

□ *Buried* □ *Cremated* □ *Disappeared* on : ....in : ....

⚭ MARITAL STATUS   □ *Civil Marriage* □ *Religious Marriage* □ *Free Union*

Date : ....in....................................   □ *Marriage contract*

Witnesses : ....

....

□ *Separation* □ *Divorce* □ *Widowhood of the groom/bride* Date : ....

👪 FAMILY EVENTS   ....

....

....

....

....

⚭ OTHER UNION(S)/ 👪 CHILDREN   ....

....

....

....

👪 SIBLINGS ▶ *Details page 477* ♂ .... ♀ .... 1....................................

2.................................... 3.................................... 4....................................

5.................................... 6.................................... 7....................................

8.................................... 9.................................... 10....................................

👤 INDIVIDUAL EVENTS   ....

....

....

⛑ MILITARY LIFE Assignment(s) : ....

Campaign(s): ....

Medal(s) : ....□ *Died in combat* □ *Injured on* : ....

952	953	954	955

476   477

238

119

📑 NOTES ....

....

....

....

♀ Surname : ....First name : ....

▶ Generation 8 - *maternal ascendant*

☐ *Implex*   Child : ☐ *Legitimate* ☐ *Natural* ☐ *Adopted* ☐ *Found* ☐ *Recognized* ☐ *Adulterated*

Born : ....in...

Baptized : ....in...

Godfather: ....Godmother : ....

Daughter of : ....and: ....

Nationality : ....Religion : ....Studies: ....

Occupation(s) : ....

Deceased : ....in...........................Cause:...........................

☐ *Buried* ☐ *Cremated* ☐ *Disappeared* on : ....in : ....

👪 CHILDREN ♂ .... ♀ ....

	Gen.	° Birth	† Death	Spouse

💍 OTHER UNION(S)/ 👪 CHILDREN ....

....

....

👪 SIBLINGS ▶ *Details page 479* ♂ .... ♀ .... 1...

2...3...4...

5...6...7...

8...9...10...

👤 INDIVIDUAL EVENTS ....

....

....

....

....

....

....

📝 NOTES ....

....

....

....

956	957	958	959

478	479

239

119

Surname: .... First name : .... ♂

▶ Generation8 – *maternal ascendant*

Child : ☐ *Legitimate* ☐ *Natural* ☐ *Adopted* ☐ *Found* ☐ *Recognized* ☐ *Adulterated*   ☐ *Implex*

Born : ....in...

Baptized : ....in..

Godfather: ....Godmother : ....

Son of : ....and:...

Nationality : ....Religion : ....Studies: ....

Occupation(s) : ....

Deceased : ....in.................................Cause:........................

☐ *Buried* ☐ *Cremated* ☐ *Disappeared* on : ....in :.........................

💍 MARITAL STATUS   ☐ *Civil Marriage*   ☐ *Religious Marriage*   ☐ *Free Union*

Date : ....in... ☐ *Marriage contract*

Witnesses : ....

....

☐ *Separation* ☐ *Divorce* ☐ *Widowhood of the groom/bride* Date : ....

👪 FAMILY EVENTS ....

....

....

....

....

💍 OTHER UNION(S)/ 👪 CHILDREN ....

....

....

....

👪 SIBLINGS   ▶ *Details page 481*   ♂ .... ♀ ....   1..................................

2.. 3............................... 4..................................

5.. 6............................... 7..................................

8.. 9............................... 10.................................

👤 INDIVIDUAL EVENTS ....

....

....

⛑ MILITARY LIFE Assignment(s) : ....

Campaign(s): ....

Medal(s) : ....☐ *Died in combat* ☐ *Injured on* : ....

....

960	961	962	963

480 — 481

240

120

📝 NOTES ....

....

....

....

....

♀ Surname : ....First name : ....

▶ Generation 8 – *maternal ascendant*

☐ *Implex*   Child : ☐ *Legitimate* ☐ *Natural* ☐ *Adopted* ☐ *Found* ☐ *Recognized* ☐ *Adulterated*

Born : ....in...

Baptized : ....in...

Godfather: ....Godmother : ....

Daughter of : ....and: ....

Nationality : ....Religion : ....Studies: ....

Occupation(s) : ....

Deceased : ....in...................................Cause:.............

☐ *Buried* ☐ *Cremated* ☐ *Disappeared* on : ....in : ....

👫 CHILDREN ♂ .... ♀	Gen.	° Birth	† Death	Spouse
....	......	....	....	....
....	......	....	....	....
....	......	....	....	....
....	......	....	....	....
....	......	....	....	....
....	......	....	....	....
....	......	....	....	....
....	......	....	....	....
....	......	....	....	....
....	......	....	....	....

💍 OTHER UNION(S)/ 👫 CHILDREN ....

....

....

....

👫 SIBLINGS ▶ *Details page 483*   ♂ .... ♀ ....   1..

2..3................................4....................................

5..6................................7....................................

8..9................................10...................................

👤 INDIVIDUAL EVENTS ....

....

....

....

....

....

....

📋 NOTES ....

....

....

....

....

964	965	966	967
	482		483
	241		
	120		

Sosa 242

Surname: .... First name : .... ♂

Child : ☐ *Legitimate* ☐ *Natural* ☐ *Adopted* ☐ *Found* ☐ *Recognized* ☐ *Adulterated*   ☐ *Implex*

Born : ....in...

Baptized : ....in...

Godfather: ....Godmother : ....

Son of : ....and: ....

Nationality : ....Religion : ....Studies: ....

Occupation(s) : ....

Deceased : ....in...Cause:...

☐ *Buried* ☐ *Cremated* ☐ *Disappeared* on : ....in : ....

⛀ MARITAL STATUS   ☐ *Civil Marriage*   ☐ *Religious Marriage*   ☐ *Free Union*

Date : ....in...   ☐ *Marriage contract*

Witnesses : ....

....

☐ *Separation* ☐ *Divorce* ☐ *Widowhood of the groom/bride*   Date : ....

👪 FAMILY EVENTS ....

....
....
....
....
....

⛀ OTHER UNION(S)/👪 CHILDREN ....

....
....
....

👪 SIBLINGS   ▶ *Details page 485*   ♂ ....   ♀ ....   1...

2... 3... 4...

5... 6... 7...

8... 9... 10...

👤 INDIVIDUAL EVENTS ....

....
....
....

⛑ MILITARY LIFE   Assignment(s) : ....

Campaign(s): ....

Medal(s) : ....☐ *Died in combat* ☐ *Injured on* : ....

968	969	970	971

📑 NOTES ....

484   485

242

121

....
....
....
....

♀ Surname : .... First name : ....

□ *Implex*

Child : □ *Legitimate* □ *Natural* □ *Adopted* □ *Found* □ *Recognized* □ *Adulterated*

Born : ....in ....

Baptized : ....in ....

Godfather: ....Godmother : ....

Daughter of : ....and: ....

Nationality : ....Religion : ....Studies: ....

Occupation(s) : ....

Deceased : ....in ....Cause:..........................

□ *Buried* □ *Cremated* □ *Disappeared* on : ....in : ....

👪 CHILDREN ♂ .... ♀	Gen.	° Birth	† Death	Spouse
....	......	....	....	....
....	......	....	....	....
....	......	....	....	....
....	......	....	....	....
....	......	....	....	....
....	......	....	....	....
....	......	....	....	....
....	......	....	....	....
....	......	....	....	....
....	......	....	....	....

💍 OTHER UNION(S)/ 👪 CHILDREN ....

....

....

👪 SIBLINGS ▶ *Details page 487* ♂ .... ♀ .... 1...

2.. 3.. 4..

5.. 6.. 7..

8.. 9.. 10..

👤 INDIVIDUAL EVENTS ....

....

....

....

....

....

....

📝 NOTES ....

....

....

....

....

972	973	974	975

486	487

243

121

Surname: .... First name : .... ♂

▶ Generation8 – *maternal ascendant*

Child : ☐ *Legitimate* ☐ *Natural* ☐ *Adopted* ☐ *Found* ☐ *Recognized* ☐ *Adulterated*   ☐ *Implex*

Born : ....in...

Baptized : ....in...

Godfather: ....Godmother : ....

Son of : ....and: ....

Nationality : ....Religion : ....Studies: ....

Occupation(s) : ....

Deceased : ....in....................................Cause:............................

☐ *Buried* ☐ *Cremated* ☐ *Disappeared* on : ....in : ....

⚭ MARITAL STATUS   ☐ *Civil Marriage* ☐ *Religious Marriage* ☐ *Free Union*

Date : ....in... ☐ *Marriage contract*

Witnesses : ....

....

☐ *Separation* ☐ *Divorce* ☐ *Widowhood of the groom/bride* Date : ....

👪 FAMILY EVENTS   ....

....

....

....

....

....

⚭ OTHER UNION(S)/👪 CHILDREN ....

....

....

....

👫 SIBLINGS   ▶ *Details page 489*   ♂ .... ♀ ....   1. ....

2.. 3.. 4...

5.. 6.. 7...

8.. 9.. 10...

👤 INDIVIDUAL EVENTS ....

....

....

....

⛑ MILITARY LIFE   Assignment(s) : ....

Campaign(s): ....

Medal(s) : ....☐ *Died in combat* ☐ *Injured on* : ....

....

| 976 | 977 | 978 | 979 |

| 488 | | 489 |

| 244 |

| 122 |

📝 NOTES ....

....

....

....

....

♀ Surname : .... First name : ....

□ *Implex*   Child : □ *Legitimate* □ *Natural* □ *Adopted* □ *Found* □ *Recognized* □ *Adulterated*

Born : .... in ....

Baptized : .... in ....

Godfather: .... Godmother : ....

Daughter of : .... and: ....

Nationality : .... Religion : .... Studies: ....

Occupation(s) : ....

Deceased : .... in .... Cause: ....

□ *Buried* □ *Cremated* □ *Disappeared* on : .... in : ....

👫 CHILDREN ♂ .... ♀ ....

	Gen.	° Birth	† Death	Spouse
....	......	....	....	....
....	......	....	....	....
....	......	....	....	....
....	......	....	....	....
....	......	....	....	....
....	......	....	....	....
....	......	....	....	....
....	......	....	....	....
....	......	....	....	....
....	......	....	....	....

💍 OTHER UNION(S)/ 👫 CHILDREN ....

....

....

....

👫 SIBLINGS ▶ *Details page 491* ♂ .... ♀ .... 1. ....

2. .... 3. .... 4. ....

5. .... 6. .... 7. ....

8. .... 9. .... 10. ....

👤 INDIVIDUAL EVENTS ....

....

....

....

....

....

....

📝 NOTES ....

....

....

....

980	981	982	983

490		491

245

122

Surname: .... First name : .... ♂

Child : ☐ *Legitimate* ☐ *Natural* ☐ *Adopted* ☐ *Found* ☐ *Recognized* ☐ *Adulterated*   ☐ *Implex*

Born : ....in..

Baptized : ....in...

Godfather: ....Godmother : ....

Son of : ....and:..

Nationality : ....Religion : ....Studies: ....

Occupation(s) : ....

Deceased : ....in.........................Cause:...........................

☐ *Buried* ☐ *Cremated* ☐ *Disappeared* on : ....in : ....

⊚ MARITAL STATUS   ☐ *Civil Marriage* ☐ *Religious Marriage* ☐ *Free Union*

Date : ....in.. ☐ *Marriage contract*

Witnesses : ....

....

☐ *Separation* ☐ *Divorce* ☐ *Widowhood of the groom/bride* Date : ....

👫 FAMILY EVENTS   ....

....
....
....
....
....

⊚ OTHER UNION(S)/👫 CHILDREN ....

....
....
....

👫 SIBLINGS   ▶ *Details page 493*   ♂ .... ♀ ....   1.................................
2..3...............................4...............................
5..6...............................7...............................
8..9...............................10..............................

👤 INDIVIDUAL EVENTS ....

....
....
....

⛑ MILITARY LIFE   Assignment(s) : ....

Campaign(s): ....

Medal(s) : ....☐ *Died in combat* ☐ *Injured on* : ....

....

984	985	986	987

```
  492        493
       246
       123
```

📝 NOTES ....

....
....
....

♀ Surname : ....First name : ....

▶ Generation 8 – *maternal ascendant*

☐ *Implex*   Child : ☐ *Legitimate* ☐ *Natural* ☐ *Adopted* ☐ *Found* ☐ *Recognized* ☐ *Adulterated*

Born : ....in...

Baptized : ....in..

Godfather: ....Godmother : ....

Daughter of : ....and: ....

Nationality : ....Religion : ....Studies: ....

Occupation(s) : ....

Deceased : ....in.....................Cause:..................

☐ *Buried* ☐ *Cremated* ☐ *Disappeared* on : ....in :..............

👪 CHILDREN ♂ .... ♀	Gen.	° Birth	† Death	Spouse
....	......	....	....	....
....	......	....	....	....
....	......	....	....	....
....	......	....	....	....
....	......	....	....	....
....	......	....	....	....
....	......	....	....	....
....	......	....	....	....
....	......	....	....	....
....	......	....	....	....

💍 OTHER UNION(S)/ 👪 CHILDREN ....

....

....

👪 SIBLINGS ▶ *Details page 495* ♂ .... ♀ .... 1...

2....................................... 3................................... 4...................................

5....................................... 6................................... 7...................................

8....................................... 9................................... 10.................................

👤 INDIVIDUAL EVENTS ....

....

....

....

....

....

....

📑 NOTES ....

....

....

....

....

988	989	990	991

494	495

247

123

Surname: .... First name : .... ♂

▶ Generation8 – *maternal ascendant*

Child : ☐ *Legitimate* ☐ *Natural* ☐ *Adopted* ☐ *Found* ☐ *Recognized* ☐ *Adulterated*   ☐ *Implex*

Born : ....in ....

Baptized : ....in ....

Godfather: ....Godmother : ....

Son of : ....and: ....

Nationality : ....Religion : ....Studies: ....

Occupation(s) : ....

Deceased : ....in................................Cause:..........................

☐ *Buried* ☐ *Cremated* ☐ *Disappeared* on : ....in :....................

⊚ MARITAL STATUS   ☐ *Civil Marriage* ☐ *Religious Marriage* ☐ *Free Union*

Date : ....in .... ☐ *Marriage contract*

Witnesses : ....

....

☐ *Separation* ☐ *Divorce* ☐ *Widowhood of the groom/bride* Date : ....

👪 FAMILY EVENTS   ....

....
....
....
....
....

⊚ OTHER UNION(S)/ 👪 CHILDREN   ....

....
....
....

👪 SIBLINGS   ▶ *Details page 497*   ♂ .... ♀ .... 1..
2... 3... 4...
5... 6... 7...
8... 9... 10...

👤 INDIVIDUAL EVENTS   ....

....
....

⛑ MILITARY LIFE   Assignment(s) : ....

Campaign(s): ....

Medal(s) : ....☐ *Died in combat* ☐ *Injured on* : ....

992	993	994	995

496		497

248

124

🗎 NOTES ....

....
....
....
....

♀ Surname : .... First name : ....

▶ Generation 8 – *maternal ascendant*

☐ *Implex*　　Child : ☐ *Legitimate* ☐ *Natural* ☐ *Adopted* ☐ *Found* ☐ *Recognized* ☐ *Adulterated*

Born : ....in...

Baptized : ....in..

Godfather: ....Godmother : ....

Daughter of : ....and: ....

Nationality : ....Religion : ....Studies: ....

Occupation(s) : ....

Deceased : ....in......................Cause:.....................

☐ *Buried* ☐ *Cremated* ☐ *Disappeared* on : ....in : ....

👫 CHILDREN ♂ .... ♀	Gen.	° Birth	† Death	Spouse
....	......	....	....	....
....	......	....	....	....
....	......	....	....	....
....	......	....	....	....
....	......	....	....	....
....	......	....	....	....
....	......	....	....	....
....	......	....	....	....
....	......	....	....	....
....	......	....	....	....

💍 OTHER UNION(S)/ 👫 CHILDREN ....

....

....

👫 SIBLINGS ▶ *Details page 499* ♂ .... ♀ .... 1..................................

2.. 3.. 4..............................

5.. 6.. 7..............................

8.. 9.. 10............................

👤 INDIVIDUAL EVENTS ....

....

....

....

....

....

....

📝 NOTES ....

....

....

....

996	997	998	999
498		499	
249			
124			

Surname: .... First name : .... ♂

▶ Generation8 – *maternal ascendant*

Child : ☐ *Legitimate* ☐ *Natural* ☐ *Adopted* ☐ *Found* ☐ *Recognized* ☐ *Adulterated*   ☐ *Implex*

Born : ....in..

Baptized : ....in..

Godfather: ....Godmother : ....

Son of : ....and: ....

Nationality : ....Religion : ....Studies: ....

Occupation(s) : ....

Deceased : ....in....................................Cause:.........................

☐ *Buried* ☐ *Cremated* ☐ *Disappeared* on : ....in :.....................

⊙ MARITAL STATUS   ☐ *Civil Marriage* ☐ *Religious Marriage* ☐ *Free Union*

Date : ....in.. ☐ *Marriage contract*

Witnesses : ....

....

☐ *Separation* ☐ *Divorce* ☐ *Widowhood of the groom/bride* Date : ....

👫 FAMILY EVENTS ....

....
....
....
....
....

⊙ OTHER UNION(S)/ 👫 CHILDREN ....

....
....
....

👫 SIBLINGS ▶ *Details page 501* ♂ .... ♀ .... 1...

2.. 3.. 4..

5.. 6.. 7..

8.. 9.. 10...

👤 INDIVIDUAL EVENTS ....

....
....
....

⛑ MILITARY LIFE Assignment(s) : ....

Campaign(s): ....

Medal(s) : ....☐ *Died in combat* ☐ *Injured on* : ....

....

1000	1001	1002	1003

500   501

250

125

📑 NOTES ....

....
....
....
....
....

♀ Surname : .... First name : ....

▶ Generation 8 – *maternal ascendant*

☐ *Implex*   Child : ☐ *Legitimate* ☐ *Natural* ☐ *Adopted* ☐ *Found* ☐ *Recognized* ☐ *Adulterated*

Born : ....in.............................

Baptized : ....in.............................

Godfather: ....Godmother : ....

Daughter of : ....and: ....

Nationality : ....Religion : ....Studies: ....

Occupation(s) : ....

Deceased : ....in.......................Cause:..........................

☐ *Buried* ☐ *Cremated* ☐ *Disappeared* on : ....in :.........................

👫 CHILDREN ♂ .... ♀	Gen.	° Birth	† Death	Spouse
....	......	....	....	....
....	......	....	....	....
....	......	....	....	....
....	......	....	....	....
....	......	....	....	....
....	......	....	....	....
....	......	....	....	....
....	......	....	....	....
....	......	....	....	....
....	......	....	....	....

💍 OTHER UNION(S)/ 👫 CHILDREN ....

....

....

👫 SIBLINGS ▶ *Details page 503*   ♂ .... ♀ .... 1...

2... 3... 4...

5... 6... 7...

8... 9... 10..

👤 INDIVIDUAL EVENTS ....

....

....

....

....

....

....

📑 NOTES ....

....

....

....

```
┌────┬────┬────┬────┐
│1004│1005│1006│1007│
└─┬──┴─┬──┴─┬──┴─┬──┘
  └ 502 ┘   └ 503 ┘
        251
        125
```

Surname: .... First name : .... ♂

Child : ☐ *Legitimate* ☐ *Natural* ☐ *Adopted* ☐ *Found* ☐ *Recognized* ☐ *Adulterated*　☐ *Implex*

Born : ....in..

Baptized : ....in..

Godfather: ....Godmother : ....

Son of : ....and: ....

Nationality : ....Religion : ....Studies: ....

Occupation(s) : ....

Deceased : ....in.....................Cause:.....................

☐ *Buried* ☐ *Cremated* ☐ *Disappeared* on : ....in :.....................

⚭ MARITAL STATUS　　　☐ *Civil Marriage* ☐ *Religious Marriage* ☐ *Free Union*

Date : ....in..☐ *Marriage contract*

Witnesses : ....

....

☐ *Separation* ☐ *Divorce* ☐ *Widowhood of the groom/bride*　Date : ....

👫 FAMILY EVENTS ....

....
....
....
....
....

⚭ OTHER UNION(S)/ 👫 CHILDREN ....

....
....
....

👫 SIBLINGS　▶ *Details page 505*　♂ ....　♀ ....　1..

2..　3..　4..

5..　6..　7..

8..　9..　10..

👤 INDIVIDUAL EVENTS ....

....
....

⛑ MILITARY LIFE　Assignment(s) : ....

Campaign(s): ....

Medal(s) : ....☐ *Died in combat* ☐ *Injured on* : ....

....

1008	1009	1010	1011

```
  504        505
       252
       126
```

🗎 NOTES ....

....
....
....
....

♀ Surname : .... First name : ....

▶ Generation 8 – *maternal ascendant*

☐ *Implex* Child : ☐ *Legitimate* ☐ *Natural* ☐ *Adopted* ☐ *Found* ☐ *Recognized* ☐ *Adulterated*

Born : ....in ....

Baptized : ....in ....

Godfather: ....Godmother : ....

Daughter of : ....and: ....

Nationality : ....Religion : ....Studies: ....

Occupation(s) : ....

Deceased : ....in ....Cause:....................

☐ *Buried* ☐ *Cremated* ☐ *Disappeared* on : ....in : ....

👫 CHILDREN ♂ .... ♀	Gen.	° Birth	† Death	Spouse
....	......	....	....	....
....	......	....	....	....
....	......	....	....	....
....	......	....	....	....
....	......	....	....	....
....	......	....	....	....
....	......	....	....	....
....	......	....	....	....
....	......	....	....	....
....	......	....	....	....

💍 OTHER UNION(S)/ 👫 CHILDREN ....

....

....

....

👫 SIBLINGS ▶ *Details page 507* ♂ .... ♀ .... 1..

2................................ 3................................ 4................................

5................................ 6................................ 7................................

8................................ 9................................ 10...............................

👤 INDIVIDUAL EVENTS ....

....

....

....

....

....

....

📑 NOTES ....

1012	1013	1014	1015

506	507

253

126

Surname: .... First name : .... ♂

▶ Generation8 – *maternal ascendant*

Child : ☐ *Legitimate* ☐ *Natural* ☐ *Adopted* ☐ *Found* ☐ *Recognized* ☐ *Adulterated*   ☐ *Implex*

Born : ....in...

Baptized : ....in...

Godfather: ....Godmother : ....

Son of : ....and:..

Nationality : ....Religion : ....Studies: ....

Occupation(s) : ....

Deceased : ....in.........................Cause:...............................

☐ *Buried* ☐ *Cremated* ☐ *Disappeared* on : ....in :.............................

⚭ MARITAL STATUS   ☐ *Civil Marriage*   ☐ *Religious Marriage*   ☐ *Free Union*

Date : ....in.. ☐ *Marriage contract*

Witnesses : ....

....

☐ *Separation* ☐ *Divorce* ☐ *Widowhood of the groom/bride*   Date : ....

👪 FAMILY EVENTS ....

....

....

....

....

....

⚭ OTHER UNION(S)/👪 CHILDREN ....

....

....

👪 SIBLINGS   ▶ *Details page 509*   ♂ .... ♀ ....   1.............................

2.......................................3......................................4............................

5.......................................6......................................7............................

8.......................................9......................................10...........................

👤 INDIVIDUAL EVENTS ....

....

....

⛑ MILITARY LIFE   Assignment(s) : ....

Campaign(s): ....

Medal(s) : ....☐ *Died in combat* ☐ *Injured on* : ....

1016	1017	1018	1019

508   509

254

127

🗒 NOTES ....

....

....

....

....

♀ Surname : .... First name : ....

▶ Generation 8 – *maternal ascendant*

☐ *Implex*   Child : ☐ *Legitimate* ☐ *Natural* ☐ *Adopted* ☐ *Found* ☐ *Recognized* ☐ *Adulterated*

Born : .... in ....
Baptized : .... in ....
Godfather: .... Godmother : ....
Daughter of : .... and: ....
Nationality : .... Religion : .... Studies: ....
Occupation(s) : ....
Deceased : .... in .... Cause: ....
☐ *Buried* ☐ *Cremated* ☐ *Disappeared* on : .... in : ....

👫 CHILDREN ♂ .... ♀ ....

	Gen.	° Birth	† Death	Spouse
....	.....	....	....	....
....	.....	....	....	....
....	.....	....	....	....
....	.....	....	....	....
....	.....	....	....	....
....	.....	....	....	....
....	.....	....	....	....
....	.....	....	....	....
....	.....	....	....	....
....	.....	....	....	....

💍 OTHER UNION(S)/ 👫 CHILDREN ....

....
....
....

👫 SIBLINGS ▶ *Details page 511*   ♂ .... ♀ ....   1. ....

2. .... 3. .... 4. ....
5. .... 6. .... 7. ....
8. .... 9. .... 10. ....

👤 INDIVIDUAL EVENTS ....

....
....
....
....
....
....

📝 NOTES ....

....
....
....
....

1020	1021	1022	1023

510		511

255

127

Sosa
256

Surname : .... First name : .... ♂

▶Generation 9 – paternal ascendant ↓Child page 128   □ Implex

Born : ....in............................□ baptized

Son of : ....and:...........................

Occupation(s) : ....

Deceased : ....in........................

💍 MARITAL STATUS   □ Civil Marriage   □ Religious Marriage   □ Free Union

Date : ....in.............................□ Marriage contract

Witnesses: ....

👪 ASCENDANCY UP TO XIVth GENERATION

4096 XIII 4097	2048 XII 2049
8194 XIV 8195	8196 XIV 8197	4098 XIII 4099
	1024 XI 1025
8192 XIV 8193	
8198 XIV 8199	GX 512 Father

Sosa 256

GX 513 Mother

2050 XII 2051	4100 XIII 4101
4102 XIII 4103	8206 XIV 8207	8200 XIV 8201
8202 XIV 8203	
8204 XIV 8205	

8210 XIV 8211	
8212 XIV 8213	
8214 XIV 8215	8208 XIV 8209	4104 XIII 4105
4106 XIII 4107	2052 XII 2053
	1026 XI 1027

8216 XIV 8217	
8222 XIV 8223	
4108 XIII 4109	8218 XIV 8219	8220 XIV 8221
2054 XII 2055	4110 XIII 4111

♀ Surname : .... First name : ....

▶Generation IX – paternal ascendant ↓Child page 128 – □ Implex

Born : ....in...□ baptized

Daughter of : ....and:..

Occupation(s) : ....

Deceased : ....in.................................

⚭ CHILDREN ....

....

👪 ASCENDANCY UP TO XIVth GENERATION

4112 XIII 4113	2056 XII 2057	2058 XII 2059
8226 XIV 8227	8228 XIV 8229	4114 XIII 4115
		1028 XI 1029
8224 XIV 8225		
	8230 XIV 8231	
⚜	GX 514 Father	8236 XIV 8237

Sosa 257

GX 515 Mother

8242 XIV 8243		8248 XIV 8249
8244 XIV 8245		
8246 XIV 8247	8240 XIV 8241	4120 XIII 4121
4122 XIII 4123	2060 XII 2061	1030 XI 1031

Right side:
4116 XIII 4117
8238 XIV 8239
8232 XIV 8233
4118 XIII 4119
8234 XIV 8235
8250 XIV 8251
8252 XIV 8253
4124 XIII 4125
8254 XIV 8255
4126 XIII 4127
2062 XII 2063

Sosa
258

Surname : .... First name : .... ♂

▶Generation 9 – paternal ascendant   ↓Child page 129   □ Implex

Born : ....in...□ baptized

Son of : ....and: ....

Occupation(s) : ....

Deceased : ....in..

💍 MARITAL STATUS   □ Civil Marriage   □ Religious Marriage   □ Free Union

Date : ....in... □ Marriage contract

Witnesses: ....

👪 ASCENDANCY UP TO XIVth GENERATION

4128 XIII 4129	2064 XII 2065
8258 XIV 8259	8260 XIV 8261
4130 XIII 4131	
	1032 XI 1033
8256 XIV 8257	
8262 XIV 8263	GX 516 Father

2066 XII 2067

4132 XIII 4133

4134 XIII 4135

8270 XIV 8271

8264 XIV 8265

8266 XIV 8267

8268 XIV 8269

Sosa 258

GX 517 Mother

8274 XIV 8275

8276 XIV 8277

8280 XIV 8281

8286 XIV 8287

1034 XI 1035

8278 XIV 8279

8272 XIV 8273

4136 XIII 4137

4138 XIII 4139

2068 XII 2069

4140 XIII 4141

8282 XIV 8283

8284 XIV 8285

4142 XIII 4143

2070 XII 2071

258

♀ Surname : ....First name : ....

▶Generation IX – paternal ascendant ↓Child page 129 –   □ Implex

Born : ....in..□ baptized

Daughter of : ....and:.................................

Occupation(s) : ....

Deceased : ....in...............................

⚭ CHILDREN ....

....

👪 ASCENDANCY UP TO XIVth GENERATION

4144 XIII 4145	2072 XII 2073
8290 XIV 8291	8292 XIV 8293
4146 XIII 4147	
1036 XI 1037	
8288 XIV 8289	
8294 XIV 8295	
GX 518 Father	
Sosa 259	
GX 519 Mother	
2074 XII 2075	
4150 XIII 4151	8302 XIV 8303	8296 XIV 8297	4148 XIII 4149
8298 XIV 8299	
8300 XIV 8301	
8306 XIV 8307	
8308 XIV 8309	
8310 XIV 8311	8304 XIV 8305
4152 XIII 4153	
4154 XIII 4155	2076 XII 2077
1038 XI 1039	
8312 XIV 8313	
8318 XIV 8319	
4156 XIII 4157	8314 XIV 8315	8316 XIV 8317	4158 XIII 4159
2078 XII 2079	

Sosa
260

Surname : .... First name : .... ♂

▶Generation 9 – paternal ascendant ↓Child page 130 □ Implex

Born : ....in..□ baptized

Son of : ....and: ....

Occupation(s) : ....

Deceased : ....in..............................

⊚ MARITAL STATUS

□ *Civil Marriage*   □ *Religious Marriage*   □ *Free Union*

Date : ....in.. □ Marriage contract

Witnesses: ....

👪 ASCENDANCY UP TO XIVth GENERATION

4160 XIII 4161	2080 XII 2081
8322 XIV 8323	8324 XIV 8325	4162 XIII 4163
	1040 XI 1041
8320 XIV 8321	
8326 XIV 8327	
	GX 520 Father

Sosa 260

	GX 521 Mother
8338 XIV 8339	
8340 XIV 8341	
8342 XIV 8343	8336 XIV 8337	4168 XIII 4169
4170 XIII 4171	2084 XII 2085
	1042 XI 1043

2082 XII 2083	4164 XIII 4165
4166 XIII 4167	8334 XIV 8335	8328 XIV 8329
	8330 XIV 8331
8332 XIV 8333	

8344 XIV 8345	
	8350 XIV 8351
4172 XIII 4173	8346 XIV 8347	8348 XIV 8349
2086 XII 2087	4174 XIII 4175

260

♀ Surname : .... First name : ....

Sosa
261

►Generation IX – paternal ascendant ↓Child page 130 –   ☐ Implex

Born : ....in................................. ☐ baptized

Daughter of : ....and:.................................

Occupation(s) : ....

Deceased : ....in.................

⚭ **CHILDREN** ....

....

⚶ ASCENDANCY UP TO XIVth GENERATION

4176 XIII 4177	2088 XII 2089
8354 XIV 8355	8356 XIV 8357	4178 XIII 4179
	2090 XII 2091
4182 XIII 4183	8366 XIV 8367	8360 XIV 8361	4180 XIII 4181

1044 XI 1045

8352 XIV 8353

8358 XIV 8359

8362 XIV 8363

8364 XIV 8365

GX 522 Father

Sosa 261

GX 523 Mother

8370 XIV 8371

8372 XIV 8373

8376 XIV 8377

8382 XIV 8383

1046 XI 1047

8374 XIV 8375

8368 XIV 8369

4184 XIII 4185

4186 XIII 4187

4188 XIII 4189

8378 XIV 8379

8380 XIV 8381

4190 XIII 4191

2092 XII 2093

2094 XII 2095

261

Sosa
262

Surname : .... First name : .... ♂

▶Generation 9 – paternal ascendant ↓Child page 131   ☐ Implex

Born : ....in..☐ baptized

Son of : ....and: ....

Occupation(s) : ....

Deceased : ....in...

⚭ MARITAL STATUS   ☐ Civil Marriage ☐ Religious Marriage ☐ Free Union

Date : ....in.. ☐ Marriage contract

Witnesses: ....

👥 ASCENDANCY UP TO XIVth GENERATION

4192 XIII 4193	2096 XII 2097
8386 XIV 8387	8388 XIV 8389	4194 XIII 4195
8384 XIV 8385	
8390 XIV 8391	

1048 XI 1049

GX 524 Father

Sosa 262

GX 525 Mother

| 2098 XII 2099 | 4196 XIII 4197 |
| 4198 XIII 4199 | 8398 XIV 8399 | 8392 XIV 8393 |
| 8394 XIV 8395 |
| 8396 XIV 8397 |

8402 XIV 8403	
8404 XIV 8405	
8406 XIV 8407	8400 XIV 8401	4200 XIII 4201
4202 XIII 4203	2100 XII 2101

1050 XI 1051

8408 XIV 8409	
8414 XIV 8415	
4204 XIII 4205	8410 XIV 8411	8412 XIV 8413
2102 XII 2103	4206 XIII 4207

262

♀ Surname : .... First name : ....

▶Generation IX – paternal ascendant ↓Child page 131 – □ Implex

Born : .... in .... □ baptized

Daughter of : .... and: ....

Occupation(s) : ....

Deceased : .... in ....

⚭ CHILDREN ....

....

ASCENDANCY UP TO XIVth GENERATION

4208 XIII 4209	2104 XII 2105
8418 XIV 8419	8420 XIV 8421
4210 XIII 4211	
	2106 XII 2107
	4212 XIII 4213
8430 XIV 8431	8424 XIV 8425
4214 XIII 4215	
1052 XI 1053	
8416 XIV 8417	8426 XIV 8427
8422 XIV 8423	8428 XIV 8429

GX 526 Father

Sosa 263

GX 527 Mother

8434 XIV 8435	8440 XIV 8441
8436 XIV 8437	8446 XIV 8447
8438 XIV 8439	8432 XIV 8433
4216 XIII 4217	8442 XIV 8443
	8444 XIV 8445
4218 XIII 4219	4220 XIII 4221
2108 XII 2109	1054 XI 1055
	2110 XII 2111
	4222 XIII 4223

Sosa
264

Surname : .... First name : .... ♂

►Generation 9 – paternal ascendant ↓Child page 132 ☐ Implex

Born : ....in...☐ baptized

Son of : ....and: ....

Occupation(s) : ....

Deceased : ....in..

⚭ MARITAL STATUS   ☐ *Civil Marriage* ☐ *Religious Marriage* ☐ *Free Union*

Date : ....in.. ☐ Marriage contract

Witnesses: ....

👪 ASCENDANCY UP TO XIVth GENERATION

2112 XII 2113	2114 XII 2115
4224 XIII 4225	4228 XIII 4229
8450 XIV 8451	8452 XIV 8453	4226 XIII 4227	4230 XIII 4231	8462 XIV 8463	8456 XIV 8457
	1056 XI 1057	
8448 XIV 8449	8458 XIV 8459
8454 XIV 8455	8460 XIV 8461

GX 528 Father

Sosa 264

GX 529 Mother

| 8466 XIV 8467 | 8472 XIV 8473 |
| 8468 XIV 8469 | 8478 XIV 8479 |

8470 XIV 8471	8464 XIV 8465	4232 XIII 4233	4236 XIII 4237	8474 XIV 8475	8476 XIV 8477
4234 XIII 4235	4238 XIII 4239
2116 XII 2117	1058 XI 1059	2118 XII 2119

♀ Surname : .... First name : ....

▶Generation IX – paternal ascendant ↓Child page 132 –   ☐ Implex

Born : ....in ....☐ baptized

Daughter of : ....and: ....

Occupation(s) : ....

Deceased : ....in ....

💍 **CHILDREN** ....

....

👪 **ASCENDANCY UP TO XIVth GENERATION**

2120 XII 2121		2122 XII 2123
4240 XIII 4241		4244 XIII 4245
8482 XIV 8483	8484 XIV 8485	4242 XIII 4243	8494 XIV 8495	8488 XIV 8489
		4246 XIII 4247

1060 XI 1061

8480 XIV 8481

8490 XIV 8491

8486 XIV 8487

8492 XIV 8493

⚜   ⚜

GX 530 Father

Sosa 265

GX 531 Mother

x

8498 XIV 8499

8504 XIV 8505

8500 XIV 8501

8510 XIV 8511

8502 XIV 8503

8496 XIV 8497

4248 XIII 4249

8506 XIV 8507

8508 XIV 8509

4250 XIII 4251

2124 XII 2125

1062 XI 1063

2126 XII 2127

4252 XIII 4253

4254 XIII 4255

Sosa
266

Surname : .... First name : .... ♂

▶Generation 9 – paternal ascendant   ↓Child page 133   □ Implex

Born : ....in...□ baptized

Son of : ....and:...

Occupation(s) : ....

Deceased : ....in..

⊚ **MARITAL STATUS**   □ *Civil Marriage*   □ *Religious Marriage*   □ *Free Union*

Date : ....in... □ Marriage contract

Witnesses: ....

⚑ ASCENDANCY UP TO XIVth GENERATION

2128 XII 2129	2130 XII 2131
4256 XIII 4257	4260 XIII 4261
8514 XIV 8515	8516 XIV 8517	4258 XIII 4259		4262 XIII 4263	8526 XIV 8527	8520 XIV 8521
	1064 XI 1065	
8512 XIV 8513		8522 XIV 8523
8518 XIV 8519	GX 532 Father	8524 XIV 8525

Sosa 266

GX 533 Mother	8536 XIV 8537
8530 XIV 8531	
8532 XIV 8533	8542 XIV 8543
8534 XIV 8535	8528 XIV 8529	4264 XIII 4265		4268 XIII 4269	8538 XIV 8539	8540 XIV 8541
4266 XIII 4267	4270 XIII 4271
2132 XII 2133	1066 XI 1067	2134 XII 2135

266

♀ Surname : .... First name : ....

▶Generation IX – paternal ascendant ↓Child page 133 –　　　　□ Implex

Born : .... in .... □ baptized

Daughter of : .... and: ....

Occupation(s) : ....

Deceased : .... in ....

○○ CHILDREN ....

....

....

👪 ASCENDANCY UP TO XIVth GENERATION

4272 XIII 4273	2136 XII 2137	8546 XIV 8547

1068 XI 1069

GX 534 Father

Sosa 267

GX 535 Mother

1070 XI 1071

2138 XII 2139

4276 XIII 4277

8558 XIV 8559

8552 XIV 8553

8548 XIV 8549

4274 XIII 4275

4278 4279

8544 XIV 8545

8550 XIV 8551

8554 XIV 8555

8556 XIV 8557

8562 XIV 8563

8564 XIV 8565

8566 XIV 8567

8560 XIV 8561

4280 XIII 4281

4282 XIII 4283

2140 XII 2141

2142 XII 2143

4284 XIII 4285

8570 XIV 8571

8572 XIV 8573

4286 XIII 4287

8568 XIV 8569

8574 XIV 8575

Sosa
268

Surname : .... First name : .... ♂

▶Generation 9 – paternal ascendant ↓Child page 134 □ Implex

Born : .... in .... □ baptized

Son of : .... and: ....

Occupation(s) : ....

Deceased : .... in ....

⚭ MARITAL STATUS

□ Civil Marriage □ Religious Marriage □ Free Union

Date : .... in .... □ Marriage contract

Witnesses: ....

ASCENDANCY UP TO XIVth GENERATION

2144 XII 2145		2146 XII 2147	
4288 XIII 4289	4290 XIII 4291	4294 XIII 4295	4292 XIII 4293
8578 XIV 8579	8580 XIV 8581	8590 XIV 8591	8584 XIV 8585
8576 XIV 8577			8586 XIV 8587
8582 XIV 8583		8588 XIV 8589	

1072 XI 1073

GX 536 Father

Sosa 268

GX 537 Mother

8594 XIV 8595		8600 XIV 8601	8606 XIV 8607
8596 XIV 8597			
8598 XIV 8599	8592 XIV 8593	4300 XIII 4301	8602 XIV 8603 / 8604 XIV 8605
4298 XIII 4299	4296 XIII 4297	2150 XII 2151	4302 XIII 4303
	2148 XII 2149		

1074 XI 1075

268

Sosa
269

♀ Surname : .... First name : ....

▶Generation IX – paternal ascendant ↓Child page 134 –   □ Implex

Born : .... in .... □ baptized

Daughter of : .... and: ....

Occupation(s) : ....

Deceased : .... in ....

⟭⟭ CHILDREN ....

....

....

⚎⚎ ASCENDANCY UP TO XIVth GENERATION

4304 XIII 4305	2152 XII 2153
8610 XIV 8611	8612 XIV 8613	4306 XIII 4307
	1076 XI 1077

2154 XII 2155

4308 XIII 4309

4310 XIII 4311 | 8622 XIV 8623 | 8616 XIV 8617

8608 XIV 8609

8618 XIV 8619

8614 XIV 8615

8620 XIV 8621

○
†
GX 538 Father

Sosa 269

GX 539 Mother
x
○
†

8626 XIV 8627

8632 XIV 8633

8628 XIV 8629

8638 XIV 8639

8630 XIV 8631 | 8624 XIV 8625 | 4312 XIII 4313

1078 XI 1079

4316 XIII 4317 | 8634 XIV 8635 | 8636 XIV 8637

4314 XIII 4315

2156 XII 2157

2158 XII 2159

4318 XIII 4319

269

Sosa
270

Surname : .... First name : .... ♂

▶Generation 9 – paternal ascendant ↓Child page 135   □ Implex

Born : ....in..□ baptized

Son of : ....and:...

Occupation(s) : ....

Deceased : ....in..

💍 MARITAL STATUS   □ *Civil Marriage* □ *Religious Marriage* □ *Free Union*

Date : ....in... □ Marriage contract

Witnesses: ....

👪 ASCENDANCY UP TO XIVth GENERATION

2160 XII 2161	2162 XII 2163
4320 XIII 4321	4324 XIII 4325
8642 XIV 8643	8654 XIV 8655
8644 XIV 8645	8648 XIV 8649
4322 XIII 4323	4326 XIII 4327
1080 XI 1081	
8640 XIV 8641	8650 XIV 8651
8646 XIV 8647	8652 XIV 8653

GX 540 Father

Sosa 270

GX 541 Mother

8658 XIV 8659	8664 XIV 8665
8660 XIV 8661	8670 XIV 8671
8662 XIV 8663	8666 XIV 8667
8656 XIV 8657	8668 XIV 8669
4328 XIII 4329	4332 XIII 4333
4330 XIII 4331	4334 XIII 4335
1082 XI 1083	
2164 XII 2165	2166 XII 2167

♀ Surname : .... First name : ....

▶Generation IX – paternal ascendant ↓Child page 135 –   ☐ Implex

Born : .... in .... ☐ baptized

Daughter of : .... and: ....

Occupation(s) : ....

Deceased : .... in ....

⚭ **CHILDREN** ....

....

....

👪 **ASCENDANCY UP TO XIVth GENERATION**

4336 XIII 4337	2168 XII 2169
8674 XIV 8675	
8676 XIV 8677	4338 XIII 4339
	2170 XII 2171
	4342 XIII 4343
	8686 XIV 8687
	8680 XIV 8681
	4340 XIII 4341

1084 **XI** 1085

8672 XIV 8673

8682 XIV 8683

8678 XIV 8679

8684 XIV 8685

GX 542 Father

Sosa 271

GX 543 Mother

8690 XIV 8691

8696 XIV 8697

8692 XIV 8693

8702 XIV 8703

1086 **XI** 1087

8694 XIV 8695	
8688 XIV 8689	4344 XIII 4345
4346 XIII 4347	2172 XII 2173
	4348 XIII 4349
	8698 XIV 8699
	8700 XIV 8701
	2174 XII 2175
	4350 XIII 4351

Surname : .... First name : .... ♂

▶Generation 9 – paternal ascendant ↓Child page 136   ☐ Implex

Born : ....in ....☐ baptized

Son of : ....and: ....

Occupation(s) : ....

Deceased : ....in...

💍 MARITAL STATUS   ☐ *Civil Marriage* ☐ *Religious Marriage* ☐ *Free Union*

Date : ....in.. ☐ Marriage contract

Witnesses: ....

🎎 ASCENDANCY UP TO XIVth GENERATION

4352 XIII 4353	
2176 XII 2177	
8706 XIV 8707	8708 XIV 8709
4354 XIII 4355	
2178 XII 2179	
4356 XIII 4357	
4358 XIII 4359	8718 XIV 8719	8712 XIV 8713
1088 XI 1089	
8704 XIV 8705	
8714 XIV 8715	
8710 XIV 8711	
GX 544 Father	
8716 XIV 8717	

Sosa 272

GX 545 Mother

8722 XIV 8723	8728 XIV 8729
8724 XIV 8725	8734 XIV 8735
8726 XIV 8727	8720 XIV 8721
4360 XIII 4361	
1090 XI 1091	
4364 XIII 4365	8730 XIV 8731	8732 XIV 8733
4362 XIII 4363	
2180 XII 2181	
2182 XII 2183	
4366 XIII 4367	

Sosa 273

♀ Surname : .... First name : ....

▶Generation IX – paternal ascendant ↓Child page 136 –   □ Implex

Born : ....in...□ baptized

Daughter of : ....and: ....

Occupation(s) : ....

Deceased : ....in.................................

⚭ CHILDREN ....

🖧 ASCENDANCY UP TO XIVth GENERATION

4368 XIII 4369	2184 XII 2185		2186 XII 2187	4372 XIII 4373
8738 XIV 8739	8740 XIV 8741	4370 XIII 4371	4374 XIII 4375	8750 XIV 8751	8744 XIV 8745

1092 XI 1093

8736 XIV 8737

8742 XIV 8743

8746 XIV 8747

8748 XIV 8749

GX 546 Father

Sosa 273

GX 547 Mother

8754 XIV 8755

8756 XIV 8757

8760 XIV 8761

8766 XIV 8767

1094 XI 1095

| 8758 XIV 8759 | 8752 XIV 8753 | 4376 XIII 4377 | 4380 XIII 4381 | 8762 XIV 8763 | 8764 XIV 8765 |

4378 XIII 4379

4382 XIII 4383

2188 XII 2189

2190 XII 2191

273

Sosa
274 Surname : ....First name : .... ♂

▸Generation 9 - paternal ascendant ↓Child page 137 ☐ Implex

Born : ....in..☐ baptized

Son of : ....and: ....

Occupation(s) : ....

Deceased : ....in..

MARITAL STATUS

☐ *Civil Marriage* ☐ *Religious Marriage* ☐ *Free Union*

Date : ....in.. ☐ Marriage contract

Witnesses: ....

ASCENDANCY UP TO XIVth GENERATION

2192 XII 2193

2194 XII 2195

4384 XIII 4385

4388 XIII 4389

8770 XIV 8771

8772 XIV 8773

4386 XIII 4387

4390 XIII 4391

8782 XIV 8783

8776 XIV 8777

1096 XI 1097

8768 XIV 8769

8778 XIV 8779

8774 XIV 8775

8780 XIV 8781

GX 548 Father

Sosa 274

GX 549 Mother

8786 XIV 8787

8792 XIV 8793

8788 XIV 8789

8798 XIV 8799

1098 XI 1099

8790 XIV 8791

8784 XIV 8785

4392 XIII 4393

4396 XIII 4397

8794 XIV 8795

8796 XIV 8797

4394 XIII 4395

4398 XIII 4399

2196 XII 2197

2198 XII 2199

Q Surname : .... First name : ....

▶Generation IX – paternal ascendant ↓Child page 137 –   □ Implex

Born : .... in .... □ baptized

Daughter of : .... and: ....

Occupation(s) : ....

Deceased : .... in ....

⚭ CHILDREN ....

....

....

👪 ASCENDANCY UP TO XIVth GENERATION

4400 XIII 4401	2200 XII 2201	
8802 XIV 8803	8804 XIV 8805	4402 XIII 4403

1100 XI 1101

2202 XII 2203	
4406 XIII 4407	8814 XIV 8815	8808 XIV 8809	4404 XIII 4405

8800 XIV 8801	
8806 XIV 8807	

GX 550 Father

Sosa 275

GX 551 Mother

8810 XIV 8811
8812 XIV 8813

8818 XIV 8819	
8820 XIV 8821	

8824 XIV 8825	
8830 XIV 8831

8822 XIV 8823	8816 XIV 8817	4408 XIII 4409
4410 XIII 4411	2204 XII 2205	

1102 XI 1103

4412 XIII 4413	8826 XIV 8827	8828 XIV 8829
2206 XII 2207	4414 XIII 4415

Surname : .... First name : .... ♂

□ Implex

Born : ....in ....□ baptized

Son of : ....and: ....

Occupation(s) : ....

Deceased : ....in...

⊘ MARITAL STATUS

□ *Civil Marriage*   □ *Religious Marriage*   □ *Free Union*

Date : ....in...

□ Marriage contract

Witnesses: ....

👪 ASCENDANCY UP TO XIVth GENERATION

4416 XIII 4417	2208 XII 2209
8834 XIV 8835	8836 XIV 8837
4418 XIII 4419	
8832 XIV 8833	
8838 XIV 8839	

1104 XI 1105

GX 552 Father

Sosa 276

GX 553 Mother

2210 XII 2211	4420 XIII 4421
4422 XIII 4423	8846 XIV 8847
8840 XIV 8841	
8842 XIV 8843	
8844 XIV 8845	

8850 XIV 8851	
8852 XIV 8853	
8854 XIV 8855	8848 XIV 8849
4424 XIII 4425	
4426 XIII 4427	

1106 XI 1107

8856 XIV 8857	
8862 XIV 8863	
4428 XIII 4429	8858 XIV 8859
8860 XIV 8861	
4430 XIII 4431	

2212 XII 2213

2214 XII 2215

♀ Surname : .... First name : ....

▶Generation IX – paternal ascendant ↓Child page 138 –   □ Implex

Born : ....in.. □ baptized

Daughter of : ....and:...

Occupation(s) : ....

Deceased : ....in..

⚭ **CHILDREN** ....
....
....

👪 ASCENDANCY UP TO XIVth GENERATION

4432 XIII 4433	2216 XII 2217
8866 XIV 8867	8868 XIV 8869	4434 XIII 4435
	1108 XI 1109
8864 XIV 8865	
8870 XIV 8871	GX 554 Father

2218 XII 2219

4438 XIII 4439   8878 XIV 8879   8872 XIV 8873   4436 XIII 4437

8874 XIV 8875

8876 XIV 8877

Sosa 277

GX 555 Mother

x

8882 XIV 8883

8884 XIV 8885

8886 XIV 8887   8880 XIV 8881   4440 XIII 4441

4442 XIII 4443

2220 XII 2221

1110 XI 1111

8888 XIV 8889

8894 XIV 8895

4444 XIII 4445   8890 XIV 8891   8892 XIV 8893

4446 XIII 4447

2222 XII 2223

Sosa
278

Surname : .... First name : .... ♂

▶Generation 9 – paternal ascendant ↓Child page 139   ☐ Implex

Born : ....in...☐ baptized

Son of : ....and:...

Occupation(s) : ....

Deceased : ....in...

💍 MARITAL STATUS   ☐ Civil Marriage ☐ Religious Marriage ☐ Free Union

Date : ....in... ☐ Marriage contract

Witnesses: ....

👪 ASCENDANCY UP TO XIVth GENERATION

2224 XII 2225		2226 XII 2227
4448 XIII 4449		4452 XIII 4453
8898 XIV 8899	8900 XIV 8901	8910 XIV 8911	8904 XIV 8905
4450 XIII 4451		4454 XIII 4455
	1112 XI 1113	
8896 XIV 8897		8906 XIV 8907
8902 XIV 8903		8908 XIV 8909

GX 556 Father

Sosa 278

GX 557 Mother

8914 XIV 8915		8920 XIV 8921
8916 XIV 8917		8926 XIV 8927
8918 XIV 8919	8912 XIV 8913	8922 XIV 8923	8924 XIV 8925
4456 XIII 4457		4460 XIII 4461
4458 XIII 4459		4462 XIII 4463
2228 XII 2229	1114 XI 1115	2230 XII 2231

♀ Surname : ....First name : ....

▶Generation IX – paternal ascendant ↓Child page 139 –   □ Implex

Born : ....in..□ baptized

Daughter of : ....and: ....

Occupation(s) : ....

Deceased : ....in...

⚭ CHILDREN ....
....
....

👪 ASCENDANCY UP TO XIVth GENERATION

4464 XIII 4465	2232 XII 2233	
8930 XIV 8931	8932 XIV 8933	4466 XIII 4467
	1116 XI 1117	
8928 XIV 8929		
8934 XIV 8935	GX 558 Father	8940 XIV 8941

Sosa 279

8946 XIV 8947	GX 559 Mother	8952 XIV 8953
8948 XIV 8949		8958 XIV 8959
	1118 XI 1119	
8950 XIV 8951	8944 XIV 8945	4472 XIII 4473
4474 XIII 4475	2236 XII 2237	

2234 XII 2235

4468 XIII 4469

8942 XIV 8943

8936 XIV 8937

8938 XIV 8939

4470 XIII 4471

4476 XIII 4477

8954 XIV 8955

8956 XIV 8957

4478 XIII 4479

2238 XII 2239

Sosa
280

Surname : .... First name : .... ♂

▶Generation 9 – paternal ascendant ↓Child page 140

☐ Implex

Born : ....in..................................☐ baptized

Son of : ....and: ....

Occupation(s) : ....

Deceased : ....in......................................

⊙ MARITAL STATUS
☐ Civil Marriage ☐ Religious Marriage ☐ Free Union

Date : ....in...☐ Marriage contract

Witnesses: ....

ASCENDANCY UP TO XIVth GENERATION

4480 XIII 4481	2240 XII 2241
8962 XIV 8963	8964 XIV 8965
4482 XIII 4483	2242 XII 2243
4486 XIII 4487	8974 XIV 8975
8968 XIV 8969	4484 XIII 4485

1120 XI 1121

8960 XIV 8961

8966 XIV 8967

8970 XIV 8971

8972 XIV 8973

GX 560 Father

Sosa 280

GX 561 Mother

8978 XIV 8979

8980 XIV 8981

8984 XIV 8985

8990 XIV 8991

8982 XIV 8983

8976 XIV 8977

4488 XIII 4489

4492 XIII 4493

8986 XIV 8987

8988 XIV 8989

4494 XIII 4495

4490 XIII 4491

2244 XII 2245

1122 XI 1123

2246 XII 2247

♀ Surname : ....First name : ....

▶Generation IX – paternal ascendant ↓Child page 140 –   □ Implex

Born : ....in..□ baptized

Daughter of : ....and: ....

Occupation(s) : ....

Deceased : ....in...

◎◎ **CHILDREN** ....
....
....

⚏ **ASCENDANCY UP TO XIVth GENERATION**

4496 XIII 4497	2248 XII 2249
8994 XIV 8995	8996 XIV 8997
4498 XIII 4499	

2250 XII 2251

4500 XIII 4501

4502 XIII 4503

9006 XIV 9007

9000 XIV 9001

1124 XI 1125

8992 XIV 8993

9002 XIV 9003

8998 XIV 8999

○

†

GX 562 Father

9004 XIV 9005

Sosa 281

GX 563 Mother

x

○

†

9010 XIV 9011

9016 XIV 9017

9012 XIV 9013

9022 XIV 9023

9014 XIV 9015

9008 XIV 9009

4504 XIII 4505

1126 XI 1127

4508 XIII 4509

9018 XIV 9019

9020 XIV 9021

4506 XIII 4507

2252 XII 2253

2254 XII 2255

4510 XIII 4511

Sosa
282

Surname : .... First name : .... ♂

▶Generation 9 – paternal ascendant ↓Child page 141

☐ Implex

Born : ....in...☐ baptized

Son of : ....and: ....

Occupation(s) : ....

Deceased : ....in...

⚭ MARITAL STATUS

☐ Civil Marriage ☐ Religious Marriage ☐ Free Union

Date : ....in.. ☐ Marriage contract

Witnesses: ....

👪 ASCENDANCY UP TO XIVth GENERATION

4512 XIII 4513	2256 XII 2257
9026 XIV 9027	9028 XIV 9029
4514 XIII 4515	2258 XII 2259
4516 XIII 4517
4518 XIII 4519	9038 XIV 9039	9032 XIV 9033

1128 XI 1129

9024 XIV 9025

9030 XIV 9031

9036 XIV 9037

9034 XIV 9035

GX 564 Father

Sosa 282

GX 565 Mother

9042 XIV 9043

9048 XIV 9049

9044 XIV 9045

9054 XIV 9055

1130 XI 1131

9046 XIV 9047

9040 XIV 9041

4520 XIII 4521

4524 XIII 4525

9050 XIV 9051

9052 XIV 9053

4522 XIII 4523

2260 XII 2261

2262 XII 2263

4526 XIII 4527

♀ Surname : ....First name : ....

▶Generation IX – paternal ascendant ↓Child page 141 –   □ Implex

Born : ....in...□ baptized

Daughter of : ....and:...

Occupation(s) : ....

Deceased : ....in...

⚭ **CHILDREN** ....

....

....

👪 **ASCENDANCY UP TO XIVth GENERATION**

4528	XIII	4529		2264	XII	2265

| 9058 | XIV | 9059 | | 9060 | XIV | 9061 | | 4530 | XIII | 4531 |

| 2266 | XII | 2267 |
| 4532 | XIII | 4533 |

| 4534 | XIII | 4535 | | 9070 | XIV | 9071 | | 9064 | XIV | 9065 |

| 1132 | XI | 1133 |

| 9056 | XIV | 9057 |

| 9066 | XIV | 9067 |

| 9062 | XIV | 9063 |

GX 566 Father

| 9068 | XIV | 9069 |

Sosa 283

GX 567 Mother

| 9074 | XIV | 9075 |

| 9080 | XIV | 9081 |

| 9076 | XIV | 9077 |

| 9086 | XIV | 9087 |

| 9078 | XIV | 9079 | | 9072 | XIV | 9073 | | 4536 | XIII | 4537 |

| 1134 | XI | 1135 |

| 4540 | XIII | 4541 | | 9082 | XIV | 9083 | | 9084 | XIV | 9085 |

| 4538 | XIII | 4539 |

| 2268 | XII | 2269 |

| 2270 | XII | 2271 |

| 4542 | XIII | 4543 |

Surname : .... First name : .... ♂

▶Generation 9 – paternal ascendant ↓Child page 142

☐ Implex

Born : ....in...☐ baptized

Son of : ....and: ....

Occupation(s) : ....

Deceased : ....in...

💍 **MARITAL STATUS**   ☐ *Civil Marriage*   ☐ *Religious Marriage*   ☐ *Free Union*

Date : ....in... ☐ Marriage contract

Witnesses: ....

👪 **ASCENDANCY UP TO XIVth GENERATION**

4544 XIII 4545	
2272 XII 2273	2274 XII 2275
9090 XIV 9091	9092 XIV 9093	4546 XIII 4547	4550 XIII 4551	9102 XIV 9103	9096 XIV 9097	4548 XIII 4549
1136 XI 1137	
9088 XIV 9089	9098 XIV 9099
9094 XIV 9095	GX 568 Father	9100 XIV 9101

Sosa 284

GX 569 Mother

9106 XIV 9107	9112 XIV 9113
9108 XIV 9109	9118 XIV 9119
9110 XIV 9111	9104 XIV 9105	4552 XIII 4553	1138 XI 1139	4556 XIII 4557	9114 XIV 9115	9116 XIV 9117	4558 XIII 4559
4554 XIII 4555	2276 XII 2277	2278 XII 2279

♀ Surname : ....First name : ....

▶Generation IX – paternal ascendant ↓Child page 142 – □ Implex

Born : ....in...□ baptized

Daughter of : ....and: ....

Occupation(s) : ....

Deceased : ....in...

⚭ CHILDREN ....

....

....

👪 ASCENDANCY UP TO XIVth GENERATION

4560 XIII 4561	2280 XII 2281
9122 XIV 9123	9124 XIV 9125
4562 XIII 4563	
9120 XIV 9121	
9126 XIV 9127	

1140 XI 1141

GX 570 Father

Sosa 285

GX 571 Mother

1142 XI 1143

2282 XII 2283	4564 XIII 4565
4566 XIII 4567	9134 XIV 9135
9128 XIV 9129	
9130 XIV 9131	
9132 XIV 9133	

9138 XIV 9139	
9140 XIV 9141	
9142 XIV 9143	9136 XIV 9137
4568 XIII 4569	
4570 XIII 4571	2284 XII 2285

9144 XIV 9145	
9150 XIV 9151	
4572 XIII 4573	9146 XIV 9147
9148 XIV 9149	
2286 XII 2287	4574 XIII 4575

285

286

Surname : .... First name : .... ♂

▶Generation 9 – paternal ascendant ↓Child page 143 □ Implex

Born : ....in...□ baptized

Son of : ....and: ....

Occupation(s) : ....

Deceased : ....in.................................

⚭ MARITAL STATUS   □ *Civil Marriage* □ *Religious Marriage* □ *Free Union*

Date : ....in... □ Marriage contract

Witnesses: ....

👪 ASCENDANCY UP TO XIVth GENERATION

2288 XII 2289	2290 XII 2291
4576 XIII 4577	4580 XIII 4581
9154 XIV 9155	9156 XIV 9157	4578 XIII 4579	4582 XIII 4583	9166 XIV 9167	9160 XIV 9161
1144 XI 1145	
9152 XIV 9153	9162 XIV 9163
9158 XIV 9159	9164 XIV 9165

GX 572 Father

Sosa 286

GX 573 Mother

9170 XIV 9171	9176 XIV 9177
9172 XIV 9173	9182 XIV 9183
9174 XIV 9175	9168 XIV 9169	4584 XIII 4585	4588 XIII 4589	9178 XIV 9179	9180 XIV 9181
1146 XI 1147	
4586 XIII 4587	4590 XIII 4591
2292 XII 2293	2294 XII 2295

♀ Surname : .... First name : ....

▶Generation IX – paternal ascendant ↓Child page 143 –   □ Implex

Born : .... in .... □ baptized

Daughter of : .... and: ....

Occupation(s) : ....

Deceased : .... in ....

◯◯ CHILDREN ....
....
....

👪 ASCENDANCY UP TO XIVth GENERATION

4592 XIII 4593	2296 XII 2297
9186 XIV 9187	
9188 XIV 9189	4594 XIII 4595
	1148 XI 1149
9184 XIV 9185	
9190 XIV 9191	GX 574 Father

Sosa 287

GX 575 Mother

2298 XII 2299	4596 XIII 4597
	9198 XIV 9199
4598 XIII 4599	9192 XIV 9193
	9194 XIV 9195
9196 XIV 9197	

9202 XIV 9203	9208 XIV 9209
9204 XIV 9205	9214 XIV 9215
9206 XIV 9207	
9200 XIV 9201	4600 XIII 4601
4602 XIII 4603	2300 XII 2301

1150 XI 1151

2302 XII 2303
4604 XIII 4605
9210 XIV 9211
9212 XIV 9213
4606 XIII 4607

Surname : .... First name : .... ♂

☐ Implex

Born : ....in ....☐ baptized

Son of : ....and: ....

Occupation(s) : ....

Deceased : ....in...

⬭ MARITAL STATUS

☐ *Civil Marriage*   ☐ *Religious Marriage*   ☐ *Free Union*

Date : ....in.. ☐ Marriage contract

Witnesses: ....

⚏ ASCENDANCY UP TO XIVth GENERATION

4608 XIII 4609	2304 XII 2305
9218 XIV 9219	9220 XIV 9221
4610 XIII 4611	

2306 XII 2307

4614 XIII 4615

9230 XIV 9231

9224 XIV 9225

4612 XIII 4613

1152 XI 1153

9216 XIV 9217

9226 XIV 9227

9222 XIV 9223

9228 XIV 9229

GX 576 Father

Sosa 288

GX 577 Mother

9234 XIV 9235

9240 XIV 9241

9236 XIV 9237

9246 XIV 9247

9238 XIV 9239

9232 XIV 9233

4616 XIII 4617

4620 XIII 4621

9242 XIV 9243

9244 XIV 9245

4618 XIII 4619

1154 XI 1155

2308 XII 2309

2310 XII 2311

4622 XIII 4623

♀ Surname : ....First name : ....

▶Generation IX – paternal ascendant ↓Child page 144 –   □ Implex

Born : ....in..□ baptized

Daughter of : ....and: ....

Occupation(s) : ....

Deceased : ....in..

⊙ **CHILDREN** ....

....

👪 **ASCENDANCY UP TO XIVth GENERATION**

4624 XIII 4625	2312 XII 2313	2314 XII 2315	4628 XIII 4629

9250 XIV 9251

9252 XIV 9253

4626 XIII 4627

9262 XIV 9263

9256 XIV 9257

4630 XIII 4631

1156 XI 1157

9248 XIV 9249

9254 XIV 9255

9258 XIV 9259

9260 XIV 9261

GX 578 Father

Sosa 289

GX 579 Mother

9266 XIV 9267

9272 XIV 9273

9268 XIV 9269

9278 XIV 9279

9270 XIV 9271

9264 XIV 9265

4632 XIII 4633

1158 XI 1159

4636 XIII 4637

9274 XIV 9275

9276 XIV 9277

4634 XIII 4635

2316 XII 2317

2318 XII 2319

4638 XIII 4639

Sosa
290

Surname : .... First name : .... ♂

▶Generation 9 – paternal ascendant ↓Child page 145 ☐ Implex

Born : .... in .... ☐ baptized

Son of : .... and : ....

Occupation(s) : ....

Deceased : .... in ....

⚭ MARITAL STATUS   ☐ Civil Marriage   ☐ Religious Marriage   ☐ Free Union

Date : .... in .... ☐ Marriage contract

Witnesses: ....

👪 ASCENDANCY UP TO XIVth GENERATION

4640 XIII 4641	
2320 XII 2321	
9282 XIV 9283	
9284 XIV 9285	
4642 XIII 4643	
2322 XII 2323	
4644 XIII 4645	
4646 XIII 4647	
9294 XIV 9295	
9288 XIV 9289	

1160 XI 1161

9280 XIV 9281	
9286 XIV 9287	
9290 XIV 9291	
9292 XIV 9293	

GX 580 Father

Sosa 290

GX 581 Mother

9298 XIV 9299	
9300 XIV 9301	
9304 XIV 9305	
9310 XIV 9311	

4650 XIII 4651	
9302 XIV 9303	
9296 XIV 9297	
4648 XIII 4649	
2324 XII 2325	
2326 XII 2327	
4652 XIII 4653	
9306 XIV 9307	
9308 XIV 9309	
4654 XIII 4655	

1162 XI 1163

♀ Surname : .... First name : ....

▶Generation IX – paternal ascendant ↓Child page 145 –   □ Implex

Born : ....in...□ baptized

Daughter of : ....and:................................

Occupation(s) : ....

Deceased : ....in...

⚭ **CHILDREN** ....
....
....

👪 **ASCENDANCY UP TO XIVth GENERATION**

4656 XIII 4657	
2328 XII 2329	
9314 XIV 9315	9316 XIV 9317
4658 XIII 4659	
2330 XII 2331	
4660 XIII 4661	
4662 XIII 4663	9326 XIV 9327
9320 XIV 9321	
9312 XIV 9313	
1164 XI 1165	
9322 XIV 9323	
9318 XIV 9319	
GX 582 Father	
9324 XIV 9325	

Sosa 291

GX 583 Mother	
9330 XIV 9331	9336 XIV 9337
9332 XIV 9333	
9342 XIV 9343	
9334 XIV 9335	9328 XIV 9329
4664 XIII 4665	
1166 XI 1167	
4668 XIII 4669	9338 XIV 9339
9340 XIV 9341	
4666 XIII 4667	
2332 XII 2333	
2334 XII 2335	
4670 XIII 4671	

Surname : .... First name : .... ♂

▶Generation 9 – paternal ascendant ↓Child page 146   □ Implex

Born : ....in...□ baptized

Son of : ....and: ....

Occupation(s) : ....

Deceased : ....in..

💍 **MARITAL STATUS**   □ *Civil Marriage*   □ *Religious Marriage*   □ *Free Union*

Date : ....in.. □ Marriage contract

Witnesses: ....

👪 ASCENDANCY UP TO XIVth GENERATION

4672 XIII 4673	
2336 XII 2337	
9346 XIV 9347	9348 XIV 9349
4674 XIII 4675	
2338 XII 2339	
9358 XIV 9359	9352 XIV 9353
4676 XIII 4677	

1168   XI   1169

9344 XIV 9345	
9350 XIV 9351	
4678 XIII 4679	
9354 XIV 9355	
9356 XIV 9357	

GX 584 Father

Sosa 292

GX 585 Mother

9362 XIV 9363	
9364 XIV 9365	
9368 XIV 9369	
9374 XIV 9375	

1170   XI   1171

9366 XIV 9367	9360 XIV 9361
4680 XIII 4681	
4682 XIII 4683	
2340 XII 2341	
4684 XIII 4685	
9370 XIV 9371	9372 XIV 9373
2342 XII 2343	
4686 XIII 4687	

♀ Surname : .... First name : ....

▶Generation IX – paternal ascendant ↓Child page 146 –   ☐ Implex

Born : .... in .... ☐ baptized

Daughter of : .... and: ....

Occupation(s) : ....

Deceased : .... in ....

CHILDREN ....

....

ASCENDANCY UP TO XIVth GENERATION

| 4688 XIII 4689 | | 2344 XII 2345 | | | 2346 XII 2347 | | 4692 XIII 4693 |

| 9378 XIV 9379 | 9380 XIV 9381 | 4690 XIII 4691 | | | 4694 XIII 4695 | 9390 XIV 9391 | 9384 XIV 9385 |

† †

1172 XI 1173

| 9376 XIV 9377 | | | | 9386 XIV 9387 |

○

| 9382 XIV 9383 | | GX 586 Father | | 9388 XIV 9389 |

†

Sosa 293

GX 587 Mother

x

| 9394 XIV 9395 | | | 9400 XIV 9401 |

| 9396 XIV 9397 | | ○ | | 9406 XIV 9407 |

†

| 9398 XIV 9399 | 9392 XIV 9393 | 4696 XIII 4697 | | | 4700 XIII 4701 | 9402 XIV 9403 | 9404 XIV 9405 |

1174 XI 1175

| 4698 XIII 4699 | | 2348 XII 2349 | | | 2350 XII 2351 | | 4702 XIII 4703 |

Sosa
294

Surname : .... First name : .... ♂

▶Generation 9 – paternal ascendant   ↓Child page 147   □ Implex

Born : .... in ....□ baptized

Son of : .... and: ....

Occupation(s) : ....

Deceased : .... in ....

⚭ MARITAL STATUS   □ *Civil Marriage*   □ *Religious Marriage*   □ *Free Union*

Date : .... in .... □ Marriage contract

Witnesses: ....

❖ ASCENDANCY UP TO XIVth GENERATION

| 4704 XIII 4705 | | 2352 XII 2353 | | | 2354 XII 2355 | | 4708 XIII 4709 |

| 9410 XIV 9411 | 9412 XIV 9413 | 4706 XIII 4707 | | | 4710 XIII 4711 | 9422 XIV 9423 | 9416 XIV 9417 |

1176 XI 1177

| 9408 XIV 9409 | | | | | | | 9418 XIV 9419 |

| | 9414 XIV 9415 | | GX 588 Father | | 9420 XIV 9421 | |

Sosa 294

GX 589 Mother

| | 9426 XIV 9427 | | | | 9432 XIV 9433 | | 9438 XIV 9439 |

| 9428 XIV 9429 | | | | | | | |

1178 XI 1179

| 4714 XIII 4715 | 9430 XIV 9431 | 9424 XIV 9425 | 4712 XIII 4713 | | 4716 XIII 4717 | 9434 XIV 9435 | 9436 XIV 9437 | 4718 XIII 4719 |

| | | 2356 XII 2357 | | | 2358 XII 2359 | | |

294

♀ Surname : .... First name : ....

Sosa
295

▶Generation IX – paternal ascendant ↓Child page 147 –   □ Implex

Born : .... in .... □ baptized

Daughter of : .... and: ....

Occupation(s) : ....

Deceased : .... in ....

⚭ CHILDREN ....
....
....

👪 ASCENDANCY UP TO XIVth GENERATION

4720 XIII 4721	2360 XII 2361	2362 XII 2363	4724 XIII 4725

9442 XIV 9443 | 9444 XIV 9445 | 4722 XIII 4723 | 1180 XI 1181 | 9454 XIV 9455 | 9448 XIV 9449

9440 XIV 9441

9446 XIV 9447

GX 590 Father

Sosa 295

GX 591 Mother

9452 XIV 9453

9450 XIV 9451

9458 XIV 9459

9460 XIV 9461

9464 XIV 9465

9470 XIV 9471

9462 XIV 9463 | 9456 XIV 9457 | 4728 XIII 4729 | 1182 XI 1183 | 9466 XIV 9467 | 9468 XIV 9469

4730 XIII 4731 | 2364 XII 2365 | 2366 XII 2367 | 4734 XIII 4735

4732 XIII 4733

295

Surname : .... First name : .... ♂

▶Generation 9 – paternal ascendant ↓Child page 148 □ Implex

Born : ....in ....□ baptized

Son of : ....and: ....

Occupation(s) : ....

Deceased : ....in ....

⚭ MARITAL STATUS □ Civil Marriage □ Religious Marriage □ Free Union

Date : ....in .... □ Marriage contract

Witnesses: ....

👪 ASCENDANCY UP TO XIVth GENERATION

4736 XIII 4737	
9474 XIV 9475	9476 XIV 9477
2368 XII 2369	4738 XIII 4739
9472 XIV 9473	
9478 XIV 9479	

1184 XI 1185

GX 592 Father

Sosa 296

GX 593 Mother

1186 XI 1187

2370 XII 2371	4740 XIII 4741
9486 XIV 9487	9480 XIV 9481
4742 XIII 4743	
9482 XIV 9483	
9484 XIV 9485	

9490 XIV 9491	
9492 XIV 9493	
9494 XIV 9495	9488 XIV 9489
4744 XIII 4745	
4746 XIII 4747	
2372 XII 2373	

9496 XIV 9497	
9502 XIV 9503	
4748 XIII 4749	
9498 XIV 9499	9500 XIV 9501
4750 XIII 4751	
2374 XII 2375	

♀ Surname : .... First name : ....

▶Generation IX – paternal ascendant ↓Child page 148 –   □ Implex

Born : ....in ....□ baptized

Daughter of : ....and: ....

Occupation(s) : ....

Deceased : ....in ....

⚭ CHILDREN ....

⚏ ASCENDANCY UP TO XIVth GENERATION

2376 XII 2377	2378 XII 2379
4752 XIII 4753	4756 XIII 4757
9506 XIV 9507	9518 XIV 9519
9508 XIV 9509	9512 XIV 9513
4754 XIII 4755	4758 XIII 4759

1188 XI 1189

GX 594 Father

Sosa 297

GX 595 Mother

9504 XIV 9505

9510 XIV 9511

9514 XIV 9515

9516 XIV 9517

9522 XIV 9523

9528 XIV 9529

9524 XIV 9525

9534 XIV 9535

9526 XIV 9527

9520 XIV 9521

4760 XIII 4761

4764 XIII 4765

9530 XIV 9531

9532 XIV 9533

4762 XIII 4763

4766 XIII 4767

2380 XII 2381

1190 XI 1191

2382 XII 2383

Surname : .... First name : .... ♂

▶Generation 9 – paternal ascendant   ↓Child page 149   □ Implex

Born : ....in..□ baptized

Son of : ....and: ....

Occupation(s) : ....

Deceased : ....in..

⚭ MARITAL STATUS   □ Civil Marriage   □ Religious Marriage   □ Free Union

Date : ....in.. □ Marriage contract

Witnesses: ....

👪 ASCENDANCY UP TO XIVth GENERATION

4768 XIII 4769	2384 XII 2385	
9538 XIV 9539	9540 XIV 9541	4770 XIII 4771
		2386 XII 2387
4774 XIII 4775	9550 XIV 9551	9544 XIV 9545	4772 XIII 4773

1192 **XI** 1193

9536 XIV 9537

9546 XIV 9547

9542 XIV 9543

GX 596 Father

9548 XIV 9549

Sosa 298

GX 597 Mother

9554 XIV 9555

9560 XIV 9561

9556 XIV 9557

9566 XIV 9567

1194 **XI** 1195

9558 XIV 9559

9552 XIV 9553

4776 XIII 4777

4780 XIII 4781

9562 XIV 9563

9564 XIV 9565

4778 XIII 4779

2388 XII 2389

2390 XII 2391

4782 XIII 4783

♀ Surname : .... First name : ....

▶Generation IX – paternal ascendant ↓Child page 149 –   ☐ Implex

Born : .... in ....☐ baptized

Daughter of : ....and: ....

Occupation(s) : ....

Deceased : ....in ....

💍 **CHILDREN** ....
....
....

👪 **ASCENDANCY UP TO XIVth GENERATION**

4784 XIII 4785	2392 XII 2393
9570 XIV 9571	9572 XIV 9573	4786 XIII 4787
	1196 XI 1197
9568 XIV 9569	
	9574 XIV 9575

GX 598 Father

Sosa 299

GX 599 Mother

2394 XII 2395	4788 XIII 4789
9582 XIV 9583	9576 XIV 9577
4790 XIII 4791	
	9578 XIV 9579
9580 XIV 9581	

9586 XIV 9587	
9588 XIV 9589	
9590 XIV 9591	9584 XIV 9585	4792 XIII 4793
4794 XIII 4795	2396 XII 2397

1198 XI 1199	

9592 XIV 9593	
	9598 XIV 9599
9596 XIV 9597	9594 XIV 9595	4796 XIII 4797
	4798 XIII 4799
9596 XIV 9597	2398 XII 2399

Sosa
300

Surname : .... First name : .... ♂

▶Generation 9 – paternal ascendant ↓Child page 150   □ Implex

Born : ....in..................................... □ baptized

Son of : ....and: ....

Occupation(s) : ....

Deceased : ....in...

💍 MARITAL STATUS   □ Civil Marriage □ Religious Marriage □ Free Union

Date : ....in.. □ Marriage contract

Witnesses: ....

👪 ASCENDANCY UP TO XIVth GENERATION

2400 XII 2401		2402 XII 2403
4800 XIII 4801	9602 XIV 9603 / 9604 XIV 9605 / 4802 XIII 4803	1200 XI 1201	4806 XIII 4807 / 9614 XIV 9615 / 9608 XIV 9609	4804 XIII 4805

9600 XIV 9601

9606 XIV 9607

9612 XIV 9613

9610 XIV 9611

GX 600 Father

Sosa 300

GX 601 Mother

9618 XIV 9619

9620 XIV 9621

9624 XIV 9625

9630 XIV 9631

9622 XIV 9623 / 9616 XIV 9617 / 4808 XIII 4809	1202 XI 1203	4812 XIII 4813 / 9626 XIV 9627 / 9628 XIV 9629
4810 XIII 4811	2404 XII 2405	2406 XII 2407	4814 XIII 4815

300

Sosa
301

♀ Surname : ....First name : ....

▶Generation IX – paternal ascendant ↓Child page 150 – □ Implex

Born : ....in.......................................□ baptized

Daughter of : ....and:...................................

Occupation(s) : ....

Deceased : ....in.......................................

⚭ CHILDREN ....
....
....

ASCENDANCY UP TO XIVth GENERATION

| 2408 XII 2409 | 2410 XII 2411 |

4816 XIII 4817
4820 XIII 4821

9634 XIV 9635
9636 XIV 9637
4818 XIII 4819
4822 XIII 4823
9646 XIV 9647
9640 XIV 9641

1204 XI 1205

9632 XIV 9633

9642 XIV 9643

9638 XIV 9639

GX 602 Father

9644 XIV 9645

Sosa 301

GX 603 Mother

9650 XIV 9651
9656 XIV 9657

9652 XIV 9653
9662 XIV 9663

9654 XIV 9655
9648 XIV 9649
4824 XIII 4825
4828 XIII 4829
9658 XIV 9659
9660 XIV 9661

4826 XIII 4827
2412 XII 2413
1206 XI 1207
2414 XII 2415
4830 XIII 4831

301

Surname : .... First name : .... ♂

□ Implex

Born : ....in...□ baptized

Son of : ....and: ....

Occupation(s) : ....

Deceased : ....in...

⚭ **MARITAL STATUS**

□ *Civil Marriage* □ *Religious Marriage* □ *Free Union*

Date : ....in... □ Marriage contract

Witnesses: ....

ASCENDANCY UP TO XIVth GENERATION

4832 XIII 4833	2416 XII 2417
9666 XIV 9667	
9668 XIV 9669	4834 XIII 4835
2418 XII 2419	4836 XIII 4837
4838 XIII 4839	9678 XIV 9679
	9672 XIV 9673

1208 XI 1209

9664 XIV 9665

9674 XIV 9675

9670 XIV 9671

9676 XIV 9677

GX 604 Father

Sosa 302

GX 605 Mother

9682 XIV 9683

9688 XIV 9689

9684 XIV 9685

9694 XIV 9695

1210 XI 1211

9686 XIV 9687	9680 XIV 9681	4840 XIII 4841

4844 XIII 4845	9690 XIV 9691	9692 XIV 9693

4842 XII 4843

2420 XII 2421

2422 XII 2423

4846 XIII 4847

♀ Surname : ....First name : ....

▶Generation IX – paternal ascendant ↓Child page 151 –   □ Implex

Born : ....in.....................................□ baptized

Daughter of : ....and:.................................

Occupation(s) : ....

Deceased : ....in...

⊚ CHILDREN ....

....

....

⚎ ASCENDANCY UP TO XIVth GENERATION

4848 XIII 4849	
2424 XII 2425	
9698 XIV 9699	
9700 XIV 9701	
4850 XIII 4851	
1212 XI 1213	
9696 XIV 9697	
9702 XIV 9703	
2426 XII 2427	
4852 XIII 4853	
9710 XIV 9711	
9704 XIV 9705	
4854 XIII 4855	
9706 XIV 9707	
9708 XIV 9709	

GX 606 Father

Sosa 303

GX 607 Mother

x

9714 XIV 9715	
9716 XIV 9717	
9718 XIV 9719	
9712 XIV 9713	
4856 XIII 4857	
4858 XIII 4859	
2428 XII 2429	
1214 XI 1215	
9720 XIV 9721	
9726 XIV 9727	
9722 XIV 9723	
9724 XIV 9725	
4860 XIII 4861	
4862 XIII 4863	
2430 XII 2431	

Surname : .... First name : .... ♂

▶Generation 9 – paternal ascendant ↓Child page 152

☐ Implex

Born : ....in...☐ baptized

Son of : ....and: ....

Occupation(s) : ....

Deceased : ....in..

💍 **MARITAL STATUS**   ☐ *Civil Marriage*   ☐ *Religious Marriage*   ☐ *Free Union*

Date : ....in.. ☐ Marriage contract

Witnesses: ....

👪 **ASCENDANCY UP TO XIVth GENERATION**

4864 XIII 4865	
2432 XII 2433	
9730 XIV 9731	9732 XIV 9733
4866 XIII 4867	
1216 XI 1217	
9728 XIV 9729	
9734 XIV 9735	
GX 608 Father	

Sosa 304

GX 609 Mother

2434 XII 2435	
4868 XIII 4869	
9742 XIV 9743	9736 XIV 9737
4870 XIII 4871	
9738 XIV 9739	
9740 XIV 9741	
9752 XIV 9753	

9746 XIV 9747	
9748 XIV 9749	
9750 XIV 9751	9744 XIV 9745
4872 XIII 4873	
4874 XIII 4875	
2436 XII 2437	
1218 XI 1219	

9758 XIV 9759	
4876 XIII 4877	
9754 XIV 9755	9756 XIV 9757
4878 XIII 4879	
2438 XII 2439	

♀ Surname : .... First name : ....

▶Generation IX – paternal ascendant ↓Child page 152 –   ☐ Implex

Born : .... in .... ☐ baptized

Daughter of : ....and: ....

Occupation(s) : ....

Deceased : .... in ....

(◯◯) **CHILDREN** ....

....

....

⚶ ASCENDANCY UP TO XIVth GENERATION

2440 XII 2441	2442 XII 2443
4880 XIII 4881	4884 XIII 4885
9762 XIV 9763	9764 XIV 9765	4882 XIII 4883	4886 XIII 4887	9774 XIV 9775	9768 XIV 9769

1220 XI 1221

9760 XIV 9761

9766 XIV 9767

9770 XIV 9771

9772 XIV 9773

GX 610 Father

Sosa 305

GX 611 Mother

9778 XIV 9779

9784 XIV 9785

9780 XIV 9781

9790 XIV 9791

1222 XI 1223

9782 XIV 9783 9776 XIV 9777 4888 XIII 4889

4892 XIII 4893 9786 XIV 9787 9788 XIV 9789

4890 XIII 4891

2444 XII 2445

2446 XII 2447

4894 XIII 4895

Surname : .... First name : .... ♂

☐ Implex

Born : ....in...☐ baptized

Son of : ....and: ....

Occupation(s) : ....

Deceased : ....in..

💍 **MARITAL STATUS**   ☐ *Civil Marriage* ☐ *Religious Marriage* ☐ *Free Union*

Date : ....in...☐ Marriage contract

Witnesses: ....

👪 ASCENDANCY UP TO XIVth GENERATION

4896 XIII 4897	2448 XII 2449
9794 XIV 9795	
9796 XIV 9797	4898 XIII 4899
	2450 XII 2451
	4902 XIII 4903
	9806 XIV 9807
	9800 XIV 9801
	4900 XIII 4901

1224 XI 1225

9792 XIV 9793	9802 XIV 9803
9798 XIV 9799	9804 XIV 9805

GX 612 Father

Sosa 306

GX 613 Mother

9810 XIV 9811	9816 XIV 9817
9812 XIV 9813	9822 XIV 9823

9814 XIV 9815	
9808 XIV 9809	4904 XIII 4905
4906 XIII 4907	2452 XII 2453

1226 XI 1227

4908 XIII 4909	9818 XIV 9819
	9820 XIV 9821
2454 XII 2455	4910 XIII 4911

♀ Surname : ....First name : ....

▶Generation IX – paternal ascendant ↓Child page 153 –　　　　□ Implex

Born : ....in...□ baptized

Daughter of : ....and:...

Occupation(s) : ....

Deceased : ....in...

⚭ **CHILDREN** ....

....

👪 **ASCENDANCY UP TO XIVth GENERATION**

4912 XIII 4913	2456 XII 2457
9826 XIV 9827	9828 XIV 9829
4914 XIII 4915	
9824 XIV 9825	
9830 XIV 9831	

1228　XI　1229

GX　614 Father

Sosa 307

GX　615 Mother

2458 XII 2459	4916 XIII 4917
9838 XIV 9839	9832 XIV 9833
4918 XIII 4919	
9834 XIV 9835	
9836 XIV 9837	

9842 XIV 9843	9848 XIV 9849
9844 XIV 9845	9854 XIV 9855
9846 XIV 9847	9840 XIV 9841
4920 XIII 4921	
4922 XIII 4923	2460 XII 2461

1230　XI　1231

4924 XIII 4925	
9850 XIV 9851	9852 XIV 9853
2462 XII 2463	4926 XIII 4927

Sosa
308

Surname : .... First name : .... ♂

▶Generation 9 – paternal ascendant   ↓Child page 154

☐ Implex

Born : ....in.................................... ☐ baptized

Son of : ....and: ....

Occupation(s) : ....

Deceased : ....in....................................

⚭ MARITAL STATUS   ☐ *Civil Marriage* ☐ *Religious Marriage* ☐ *Free Union*

Date : ....in.................................... ☐ Marriage contract

Witnesses: ....

🏃 ASCENDANCY UP TO XIVth GENERATION

4928 XIII 4929	2464 XII 2465
9858 XIV 9859	2466 XII 2467
9860 XIV 9861	4932 XIII 4933
4930 XIII 4931	4934 XIII 4935
	9870 XIV 9871
	9864 XIV 9865

1232 XI 1233

9856 XIV 9857

9862 XIV 9863

9866 XIV 9867

9868 XIV 9869

GX 616 Father

Sosa 308

GX 617 Mother

9874 XIV 9875

9880 XIV 9881

9876 XIV 9877

9886 XIV 9887

9878 XIV 9879

9872 XIV 9873

4936 XIII 4937

4938 XII 4939

1234 XI 1235

4940 XIII 4941

9882 XIV 9883

9884 XIV 9885

4942 XIII 4943

2468 XII 2469

2470 XII 2471

308

♀ Surname : .... First name : ....

▶Generation IX – paternal ascendant ↓Child page 154 –   □ Implex

Born : .... in .... □ baptized

Daughter of : .... and: ....

Occupation(s) : ....

Deceased : .... in ....

💍 **CHILDREN** ....
....
....

👪 **ASCENDANCY UP TO XIVth GENERATION**

4944 XIII 4945	
9890 XIV 9891	2472 XII 2473
9892 XIV 9893	4946 XIII 4947
9888 XIV 9889	
9894 XIV 9895	

1236 XI 1237

2474 XII 2475

4948 XIII 4949

9902 XIV 9903

9896 XIV 9897

4950 XIII 4951

9898 XIV 9899

9900 XIV 9901

GX 618 Father

Sosa 309

GX 619 Mother

x

9906 XIV 9907

9908 XIV 9909

9912 XIV 9913

9918 XIV 9919

9910 XIV 9911

9904 XIV 9905

4952 XIII 4953

4954 XIII 4955

2476 XII 2477

1238 XI 1239

4956 XIII 4957

9914 XIV 9915

9916 XIV 9917

4958 XIII 4959

2478 XII 2479

Sosa
310

Surname : .... First name : .... ♂

▶Generation 9 – paternal ascendant ↓Child page 155

☐ Implex

Born : .... in .... ☐ baptized

Son of : .... and: ....

Occupation(s) : ....

Deceased : .... in ....

⚭ MARITAL STATUS

☐ Civil Marriage   ☐ Religious Marriage   ☐ Free Union

Date : .... in .... ☐ Marriage contract

Witnesses: ....

👪 ASCENDANCY UP TO XIVth GENERATION

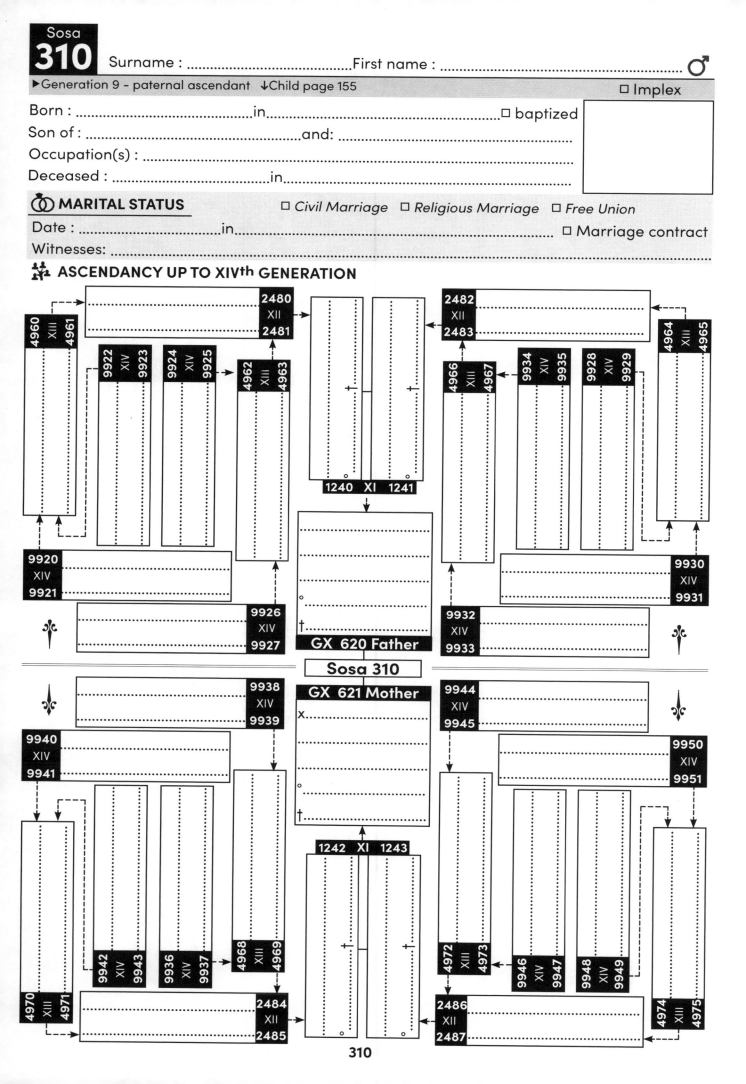

4960 XIII 4961	2480 XII 2481
9922 XIV 9923	9924 XIV 9925
4962 XIII 4963	

2482 XII 2483

4966 XIII 4967

9934 XIV 9935 | 9928 XIV 9929

4964 XIII 4965

9920 XIV 9921

9930 XIV 9931

9926 XIV 9927

1240 XI 1241

GX 620 Father

9932 XIV 9933

Sosa 310

GX 621 Mother

9938 XIV 9939

9944 XIV 9945

9940 XIV 9941

9950 XIV 9951

9942 XIV 9943 | 9936 XIV 9937

4968 XIII 4969

4970 XIII 4971

2484 XII 2485

1242 XI 1243

4972 XIII 4973

9946 XIV 9947 | 9948 XIV 9949

2486 XII 2487

4974 XIII 4975

310

♀ Surname : .... First name : ....

▶Generation IX – paternal ascendant ↓Child page 155 –   □ Implex

Born : ....in................................... □ baptized

Daughter of : ....and: ....

Occupation(s) : ....

Deceased : ....in...................................

⚭ **CHILDREN** ....
....
....

🏃 ASCENDANCY UP TO XIVth GENERATION

2488 XII 2489		2490 XII 2491
4976 XIII 4977		4980 XIII 4981
9954 XIV 9955	9956 XIV 9957	4978 XIII 4979	4982 XIII 4983	9966 XIV 9967	9960 XIV 9961
	1244 XI 1245	
9952 XIV 9953		9962 XIV 9963
9958 XIV 9959	GX 622 Father	9964 XIV 9965

Sosa 311

GX 623 Mother

9970 XIV 9971		9976 XIV 9977
9972 XIV 9973		9982 XIV 9983
	1246 XI 1247	
9974 XIV 9975	9968 XIV 9969	4984 XIII 4985	4988 XIII 4989	9978 XIV 9979	9980 XIV 9981
4986 XIII 4987		4990 XIII 4991
2492 XII 2493		2494 XII 2495

Surname : .... First name : .... ♂

▶Generation 9 – paternal ascendant ↓Child page 156

☐ Implex

Born : .... in .... ☐ baptized

Son of : .... and: ....

Occupation(s) : ....

Deceased : .... in ....

⚭ MARITAL STATUS

☐ *Civil Marriage*   ☐ *Religious Marriage*   ☐ *Free Union*

Date : .... in .... ☐ Marriage contract

Witnesses: ....

👪 ASCENDANCY UP TO XIVth GENERATION

4992 XIII 4993	2496 XII 2497
9986 XIV 9987	9988 XIV 9989
4994 XIII 4995	

1248 XI 1249

9984 XIV 9985

9990 XIV 9991

GX 624 Father

2498 XII 2499

4998 XIII 4999

9998 XIV 9999

9992 XIV 9993

4996 XIII 4997

9994 XIV 9995

9996 XIV 9997

Sosa 312

GX 625 Mother

10002 XIV 10003

10004 XIV 10005

10006 XIV 10007

10000 XIV 10001

5000 XIII 5001

5002 XIII 5003

2500 XII 2501

1250 XI 1251

10008 XIV 10009

10014 XIV 10015

10010 XIV 10011

10012 XIV 10013

5004 XIII 5005

5006 XIII 5007

2502 XII 2503

♀ Surname : .... First name : ....

▶Generation IX – paternal ascendant ↓Child page 156 –   □ Implex

Born : .... in .... □ baptized

Daughter of : .... and: ....

Occupation(s) : ....

Deceased : .... in ....

⚭ **CHILDREN** ....

....

....

👪 **ASCENDANCY UP TO XIVth GENERATION**

2504 XII 2505	2506 XII 2507
5008 XIII 5009	5012 XIII 5013
10018 XIV 10019	10030 XIV 10031
10020 XIV 10021	10024 XIV 10025
5010 XIII 5011	5014 XIII 5015

1252 XI 1253

GX 626 Father

10016 XIV 10017	10026 XIV 10027
10022 XIV 10023	10028 XIV 10029

Sosa 313

GX 627 Mother

10034 XIV 10035	10040 XIV 10041
10036 XIV 10037	10046 XIV 10047

1254 XI 1255

10038 XIV 10039	10042 XIV 10043
10032 XIV 10033	10044 XIV 10045
5016 XIII 5017	5020 XIII 5021
5018 XIII 5019	5022 XIII 5023
2508 XII 2509	2510 XII 2511

Surname : .... First name : .... ♂

□ Implex

Born : ....in..□ baptized

Son of : ....and: ....

Occupation(s) : ....

Deceased : ....in...

⚭ **MARITAL STATUS** □ *Civil Marriage* □ *Religious Marriage* □ *Free Union*

Date : ....in.. □ Marriage contract

Witnesses: ....

ASCENDANCY UP TO XIVth GENERATION

2512 XII 2513	2514 XII 2515
5024 XIII 5025	5028 XIII 5029
10050 XIV 10051	10052 XIV 10053	5026 XIII 5027	5030 XIII 5031	10062 XIV 10063	10056 XIV 10057
	1256 XI 1257	
10048 XIV 10049	10058 XIV 10059
10054 XIV 10055	GX 628 Father	10060 XIV 10061

Sosa 314

GX 629 Mother

10066 XIV 10067	10072 XIV 10073
10068 XIV 10069	10078 XIV 10079
	1258 XI 1259	
10070 XIV 10071	10064 XIV 10065	5032 XIII 5033	5036 XIII 5037	10074 XIV 10075	10076 XIV 10077
5034 XIII 5035	2516 XII 2517	2518 XII 2519	5038 XIII 5039

♀ Surname : .... First name : ....

315

▶Generation IX – paternal ascendant ↓Child page 157 –   ☐ Implex

Born : .... in .... ☐ baptized

Daughter of : .... and: ....

Occupation(s) : ....

Deceased : .... in ....

⚭ CHILDREN ....
....

👪 ASCENDANCY UP TO XIVth GENERATION

5040 XIII 5041	2520 XII 2521
10082 XIV 10083	10084 XIV 10085
5042 XIII 5043	
1260 XI 1261	
10080 XIV 10081	
10086 XIV 10087	
GX 630 Father	
Sosa 315	
GX 631 Mother	
2522 XII 2523	
5044 XIII 5045	
5046 XIII 5047	10094 XIV 10095	10088 XIV 10089
10090 XIV 10091	
10092 XIV 10093	
10098 XIV 10099	10104 XIV 10105
10100 XIV 10101	10110 XIV 10111
10102 XIV 10103	10096 XIV 10097
5048 XIII 5049	
1262 XI 1263	
5050 XIII 5051	2524 XII 2525
5052 XIII 5053	10106 XIV 10107	10108 XIV 10109
2526 XII 2527	5054 XIII 5055

315

Surname : .... First name : .... ♂

□ Implex

Born : ....in....................................... □ baptized

Son of : ....and: ....

Occupation(s) : ....

Deceased : ....in...................................

💍 **MARITAL STATUS**   □ *Civil Marriage*   □ *Religious Marriage*   □ *Free Union*

Date : ....in... □ Marriage contract

Witnesses: ....

👪 **ASCENDANCY UP TO XIVth GENERATION**

5056 XIII 5057	2528 XII 2529
10114 XIV 10115	
10116 XIV 10117	5058 XIII 5059
	1264 XI 1265
10112 XIV 10113	
10118 XIV 10119	

GX 632 Father

Sosa 316

GX 633 Mother

2530 XII 2531	5060 XIII 5061
10126 XIV 10127	10120 XIV 10121
5062 XIII 5063	
	10122 XIV 10123
10124 XIV 10125	

10130 XIV 10131	10136 XIV 10137
10132 XIV 10133	10142 XIV 10143
	1266 XI 1267
10134 XIV 10135	
10128 XIV 10129	5064 XIII 5065
5066 XIII 5067	2532 XII 2533

5068 XIII 5069	5070 XIII 5071
10138 XIV 10139	10140 XIV 10141
2534 XII 2535	

♀ Surname : ....First name : ....

▶Generation IX – paternal ascendant ↓Child page 158 –   □ Implex

Born : ....in...□ baptized

Daughter of : ....and: ....

Occupation(s) : ....

Deceased : ....in...

◎◎ **CHILDREN** ....

....

....

👥 **ASCENDANCY UP TO XIVth GENERATION**

5072 XIII 5073	2536 XII 2537
10146 XIV 10147	10148 XIV 10149
5074 XIII 5075	2538 XII 2539
	5076 XIII 5077

1268 XI 1269

10144 XIV 10145

10150 XIV 10151

GX 634 Father

5078 XIII 5079

10158 XIV 10159

10152 XIV 10153

10154 XIV 10155

10156 XIV 10157

Sosa 317

GX 635 Mother

10162 XIV 10163

10164 XIV 10165

10168 XIV 10169

10174 XIV 10175

1270 XI 1271

5082 XIII 5083

10166 XIV 10167

10160 XIV 10161

5080 XIII 5081

2540 XII 2541

5084 XIII 5085

10170 XIV 10171

10172 XIV 10173

2542 XII 2543

5086 XIII 5087

Surname : .... First name : .... ♂

▶Generation 9 – paternal ascendant ↓Child page 159   □ Implex

Born : ....in...□ baptized

Son of : ....and: ....

Occupation(s) : ....

Deceased : ....in...

💍 MARITAL STATUS   □ *Civil Marriage*   □ *Religious Marriage*   □ *Free Union*

Date : ....in.. □ Marriage contract

Witnesses: ....

👪 ASCENDANCY UP TO XIVth GENERATION

5088 XIII 5089	2544 XII 2545
10178 XIV 10179	2546 XII 2547
10180 XIV 10181	5092 XIII 5093
5090 XIII 5091	5094 XIII 5095
	10190 XIV 10191
	10184 XIV 10185

1272 XI 1273

10176 XIV 10177

10186 XIV 10187

10182 XIV 10183

10188 XIV 10189

GX 636 Father

Sosa 318

GX 637 Mother

10194 XIV 10195

10200 XIV 10201

10196 XIV 10197

10206 XIV 10207

10198 XIV 10199

10192 XIV 10193

5096 XIII 5097

1274 XI 1275

5100 XIII 5101

10202 XIV 10203

10204 XIV 10205

5098 XIII 5099

2548 XII 2549

2550 XII 2551

5102 XIII 5103

♀ Surname : .... First name : ....

▶Generation IX – paternal ascendant ↓Child page 159 –   □ Implex

Born : .... in .... □ baptized

Daughter of : .... and: ....

Occupation(s) : ....

Deceased : .... in ....

💍 CHILDREN ....
....
....

👪 ASCENDANCY UP TO XIVth GENERATION

2552 XII 2553	
5104 XIII 5105	
10210 XIV 10211	10212 XIV 10213
5106 XIII 5107	
2554 XII 2555	
5108 XIII 5109	
5110 XIII 5111	
10222 XIV 10223	10216 XIV 10217

1276 XI 1277

GX 638 Father

Sosa 319

GX 639 Mother

1278 XI 1279

10208 XIV 10209

10214 XIV 10215

10220 XIV 10221

10218 XIV 10219

10226 XIV 10227

10232 XIV 10233

10228 XIV 10229

10238 XIV 10239

10230 XIV 10231

10224 XIV 10225

5112 XIII 5113

10234 XIV 10235

10236 XIV 10237

5116 XIII 5117

5114 XIII 5115

2556 XII 2557

2558 XII 2559

5118 XIII 5119

Surname : .... First name : .... ♂

☐ Implex

Born : ....in...☐ baptized

Son of : ....and: ....

Occupation(s) : ....

Deceased : ....in...

💍 MARITAL STATUS

☐ Civil Marriage ☐ Religious Marriage ☐ Free Union

Date : ....in.. ☐ Marriage contract

Witnesses: ....

👪 ASCENDANCY UP TO XIVth GENERATION

5120 XIII 5121	
2560 XII 2561	2562 XII 2563
10242 XIV 10243	10244 XIV 10245	5122 XIII 5123		5126 XIII 5127	10254 XIV 10255	10248 XIV 10249	5124 XIII 5125
1280 XI 1281	
10240 XIV 10241	
10246 XIV 10247	10250 XIV 10251
GX 640 Father	10252 XIV 10253

Sosa 320

GX 641 Mother	10258 XIV 10259	10264 XIV 10265
10260 XIV 10261	10270 XIV 10271
1282 XI 1283	
10262 XIV 10263	10256 XIV 10257	5128 XIII 5129		5132 XIII 5133	10266 XIV 10267	10268 XIV 10269	5134 XIII 5135
5130 XIII 5131	2564 XII 2565	2566 XII 2567

♀ Surname : ....First name : ....

▶Generation IX – paternal ascendant ↓Child page 160 –
☐ Implex

Born : ....in ....☐ baptized

Daughter of : ....and: ....

Occupation(s) : ....

Deceased : ....in ....

⚭ **CHILDREN** ....

....

👪 ASCENDANCY UP TO XIVth GENERATION

5136 XIII 5137	2568 XII 2569
10274 XIV 10275	
10276 XIV 10277	5138 XIII 5139
10272 XIV 10273	
10278 XIV 10279	

1284 XI 1285

GX 642 Father

Sosa 321

GX 643 Mother

2570 XII 2571

5142 XIII 5143

10286 XIV 10287

10280 XIV 10281

5140 XIII 5141

10282 XIV 10283

10284 XIV 10285

10290 XIV 10291

10292 XIV 10293

10294 XIV 10295

10288 XIV 10289

5144 XIII 5145

5146 XIII 5147

2572 XII 2573

1286 XI 1287

10296 XIV 10297

10302 XIV 10303

5148 XIII 5149

10298 XIV 10299

10300 XIV 10301

5150 XIII 5151

2574 XII 2575

Sosa
322

Surname : .... First name : .... ♂

► Generation 9 – paternal ascendant   ↓Child page 161   ☐ Implex

Born : ....in..☐ baptized

Son of : ....and: ....

Occupation(s) : ....

Deceased : ....in...

⚭ MARITAL STATUS   ☐ Civil Marriage   ☐ Religious Marriage   ☐ Free Union

Date : ....in.. ☐ Marriage contract

Witnesses: ....

👪 ASCENDANCY UP TO XIVth GENERATION

5152 XIII 5153	2576 XII 2577	1288 XI 1289
10306 XIV 10307	10308 XIV 10309	5154 XIII 5155
10304 XIV 10305		
10310 XIV 10311	GX 644 Father	

Sosa 322

GX 645 Mother

| 2578 XII 2579 | 5156 XIII 5157 |
| 5158 XIII 5159 | 10318 XIV 10319 | 10312 XIV 10313 |
| 10314 XIV 10315 |
| 10316 XIV 10317 |

10322 XIV 10323	10328 XIV 10329
10324 XIV 10325	10334 XIV 10335
10326 XIV 10327	10320 XIV 10321	5160 XIII 5161
5162 XIII 5163	2580 XII 2581	1290 XI 1291
5164 XIII 5165	10330 XIV 10331	10332 XIV 10333
5166 XIII 5167
2582 XII 2583

322

♀ Surname : .... First name : ....

▶Generation IX – paternal ascendant ↓Child page 161 – □ Implex

Born : .... in .... □ baptized

Daughter of : .... and: ....

Occupation(s) : ....

Deceased : .... in ....

⚭ CHILDREN ....
....
....

⚏ ASCENDANCY UP TO XIVth GENERATION

5168 XIII **5169**	**2584** XII **2585**
10338 XIV **10339**	**10340** XIV **10341**
	5170 XIII **5171**
10336 XIV **10337**	
	10342 XIV **10343**

2586 XII **2587**

5174 XIII **5175**	**5172** XIII **5173**
10350 XIV **10351**	**10344** XIV **10345**
10346 XIV **10347**	
10348 XIV **10349**	

1292 XI 1293

GX 646 Father

Sosa 323

GX 647 Mother

10354 XIV **10355**	**10360** XIV **10361**
10356 XIV **10357**	**10366** XIV **10367**

10358 XIV **10359**	**10362** XIV **10363**
10352 XIV **10353**	**10364** XIV **10365**
5176 XIII **5177**	**5180** XIII **5181**
5178 XIII **5179**	**5182** XIII **5183**
2588 XII **2589**	**2590** XII **2591**

1294 XI 1295

Surname : .... First name : .... ♂

□ Implex

Born : ....in..□ baptized

Son of : ....and: ....

Occupation(s) : ....

Deceased : ....in...

⊙⊙ MARITAL STATUS   □ Civil Marriage   □ Religious Marriage   □ Free Union

Date : ....in... □ Marriage contract

Witnesses: ....

👪 ASCENDANCY UP TO XIVth GENERATION

2592 XII 2593	5184 XIII 5185
10370 XIV 10371	10372 XIV 10373
5186 XIII 5187	
10368 XIV 10369	
10374 XIV 10375	

1296 **XI** 1297

GX 648 Father

Sosa 324

GX 649 Mother

2594 XII 2595

5188 XIII 5189

10382 XIV 10383

10376 XIV 10377

5190 XIII 5191

10378 XIV 10379

10380 XIV 10381

10386 XIV 10387

10388 XIV 10389

10392 XIV 10393

10398 XIV 10399

10390 XIV 10391

10384 XIV 10385

5192 XIII 5193

5194 XIII 5195

2596 XII 2597

1298 **XI** 1299

5196 XIII 5197

10394 XIV 10395

10396 XIV 10397

5198 XIII 5199

2598 XII 2599

♀ Surname : .... First name : ....

▶Generation IX – paternal ascendant ↓Child page 162 –　　　　　□ Implex

Born : .... in .... □ baptized

Daughter of : .... and: ....

Occupation(s) : ....

Deceased : .... in ....

⊘⊘ CHILDREN ....

....

....

👪 ASCENDANCY UP TO XIVth GENERATION

2600 / XII / 2601	
5200 / XIII / 5201	
10402 / XIV / 10403	
10404 / XIV / 10405	
5202 / XIII / 5203	
1300 XI 1301	
2602 / XII / 2603	
5204 / XIII / 5205	
5206 / XIII / 5207	
10414 / XIV / 10415	
10408 / XIV / 10409	
10400 / XIV / 10401	
10406 / XIV / 10407	
10410 / XIV / 10411	
10412 / XIV / 10413	

GX 650 Father

Sosa 325

GX 651 Mother

10418 / XIV / 10419	
10420 / XIV / 10421	
10422 / XIV / 10423	
10416 / XIV / 10417	
5208 / XIII / 5209	
1302 XI 1303	
10424 / XIV / 10425	
10430 / XIV / 10431	
5212 / XIII / 5213	
10426 / XIV / 10427	
10428 / XIV / 10429	
5210 / XIII / 5211	
2604 / XII / 2605	
2606 / XII / 2607	
5214 / XIII / 5215	

Surname : .... First name : .... ♂

▶Generation 9 – paternal ascendant   ↓Child page 163

□ Implex

Born : ....in ....□ baptized

Son of : ....and: ....

Occupation(s) : ....

Deceased : ....in..

⚭ MARITAL STATUS

□ *Civil Marriage*   □ *Religious Marriage*   □ *Free Union*

Date : ....in.. □ Marriage contract

Witnesses: ....

👪 ASCENDANCY UP TO XIVth GENERATION

5216 XIII 5217	
2608 XII 2609	
10434 XIV 10435	10436 XIV 10437
5218 XIII 5219	
10432 XIV 10433	
10438 XIV 10439	

1304 XI 1305

GX 652 Father

2610 XII 2611	5220 XIII 5221
5222 XIII 5223	
10446 XIV 10447	10440 XIV 10441
10442 XIV 10443	
10444 XIV 10445	

Sosa 326

GX 653 Mother

10450 XIV 10451	
10452 XIV 10453	
10454 XIV 10455	10448 XIV 10449
5224 XIII 5225	
5226 XIII 5227	
2612 XII 2613	

1306 XI 1307

10456 XIV 10457	
10462 XIV 10463	
5228 XIII 5229	10458 XIV 10459
10460 XIV 10461	
5230 XIII 5231	
2614 XII 2615	

♀ Surname : .... First name : ....

▶Generation IX – paternal ascendant ↓Child page 163 –   □ Implex

Born : .... in .... □ baptized

Daughter of : .... and: ....

Occupation(s) : ....

Deceased : .... in ....

⚭ CHILDREN ....

....

....

👪 ASCENDANCY UP TO XIVth GENERATION

5232 XIII 5233	
2616 XII 2617	2618 XII 2619
10466 XIV 10467	5236 XIII 5237
10468 XIV 10469	5238 XIII 5239
5234 XIII 5235	10478 XIV 10479
	10472 XIV 10473

1308　XI　1309

10464 XIV 10465

10470 XIV 10471

10474 XIV 10475

10476 XIV 10477

GX 654 Father

Sosa 327

GX 655 Mother

x

°

†

10482 XIV 10483	10488 XIV 10489
10484 XIV 10485	10494 XIV 10495
10486 XIV 10487	10490 XIV 10491
10480 XIV 10481	10492 XIV 10493
5240 XIII 5241	5244 XIII 5245
5242 XIII 5243	5246 XIII 5247

1310　XI　1311

2620 XII 2621

2622 XII 2623

Sosa
328

Surname : .... First name : .... ♂

▶Generation 9 – paternal ascendant   ↓Child page 164   □ Implex

Born : ....in ....□ baptized

Son of : ....and: ....

Occupation(s) : ....

Deceased : ....in ....

⚭ MARITAL STATUS   □ Civil Marriage   □ Religious Marriage   □ Free Union

Date : ....in..   □ Marriage contract

Witnesses: ....

👪 ASCENDANCY UP TO XIVth GENERATION

5248 XIII 5249	
2624 XII 2625	
10498 XIV 10499	10500 XIV 10501
5250 XIII 5251	
1312 XI 1313	
10496 XIV 10497	
10502 XIV 10503	

2626 XII 2627	5252 XIII 5253
5254 XIII 5255	
10510 XIV 10511	10504 XIV 10505
10506 XIV 10507	
10508 XIV 10509	

GX 656 Father

Sosa 328

GX 657 Mother

10514 XIV 10515	
10516 XIV 10517	
10518 XIV 10519	10512 XIV 10513
5256 XIII 5257	
5258 XIII 5259	
2628 XII 2629	
1314 XI 1315	

10520 XIV 10521	
10526 XIV 10527	
5260 XIII 5261	
10522 XIV 10523	10524 XIV 10525
2630 XII 2631	5262 XIII 5263

328

♀ Surname : ....First name : ....

▶Generation IX – paternal ascendant ↓Child page 164 –   □ Implex

Born : ....in...□ baptized

Daughter of : ....and: ....

Occupation(s) : ....

Deceased : ....in.............................

⚭ CHILDREN ....
....
....

⚶ ASCENDANCY UP TO XIVth GENERATION

2632 XII 2633	
5264 XIII 5265	
10530 XIV 10531	
10532 XIV 10533	
5266 XIII 5267	
2634 XII 2635	
5268 XIII 5269	
5270 XIII 5271	
10542 XIV 10543	
10536 XIV 10537	

1316 XI 1317

10528 XIV 10529

10534 XIV 10535

GX 658 Father

Sosa 329

GX 659 Mother

10538 XIV 10539

10540 XIV 10541

10546 XIV 10547

10548 XIV 10549

10552 XIV 10553

10558 XIV 10559

1318 XI 1319

| 10550 XIV 10551 | 10544 XIV 10545 | 5272 XIII 5273 | | 5276 XIII 5277 | 10554 XIV 10555 | 10556 XIV 10557 | 5278 XIII 5279 |

5274 XIII 5275

2636 XII 2637

2638 XII 2639

329

330

Surname : .... First name : .... ♂

☐ Implex

Born : .... in .... ☐ baptized

Son of : .... and: ....

Occupation(s) : ....

Deceased : .... in ....

⊘ MARITAL STATUS

☐ Civil Marriage   ☐ Religious Marriage   ☐ Free Union

Date : .... in .... ☐ Marriage contract

Witnesses: ....

🏃 ASCENDANCY UP TO XIVth GENERATION

5280 XIII 5281	
10562 XIV 10563	10564 XIV 10565
5282 XIII 5283	
2640 XII 2641	
2642 XII 2643	
5286 XIII 5287	
10574 XIV 10575	10568 XIV 10569
5284 XIII 5285	

1320 XI 1321

| 10560 XIV 10561 | |
| 10566 XIV 10567 | |

GX 660 Father

| 10570 XIV 10571 | |
| 10572 XIV 10573 | |

Sosa 330

GX 661 Mother

10578 XIV 10579	
10580 XIV 10581	
10582 XIV 10583	10576 XIV 10577
5288 XIII 5289	

10584 XIV 10585	
10590 XIV 10591	
5292 XIII 5293	
10586 XIV 10587	10588 XIV 10589

1322 XI 1323

5290 XIII 5291	
2644 XII 2645	
2646 XII 2647	
5294 XIII 5295	

♀ Surname : .... First name : ....

►Generation IX – paternal ascendant ↓Child page 165 – □ Implex

Born : .... in .... □ baptized

Daughter of : .... and: ....

Occupation(s) : ....

Deceased : .... in ....

◎ CHILDREN ....
....
....

🏃 ASCENDANCY UP TO XIVth GENERATION

5296 XIII 5297	2648 XII 2649	2650 XII 2651	5300 XIII 5301

10594 XIV 10595 · 10596 XIV 10597 · 5298 XIII 5299 · 5302 XIII 5303 · 10606 XIV 10607 · 10600 XIV 10601

1324 **XI** 1325

10592 XIV 10593

10598 XIV 10599

10602 XIV 10603

10604 XIV 10605

GX 662 Father

Sosa 331

GX 663 Mother

10610 XIV 10611

10616 XIV 10617

10612 XIV 10613

10622 XIV 10623

10614 XIV 10615 · 10608 XIV 10609 · 5304 XIII 5305 · 5308 XIII 5309 · 10618 XIV 10619 · 10620 XIV 10621

1326 **XI** 1327

5306 XIII 5307

2652 XII 2653

2654 XII 2655

5310 XIII 5311

Surname : .... First name : .... ♂

□ Implex

Born : ....in...□ baptized

Son of : ....and: ....

Occupation(s) : ....

Deceased : ....in.............................

⊚ MARITAL STATUS
□ *Civil Marriage* □ *Religious Marriage* □ *Free Union*

Date : ....in.. □ Marriage contract

Witnesses: ....

👪 ASCENDANCY UP TO XIVth GENERATION

5312 XIII 5313	2656 XII 2657
10626 XIV 10627	
10628 XIV 10629	5314 XIII 5315
10624 XIV 10625	
10630 XIV 10631	

1328 XI 1329

GX 664 Father

2658 XII 2659	5316 XIII 5317
10638 XIV 10639	
10632 XIV 10633	
5318 XIII 5319	10634 XIV 10635
10636 XIV 10637	

Sosa 332

GX 665 Mother

10642 XIV 10643	
10644 XIV 10645	
10646 XIV 10647	
10640 XIV 10641	5320 XIII 5321
5322 XIII 5323	2660 XII 2661

1330 XI 1331

10648 XIV 10649	
10654 XIV 10655	
5324 XIII 5325	
10650 XIV 10651	
10652 XIV 10653	5326 XIII 5327
2662 XII 2663	

♀ Surname : .... First name : ....

Sosa
333

▶Generation IX – paternal ascendant ↓Child page 166 – ☐ Implex

Born : .... in .... ☐ baptized

Daughter of : .... and: ....

Occupation(s) : ....

Deceased : .... in ....

⚭ CHILDREN ....

👪 ASCENDANCY UP TO XIVth GENERATION

5328 XIII 5329	2664 XII 2665
10658 XIV 10659	
10660 XIV 10661	5330 XIII 5331
10656 XIV 10657	
10662 XIV 10663	

1332 XI 1333

GX 666 Father

Sosa 333

GX 667 Mother

2666 XII 2667	5332 XIII 5333
5334 XIII 5335	10670 XIV 10671
	10664 XIV 10665
10666 XIV 10667	
10668 XIV 10669	

10674 XIV 10675	
10676 XIV 10677	
10678 XIV 10679	5336 XIII 5337
10672 XIV 10673	
5338 XIII 5339	2668 XII 2669

1334 XI 1335

10680 XIV 10681	
10686 XIV 10687	
5340 XIII 5341	10682 XIV 10683
	10684 XIV 10685
2670 XII 2671	5342 XIII 5343

333

Sosa
334

Surname : .... First name : .... ♂

▶Generation 9 – paternal ascendant   ↓Child page 167   □ Implex

Born : ....in ....□ baptized

Son of : ....and: ....

Occupation(s) : ....

Deceased : ....in....................................

💍 MARITAL STATUS   □ *Civil Marriage*   □ *Religious Marriage*   □ *Free Union*

Date : ....in.................................... □ Marriage contract

Witnesses: ....

👪 ASCENDANCY UP TO XIVth GENERATION

| 5344 XIII 5345 | | 2672 XII 2673 | | | | 2674 XII 2675 | | 5348 XIII 5349 |

| 10690 XIV 10691 | 10692 XIV 10693 | 5346 XIII 5347 | | | 5350 XIII 5351 | 10702 XIV 10703 | 10696 XIV 10697 | |

1336 XI 1337

| 10688 XIV 10689 | | | 10698 XIV 10699 |

| 10694 XIV 10695 | | 10700 XIV 10701 |

GX 668 Father

Sosa 334

GX 669 Mother

| 10706 XIV 10707 | | 10712 XIV 10713 |

| 10708 XIV 10709 | | 10718 XIV 10719 |

1338 XI 1339

| 5354 XIII 5355 | 10710 XIV 10711 | 10704 XIV 10705 | 5352 XIII 5353 | | 5356 XIII 5357 | 10714 XIV 10715 | 10716 XIV 10717 | 5358 XIII 5359 |

| 2676 XII 2677 | | | 2678 XII 2679 |

334

♀ Surname : ....First name : ....

▶Generation IX – paternal ascendant ↓Child page 167 –   □ Implex

Born : ....in...□ baptized

Daughter of : ....and: ....

Occupation(s) : ....

Deceased : ....in...

💍 CHILDREN ....
....
....

👪 ASCENDANCY UP TO XIVth GENERATION

2680 XII 2681		2682 XII 2683
5360 XIII 5361		5364 XIII 5365
10722 XIV 10723	10724 XIV 10725	5362 XIII 5363	5366 XIII 5367	10734 XIV 10735	10728 XIV 10729
		1340 XI 1341	
10720 XIV 10721		10730 XIV 10731
10726 XIV 10727	GX 670 Father	10732 XIV 10733

Sosa 335

GX 671 Mother

10738 XIV 10739		10744 XIV 10745
10740 XIV 10741		10750 XIV 10751
10742 XIV 10743	10736 XIV 10737	5368 XIII 5369	5372 XIII 5373	10746 XIV 10747	10748 XIV 10749
5370 XIII 5371	2684 XII 2685	1342 XI 1343	2686 XII 2687	5374 XIII 5375

Sosa
336

Surname : .... First name : .... ♂

▶Generation 9 – paternal ascendant ↓Child page 168

☐ Implex

Born : ....in .... ☐ baptized

Son of : ....and: ....

Occupation(s) : ....

Deceased : ....in...

💍 MARITAL STATUS

☐ *Civil Marriage* ☐ *Religious Marriage* ☐ *Free Union*

Date : ....in... ☐ Marriage contract

Witnesses: ....

👥 ASCENDANCY UP TO XIVth GENERATION

5376 XIII 5377	2688 XII 2689
10754 XIV 10755	
10756 XIV 10757	5378 XIII 5379
10752 XIV 10753	
10758 XIV 10759	

2690 XII 2691

5382 XIII 5383

10766 XIV 10767

10760 XIV 10761

5380 XIII 5381

10762 XIV 10763

10764 XIV 10765

1344 XI 1345

GX 672 Father

Sosa 336

GX 673 Mother

10770 XIV 10771

10772 XIV 10773

10774 XIV 10775

10768 XIV 10769

5384 XIII 5385

5386 XIII 5387

2692 XII 2693

1346 XI 1347

10776 XIV 10777

10782 XIV 10783

10778 XIV 10779

10780 XIV 10781

5388 XIII 5389

2694 XII 2695

5390 XIII 5391

336

♀ Surname : ....First name : ....

▶Generation IX – paternal ascendant ↓Child page 168 –   ☐ Implex

Born : ....in...☐ baptized

Daughter of : ....and:..

Occupation(s) : ....

Deceased : ....in...

⚭ CHILDREN ....

....

....

👪 ASCENDANCY UP TO XIVth GENERATION

2696 XII 2697	2698 XII 2699
5392 XIII 5393	5396 XIII 5397
10786 XIV 10787	10798 XIV 10799
10788 XIV 10789	10792 XIV 10793
5394 XIII 5395	5398 XIII 5399

1348 XI 1349

10784 XIV 10785

10790 XIV 10791

10794 XIV 10795

10796 XIV 10797

GX 674 Father

Sosa 337

GX 675 Mother

10802 XIV 10803

10808 XIV 10809

10804 XIV 10805

10814 XIV 10815

10806 XIV 10807

10800 XIV 10801

5400 XIII 5401

1350 XI 1351

5404 XIII 5405

10810 XIV 10811

10812 XIV 10813

5402 XIII 5403

2700 XII 2701

2702 XII 2703

5406 XIII 5407

Surname : .... First name : .... ♂

▶Generation 9 – paternal ascendant ↓Child page 169

□ Implex

Born : ....in...□ baptized

Son of : ....and: ....

Occupation(s) : ....

Deceased : ....in.............................

🔗 **MARITAL STATUS**   □ *Civil Marriage* □ *Religious Marriage* □ *Free Union*

Date : ....in.. □ Marriage contract

Witnesses: ....

ASCENDANCY UP TO XIVth GENERATION

5408 XIII 5409	2704 XII 2705
10818 XIV 10819	10820 XIV 10821
5410 XIII 5411	
	1352 XI 1353
10816 XIV 10817	
10822 XIV 10823	GX 676 Father

2706 XII 2707	5412 XIII 5413
5414 XIII 5415	10830 XIV 10831
10824 XIV 10825	
	10826 XIV 10827
10828 XIV 10829	

Sosa 338

GX 676 Father

GX 677 Mother

10834 XIV 10835	10840 XIV 10841
10836 XIV 10837	10846 XIV 10847
	1354 XI 1355
10838 XIV 10839	10832 XIV 10833
5416 XIII 5417	
5418 XIII 5419	2708 XII 2709

5420 XIII 5421	
10842 XIV 10843	10844 XIV 10845
2710 XII 2711	5422 XIII 5423

♀ Surname : .... First name : ....

▶Generation IX – paternal ascendant ↓Child page 169 –   □ Implex

Born : ....in ....□ baptized

Daughter of : ....and: ....

Occupation(s) : ....

Deceased : ....in ....

⚭ **CHILDREN** ....

....

....

👪 **ASCENDANCY UP TO XIVth GENERATION**

5424 XIII 5425	2712 XII 2713
10850 XIV 10851	10852 XIV 10853	5426 XIII 5427
1356 XI 1357
10848 XIV 10849
10854 XIV 10855
GX 678 Father
Sosa 339
GX 679 Mother

2714 XII 2715	5428 XIII 5429
10862 XIV 10863	10856 XIV 10857	5430 XIII 5431
10858 XIV 10859
10860 XIV 10861

10866 XIV 10867
10868 XIV 10869
10870 XIV 10871	10864 XIV 10865	5432 XIII 5433
5434 XIII 5435	2716 XII 2717
1358 XI 1359

10872 XIV 10873
10878 XIV 10879
5436 XIII 5437	10874 XIV 10875	10876 XIV 10877
2718 XII 2719	5438 XIII 5439

Sosa
340

Surname : .... First name : .... ♂

□ Implex

Born : ....in...□ baptized

Son of : ....and: ....

Occupation(s) : ....

Deceased : ....in..

💍 MARITAL STATUS   □ Civil Marriage   □ Religious Marriage   □ Free Union

Date : ....in.. □ Marriage contract

Witnesses: ....

👪 ASCENDANCY UP TO XIVth GENERATION

5440 XIII **5441**	**2720** XII **2721**
10882 XIV **10883**	
10884 XIV **10885**	**5442** XIII **5443**
	1360 XI 1361
10880 XIV **10881**	
10886 XIV **10887**	**GX 680 Father**

2722 XII **2723**

5446 XIII **5447**

10894 XIV **10895**

10888 XIV **10889**

5444 XIII **5445**

10890 XIV **10891**

10892 XIV **10893**

Sosa 340

GX 681 Mother

10898 XIV **10899**

10900 XIV **10901**

10902 XIV **10903**

10896 XIV **10897**

5448 XIII **5449**

5450 XIII **5451**

2724 XII **2725**

1362 XI 1363

10904 XIV **10905**

10910 XIV **10911**

5452 XIII **5453**

10906 XIV **10907**

10908 XIV **10909**

5454 XIII **5455**

2726 XII **2727**

340

♀ Surname : .... First name : ....

▶Generation IX – paternal ascendant ↓Child page 170 – □ Implex

Born : ....in..□ baptized

Daughter of : ....and: ....

Occupation(s) : ....

Deceased : ....in...........................

👥 CHILDREN ....
....
....

👪 ASCENDANCY UP TO XIVth GENERATION

5456 XIII 5457	2728 XII 2729
10914 XIV 10915	2730 XII 2731
10916 XIV 10917	5458 XIII 5459
	5460 XIII 5461
	5462 XIII 5463
10926 XIV 10927	10920 XIV 10921

1364 XI 1365

10912 XIV 10913

10918 XIV 10919

10922 XIV 10923

10924 XIV 10925

GX 682 Father

Sosa 341

GX 683 Mother

10930 XIV 10931

10932 XIV 10933

10936 XIV 10937

10942 XIV 10943

1366 XI 1367

10934 XIV 10935

10928 XIV 10929

5464 XIII 5465

5468 XIII 5469

10938 XIV 10939

10940 XIV 10941

5466 XIII 5467

2732 XII 2733

2734 XII 2735

5470 XIII 5471

Sosa
342

Surname : .... First name : .... ♂

▶Generation 9 – paternal ascendant ↓Child page 171 □ Implex

Born : ....in................................ □ baptized

Son of : ....and:....................................

Occupation(s) : ....

Deceased : ....in...

⚭ MARITAL STATUS

□ Civil Marriage   □ Religious Marriage   □ Free Union

Date : ....in.. □ Marriage contract

Witnesses: ....

👪 ASCENDANCY UP TO XIVth GENERATION

5472 XIII **5473**	**2736** XII **2737**
10946 XIV **10947**	
10948 XIV **10949**	**5474** XIII **5475**
2738 XII **2739**	**5476** XIII **5477**
5478 XIII **5479**	**10958** XIV **10959**
10952 XIV **10953**	

1368 XI 1369

10944 XIV **10945**

10954 XIV **10955**

10950 XIV **10951**

10956 XIV **10957**

GX 684 Father

Sosa 342

GX 685 Mother

10962 XIV **10963**

10968 XIV **10969**

10964 XIV **10965**

10974 XIV **10975**

10966 XIV **10967**	**5480** XIII **5481**
10960 XIV **10961**	
5482 XIII **5483**	

1370 XI 1371

5484 XIII **5485**

10970 XIV **10971**

10972 XIV **10973**

5486 XIII **5487**

2740 XII **2741**

2742 XII **2743**

342

♀ Surname : .... First name : ....

□ Implex

Born : .... in .... □ baptized

Daughter of : .... and: ....

Occupation(s) : ....

Deceased : .... in ....

⊚ CHILDREN ....

....

....

👪 ASCENDANCY UP TO XIVth GENERATION

2744 XII 2745		2746 XII 2747
5488 XIII 5489		5492 XIII 5493
10978 XIV 10979	10980 XIV 10981	5490 XIII 5491	5494 XIII 5495	10990 XIV 10991	10984 XIV 10985

1372　XI　1373

| 10976 XIV 10977 | | 10986 XIV 10987 |
| 10982 XIV 10983 | 10988 XIV 10989 |

GX 686 Father

Sosa 343

GX 687 Mother

| 10994 XIV 10995 | | 11000 XIV 11001 |
| 10996 XIV 10997 | | 11006 XIV 11007 |

x

1374　XI　1375

10998 XIV 10999	10992 XIV 10993	5496 XIII 5497	5500 XIII 5501	11002 XIV 11003	11004 XIV 11005
5498 XIII 5499		5502 XIII 5503
2748 XII 2749		2750 XII 2751

Sosa
344

Surname : .... First name : .... ♂

▶Generation 9 – paternal ascendant ↓Child page 172   ☐ Implex

Born : ....in...................................☐ baptized

Son of : ....and: ....

Occupation(s) : ....

Deceased : ....in...........................

💍 MARITAL STATUS   ☐ Civil Marriage ☐ Religious Marriage ☐ Free Union

Date : ....in.. ☐ Marriage contract

Witnesses: ....

👪 ASCENDANCY UP TO XIVth GENERATION

5504 XIII 5505	2752 XII 2753	2754 XII 2755	5508 XIII 5509

11010 XIV 11011   11012 XIV 11013   5506 XIII 5507

5510 XIII 5511   11022 XIV 11023   11016 XIV 11017

1376 XI 1377

11008 XIV 11009

11014 XIV 11015

11018 XIV 11019

11020 XIV 11021

GX 688 Father

Sosa 344

GX 689 Mother

11026 XIV 11027

11028 XIV 11029

11032 XIV 11033

11038 XIV 11039

11030 XIV 11031   11024 XIV 11025   5512 XIII 5513

5514 XIII 5515

1378 XI 1379

5516 XIII 5517   11034 XIV 11035   11036 XIV 11037

5518 XIII 5519

2756 XII 2757

2758 XII 2759

344

♀ Surname : ....First name : ....

▶Generation IX – paternal ascendant ↓Child page 172 –   □ Implex

Born : ....in..□ baptized

Daughter of : ....and: ....

Occupation(s) : ....

Deceased : ....in...

👭 CHILDREN ....

....

🏃 ASCENDANCY UP TO XIVth GENERATION

2760 XII **2761**		**2762** XII **2763**
5520 XIII **5521**		**5524** XIII **5525**
11042 XIV **11043**		**11054** XIV **11055**
11044 XIV **11045**	**5522** XIII **5523**	**11048** XIV **11049**
		5526 XIII **5527**
	1380 XI **1381**	
11040 XIV **11041**		**11050** XIV **11051**
11046 XIV **11047**		**11052** XIV **11053**

GX 690 Father

Sosa 345

GX 691 Mother

11058 XIV **11059**		**11064** XIV **11065**
11060 XIV **11061**		**11070** XIV **11071**
11062 XIV **11063**		**11066** XIV **11067**
11056 XIV **11057**	**5528** XIII **5529**	**11068** XIV **11069**
	1382 XI **1383**	**5532** XIII **5533**
5530 XIII **5531**		**5534** XIII **5535**
	2764 XII **2765**	**2766** XII **2767**

345

Sosa
346

Surname : .... First name : .... ♂

▶Generation 9 – paternal ascendant ↓Child page 173

☐ Implex

Born : ....in ....☐ baptized

Son of : ....and: ....

Occupation(s) : ....

Deceased : ....in...................................

💍 MARITAL STATUS

☐ *Civil Marriage*   ☐ *Religious Marriage*   ☐ *Free Union*

Date : ....in... ☐ Marriage contract

Witnesses: ....

👪 ASCENDANCY UP TO XIVth GENERATION

5536 XIII 5537	
2768 XII 2769	
11074 XIV 11075	
11076 XIV 11077	
5538 XIII 5539	
2770 XII 2771	
5542 XIII 5543	
11086 XIV 11087	
11080 XIV 11081	
5540 XIII 5541	

† † 1384 XI 1385

○ †

11072 XIV 11073

11078 XIV 11079

11082 XIV 11083

11084 XIV 11085

GX 692 Father

Sosa 346

GX 693 Mother

x

○ †

11090 XIV 11091

11092 XIV 11093

11096 XIV 11097

11102 XIV 11103

1386 XI 1387

† †

11094 XIV 11095

11088 XIV 11089

5544 XIII 5545

5548 XIII 5549

11098 XIV 11099

11100 XIV 11101

5546 XIII 5547

2772 XII 2773

2774 XII 2775

5550 XIII 5551

○ ○

346

347

♀ Surname : .... First name : ....

▶Generation IX – paternal ascendant ↓Child page 173 –   □ Implex

Born : ....in...□ baptized

Daughter of : ....and: ....

Occupation(s) : ....

Deceased : ....in...

⚭ CHILDREN ....
....
....

⚎ ASCENDANCY UP TO XIVth GENERATION

5552 XIII 5553	2776 XII 2777
11106 XIV 11107	11108 XIV 11109	5554 XIII 5555
2778 XII 2779	5556 XIII 5557
5558 XIII 5559	11118 XIV 11119	11112 XIV 11113

1388 XI 1389

11104 XIV 11105

11110 XIV 11111

11116 XIV 11117

11114 XIV 11115

GX 694 Father

Sosa 347

GX 695 Mother

11122 XIV 11123

11128 XIV 11129

11124 XIV 11125

11134 XIV 11135

11126 XIV 11127

11120 XIV 11121

5560 XIII 5561

5564 XIII 5565

11130 XIV 11131

11132 XIV 11133

5562 XIII 5563

2780 XII 2781

1390 XI 1391

2782 XII 2783

5566 XIII 5567

347

Surname : .... First name : .... ♂

▶Generation 9 – paternal ascendant   ↓Child page 174   ☐ Implex

Born : .... in .... ☐ baptized

Son of : .... and: ....

Occupation(s) : ....

Deceased : .... in ....

💍 **MARITAL STATUS**   ☐ *Civil Marriage* ☐ *Religious Marriage* ☐ *Free Union*

Date : .... in .... ☐ Marriage contract

Witnesses: ....

👪 **ASCENDANCY UP TO XIVth GENERATION**

5568 XIII 5569	2784 XII 2785
11138 XIV 11139	
11140 XIV 11141	5570 XIII 5571
11136 XIV 11137	
11142 XIV 11143	

1392 XI 1393

GX 696 Father

Sosa 348

GX 697 Mother

2786 XII 2787	5572 XIII 5573
5574 XIII 5575	
11150 XIV 11151	
11144 XIV 11145	
11146 XIV 11147	
11148 XIV 11149	

11154 XIV 11155	11160 XIV 11161
11156 XIV 11157	
11158 XIV 11159	
11152 XIV 11153	5576 XIII 5577

1394 XI 1395

11166 XIV 11167	
5580 XIII 5581	
11162 XIV 11163	
11164 XIV 11165	
5582 XIII 5583	

| 5578 XIII 5579 | 2788 XII 2789 |

| 2790 XII 2791 | |

Sosa
349

♀ Surname : .... First name : ....

▶Generation IX – paternal ascendant ↓Child page 174 – ☐ Implex

Born : .... in.. ☐ baptized

Daughter of : ....and: ....

Occupation(s) : ....

Deceased : .... in.......................................

⚭ CHILDREN ....
....
....

👪 ASCENDANCY UP TO XIVth GENERATION

5584 XIII 5585	2792 XII 2793
11170 XIV 11171	11172 XIV 11173	5586 XIII 5587
	1396 XI 1397
11168 XIV 11169	
11174 XIV 11175	GX 698 Father

Sosa 349

GX 699 Mother

| 2794 XII 2795 | 5588 XIII 5589 |
| 5590 XIII 5591 | 11182 XIV 11183 | 11176 XIV 11177 |
| 11178 XIV 11179 |
| 11180 XIV 11181 |

11186 XIV 11187	11192 XIV 11193
11188 XIV 11189	11198 XIV 11199
11190 XIV 11191	11184 XIV 11185	5592 XIII 5593
1398 XI 1399
5594 XIII 5595	2796 XII 2797
5596 XIII 5597	11194 XIV 11195	11196 XIV 11197
2798 XII 2799	5598 XIII 5599

349

Surname : .... First name : .... ♂

Born : ....in...☐ baptized

Son of : ....and: ....

Occupation(s) : ....

Deceased : ....in...

💍 MARITAL STATUS   ☐ Civil Marriage   ☐ Religious Marriage   ☐ Free Union

Date : ....in...☐ Marriage contract

Witnesses: ....

👪 ASCENDANCY UP TO XIVth GENERATION

5600 XIII 5601	
2800 XII 2801	2802 XII 2803
11202 XIV 11203	11204 XIV 11205
5602 XIII 5603	5606 XIII 5607
	11214 XIV 11215	11208 XIV 11209
	5604 XIII 5605
1400 XI 1401	
11200 XIV 11201	11210 XIV 11211
11206 XIV 11207	11212 XIV 11213
GX 700 Father	

Sosa 350

GX 701 Mother	
11218 XIV 11219	11224 XIV 11225
11220 XIV 11221	11230 XIV 11231
11222 XIV 11223	11216 XIV 11217
5608 XIII 5609	11226 XIV 11227	11228 XIV 11229
1402 XI 1403	5612 XIII 5613
5610 XIII 5611	5614 XIII 5615
2804 XII 2805	2806 XII 2807

♀ Surname : .... First name : ....

▶Generation IX – paternal ascendant ↓Child page 175 –   ☐ Implex

Born : .... in ....☐ baptized

Daughter of : ....and: ....

Occupation(s) : ....

Deceased : .... in ....

⚭ **CHILDREN** ....
....
....

👪 **ASCENDANCY UP TO XIVth GENERATION**

| 2808 XII 2809 |
| 5616 XIII 5617 |
| 11234 XIV 11235 |
| 11236 XIV 11237 |
| 5618 XIII 5619 |
| 2810 XII 2811 |
| 5620 XIII 5621 |
| 5622 XIII 5623 |
| 11246 XIV 11247 |
| 11240 XIV 11241 |

1404 XI 1405

| 11232 XIV 11233 |
| 11242 XIV 11243 |
| 11238 XIV 11239 |
| 11244 XIV 11245 |

GX 702 Father

Sosa 351

GX 703 Mother

| 11250 XIV 11251 |
| 11256 XIV 11257 |
| 11252 XIV 11253 |
| 11262 XIV 11263 |

| 11254 XIV 11255 |
| 11248 XIV 11249 |
| 5624 XIII 5625 |
| 5628 XIII 5629 |
| 11258 XIV 11259 |
| 11260 XIV 11261 |

1406 XI 1407

| 5626 XIII 5627 |
| 2812 XII 2813 |
| 2814 XII 2815 |
| 5630 XIII 5631 |

Sosa 352

Surname : .... First name : .... ♂

▶Generation 9 – paternal ascendant   ↓Child page 176

☐ Implex

Born : ....in.................................. ☐ baptized

Son of : ....and: ....

Occupation(s) : ....

Deceased : ....in..................................

⚭ MARITAL STATUS
☐ *Civil Marriage*   ☐ *Religious Marriage*   ☐ *Free Union*

Date : ....in.................................. ☐ Marriage contract

Witnesses: ....

👪 ASCENDANCY UP TO XIVth GENERATION

5632 XIII 5633	2816 XII 2817	2818 XII 2819	5636 XIII 5637
11266 XIV 11267	11268 XIV 11269	5634 XIII 5635	5638 XIII 5639	11278 XIV 11279	11272 XIV 11273
	1408 XI 1409	
11264 XIV 11265		11274 XIV 11275
11270 XIV 11271	GX 704 Father	11276 XIV 11277

Sosa 352

GX 705 Mother

11282 XIV 11283	11288 XIV 11289
11284 XIV 11285	11294 XIV 11295
	1410 XI 1411	
11286 XIV 11287	11280 XIV 11281	5640 XIII 5641	5644 XIII 5645	11290 XIV 11291	11292 XIV 11293
5642 XIII 5643	2820 XII 2821	2822 XII 2823	5646 XIII 5647

352

♀ Surname : .... First name : ....

▶Generation IX – paternal ascendant ↓Child page 176 –   ☐ Implex

Born : .... in .... ☐ baptized

Daughter of : .... and: ....

Occupation(s) : ....

Deceased : .... in ....

⚭ **CHILDREN** ....

....

....

⚒ ASCENDANCY UP TO XIVth GENERATION

5648 XIII 5649	2824 XII 2825
11298 XIV 11299	11300 XIV 11301
5650 XIII 5651	
2826 XII 2827	5652 XIII 5653
5654 XIII 5655	11310 XIV 11311
11304 XIV 11305	

1412 XI 1413

1414 XI 1415

11296 XIV 11297

11302 XIV 11303

11306 XIV 11307

11308 XIV 11309

GX 706 Father

Sosa 353

GX 707 Mother

11314 XIV 11315

11316 XIV 11317

11320 XIV 11321

11326 XIV 11327

11318 XIV 11319

11312 XIV 11313

5656 XIII 5657

5660 XIII 5661

11322 XIV 11323

11324 XIV 11325

5658 XIII 5659

2828 XII 2829

2830 XII 2831

5662 XIII 5663

Surname : .... First name : .... ♂

▶Generation 9 – paternal ascendant   ↓Child page 177

☐ Implex

Born : ....in...☐ baptized

Son of : ....and: ....

Occupation(s) : ....

Deceased : ....in...

💍 **MARITAL STATUS**   ☐ *Civil Marriage*   ☐ *Religious Marriage*   ☐ *Free Union*

Date : ....in.. ☐ Marriage contract

Witnesses: ....

👪 **ASCENDANCY UP TO XIVth GENERATION**

2832 XII 2833	
5664 XIII 5665	
11330 XIV 11331	11332 XIV 11333
5666 XIII 5667	
2834 XII 2835	
5668 XIII 5669	
5670 XIII 5671	11342 XIV 11343
11336 XIV 11337	
11328 XIV 11329	
1416 XI 1417	
11334 XIV 11335	
11338 XIV 11339	
11340 XIV 11341	

GX 708 Father

Sosa 354

GX 709 Mother

11346 XIV 11347	11352 XIV 11353
11348 XIV 11349	11358 XIV 11359
11350 XIV 11351	11344 XIV 11345
5672 XIII 5673	
1418 XI 1419	
5674 XIII 5675	
2836 XII 2837	2838 XII 2839
5676 XIII 5677	11354 XIV 11355
11356 XIV 11357	5678 XIII 5679

⚲ Surname : .... First name : ....

▶Generation IX – paternal ascendant ↓Child page 177 –   □ Implex

Born : ....in..□ baptized

Daughter of : ....and: ....

Occupation(s) : ....

Deceased : ....in.................................

⚭ **CHILDREN** ....

....

👪 ASCENDANCY UP TO XIVth GENERATION

2840 XII 2841	2842 XII 2843
5680 XIII 5681	5684 XIII 5685
11362 XIV 11363	11374 XIV 11375
11364 XIV 11365	11368 XIV 11369
5682 XIII 5683	5686 XIII 5687

1420 XI 1421

11360 XIV 11361	11370 XIV 11371
11366 XIV 11367	11372 XIV 11373

GX 710 Father

Sosa 355

GX 711 Mother

11378 XIV 11379	11384 XIV 11385
11380 XIV 11381	11390 XIV 11391

11382 XIV 11383	11386 XIV 11387
11376 XIV 11377	11388 XIV 11389
5688 XIII 5689	5692 XIII 5693

1422 XI 1423

5690 XIII 5691	5694 XIII 5695
2844 XII 2845	2846 XII 2847

Surname : .... First name : .... ♂

▶Generation 9 – paternal ascendant ↓Child page 178

☐ Implex

Born : ....in..☐ baptized

Son of : ....and:..

Occupation(s) : ....

Deceased : ....in..

⚭ MARITAL STATUS

☐ *Civil Marriage* ☐ *Religious Marriage* ☐ *Free Union*

Date : ....in.. ☐ Marriage contract

Witnesses: ....

👪 ASCENDANCY UP TO XIVth GENERATION

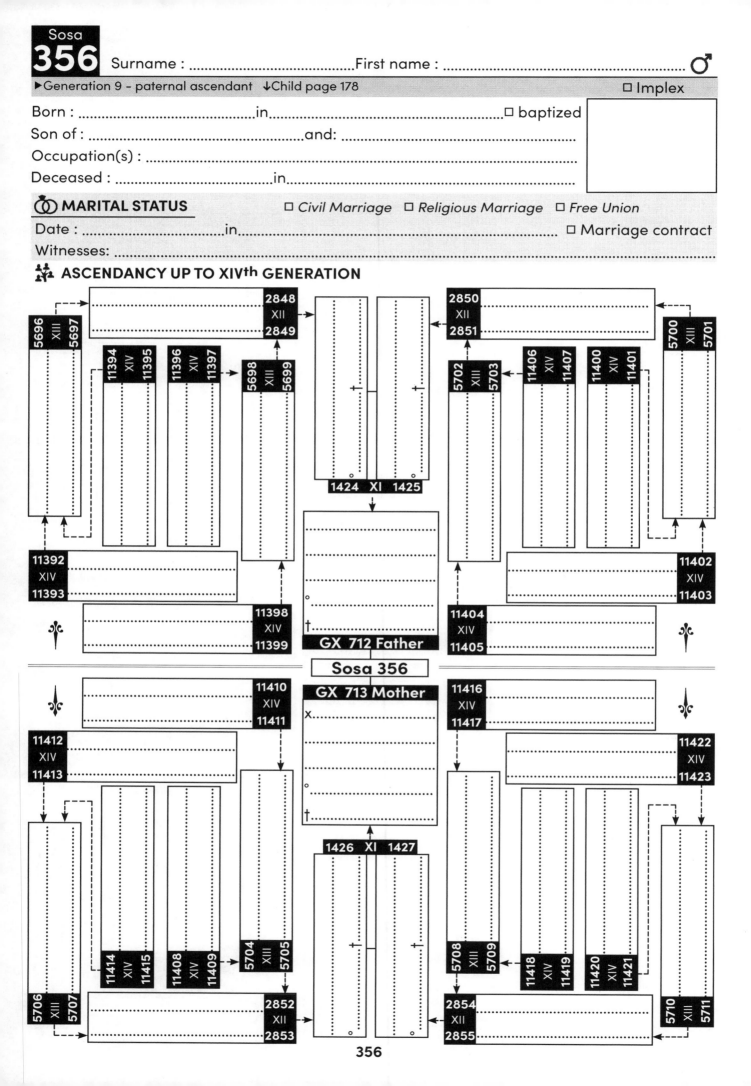

5696 XIII 5697	2848 XII 2849
11394 XIV 11395	11396 XIV 11397
	5698 XIII 5699
11392 XIV 11393	2850 XII 2851
11398 XIV 11399	5702 XIII 5703

2850 XII 2851

5700 XIII 5701

11406 XIV 11407

11400 XIV 11401

1424 XI 1425

5702 XIII 5703

11402 XIV 11403

11404 XIV 11405

GX 712 Father

Sosa 356

GX 713 Mother

11410 XIV 11411

11412 XIV 11413

11416 XIV 11417

11422 XIV 11423

11414 XIV 11415

11408 XIV 11409

5704 XIII 5705

1426 XI 1427

5708 XIII 5709

11448 XIV 11449

11420 XIV 11421

5706 XIII 5707

2852 XII 2853

2854 XII 2855

5710 XIII 5711

♀ Surname : ....First name : ....

Sosa
357

▶Generation IX – paternal ascendant ↓Child page 178 –   □ Implex

Born : ....in...□ baptized

Daughter of : ....and: ....

Occupation(s) : ....

Deceased : ....in...

⚭ **CHILDREN** ....
....
....

⚶ ASCENDANCY UP TO XIVth GENERATION

5712 XIII 5713	2856 XII 2857	2858 XII 2859
		5716 XIII 5717
11426 XIV 11427	11428 XIV 11429	5714 XIII 5715
		11438 XIV 11439
		11432 XIV 11433
	1428 XI 1429	5718 XIII 5719
11424 XIV 11425		
		11434 XIV 11435
11430 XIV 11431		11436 XIV 11437
	GX 714 Father	

Sosa 357

GX 715 Mother

11442 XIV 11443		11448 XIV 11449
11444 XIV 11445		11454 XIV 11455
	1430 XI 1431	
11446 XIV 11447		11450 XIV 11451
11440 XIV 11441	5720 XIII 5721	11452 XIV 11453
		5724 XIII 5725
5722 XIII 5723	2860 XII 2861	5726 XIII 5727
		2862 XII 2863

357

Surname : .... First name : .... ♂

▶Generation 9 – paternal ascendant ↓Child page 179

☐ Implex

Born : .... in..................................... ☐ baptized

Son of : .... and: ....

Occupation(s) : ....

Deceased : .... in...

⚭ MARITAL STATUS

☐ Civil Marriage ☐ Religious Marriage ☐ Free Union

Date : ....in... ☐ Marriage contract

Witnesses: ....

👪 ASCENDANCY UP TO XIVth GENERATION

5728 XIII 5729	
	2864 XII 2865
11458 XIV 11459	
11460 XIV 11461	
	5730 XIII 5731
11456 XIV 11457	
	11462 XIV 11463

2866 XII 2867

5732 XIII 5733

5734 XIII 5735

11470 XIV 11471

11464 XIV 11465

11466 XIV 11467

11468 XIV 11469

1432 XI 1433

† †

○ ○

GX 716 Father

Sosa 358

GX 717 Mother

11474 XIV 11475

11476 XIV 11477

11480 XIV 11481

11486 XIV 11487

11478 XIV 11479

11472 XIV 11473

5736 XIII 5737

11482 XIV 11483

11484 XIV 11485

5738 XIII 5739

2868 XII 2869

1434 XI 1435

5740 XIII 5741

2870 XII 2871

5742 XIII 5743

x

○

†

† †

○ ○

Sosa
359

♀ Surname : ....First name : ....

►Generation IX – paternal ascendant ↓Child page 179 –

☐ Implex

Born : ....in...☐ baptized

Daughter of : ....and: ....

Occupation(s) : ....

Deceased : ....in...

💍 CHILDREN ....
....
....

👪 ASCENDANCY UP TO XIVth GENERATION

| 5744 XIII 5745 | 2872 XII 2873 | | 2874 XII 2875 | 5748 XIII 5749 |

| 11490 XIV 11491 | 11492 XIV 11493 | 5746 XIII 5747 | | 5750 XIII 5751 | 11502 XIV 11503 | 11496 XIV 11497 |

† †

1436 XI 1437

| 11488 XIV 11489 | | | 11498 XIV 11499 |

○

| 11494 XIV 11495 | | 11500 XIV 11501 |

○

†

GX 718 Father

Sosa 359

GX 719 Mother

| 11506 XIV 11507 | | 11512 XIV 11513 |

| 11508 XIV 11509 | | 11518 XIV 11519 |

x

○

†

1438 XI 1439

| 11510 XIV 11511 | 11504 XIV 11505 | 5752 XIII 5753 | | 5756 XIII 5757 | 11514 XIV 11515 | 11516 XIV 11517 |

† †

| 5754 XIII 5755 | 2876 XII 2877 | | 2878 XII 2879 | 5758 XIII 5759 |

○ ○

359

Surname : .... First name : .... ♂

▶Generation 9 – paternal ascendant ↓Child page 180

☐ Implex

Born : ....in..............................☐ baptized

Son of : ....and: ....

Occupation(s) : ....

Deceased : ....in..............................

💍 **MARITAL STATUS**   ☐ *Civil Marriage* ☐ *Religious Marriage* ☐ *Free Union*

Date : ....in.............................. ☐ Marriage contract

Witnesses: ....

👫 ASCENDANCY UP TO XIVth GENERATION

5760 XIII 5761	2880 XII 2881
11522 XIV 11523	11524 XIV 11525
5762 XIII 5763	
11520 XIV 11521	
11526 XIV 11527	

1440 XI 1441

GX 720 Father

Sosa 360

GX 721 Mother

2882 XII 2883	5764 XIII 5765
5766 XIII 5767	11534 XIV 11535	11528 XIV 11529
11530 XIV 11531	
11532 XIV 11533	

11538 XIV 11539	11544 XIV 11545
11540 XIV 11541	11550 XIV 11551
11542 XIV 11543	11536 XIV 11537	5768 XIII 5769
5770 XIII 5771	2884 XII 2885

1442 XI 1443

5772 XIII 5773	11546 XIV 11547	11548 XIV 11549
5774 XIII 5775	
2886 XII 2887	

♀ Surname : .... First name : ....

►Generation IX – paternal ascendant ↓Child page 180 –

□ Implex

Born : ....in... □ baptized

Daughter of : ....and: ....

Occupation(s) : ....

Deceased : ....in ....

⚭ CHILDREN ....
....
....

👪 ASCENDANCY UP TO XIVth GENERATION

2888 XII 2889	2890 XII 2891
5776 XIII 5777	5780 XIII 5781
11554 XIV 11555	11566 XIV 11567
11556 XIV 11557	11560 XIV 11561
5778 XIII 5779	5782 XIII 5783

1444 XI 1445

11552 XIV 11553

11558 XIV 11559

11562 XIV 11563

11564 XIV 11565

GX 722 Father

Sosa 361

GX 723 Mother

11570 XIV 11571

11576 XIV 11577

11572 XIV 11573

11582 XIV 11583

1446 XI 1447

11574 XIV 11575	5788 XIII 5789
11568 XIV 11569	11578 XIV 11579
5784 XIII 5785	11580 XIV 11581
5786 XIII 5787	5790 XIII 5791

2892 XII 2893

2894 XII 2895

Sosa
362

Surname : .... First name : .... ♂

▶Generation 9 – paternal ascendant ↓Child page 181

□ Implex

Born : .... in .... □ baptized

Son of : .... and: ....

Occupation(s) : ....

Deceased : .... in ....

⚭ MARITAL STATUS

□ Civil Marriage   □ Religious Marriage   □ Free Union

Date : .... in ....

□ Marriage contract

Witnesses: ....

👪 ASCENDANCY UP TO XIVth GENERATION

5792 XIII 5793	2896 XII 2897	
11586 XIV 11587	11588 XIV 11589	5794 XIII 5795
	1448 XI 1449	
11584 XIV 11585		
11590 XIV 11591	GX 724 Father	

2898 XII 2899	5796 XIII 5797	
5798 XIII 5799	11598 XIV 11599	11592 XIV 11593
	11594 XIV 11595	
11596 XIV 11597		

Sosa 362

GX 725 Mother
x
°
†

11602 XIV 11603		
11604 XIV 11605		
11606 XIV 11607	11600 XIV 11601	5800 XIII 5801
5802 XIII 5803	2900 XII 2901	
	1450 XI 1451	

11608 XIV 11609		
11614 XIV 11615		
11610 XIV 11611	11612 XIV 11613	5806 XIII 5807
5804 XIII 5805	2902 XII 2903	

♀ Surname : ....First name : ....

▶Generation IX – paternal ascendant ↓Child page 181 –   □ Implex

Born : ....in...□ baptized

Daughter of : ....and:...

Occupation(s) : ....

Deceased : ....in.............................

💍 CHILDREN ....
....
....

🏃 ASCENDANCY UP TO XIVth GENERATION

5808 XIII 5809	2904 XII 2905
11618 XIV 11619	11620 XIV 11621	5810 XIII 5811
2906 XII 2907	5812 XIII 5813
5814 XIII 5815	11630 XIV 11631	11624 XIV 11625

1452 XI 1453

11616 XIV 11617

11622 XIV 11623

11626 XIV 11627

11628 XIV 11629

GX 726 Father

Sosa 363

GX 727 Mother

11634 XIV 11635

11636 XIV 11637

11640 XIV 11641

11646 XIV 11647

1454 XI 1455

| 11638 XIV 11639 | 11632 XIV 11633 | 5816 XIII 5817 |
| 5820 XIII 5821 | 11642 XIV 11643 | 11644 XIV 11645 |

5818 XIII 5819

5822 XIII 5823

| 2908 XII 2909 | 2910 XII 2911 |

Surname : .... First name : .... ♂

▶Generation 9 – paternal ascendant   ↓Child page 182

☐ Implex

Born : .... in .... ☐ baptized

Son of : .... and: ....

Occupation(s) : ....

Deceased : .... in ....

⚭ MARITAL STATUS

☐ *Civil Marriage* ☐ *Religious Marriage* ☐ *Free Union*

Date : ....in .... ☐ Marriage contract

Witnesses: ....

👪 ASCENDANCY UP TO XIVth GENERATION

5824 XIII 5825	2912 XII 2913	2914 XII 2915	5828 XIII 5829

11650 XIV 11651 | 11652 XIV 11653 | 5826 XIII 5827

5830 XIII 5831 | 11662 XIV 11663 | 11656 XIV 11657

1456 XI 1457

11648 XIV 11649

11658 XIV 11659

11654 XIV 11655

GX 728 Father

11660 XIV 11661

Sosa 364

GX 729 Mother

11666 XIV 11667

11672 XIV 11673

11668 XIV 11669

11678 XIV 11679

1458 XI 1459

11670 XIV 11671 | 11664 XIV 11665 | 5832 XIII 5833

5836 XIII 5837 | 11674 XIV 11675 | 11676 XIV 11677

5834 XIII 5835

2916 XII 2917

2918 XII 2919

5838 XIII 5839

♀ Surname : ....First name : ....

☐ Implex

Born : ....in...☐ baptized

Daughter of : ....and: ....

Occupation(s) : ....

Deceased : ....in...

⚭ **CHILDREN** ....

....

....

👪 **ASCENDANCY UP TO XIVth GENERATION**

5840 XIII **5841**	**2920** XII **2921**
11682 XIV **11683**	
11684 XIV **11685**	**5842** XIII **5843**
11680 XIV **11681**	
11686 XIV **11687**	

1460 XI 1461

GX 730 Father

Sosa 365

GX 731 Mother

2922 XII **2923**	**5844** XIII **5845**
	11694 XIV **11695**
5846 XIII **5847**	**11688** XIV **11689**
	11690 XIV **11691**
11692 XIV **11693**	

11698 XIV **11699**	
11700 XIV **11701**	
11702 XIV **11703**	
11696 XIV **11697**	**5848** XIII **5849**
5850 XIII **5851**	**2924** XII **2925**

1462 XI 1463

11704 XIV **11705**	
	11710 XIV **11711**
5852 XIII **5853**	**11706** XIV **11707**
	11708 XIV **11709**
2926 XII **2927**	**5854** XIII **5855**

Sosa
366

Surname : .... First name : .... ♂

▶Generation 9 – paternal ascendant ↓Child page 183   □ Implex

Born : .... in .... □ baptized

Son of : .... and: ....

Occupation(s) : ....

Deceased : .... in ....

⚭ MARITAL STATUS   □ Civil Marriage □ Religious Marriage □ Free Union

Date : .... in ....   □ Marriage contract

Witnesses: ....

👪 ASCENDANCY UP TO XIVth GENERATION

5856 XIII 5857	2928 XII 2929	
11714 XIV 11715		2930 XII 2931
11716 XIV 11717	5858 XIII 5859	5862 XIII 5863
		11726 XIV 11727
	1464 XI 1465	11720 XIV 11721
5860 XIII 5861		
11712 XIV 11713		11722 XIV 11723
11718 XIV 11719		11724 XIV 11725
	GX 732 Father	
	Sosa 366	
	GX 733 Mother	
11730 XIV 11731		11736 XIV 11737
11732 XIV 11733		11742 XIV 11743
11734 XIV 11735	5864 XIII 5865	5868 XIII 5869
11728 XIV 11729		11738 XIV 11739
5866 XIII 5867	2932 XII 2933	11740 XIV 11741
	1466 XI 1467	5870 XIII 5871
		2934 XII 2935

366

♀ Surname : .... First name : ....

►Generation IX – paternal ascendant ↓Child page 183 –   □ Implex

Born : ....in..□ baptized

Daughter of : ....and: ....

Occupation(s) : ....

Deceased : ....in..

⚭ CHILDREN ....
....

⚛ ASCENDANCY UP TO XIVth GENERATION

5872 XIII 5873	
2936 XII 2937	
11746 XIV 11747	
11748 XIV 11749	
5874 XIII 5875	
2938 XII 2939	
5876 XIII 5877	
5878 XIII 5879	
11758 XIV 11759	
11752 XIV 11753	

1468   XI   1469

11744 XIV 11745

11750 XIV 11751

GX 734 Father

11756 XIV 11757

11754 XIV 11755

Sosa 367

GX 735 Mother

11762 XIV 11763

11768 XIV 11769

11764 XIV 11765

11774 XIV 11775

1470   XI   1471

5882 XIII 5883

11766 XIV 11767

11760 XIV 11761

5880 XIII 5881

2940 XII 2941

5884 XIII 5885

11770 XIV 11771

11772 XIV 11773

5886 XIII 5887

2942 XII 2943

Sosa
368

Surname : .... First name : .... ♂

▶Generation 9 – paternal ascendant ↓Child page 184   □ Implex

Born : .... in .... □ baptized

Son of : .... and: ....

Occupation(s) : ....

Deceased : .... in ....

⚭ **MARITAL STATUS**   □ *Civil Marriage* □ *Religious Marriage* □ *Free Union*

Date : .... in .... □ Marriage contract

Witnesses: ....

ASCENDANCY UP TO XIVth GENERATION

5888 XIII 5889		
2944 XII 2945		
11778 XIV 11779	11780 XIV 11781	5890 XIII 5891
2946 XII 2947		
5892 XIII 5893		
5894 XIII 5895	11790 XIV 11791	11784 XIV 11785

1472 XI 1473

GX 736 Father

Sosa 368

GX 737 Mother

1474 XI 1475

11776 XIV 11777

11782 XIV 11783

11788 XIV 11789

11786 XIV 11787

11794 XIV 11795

11800 XIV 11801

11796 XIV 11797

11806 XIV 11807

11798 XIV 11799 | 11792 XIV 11793 | 5896 XIII 5897

5898 XIII 5899

2948 XII 2949

5900 XIII 5901 | 11802 XIV 11803 | 11804 XIV 11805

2950 XII 2951

5902 XIII 5903

368

♀ Surname : ....First name : ....

▶Generation IX – paternal ascendant ↓Child page 184 –   □ Implex

Born : ....in...□ baptized

Daughter of : ....and: ....

Occupation(s) : ....

Deceased : ....in..

⚭ CHILDREN ....

....

👪 ASCENDANCY UP TO XIVth GENERATION

5904 XIII 5905	2952 XII 2953
11810 XIV 11811	
11812 XIV 11813	5906 XIII 5907
	1476 XI 1477
11808 XIV 11809	
11814 XIV 11815	

2954 XII 2955

5910 XIII 5911

11822 XIV 11823

11816 XIV 11817

5908 XIII 5909

11818 XIV 11819

11820 XIV 11821

GX 738 Father

Sosa 369

GX 739 Mother

11826 XIV 11827

11828 XIV 11829

11832 XIV 11833

11838 XIV 11839

11830 XIV 11831

11824 XIV 11825

5912 XIII 5913

1478 XI 1479

5916 XIII 5917

11834 XIV 11835

11836 XIV 11837

5918 XIII 5919

5914 XIII 5915

2956 XII 2957

2958 XII 2959

Surname : .... First name : .... ♂

▶Generation 9 – paternal ascendant ↓Child page 185

□ Implex

Born : ....in.. □ baptized

Son of : ....and:..................................

Occupation(s) : ....

Deceased : ....in...............................

⚭ **MARITAL STATUS**   □ *Civil Marriage*   □ *Religious Marriage*   □ *Free Union*

Date : ....in.. □ Marriage contract

Witnesses: ....

ASCENDANCY UP TO XIVth GENERATION

5920 XIII 5921	2960 XII 2961
11842 XIV 11843	11844 XIV 11845
5922 XIII 5923	
11840 XIV 11841	
11846 XIV 11847	

1480 XI 1481

GX 740 Father

Sosa 370

GX 741 Mother

2962 XII 2963

5926 XIII 5927

11854 XIV 11855

11848 XIV 11849

5924 XIII 5925

11850 XIV 11851

11852 XIV 11853

11858 XIV 11859

11860 XIV 11861

11862 XIV 11863

11856 XIV 11857

5928 XIII 5929

5930 XIII 5931

2964 XII 2965

1482 XI 1483

11864 XIV 11865

11870 XIV 11871

11866 XIV 11867

11868 XIV 11869

5932 XIII 5933

5934 XIII 5935

2966 XII 2967

♀ Surname : ....First name : ....

▶Generation IX – paternal ascendant ↓Child page 185 –

☐ Implex

Born : ....in...☐ baptized

Daughter of : ....and: ....

Occupation(s) : ....

Deceased : ....in..

⚭ CHILDREN ....

....

....

⚑ ASCENDANCY UP TO XIVth GENERATION

5936 XIII 5937	
2968 XII 2969	2970 XII 2971
11874 XIV 11875	11876 XIV 11877
5938 XIII 5939	5942 XIII 5943
11886 XIV 11887	11880 XIV 11881
5940 XIII 5941	

1484 XI 1485

| 11872 XIV 11873 | 11882 XIV 11883 |

| 11878 XIV 11879 | 11884 XIV 11885 |

GX 742 Father

Sosa 371

GX 743 Mother

| 11890 XIV 11891 | 11896 XIV 11897 |

| 11892 XIV 11893 | 11902 XIV 11903 |

1486 XI 1487

11894 XIV 11895	11888 XIV 11889
5944 XIII 5945	5948 XIII 5949
	11898 XIV 11899	11900 XIV 11901
5946 XIII 5947	5950 XIII 5951

| 2972 XII 2973 | 2974 XII 2975 |

Surname : .... First name : .... ♂

☐ Implex

Born : ....in...☐ baptized

Son of : ....and: ....

Occupation(s) : ....

Deceased : ....in...

⚭ **MARITAL STATUS**   ☐ *Civil Marriage*   ☐ *Religious Marriage*   ☐ *Free Union*

Date : ....in...☐ Marriage contract

Witnesses: ....

👪 **ASCENDANCY UP TO XIVth GENERATION**

5952 XIII 5953	2976 XII 2977
11906 XIV 11907	11908 XIV 11909	5954 XIII 5955
11904 XIV 11905	
11910 XIV 11911	

1488 XI 1489

GX 744 Father

Sosa 372

GX 745 Mother

2978 XII 2979

5956 XIII 5957

5958 XIII 5959 | 11918 XIV 11919 | 11912 XIV 11913

11914 XIV 11915

11916 XIV 11917

11922 XIV 11923

11924 XIV 11925

11926 XIV 11927 | 11920 XIV 11921 | 5960 XIII 5961

5962 XIII 5963

2980 XII 2981

1490 XI 1491

11928 XIV 11929

11934 XIV 11935

5964 XIII 5965 | 11930 XIV 11931 | 11932 XIV 11933

5966 XIII 5967

2982 XII 2983

♀ Surname : .... First name : ....

▶Generation IX – paternal ascendant ↓Child page 186 –   □ Implex

Born : ....in...□ baptized

Daughter of : ....and: ....

Occupation(s) : ....

Deceased : ....in..

⚭ **CHILDREN** ....

....

....

👪 ASCENDANCY UP TO XIVth GENERATION

5968 XIII 5969		2984 XII 2985			2986 XII 2987		5972 XIII 5973

| 11938 XIV 11939 | 11940 XIV 11941 | 5970 XIII 5971 | | 5974 XIII 5975 | 11950 XIV 11951 | 11944 XIV 11945 | |

1492 XI 1493

| 11936 XIV 11937 | | | | 11946 XIV 11947 |

| 11942 XIV 11943 | | 11948 XIV 11949 |

GX 746 Father

Sosa 373

GX 747 Mother

x.

| 11954 XIV 11955 | | 11960 XIV 11961 |

| 11956 XIV 11957 | | | | 11966 XIV 11967 |

1494 XI 1495

| 11958 XIV 11959 | 11952 XIV 11953 | 5976 XIII 5977 | | 5980 XIII 5981 | 11962 XIV 11963 | 11964 XIV 11965 | |

| 5978 XIII 5979 | | 2988 XII 2989 | | | 2990 XII 2991 | | 5982 XIII 5983 |

Sosa 374

♂

Surname : .... **First name :** ....

▶Generation 9 – paternal ascendant   ↓Child page 187

☐ Implex

Born : .... **in** .... ☐ baptized

Son of : .... **and:** ....

Occupation(s) : ....

Deceased : .... **in** ....

💍 MARITAL STATUS   ☐ Civil Marriage   ☐ Religious Marriage   ☐ Free Union

Date : .... **in** ....

☐ Marriage contract

Witnesses: ....

👪 ASCENDANCY UP TO XIVth GENERATION

2992 XII 2993		2994 XII 2995
5984 XIII 5985		5988 XIII 5989
11970 XIV 11971	5986 XIII 5987	5990 XIII 5991
11972 XIV 11973		11982 XIV 11983
		11976 XIV 11977

1496 XI 1497

11968 XIV 11969

11974 XIV 11975

11978 XIV 11979

11980 XIV 11981

GX 748 Father

Sosa 374

GX 749 Mother

x..

11986 XIV 11987

11992 XIV 11993

11988 XIV 11989

11998 XIV 11999

11990 XIV 11991   11984 XIV 11985   5992 XIII 5993

1498 XI 1499

5996 XIII 5997

11994 XIV 11995   11996 XIV 11997

5994 XIII 5995

2996 XII 2997

2998 XII 2999

5998 XIII 5999

374

♀ Surname : ....First name : ....

☐ Implex

▶Generation IX – paternal ascendant ↓Child page 187 –

Born : ....in...☐ baptized

Daughter of : ....and: ....

Occupation(s) : ....

Deceased : ....in...

⚭ **CHILDREN** ....

....

🎎 **ASCENDANCY UP TO XIVth GENERATION**

6000 XIII 6001	
12002 XIV 12003	3000 XII 3001
12004 XIV 12005	6002 XIII 6003
	1500 XI 1501
12000 XIV 12001	
12006 XIV 12007	GX 750 Father

Sosa 375

	GX 751 Mother
12018 XIV 12019	
12020 XIV 12021	
12022 XIV 12023	
12016 XIV 12017	6008 XIII 6009
6010 XIII 6011	3004 XII 3005
	1502 XI 1503

3002 XII 3003
6004 XIII 6005
6006 XIII 6007
12014 XIV 12015
12008 XIV 12009
12010 XIV 12011
12012 XIV 12013
12024 XIV 12025
12030 XIV 12031
6012 XIII 6013
12026 XIV 12027
12028 XIV 12029
6014 XIII 6015
3006 XII 3007

Sosa
376

Surname : .... First name : ....♂

☐ Implex

Born : ....in...☐ baptized

Son of : ....and:...

Occupation(s) : ....

Deceased : ....in...

⚭ MARITAL STATUS
☐ Civil Marriage   ☐ Religious Marriage   ☐ Free Union

Date : ....in.. ☐ Marriage contract

Witnesses: ....

🛐 ASCENDANCY UP TO XIVth GENERATION

6016 XIII 6017	3008 XII 3009
12034 XIV 12035	6018 XIII 6019
12036 XIV 12037	
12032 XIV 12033	
12038 XIV 12039	

1504 XI 1505

3010 XII 3011

6022 XIII 6023

12046 XIV 12047

12040 XIV 12041

6020 XIII 6021

12042 XIV 12043

12044 XIV 12045

GX 752 Father

Sosa 376

GX 753 Mother

12050 XIV 12051

12052 XIV 12053

12056 XIV 12057

12062 XIV 12063

12054 XIV 12055

12048 XIV 12049

6024 XIII 6025

6026 XIII 6027

3012 XII 3013

1506 XI 1507

6028 XIII 6029

12058 XIV 12059

12060 XIV 12061

6030 XIII 6031

3014 XII 3015

♀ Surname : ....First name : ....

▶Generation IX – paternal ascendant ↓Child page 188 –

□ Implex

Born : ....in...□ baptized

Daughter of : ....and: ....

Occupation(s) : ....

Deceased : ....in...

⚭ CHILDREN ....
....
....

ASCENDANCY UP TO XIVth GENERATION

| 6032 XIII 6033 | | 3016 XII 3017 | | 3018 XII 3019 | | 6036 XIII 6037 |

| 12066 XIV 12067 | 12068 XIV 12069 | 6034 XIII 6035 | | | 6038 XIII 6039 | 12078 XIV 12079 | 12072 XIV 12073 | |

1508 XI 1509

| 12064 XIV 12065 | | | | | | | 12074 XIV 12075 |

GX 754 Father

| 12070 XIV 12071 | | 12076 XIV 12077 | |

❀

Sosa 377

GX 755 Mother

| 12082 XIV 12083 | | | 12088 XIV 12089 | ❀

| 12084 XIV 12085 | | | | | | 12094 XIV 12095 |

| | | 1510 XI 1511 | | |

| 12086 XIV 12087 | 12080 XIV 12081 | 6040 XIII 6041 | | 6044 XIII 6045 | 12090 XIV 12091 | 12092 XIV 12093 | |

| 6042 XIII 6043 | | 3020 XII 3021 | | 3022 XII 3023 | | 6046 XIII 6047 |

Surname : .... First name : .... ♂

▶Generation 9 – paternal ascendant ↓Child page 189

□ Implex

Born : .... in.. □ baptized

Son of : .... and: ....

Occupation(s) : ....

Deceased : .... in..

⚭ MARITAL STATUS   □ Civil Marriage   □ Religious Marriage   □ Free Union

Date : ....in.. □ Marriage contract

Witnesses: ....

👪 ASCENDANCY UP TO XIVth GENERATION

3024 XII 3025
6048 XIII 6049
12098 XIV 12099
12100 XIV 12101
6050 XIII 6051
3026 XII 3027
6052 XIII 6053
6054 XIII 6055
12110 XIV 12111
12104 XIV 12105
1512 XI 1513
12096 XIV 12097
12106 XIV 12107
12102 XIV 12103
12108 XIV 12109

GX 756 Father

Sosa 378

GX 757 Mother

12114 XIV 12115
12116 XIV 12117
12120 XIV 12121
12126 XIV 12127
1514 XI 1515
12118 XIV 12119
12112 XIV 12113
6056 XIII 6057
6058 XIII 6059
3028 XII 3029
3030 XII 3031
6060 XIII 6061
12122 XIV 12123
12124 XIV 12125
6062 XIII 6063

♀ Surname : .... First name : ....

►Generation IX – paternal ascendant ↓Child page 189 –

☐ Implex

Born : ....in... ☐ baptized

Daughter of : ....and: ....

Occupation(s) : ....

Deceased : ....in...

⚭ **CHILDREN** ....
....
....

👪 **ASCENDANCY UP TO XIVth GENERATION**

6064 XIII 6065	
3032 XII 3033	
12130 XIV 12131	
12132 XIV 12133	
6066 XIII 6067	
1516 XI 1517	
12128 XIV 12129	
12134 XIV 12135	
GX 758 Father	
Sosa 379	
GX 759 Mother	
12146 XIV 12147	
12148 XIV 12149	
12150 XIV 12151	
12144 XIV 12145	
6072 XIII 6073	
1518 XI 1519	
6074 XIII 6075	
3036 XII 3037	
3034 XII 3035	
6070 XIII 6071	
12142 XIV 12143	
12136 XIV 12137	
6068 XIII 6069	
12138 XIV 12139	
12140 XIV 12141	
12152 XIV 12153	
12158 XIV 12159	
6076 XIII 6077	
12154 XIV 12155	
12156 XIV 12157	
6078 XIII 6079	
3038 XII 3039	

380

Surname : .... First name : .... ♂

□ Implex

Born : ....in..□ baptized

Son of : ....and:...

Occupation(s) : ....

Deceased : ....in..

⚭ MARITAL STATUS   □ *Civil Marriage*   □ *Religious Marriage*   □ *Free Union*

Date : ....in... □ Marriage contract

Witnesses: ....

👪 ASCENDANCY UP TO XIVth GENERATION

6080 XIII 6081	3040 XII 3041
12162 XIV 12163	12164 XIV 12165
6082 XIII 6083	3042 XII 3043
12160 XIV 12161	6086 XIII 6087

3040 XII 3041

3042 XII 3043

6080 XIII 6081

12162 XIV 12163

12164 XIV 12165

6082 XIII 6083

6086 XIII 6087

12174 XIV 12175

12168 XIV 12169

6084 XIII 6085

12160 XIV 12161

12170 XIV 12171

12166 XIV 12167

12172 XIV 12173

1520 XI 1521

GX 760 Father

Sosa 380

GX 761 Mother

12178 XIV 12179

12184 XIV 12185

12180 XIV 12181

12190 XIV 12191

12182 XIV 12183

12176 XIV 12177

6088 XIII 6089

6090 XIII 6091

6092 XIII 6093

12186 XIV 12187

12188 XIV 12189

6094 XIII 6095

1522 XI 1523

3044 XII 3045

3046 XII 3047

♀ Surname : .... First name : ....

▶Generation IX – paternal ascendant ↓Child page 190 –

☐ Implex

Born : ....in.............................☐ baptized

Daughter of : ....and: ....

Occupation(s) : ....

Deceased : ....in.............................

◉ CHILDREN ....

....

....

⚏ ASCENDANCY UP TO XIVth GENERATION

| 6096 XIII 6097 | 3048 XII 3049 | | 3050 XII 3051 | 6100 XIII 6101 |

12194 XIV 12195 | 12196 XIV 12197 | 6098 XIII 6099 | | 6102 XIII 6103 | 12206 XIV 12207 | 12200 XIV 12201 |

1524 XI 1525

12192 XIV 12193

12198 XIV 12199

12202 XIV 12203

12204 XIV 12205

GX 762 Father

Sosa 381

GX 763 Mother

12210 XIV 12211

12216 XIV 12217

12212 XIV 12213

12222 XIV 12223

1526 XI 1527

12214 XIV 12215 | 12208 XIV 12209 | 6104 XIII 6105 | | 6108 XIII 6109 | 12218 XIV 12219 | 12220 XIV 12221 |

6106 XIII 6107 | 3052 XII 3053 | | 3054 XII 3055 | 6110 XIII 6111 |

Sosa
382

Surname : .... First name : .... ♂

▶ Generation 9 – paternal ascendant ↓ Child page 191

☐ Implex

Born : .... in .... ☐ baptized

Son of : .... and: ....

Occupation(s) : ....

Deceased : .... in ....

⚭ MARITAL STATUS   ☐ *Civil Marriage* ☐ *Religious Marriage* ☐ *Free Union*

Date : .... in .... ☐ Marriage contract

Witnesses: ....

👫 ASCENDANCY UP TO XIVth GENERATION

6112 XIII 6113	3056 XII 3057	3058 XII 3059	6116 XIII 6117

| 12226 XIV 12227 | 12228 XIV 12229 | 6114 XIII 6115 | 12238 XIV 12239 | 12232 XIV 12233 |

| 6118 XIII 6119 |

| 1528 XI 1529 |

| 12224 XIV 12225 | | 12234 XIV 12235 |

| 12230 XIV 12231 | 12236 XIV 12237 |

GX 764 Father

Sosa 382

GX 765 Mother

| 12242 XIV 12243 | 12248 XIV 12249 |

| 12244 XIV 12245 | 12254 XIV 12255 |

| 1530 XI 1531 |

| 12246 XIV 12247 | 12240 XIV 12241 | 6120 XIII 6121 | 6124 XIII 6125 | 12250 XIV 12251 | 12252 XIV 12253 |

| 6122 XIII 6123 | 3060 XII 3061 | 3062 XII 3063 | 6126 XIII 6127 |

382

♀ Surname : .... First name : ....

▶Generation IX – paternal ascendant ↓Child page 191 –   □ Implex

Born : ....in...□ baptized

Daughter of : ....and:...

Occupation(s) : ....

Deceased : ....in...

⚭ **CHILDREN** ....

....

....

🧬 **ASCENDANCY UP TO XIVth GENERATION**

6128 XIII 6129	3064 XII 3065
12258 XIV 12259	12260 XIV 12261
6130 XIII 6131	
12256 XIV 12257	
12262 XIV 12263	

1532 XI 1533

GX 766 Father

Sosa 383

GX 767 Mother

3066 XII 3067	6132 XIII 6133
6134 XIII 6135	12270 XIV 12271	12264 XIV 12265
12266 XIV 12267	
12268 XIV 12269	

12274 XIV 12275	12280 XIV 12281
12276 XIV 12277	12286 XIV 12287
12278 XIV 12279	12272 XIV 12273
6136 XIII 6137	
6138 XIII 6139	3068 XII 3069

1534 XI 1535

6140 XIII 6141	12282 XIV 12283	12284 XIV 12285
3070 XII 3071	6142 XIII 6143

Sosa
384

Surname : .... First name : .... ♂

▶Generation 9 – maternal ascendant ↓Child page 192 □ Implex

Born : ....in..□ baptized

Son of : ....and: ....

Occupation(s) : ....

Deceased : ....in..

💍 MARITAL STATUS   □ Civil Marriage   □ Religious Marriage   □ Free Union

Date : ....in..   □ Marriage contract

Witnesses: ....

👪 ASCENDANCY UP TO XIVth GENERATION

6144 XIII 6145	
12290 XIV 12291	3072 XII 3073
12292 XIV 12293	6146 XIII 6147
	1536 XI 1537
12288 XIV 12289	
12294 XIV 12295	GX 768 Father

Sosa 384

GX 769 Mother

3074 XII 3075	6148 XIII 6149
6150 XIII 6151	12302 XIV 12303
	12296 XIV 12297
12298 XIV 12299	
12300 XIV 12301	

12306 XIV 12307	
12308 XIV 12309	
12310 XIV 12311	
12304 XIV 12305	6152 XIII 6153
6154 XIII 6155	3076 XII 3077
	1538 XI 1539

12312 XIV 12313	
	12318 XIV 12319
6156 XIII 6157	12314 XIV 12315
	12316 XIV 12317
3078 XII 3079	6158 XIII 6159

384

♀ Surname : .... First name : ....

►Generation IX – maternal ascendant ↓Child page 192 –

□ Implex

Born : ....in...□ baptized

Daughter of : ....and: ....

Occupation(s) : ....

Deceased : ....in...

⚭ **CHILDREN** ....

....

....

🏃 **ASCENDANCY UP TO XIVth GENERATION**

6160 XIII 6161	3080 XII 3081
12322 XIV 12323	
12324 XIV 12325	6162 XIII 6163
12320 XIV 12321	
	12326 XIV 12327
⚜	**GX 770 Father**

Sosa 385

	GX 771 Mother
12338 XIV 12339	
12340 XIV 12341	
⚜	1542 XI 1543
12342 XIV 12343	
12336 XIV 12337	6168 XIII 6169
6170 XIII 6171	3084 XII 3085

3082 XII 3083	6164 XIII 6165
12334 XIV 12335	12328 XIV 12329
6166 XIII 6167	
	12330 XIV 12331
12332 XIV 12333	⚜

12344 XIV 12345	⚜
	12350 XIV 12351
6172 XIII 6173	
12346 XIV 12347	
3086 XII 3087	12348 XIV 12349
	6174 XIII 6175

1540 XI 1541

Surname : .... First name : .... ♂

☐ Implex

Born : ....in...☐ baptized

Son of : ....and: ....

Occupation(s) : ....

Deceased : ....in...

⚭ MARITAL STATUS   ☐ Civil Marriage ☐ Religious Marriage ☐ Free Union

Date : ....in...

☐ Marriage contract

Witnesses: ....

👪 ASCENDANCY UP TO XIVth GENERATION

6176 XIII 6177	3088 XII 3089
12354 XIV 12355	
12356 XIV 12357	6178 XIII 6179
12352 XIV 12353	
12358 XIV 12359	

1544 XI 1545

3090 XII 3091

6180 XIII 6181

6182 XIII 6183

12366 XIV 12367

12360 XIV 12361

12362 XIV 12363

12364 XIV 12365

GX 772 Father

Sosa 386

GX 773 Mother

12370 XIV 12371

12372 XIV 12373

12376 XIV 12377

12382 XIV 12383

12374 XIV 12375

12368 XIV 12369

6184 XIII 6185

1546 XI 1547

6188 XIII 6189

12378 XIV 12379

12380 XIV 12381

6186 XIII 6187

3092 XII 3093

3094 XII 3095

6190 XIII 6191

♀ Surname : ....First name : ....

▶Generation IX – maternal ascendant ↓Child page 193 –

☐ Implex

Born : ....in...☐ baptized

Daughter of : ....and:...

Occupation(s) : ....

Deceased : ....in...

⚭ CHILDREN ....

⚛ ASCENDANCY UP TO XIVth GENERATION

6192 XIII 6193	3096 XII 3097	
12386 XIV 12387	12388 XIV 12389	6194 XIII 6195
		3098 XII 3099
	12398 XIV 12399	12392 XIV 12393
	6196 XIII 6197	
	6198 XIII 6199	

1548 XI 1549

12384 XIV 12385

12390 XIV 12391

12394 XIV 12395

12396 XIV 12397

GX 774 Father

Sosa 387

GX 775 Mother

12402 XIV 12403

12408 XIV 12409

12404 XIV 12405

12414 XIV 12415

1550 XI 1551

12406 XIV 12407

12400 XIV 12401

6200 XIII 6201

6204 XIII 6205

12410 XIV 12411

12412 XIV 12413

6202 XIII 6203

3100 XII 3101

3102 XII 3103

6206 XIII 6207

Sosa
388

Surname : .... First name : .... ♂

▶Generation 9 – maternal ascendant ↓Child page 194   ☐ Implex

Born : .... in.. ☐ baptized

Son of : .... and: ....

Occupation(s) : ....

Deceased : .... in..

⚭ MARITAL STATUS   ☐ *Civil Marriage* ☐ *Religious Marriage* ☐ *Free Union*

Date : .... in..   ☐ Marriage contract

Witnesses: ....

👪 ASCENDANCY UP TO XIVth GENERATION

6208 XIII 6209	3104 XII 3105	3106 XII 3107	6212 XIII 6213

12418 XIV 12419   12420 XIV 12421   6210 XIII 6211

1552 XI 1553

6214 XIII 6215   12430 XIV 12431   12424 XIV 12425

12416 XIV 12417

12426 XIV 12427

12422 XIV 12423

GX 776 Father

12428 XIV 12429

Sosa 388

GX 777 Mother

12434 XIV 12435

12436 XIV 12437

12440 XIV 12441

12446 XIV 12447

1554 XI 1555

12438 XIV 12439   12432 XIV 12433   6216 XIII 6217

6220 XIII 6221   12442 XIV 12443   12444 XIV 12445

6218 XIII 6219

3108 XII 3109

3110 XII 3111

6222 XIII 6223

♀ Surname : .... First name : ....

►Generation IX – maternal ascendant ↓Child page 194 –   □ Implex

Born : ....in..□ baptized

Daughter of : ....and: ....

Occupation(s) : ....

Deceased : ....in..

⚭ CHILDREN ....

....

....

👪 ASCENDANCY UP TO XIVth GENERATION

6224 XIII 6225	3112 XII 3113
12450 XIV 12451	12452 XIV 12453
	6226 XIII 6227
12448 XIV 12449	
12454 XIV 12455	

1556 XI 1557

GX 778 Father

Sosa 389

GX 779 Mother

3114 XII 3115

6228 XIII 6229

6230 XIII 6231

12462 XIV 12463 | 12456 XIV 12457

12458 XIV 12459

12460 XIV 12461

12466 XIV 12467

12468 XIV 12469

12470 XIV 12471 | 12464 XIV 12465

6232 XIII 6233

6234 XIII 6235

3116 XII 3117

1558 XI 1559

12472 XIV 12473

12478 XIV 12479

6236 XIII 6237

12474 XIV 12475 | 12476 XIV 12477

6238 XIII 6239

3118 XII 3119

Surname : .... First name : .... ♂

□ Implex

Born : ....in..□ baptized

Son of : ....and: ....

Occupation(s) : ....

Deceased : ....in..

⚭ **MARITAL STATUS**   □ Civil Marriage   □ Religious Marriage   □ Free Union

Date : ....in... □ Marriage contract

Witnesses: ....

ASCENDANCY UP TO XIVth GENERATION

6240 XIII 6241	3120 XII 3121
12482 XIV 12483	
12484 XIV 12485	6242 XIII 6243
	3122 XII 3123
	6246 XIII 6247
12494 XIV 12495	
12488 XIV 12489	
6244 XIII 6245	

1560 XI 1561

12480 XIV 12481

12486 XIV 12487

12490 XIV 12491

12492 XIV 12493

GX 780 Father

Sosa 390

GX 781 Mother

12498 XIV 12499

12500 XIV 12501

12504 XIV 12505

12510 XIV 12511

1562 XI 1563

12502 XIV 12503

12496 XIV 12497

6248 XIII 6249

6252 XIII 6253

12506 XIV 12507

12508 XIV 12509

6250 XIII 6251

3124 XII 3125

3126 XII 3127

6254 XIII 6255

♀ Surname : .... First name : ....

▶Generation IX – maternal ascendant ↓Child page 195 –   □ Implex

Born : ....in.. □ baptized

Daughter of : ....and:..

Occupation(s) : ....

Deceased : ....in..

⚭ **CHILDREN** ....

....

ASCENDANCY UP TO XIVth GENERATION

6256 XIII 6257	3128 XII 3129
12514 XIV 12515	12516 XIV 12517
	6258 XIII 6259
3130 XII 3131	6260 XIII 6261
6262 XIII 6263	12526 XIV 12527
12520 XIV 12521	

1564 XI 1565

12512 XIV 12513

12518 XIV 12519

12522 XIV 12523

12524 XIV 12525

GX 782 Father

Sosa 391

GX 783 Mother

12530 XIV 12531

12536 XIV 12537

12532 XIV 12533

12542 XIV 12543

1566 XI 1567

12534 XIV 12535

12528 XIV 12529

6264 XIII 6265

6268 XIII 6269

12538 XIV 12539

12540 XIV 12541

6266 XIII 6267

3132 XII 3133

3134 XII 3135

6270 XIII 6271

Sosa
392

Surname : .... First name : .... ♂

▶Generation 9 – maternal ascendant ↓Child page 196 ☐ Implex

Born : .... in...☐ baptized

Son of : ....and: ....

Occupation(s) : ....

Deceased : .... in...

⚭ MARITAL STATUS ☐ Civil Marriage ☐ Religious Marriage ☐ Free Union

Date : ....in.. ☐ Marriage contract

Witnesses: ....

👪 ASCENDANCY UP TO XIVth GENERATION

6272 XIII 6273	
3136 XII 3137	3138 XII 3139
12546 XIV 12547	12548 XIV 12549
6274 XIII 6275	6278 XIII 6279
6276 XIII 6277	
12558 XIV 12559	12552 XIV 12553

1568 XI 1569

12544 XIV 12545

12554 XIV 12555

12550 XIV 12551

GX 784 Father

12556 XIV 12557

Sosa 392

GX 785 Mother

12562 XIV 12563

12568 XIV 12569

12564 XIV 12565

12574 XIV 12575

1570 XI 1571

12566 XIV 12567

12560 XIV 12561

6280 XIII 6281

12570 XIV 12571

12572 XIV 12573

6284 XIII 6285

6282 XIII 6283

3140 XII 3141

3142 XII 3143

6286 XIII 6287

392

♀ Surname : .... First name : ....

□ Implex

Born : ....in.. □ baptized

Daughter of : ....and: ....

Occupation(s) : ....

Deceased : ....in..

⚭ **CHILDREN** ....

....

....

👪 ASCENDANCY UP TO XIVth GENERATION

6288 XIII 6289	3144 XII 3145
12578 XIV 12579	12580 XIV 12581
6290 XIII 6291	

1572 **XI** 1573

| 3146 XII 3147 | 6292 XIII 6293 |
| 6294 XIII 6295 | 12590 XIV 12591 | 12584 XIV 12585 |

12576 XIV 12577

12586 XIV 12587

12582 XIV 12583

12588 XIV 12589

GX 786 Father

Sosa 393

GX 787 Mother

x

12594 XIV 12595

12600 XIV 12601

12596 XIV 12597

12606 XIV 12607

1574 **XI** 1575

| 12598 XIV 12599 | 12592 XIV 12593 | 6296 XIII 6297 |

| 6300 XIII 6301 | 12602 XIV 12603 | 12604 XIV 12605 |

6298 XIII 6299

3148 XII 3149

3150 XII 3151

6302 XIII 6303

Surname : .... First name : .... ♂

▶Generation 9 – maternal ascendant ↓Child page 197 ☐ Implex

Born : ....in...☐ baptized

Son of : ....and: ....

Occupation(s) : ....

Deceased : ....in..

⚭ **MARITAL STATUS** ☐ *Civil Marriage* ☐ *Religious Marriage* ☐ *Free Union*

Date : ....in... ☐ Marriage contract

Witnesses: ....

ASCENDANCY UP TO XIVth GENERATION

6304 XIII 6305	3152 XII 3153
12610 XIV 12611	12612 XIV 12613	6306 XIII 6307
	1576 XI 1577
12608 XIV 12609	
	12614 XIV 12615
	GX 788 Father

Sosa 394

3154 XII 3155	6308 XIII 6309
6310 XIII 6311	12622 XIV 12623	12616 XIV 12617
	12618 XIV 12619
12620 XIV 12621	

GX 789 Mother

x.....................

| 12626 XIV 12627 |
| 12628 XIV 12629 |
| 12632 XIV 12633 |
| 12638 XIV 12639 |

| 6314 XIII 6315 | 12630 XIV 12631 | 12624 XIV 12625 | 6312 XIII 6313 |
| 3156 XII 3157 |

| 1578 XI 1579 |

| 6316 XIII 6317 | 12634 XIV 12635 | 12636 XIV 12637 |
| 3158 XII 3159 | 6318 XIII 6319 |

♀ Surname : ....First name : ....

▶Generation IX – maternal ascendant ↓Child page 197 –

☐ Implex

Born : ....in...☐ baptized

Daughter of : ....and: ....

Occupation(s) : ....

Deceased : ....in...

⚭ CHILDREN ....
....
....

⚶ ASCENDANCY UP TO XIVth GENERATION

6320 XIII 6321	3160 XII 3161	3162 XII 3163	6324 XIII 6325

12642 XIV 12643
12644 XIV 12645
6322 XIII 6323

12654 XIV 12655
12648 XIV 12649
6326 XIII 6327

1580 XI 1581

12640 XIV 12641

12646 XIV 12647

GX 790 Father

12650 XIV 12651

12652 XIV 12653

Sosa 395

GX 791 Mother

x...

°

†

12658 XIV 12659

12660 XIV 12661

12664 XIV 12665

12670 XIV 12671

1582 XI 1583

12662 XIV 12663
12656 XIV 12657
6328 XIII 6329

6332 XIII 6333
12666 XIV 12667
12668 XIV 12669

6330 XIII 6331

3164 XII 3165

3166 XII 3167

6334 XIII 6335

Sosa
396

Surname : .... First name : .... ♂

►Generation 9 – maternal ascendant ↓Child page 198 □ Implex

Born : ....in..□ baptized

Son of : ....and: ....

Occupation(s) : ....

Deceased : ....in...

⚭ MARITAL STATUS   □ *Civil Marriage* □ *Religious Marriage* □ *Free Union*

Date : ....in.. □ Marriage contract

Witnesses: ....

👪 ASCENDANCY UP TO XIVth GENERATION

6336 XIII 6337	3168 XII 3169
12674 XIV 12675	12676 XIV 12677	6338 XIII 6339
12672 XIV 12673	
12678 XIV 12679	

3170 XII 3171

6340 XIII 6341

6342 XIII 6343 | 12686 XIV 12687 | 12680 XIV 12681

12682 XIV 12683

12684 XIV 12685

1584 XI 1585

GX 792 Father

Sosa 396

GX 793 Mother

1586 XI 1587

12690 XIV 12691

12692 XIV 12693

6346 XIII 6347 | 12694 XIV 12695 | 12688 XIV 12689 | 6344 XIII 6345

3172 XII 3173

3174 XII 3175

6348 XIII 6349 | 12698 XIV 12699 | 12700 XIV 12701

6350 XIII 6351

12696 XIV 12697

12702 XIV 12703

396

♀ Surname : .... First name : ....

►Generation IX – maternal ascendant ↓Child page 198 –

☐ Implex

Born : ....in...☐ baptized

Daughter of : ....and:.................................

Occupation(s) : ....

Deceased : ....in..

💍 **CHILDREN** ....

....

....

🏃 **ASCENDANCY UP TO XIVth GENERATION**

6352 XIII 6353	3176 XII 3177
12706 XIV 12707	
12708 XIV 12709	6354 XIII 6355
12704 XIV 12705	
12710 XIV 12711	

1588 XI 1589

GX 794 Father

Sosa 397

GX 795 Mother

1590 XI 1591

3178 XII 3179	6356 XIII 6357
6358 XIII 6359	12718 XIV 12719
	12712 XIV 12713
	12714 XIV 12715
12716 XIV 12717	

12722 XIV 12723
12724 XIV 12725
12726 XIV 12727
12720 XIV 12721
6360 XIII 6361
6362 XIII 6363
3180 XII 3181

12728 XIV 12729
12734 XIV 12735
12730 XIV 12731
12732 XIV 12733
6364 XIII 6365
6366 XIII 6367
3182 XII 3183

397

Surname : .... First name : .... ♂

▶Generation 9 – maternal ascendant ↓Child page 199

□ Implex

Born : .... in.. □ baptized

Son of : ....and: ....

Occupation(s) : ....

Deceased : .... in...

⚭ **MARITAL STATUS**   □ *Civil Marriage*   □ *Religious Marriage*   □ *Free Union*

Date : ....in.. □ Marriage contract

Witnesses: ....

👪 **ASCENDANCY UP TO XIVth GENERATION**

| 6368 XIII 6369 |
| 12738 XIV 12739 | 12740 XIV 12741 |
| 3184 XII 3185 |
| 6370 XIII 6371 |
| 3186 XII 3187 |
| 6374 XIII 6375 |
| 12750 XIV 12751 | 12744 XIV 12745 |
| 6372 XIII 6373 |

1592 XI 1593

| 12736 XIV 12737 |
| 12742 XIV 12743 |
| 12746 XIV 12747 |
| 12748 XIV 12749 |

GX 796 Father

Sosa 398

GX 797 Mother

| 12754 XIV 12755 |
| 12756 XIV 12757 |
| 12760 XIV 12761 |
| 12766 XIV 12767 |

| 6378 XIII 6379 |
| 12758 XIV 12759 | 12752 XIV 12753 |
| 6376 XIII 6377 |
| 3188 XII 3189 |

1594 XI 1595

| 6380 XIII 6381 |
| 12762 XIV 12763 | 12764 XIV 12765 |
| 6382 XIII 6383 |
| 3190 XII 3191 |

♀ Surname : .... First name : ....

▶Generation IX – maternal ascendant ↓Child page 199 –

☐ Implex

Born : ....in..☐ baptized

Daughter of : ....and: ....

Occupation(s) : ....

Deceased : ....in..

💍 CHILDREN ....

....

🧍 ASCENDANCY UP TO XIVth GENERATION

6384 XIII 6385	3192 XII 3193
12770 XIV 12771	
12772 XIV 12773	6386 XIII 6387
12768 XIV 12769	
12774 XIV 12775	**1596 XI 1597**

GX 798 Father

Sosa 399

GX 799 Mother

3194 XII 3195	6388 XIII 6389
6390 XIII 6391	12782 XIV 12783
	12776 XIV 12777
	12778 XIV 12779
12780 XIV 12781	

12786 XIV 12787	
12788 XIV 12789	
12790 XIV 12791	
12784 XIV 12785	6392 XIII 6393
6394 XIII 6395	3196 XII 3197

1598 XI 1599

12792 XIV 12793	
	12798 XIV 12799
6396 XIII 6397	12794 XIV 12795
	12796 XIV 12797
3198 XII 3199	6398 XIII 6399

Sosa 400

Surname : .... First name : .... ♂

▶Generation 9 – maternal ascendant ↓Child page 200

☐ Implex

Born : .... in .... ☐ baptized

Son of : .... and: ....

Occupation(s) : ....

Deceased : .... in ....

⚭ MARITAL STATUS

☐ *Civil Marriage*   ☐ *Religious Marriage*   ☐ *Free Union*

Date : .... in ....   ☐ Marriage contract

Witnesses: ....

👪 ASCENDANCY UP TO XIVth GENERATION

6400 XIII 6401	3200 XII 3201
12802 XIV 12803	
12804 XIV 12805	6402 XIII 6403
	1600 XI 1601
12800 XIV 12801	
12806 XIV 12807	
	GX 800 Father

Sosa 400

GX 801 Mother

3202 XII 3203	
6406 XIII 6407	12814 XIV 12815
	12808 XIV 12809
6404 XIII 6405	
12810 XIV 12811	
12812 XIV 12813	

12818 XIV 12819	
12820 XIV 12821	
	12822 XIV 12823
	12816 XIV 12817
6410 XIII 6411	6408 XIII 6409
3204 XII 3205	1602 XI 1603

12824 XIV 12825	
	12830 XIV 12831
6412 XIII 6413	12826 XIV 12827
	12828 XIV 12829
3206 XII 3207	6414 XIII 6415

400

♀ Surname : ....First name : ....

▶Generation IX – maternal ascendant ↓Child page 200 –

☐ Implex

Born : ....in...☐ baptized

Daughter of : ....and: ....

Occupation(s) : ....

Deceased : ....in...

⚭ CHILDREN ....

....

👪 ASCENDANCY UP TO XIVth GENERATION

3208 XII 3209	3210 XII 3211
6416 XIII 6417	6420 XIII 6421
12834 XIV 12835	12846 XIV 12847
12836 XIV 12837	12840 XIV 12841
6418 XIII 6419	6422 XIII 6423

1604 XI 1605

12832 XIV 12833

12838 XIV 12839

12842 XIV 12843

12844 XIV 12845

GX 802 Father

Sosa 401

GX 803 Mother

12850 XIV 12851

12852 XIV 12853

12856 XIV 12857

12862 XIV 12863

| 12854 XIV 12855 | 12858 XIV 12859 |
| 12848 XIV 12849 | 12860 XIV 12861 |

6424 XIII 6425

6428 XIII 6429

1606 XI 1607

6426 XIII 6427

3212 XII 3213

3214 XII 3215

6430 XIII 6431

401

Surname : .... First name : .... ♂

▶Generation 9 – maternal ascendant ↓Child page 201

☐ Implex

Born : .... in .... ☐ baptized

Son of : .... and: ....

Occupation(s) : ....

Deceased : .... in ....

💍 MARITAL STATUS

☐ *Civil Marriage*   ☐ *Religious Marriage*   ☐ *Free Union*

Date : .... in .... ☐ Marriage contract

Witnesses: ....

👪 ASCENDANCY UP TO XIVth GENERATION

6432 / XIII / 6433	
3216 / XII / 3217	
12866 / XIV / 12867	
12868 / XIV / 12869	
6434 / XIII / 6435	
3218 / XII / 3219	
6438 / XIII / 6439	
12878 / XIV / 12879	
12872 / XIV / 12873	
6436 / XIII / 6437	
1608 XI 1609	
12864 / XIV / 12865	
12874 / XIV / 12875	
12870 / XIV / 12871	
12876 / XIV / 12877	

GX 804 Father

Sosa 402

GX 805 Mother

x

12882 / XIV / 12883	
12884 / XIV / 12885	
12888 / XIV / 12889	
12894 / XIV / 12895	
1610 XI 1611	
12886 / XIV / 12887	
12880 / XIV / 12881	
6440 / XIII / 6441	
6442 / XIII / 6443	
3220 / XII / 3221	
6444 / XIII / 6445	
12890 / XIV / 12891	
12892 / XIV / 12893	
6446 / XIII / 6447	
3222 / XII / 3223	

♀ Surname : .... First name : ....

▶Generation IX – maternal ascendant ↓Child page 201 –
□ Implex

Born : .... in .... □ baptized

Daughter of : .... and: ....

Occupation(s) : ....

Deceased : .... in ....

⚭ CHILDREN ....
....
....

🐾 ASCENDANCY UP TO XIVth GENERATION

6448 XIII 6449	3224 XII 3225
12898 XIV 12899	
12900 XIV 12901	6450 XIII 6451
12896 XIV 12897	1612 XI 1613
12902 XIV 12903	GX 806 Father

Sosa 403

GX 807 Mother

3226 XII 3227	
6454 XIII 6455	6452 XIII 6453
12910 XIV 12911	
12904 XIV 12905	
12906 XIV 12907	
12908 XIV 12909	

12914 XIV 12915	12920 XIV 12921
12916 XIV 12917	
12918 XIV 12919	
12912 XIV 12913	6456 XIII 6457
6458 XIII 6459	3228 XII 3229

1614 XI 1615

6460 XIII 6461	12926 XIV 12927
12922 XIV 12923	
12924 XIV 12925	
3230 XII 3231	6462 XIII 6463

Sosa
404

Surname : .... First name : .... ♂

▶Generation 9 – maternal ascendant ↓Child page 202

□ Implex

Born : ....in..□ baptized

Son of : ....and:..

Occupation(s) : ....

Deceased : ....in..

⊙⊙ **MARITAL STATUS**   □ *Civil Marriage* □ *Religious Marriage* □ *Free Union*

Date : ....in..   □ Marriage contract

Witnesses: ....

👪 ASCENDANCY UP TO XIVth GENERATION

6464 XIII 6465	
3232 XII 3233	3234 XII 3235
12930 XIV 12931	12932 XIV 12933
6466 XIII 6467	6468 XIII 6469
12942 XIV 12943	12936 XIV 12937
6470 XIII 6471	

1616 XI 1617

12928 XIV 12929

12934 XIV 12935

12938 XIV 12939

12940 XIV 12941

GX 808 Father

Sosa 404

GX 809 Mother

12946 XIV 12947

12948 XIV 12949

12952 XIV 12953

12958 XIV 12959

1618 XI 1619

12950 XIV 12951	12944 XIV 12945
6472 XIII 6473	
6474 XIII 6475	
3236 XII 3237	
12954 XIV 12955	12956 XIV 12957
6476 XIII 6477	
3238 XII 3239	
6478 XIII 6479	

404

♀ Surname : ....First name : ....

▶Generation IX – maternal ascendant ↓Child page 202 –

□ Implex

Born : ....in...□ baptized

Daughter of : ....and: ....

Occupation(s) : ....

Deceased : ....in...

⚭ **CHILDREN** ....

....

👪 ASCENDANCY UP TO XIVth GENERATION

6480 XIII 6481	3240 XII 3241
12962 XIV 12963	
12964 XIV 12965	6482 XIII 6483
12960 XIV 12961	
12966 XIV 12967	

1620 **XI** 1621

GX 810 Father

Sosa 405

3242 XII 3243	6484 XIII 6485
6486 XIII 6487	12974 XIV 12975
12968 XIV 12969	
12970 XIV 12971	
12972 XIV 12973	

GX 811 Mother

12978 XIV 12979	12984 XIV 12985
12980 XIV 12981	12990 XIV 12991
12982 XIV 12983	
12976 XIV 12977	6488 XIII 6489
6490 XIII 6491	3244 XII 3245

1622 **XI** 1623

12986 XIV 12987	
12988 XIV 12989	
6492 XIII 6493	
6494 XIII 6495	
3246 XII 3247	

Sosa
406

Surname : .... First name : .... ♂

▶Generation 9 – maternal ascendant ↓Child page 203

☐ Implex

Born : ....in..☐ baptized

Son of : ....and: ....

Occupation(s) : ....

Deceased : ....in...

💍 MARITAL STATUS   ☐ *Civil Marriage* ☐ *Religious Marriage* ☐ *Free Union*

Date : ....in... ☐ Marriage contract

Witnesses: ....

👪 ASCENDANCY UP TO XIVth GENERATION

6496	XIII	6497
3248	XII	3249
12994	XIV	12995
12996	XIV	12997
6498	XIII	6499
3250	XII	3251
6502	XIII	6503
13006	XIV	13007
13000	XIV	13001
6500	XIII	6501

1624 XI 1625

12992	XIV	12993
12998	XIV	12999
13002	XIV	13003
13004	XIV	13005

GX 812 Father

Sosa 406

GX 813 Mother

13010	XIV	13011
13012	XIV	13013
13016	XIV	13017
13022	XIV	13023

1626 XI 1627

6506	XIII	6507
13014	XIV	13015
13008	XIV	13009
6504	XIII	6505
3252	XII	3253
3254	XII	3255
6508	XIII	6509
13018	XIV	13019
13020	XIV	13021
6510	XIII	6511

406

♀ Surname : .... First name : ....

▶Generation IX – maternal ascendant ↓Child page 203 –   ☐ Implex

Born : .... in ....☐ baptized

Daughter of : ....and: ....

Occupation(s) : ....

Deceased : ....in...

⚭ **CHILDREN** ....

....

🎋 **ASCENDANCY UP TO XIVth GENERATION**

6512 XIII 6513	3256 XII 3257
13026 XIV 13027	6514 XIII 6515
13028 XIV 13029	
13024 XIV 13025	
13030 XIV 13031	
	1628 XI 1629

GX 814 Father

Sosa 407

GX 815 Mother

x.......

3258 XII 3259	6516 XIII 6517
6518 XIII 6519	13038 XIV 13039
	13032 XIV 13033
	13034 XIV 13035
13036 XIV 13037	

13042 XIV 13043	
13044 XIV 13045	
13046 XIV 13047	
13040 XIV 13041	6520 XIII 6521
6522 XIII 6523	
	3260 XII 3261
	1630 XI 1631

13048 XIV 13049	
	13054 XIV 13055
6524 XIII 6525	13050 XIV 13051
	13052 XIV 13053
3262 XII 3263	6526 XIII 6527

Sosa
408

Surname : .... First name : .... ♂

▶Generation 9 – maternal ascendant ↓Child page 204

☐ Implex

Born : ....in...☐ baptized

Son of : ....and:...

Occupation(s) : ....

Deceased : ....in...

💍 MARITAL STATUS   ☐ *Civil Marriage*   ☐ *Religious Marriage*   ☐ *Free Union*

Date : ....in.. ☐ Marriage contract

Witnesses: ....

👪 ASCENDANCY UP TO XIVth GENERATION

6528 XIII 6529	3264 XII 3265	
13058 XIV 13059	13060 XIV 13061	6530 XIII 6531
		3266 XII 3267
	6534 XIII 6535	13070 XIV 13071
13064 XIV 13065	6532 XIII 6533	

1632 XI 1633

GX 816 Father

Sosa 408

GX 817 Mother

13056 XIV 13057	
13062 XIV 13063	
13068 XIV 13069	13066 XIV 13067

| 13074 XIV 13075 | 13080 XIV 13081 |
| 13076 XIV 13077 | 13086 XIV 13087 |

1634 XI 1635

13078 XIV 13079	13072 XIV 13073	6536 XIII 6537
		6540 XIII 6541
13082 XIV 13083	13084 XIV 13085	6542 XIII 6543
6538 XIII 6539	3268 XII 3269	3270 XII 3271

408

♀ Surname : ....First name : ....

▶Generation IX – maternal ascendant ↓Child page 204 –

☐ Implex

Born : ....in...☐ baptized

Daughter of : ....and: ....

Occupation(s) : ....

Deceased : ....in...

⚭ CHILDREN ....
....
....

👪 ASCENDANCY UP TO XIVth GENERATION

6544 XIII 6545	
	3272 XII 3273
13090 XIV 13091	
13092 XIV 13093	
	6546 XIII 6547
13088 XIV 13089	
	13094 XIV 13095

1636 XI 1637

GX 818 Father

Sosa 409

GX 819 Mother

3274 XII 3275

6550 XIII 6551

13102 XIV 13103

13096 XIV 13097

6548 XIII 6549

13098 XIV 13099

13100 XIV 13101

13106 XIV 13107

13108 XIV 13109

13110 XIV 13111

13104 XIV 13105

6552 XIII 6553

13112 XIV 13113

13118 XIV 13119

13114 XIV 13115

13116 XIV 13117

6556 XIII 6557

6558 XIII 6559

6554 XIII 6555

3276 XII 3277

1638 XI 1639

3278 XII 3279

Sosa
410

Surname : .... First name : .... ♂

□ Implex

Born : ....in.................................□ baptized

Son of : ....and: ....

Occupation(s) : ....

Deceased : ....in...

⚭ **MARITAL STATUS**   □ *Civil Marriage*   □ *Religious Marriage*   □ *Free Union*

Date : ....in.. □ Marriage contract

Witnesses: ....

👪 ASCENDANCY UP TO XIVth GENERATION

6560 XIII 6561	3280 XII 3281	
13122 XIV 13123	13124 XIV 13125	6562 XIII 6563
	1640 XI 1641	
13120 XIV 13121		
13126 XIV 13127	**GX 820 Father**	

Sosa 410

3282 XII 3283	6564 XIII 6565	
6566 XIII 6567	13134 XIV 13135	13128 XIV 13129
	13130 XIV 13131	
13132 XIV 13133		

GX 821 Mother

x

13138 XIV 13139	13144 XIV 13145	
13140 XIV 13141		13150 XIV 13151
13142 XIV 13143	13136 XIV 13137	6568 XIII 6569
6570 XIII 6571	3284 XII 3285	

1642 XI 1643		
6572 XIII 6573	13146 XIV 13147	13148 XIV 13149
3286 XII 3287	6574 XIII 6575	

♀ Surname : .... First name : ....

▶Generation IX – maternal ascendant ↓Child page 205 –   □ Implex

Born : ....in...□ baptized

Daughter of : ....and: ....

Occupation(s) : ....

Deceased : ....in...

⚭ **CHILDREN** ....

....

....

👪 **ASCENDANCY UP TO XIVth GENERATION**

6576 XIII 6577	3288 XII 3289
13154 XIV 13155	13156 XIV 13157
6578 XIII 6579	

3290 XII 3291

6580 XIII 6581

6582 XIII 6583

13166 XIV 13167

13160 XIV 13161

1644 XI 1645

13152 XIV 13153

13158 XIV 13159

13164 XIV 13165

13162 XIV 13163

GX 822 Father

Sosa 411

GX 823 Mother

13170 XIV 13171

13172 XIV 13173

13176 XIV 13177

13182 XIV 13183

1646 XI 1647

13174 XIV 13175

13168 XIV 13169

6584 XIII 6585

6586 XIII 6587

3292 XII 3293

6588 XIII 6589

13178 XIV 13179

13180 XIV 13181

3294 XII 3295

6590 XIII 6591

Sosa 412

Surname : .... First name : .... ♂

Generation 9 - maternal ascendant ↓Child page 206

☐ Implex

Born : .... in .... ☐ baptized

Son of : .... and: ....

Occupation(s) : ....

Deceased : .... in ....

⚭ MARITAL STATUS
☐ Civil Marriage ☐ Religious Marriage ☐ Free Union

Date : .... in .... ☐ Marriage contract

Witnesses: ....

👪 ASCENDANCY UP TO XIVth GENERATION

6592 XIII 6593	3296 XII 3297
13186 XIV 13187	3298 XII 3299
13188 XIV 13189	6594 XIII 6595
13184 XIV 13185	6596 XIII 6597
13190 XIV 13191	6598 XIII 6599

1648 XI 1649

13198 XIV 13199
13192 XIV 13193
13194 XIV 13195
13196 XIV 13197

GX 824 Father

Sosa 412

GX 825 Mother

13202 XIV 13203
13204 XIV 13205
13206 XIV 13207
13200 XIV 13201
6600 XIII 6601
6602 XIII 6603
3300 XII 3301

1650 XI 1651

13208 XIV 13209
13214 XIV 13215
13210 XIV 13211
13212 XIV 13213
6604 XIII 6605
6606 XIII 6607
3302 XII 3303

412

♀ Surname : .... First name : ....

► Generation IX – maternal ascendant ↓ Child page 206 –   □ Implex

Born : ....in...□ baptized

Daughter of : ....and: ....

Occupation(s) : ....

Deceased : ....in...

⚭ **CHILDREN** ....
....
....

♟ **ASCENDANCY UP TO XIVth GENERATION**

6608 XIII 6609	3304 XII 3305	
13218 XIV 13219	13220 XIV 13221	6610 XIII 6611

3306 XII 3307

6614 XIII 6615 | 13230 XIV 13231 | 13224 XIV 13225 | 6612 XIII 6613

1652 XI 1653

13216 XIV 13217

13222 XIV 13223

13226 XIV 13227

13228 XIV 13229

GX 826 Father

Sosa 413

GX 827 Mother

x

13234 XIV 13235

13240 XIV 13241

13236 XIV 13237

13246 XIV 13247

°

†

1654 XI 1655

13238 XIV 13239 | 13232 XIV 13233 | 6616 XIII 6617

6620 XIII 6621 | 13242 XIV 13243 | 13244 XIV 13245 | 6622 XIII 6623

6618 XIII 6619 | 3308 XII 3309

3310 XII 3311

Sosa
414

Surname : .... First name : .... ♂

► Generation 9 – maternal ascendant   ↓Child page 207

☐ Implex

Born : .... in ....☐ baptized

Son of : ....and: ....

Occupation(s) : ....

Deceased : ....in.......................................

⚭ MARITAL STATUS
☐ Civil Marriage ☐ Religious Marriage ☐ Free Union

Date : ....in....................................... ☐ Marriage contract

Witnesses: ....

👪 ASCENDANCY UP TO XIVth GENERATION

6624 XIII 6625	
3312 XII 3313	3314 XII 3315
13250 XIV 13251	13252 XIV 13253
6626 XIII 6627	6630 XIII 6631
6628 XIII 6629	
13262 XIV 13263	13256 XIV 13257
1656 XI 1657	
13248 XIV 13249	13258 XIV 13259
13254 XIV 13255	13260 XIV 13261

GX 828 Father

Sosa 414

GX 829 Mother

13266 XIV 13267	13272 XIV 13273
13268 XIV 13269	13278 XIV 13279
1658 XI 1659	
13270 XIV 13271	13264 XIV 13265
6632 XIII 6633	6636 XIII 6637
13274 XIV 13275	13276 XIV 13277
6634 XIII 6635	6638 XIII 6639
3316 XII 3317	3318 XII 3319

414

♀ Surname : .... First name : ....

▶Generation IX – maternal ascendant ↓Child page 207 –   □ Implex

Born : .... in.. □ baptized

Daughter of : .... and: ....

Occupation(s) : ....

Deceased : .... in..

⚭ **CHILDREN** ....

....

....

👪 ASCENDANCY UP TO XIVth GENERATION

6640 XIII 6641	3320 XII 3321
13282 XIV 13283	
13284 XIV 13285	6642 XIII 6643
13280 XIV 13281	
13286 XIV 13287	

1660 XI 1661

GX 830 Father

Sosa 415

GX 831 Mother

3322 XII 3323	6644 XIII 6645
6646 XIII 6647	13294 XIV 13295	13288 XIV 13289
13290 XIV 13291	
13292 XIV 13293	

13298 XIV 13299	
13300 XIV 13301	
13302 XIV 13303	13296 XIV 13297	6648 XIII 6649
6650 XIII 6651	3324 XII 3325

1662 XI 1663

13304 XIV 13305	
13310 XIV 13311	
6652 XIII 6653	13306 XIV 13307	13308 XIV 13309	6654 XIII 6655
3326 XII 3327	

Sosa
416

Surname : .... First name : .... ♂

▶Generation 9 – maternal ascendant ↓Child page 208 ☐ Implex

Born : .... in...☐ baptized

Son of : ....and: ....

Occupation(s) : ....

Deceased : ....in...

⚭ MARITAL STATUS   ☐ Civil Marriage ☐ Religious Marriage ☐ Free Union

Date : ....in.. ☐ Marriage contract

Witnesses: ....

👪 ASCENDANCY UP TO XIVth GENERATION

6656 XIII 6657	3328 XII 3329
13314 XIV 13315	13316 XIV 13317
	6658 XIII 6659
13312 XIV 13313	
	13318 XIV 13319

1664 XI 1665

3330 XII 3331

| 6662 XIII 6663 | 13326 XIV 13327 | 13320 XIV 13321 | 6660 XIII 6661 |

| 13322 XIV 13323 |
| 13324 XIV 13325 |

GX 832 Father

Sosa 416

GX 833 Mother

13330 XIV 13331	
13332 XIV 13333	
	13334 XIV 13335
	13328 XIV 13329
	6664 XIII 6665
6666 XIII 6667	3332 XII 3333

1666 XI 1667

13336 XIV 13337	
	13342 XIV 13343
6668 XIII 6669	13338 XIV 13339	13340 XIV 13341	6670 XIII 6671
3334 XII 3335	

416

♀ Surname : .... First name : ....

▶Generation IX – maternal ascendant ↓Child page 208 –   □ Implex

Born : ....in.. □ baptized

Daughter of : ....and: ....

Occupation(s) : ....

Deceased : ....in..

💍 **CHILDREN** ....

....

....

👪 **ASCENDANCY UP TO XIVth GENERATION**

3336 XII 3337	3338 XII 3339
6672 XIII 6673	6676 XIII 6677
13346 XIV 13347	13348 XIV 13349	6674 XIII 6675	6678 XIII 6679	13358 XIV 13359	13352 XIV 13353

1668 XI 1669

13344 XIV 13345

13354 XIV 13355

13350 XIV 13351

13356 XIV 13357

GX 834 Father

Sosa 417

GX 835 Mother

x

13362 XIV 13363

13368 XIV 13369

13364 XIV 13365

13374 XIV 13375

1670 XI 1671

13366 XIV 13367

13360 XIV 13361

6680 XIII 6681

6684 XIII 6685

13370 XIV 13371

13372 XIV 13373

6682 XIII 6683

3340 XII 3341

3342 XII 3343

6686 XIII 6687

Surname : .... First name : .... ♂

□ Implex

Born : ....in..................................□ baptized

Son of : ....and: ....

Occupation(s) : ....

Deceased : ....in..................................

⚭ **MARITAL STATUS**   □ *Civil Marriage*   □ *Religious Marriage*   □ *Free Union*

Date : ....in..................................□ Marriage contract

Witnesses: ....

ASCENDANCY UP TO XIVth GENERATION

3344 XII 3345	3346 XII 3347
6688 XIII 6689	6692 XIII 6693
13378 XIV 13379	13380 XIV 13381	6690 XIII 6691	6694 XIII 6695	13390 XIV 13391	13384 XIV 13385
13376 XIV 13377	13386 XIV 13387
13382 XIV 13383	13388 XIV 13389

1672 XI 1673

GX 836 Father

Sosa 418

GX 837 Mother

13394 XIV 13395	13400 XIV 13401
13396 XIV 13397	13406 XIV 13407
13398 XIV 13399	13392 XIV 13393	6696 XIII 6697	6700 XIII 6701	13402 XIV 13403	13404 XIV 13405
6698 XIII 6699	6702 XIII 6703
3348 XII 3349	3350 XII 3351

1674 XI 1675

♀ Surname : .... First name : ....

▶Generation IX – maternal ascendant ↓Child page 209 –   □ Implex

Born : ....in..□ baptized

Daughter of : ....and: ....

Occupation(s) : ....

Deceased : ....in...

⚭ CHILDREN ....

....

....

👪 ASCENDANCY UP TO XIVth GENERATION

| 6704 XIII 6705 | | 3352 XII 3353 | | | | 3354 XII 3355 | | 6708 XIII 6709 |

| 13410 XIV 13411 | 13412 XIV 13413 | 6706 XIII 6707 | | | | 6710 XIII 6711 | 13422 XIV 13423 | 13416 XIV 13417 |

1676 XI 1677

| 13408 XIV 13409 | | | | | | | | 13418 XIV 13419 |

| 13414 XIV 13415 | | | | | 13420 XIV 13421 |

GX 838 Father

Sosa 419

GX 839 Mother

| 13426 XIV 13427 | | | | 13432 XIV 13433 |

| 13428 XIV 13429 | | | | | | 13438 XIV 13439 |

1678 XI 1679

| 13430 XIV 13431 | 13424 XIV 13425 | 6712 XIII 6713 | | | | 6716 XIII 6717 | 13434 XIV 13435 | 13436 XIV 13437 |

| 6714 XIII 6715 | | 3356 XII 3357 | | | | 3358 XII 3359 | | 6718 XIII 6719 |

Surname : .... First name : .... ♂

▶Generation 9 – maternal ascendant ↓Child page 210

☐ Implex

Born : .... in..☐ baptized

Son of : ....and: ....

Occupation(s) : ....

Deceased : ....in...

⚭ MARITAL STATUS

☐ Civil Marriage   ☐ Religious Marriage   ☐ Free Union

Date : ....in..☐ Marriage contract

Witnesses: ....

👪 ASCENDANCY UP TO XIVth GENERATION

3360 XII 3361		3362 XII 3363
6720 XIII 6721		6724 XIII 6725
13442 XIV 13443	13444 XIV 13445	6722 XIII 6723	6726 XIII 6727	13454 XIV 13455	13448 XIV 13449
	1680 XI 1681	
13440 XIV 13441		13450 XIV 13451
13446 XIV 13447	GX 840 Father	13452 XIV 13453

Sosa 420

GX 841 Mother

13458 XIV 13459		13464 XIV 13465
13460 XIV 13461		13470 XIV 13471
13462 XIV 13463	13456 XIV 13457	6728 XIII 6729	1682 XI 1683	6732 XIII 6733	13466 XIV 13467	13468 XIV 13469
6730 XIII 6731	3364 XII 3365	3366 XII 3367	6734 XIII 6735

♀ Surname : ....First name : ....

☐ Implex

Born : ....in...☐ baptized

Daughter of : ....and: ....

Occupation(s) : ....

Deceased : ....in..

💍 **CHILDREN** ....
....
....

🏃 **ASCENDANCY UP TO XIVth GENERATION**

6736 XIII 6737	
3368 XII 3369	
13474 XIV 13475	
13476 XIV 13477	
6738 XIII 6739	
3370 XII 3371	
6740 XIII 6741	
6742 XIII 6743	
13486 XIV 13487	
13480 XIV 13481	
13472 XIV 13473	
13482 XIV 13483	
13478 XIV 13479	
13484 XIV 13485	
1684 XI 1685	
GX 842 Father	

Sosa 421

GX 843 Mother

X

13490 XIV 13491	
13496 XIV 13497	
13492 XIV 13493	
13502 XIV 13503	
13494 XIV 13495	
13488 XIV 13489	
6744 XIII 6745	
6748 XIII 6749	
13498 XIV 13499	
13500 XIV 13501	
6746 XIII 6747	
6750 XIII 6751	
3372 XII 3373	
3374 XII 3375	
1686 XI 1687	

Sosa
422

Surname : .... First name : .... ♂

▶Generation 9 – maternal ascendant ↓Child page 211

□ Implex

Born : .... in..□ baptized

Son of : ....and: ....

Occupation(s) : ....

Deceased : ....in..

⚭ MARITAL STATUS

□ Civil Marriage   □ Religious Marriage   □ Free Union

Date : ....in.. □ Marriage contract

Witnesses: ....

👪 ASCENDANCY UP TO XIVth GENERATION

6752 XIII 6753	3376 XII 3377	3378 XII 3379	6756 XIII 6757

13506 XIV 13507 | 13508 XIV 13509 | 6754 XIII 6755

6758 XIII 6759 | 13518 XIV 13519 | 13512 XIV 13513

13504 XIV 13505

1688 XI 1689

13514 XIV 13515

13510 XIV 13511

13516 XIV 13517

GX 844 Father

Sosa 422

GX 845 Mother

13522 XIV 13523

13528 XIV 13529

13524 XIV 13525

13534 XIV 13535

13526 XIV 13527 | 13520 XIV 13521 | 6760 XIII 6761

1690 XI 1691

6764 XIII 6765 | 13530 XIV 13531 | 13532 XIV 13533

6762 XIII 6763

3380 XII 3381

3382 XII 3383

6766 XIII 6767

422

♀ Surname : .... First name : ....

▶Generation IX – maternal ascendant ↓Child page 211 –

☐ Implex

Born : ....in...☐ baptized

Daughter of : ....and: ....

Occupation(s) : ....

Deceased : ....in...

💍 CHILDREN ....

....
....

👪 ASCENDANCY UP TO XIVth GENERATION

6768 XIII 6769	3384 XII 3385
13538 XIV 13539	13540 XIV 13541	6770 XIII 6771
	1692 XI 1693
13536 XIV 13537	
13542 XIV 13543	GX 846 Father

Sosa 423

GX 847 Mother

13554 XIV 13555	
13556 XIV 13557	
	1694 XI 1695
13558 XIV 13559	13552 XIV 13553	6776 XIII 6777
6778 XIII 6779	3388 XII 3389

3386 XII 3387

6774 XIII 6775 | 13550 XIV 13551 | 13544 XIV 13545 | 6772 XIII 6773

13546 XIV 13547

13548 XIV 13549

13560 XIV 13561

13566 XIV 13567

6780 XIII 6781 | 13562 XIV 13563 | 13564 XIV 13565 | 6782 XIII 6783

3390 XII 3391

Sosa
424

Surname : .... First name : .... ♂

▶Generation 9 – maternal ascendant ↓Child page 212 ☐ Implex

Born : ....in...☐ baptized

Son of : ....and:..

Occupation(s) : ....

Deceased : ....in...

⚭ MARITAL STATUS   ☐ Civil Marriage   ☐ Religious Marriage   ☐ Free Union

Date : ....in...☐ Marriage contract

Witnesses: ....

👪 ASCENDANCY UP TO XIVth GENERATION

6784 XIII 6785	3392 XII 3393	
13570 XIV 13571	13572 XIV 13573	6786 XIII 6787
		3394 XII 3395
	1696 XI 1697	6790 XIII 6791
		13582 XIV 13583
		13576 XIV 13577
		6788 XIII 6789

GX 848 Father

13568 XIV 13569

13574 XIV 13575

13578 XIV 13579

13580 XIV 13581

Sosa 424

GX 849 Mother

13586 XIV 13587

13588 XIV 13589

13592 XIV 13593

13598 XIV 13599

13590 XIV 13591

13584 XIV 13585

6792 XIII 6793

1698 XI 1699

6796 XIII 6797

13594 XIV 13595

13596 XIV 13597

6794 XIII 6795

3396 XII 3397

3398 XII 3399

6798 XIII 6799

♀ Surname : .... First name : ....

☐ Implex

Born : ....in...☐ baptized

Daughter of : ....and: ....

Occupation(s) : ....

Deceased : ....in...

⚭ **CHILDREN** ....

....

🏃 ASCENDANCY UP TO XIVth GENERATION

6800 XIII 6801	3400 XII 3401
13602 XIV 13603	
13604 XIV 13605	6802 XIII 6803
13600 XIV 13601	1700 XI 1701
13606 XIV 13607	GX 850 Father

Sosa 425

GX 851 Mother

3402 XII 3403	6804 XIII 6805
6806 XIII 6807	13614 XIV 13615
	13608 XIV 13609
13610 XIV 13611	
13612 XIV 13613	

13618 XIV 13619	13624 XIV 13625
13620 XIV 13621	13630 XIV 13631
13622 XIV 13623	
13616 XIV 13617	
6808 XIII 6809	
6810 XIII 6811	3404 XII 3405

1702 XI 1703	

6812 XIII 6813	
13626 XIV 13627	13628 XIV 13629
3406 XII 3407	6814 XIII 6815

Surname : .... First name : .... ♂

▶Generation 9 – maternal ascendant ↓Child page 213 □ Implex

Born : .... in .... □ baptized

Son of : .... and: ....

Occupation(s) : ....

Deceased : .... in ....

⚭ **MARITAL STATUS** □ *Civil Marriage* □ *Religious Marriage* □ *Free Union*

Date : .... in .... □ Marriage contract

Witnesses: ....

👪 **ASCENDANCY UP TO XIVth GENERATION**

3408 XII 3409	3410 XII 3411
6816 XIII 6817	6820 XIII 6821
13634 XIV 13635	13636 XIV 13637	6818 XIII 6819	6822 XIII 6823	13646 XIV 13647	13640 XIV 13641
1704 XI 1705	
13632 XIV 13633	13642 XIV 13643
13638 XIV 13639	13644 XIV 13645

GX 852 Father

Sosa 426

GX 853 Mother

13650 XIV 13651	13656 XIV 13657
13652 XIV 13653	13662 XIV 13663
13654 XIV 13655	13648 XIV 13649	6824 XIII 6825	6828 XIII 6829	13658 XIV 13659	13660 XIV 13661
1706 XI 1707	
6826 XIII 6827	6830 XIII 6831
3412 XII 3413	3414 XII 3415

⚲ Surname : .... First name : ....

▶Generation IX – maternal ascendant ↓Child page 213 –   □ Implex

Born : ....in.................................... □ baptized

Daughter of : ....and: ....

Occupation(s) : ....

Deceased : ....in....................

⚭ **CHILDREN** ....
....
....

⚒ **ASCENDANCY UP TO XIVth GENERATION**

6832 XIII 6833	3416 XII 3417
13666 XIV 13667	
13668 XIV 13669	6834 XIII 6835
13664 XIV 13665	
13670 XIV 13671	

1708 XI 1709

GX 854 Father

Sosa 427

GX 855 Mother

3418 XII 3419	6836 XIII 6837
6838 XIII 6839	13678 XIV 13679	13672 XIV 13673
13674 XIV 13675	
13676 XIV 13677	

13682 XIV 13683	13688 XIV 13689
13684 XIV 13685	13694 XIV 13695
13686 XIV 13687	13680 XIV 13681	6840 XIII 6841
6842 XIII 6843	3420 XII 3421

1710 XI 1711

6844 XIII 6845	13690 XIV 13691	13692 XIV 13693
3422 XII 3423	6846 XIII 6847

427

Sosa
428

Surname : .... First name : .... ♂

▶Generation 9 – maternal ascendant   ↓Child page 214

☐ Implex

Born : ....in...☐ baptized

Son of : ....and: ....

Occupation(s) : ....

Deceased : ....in...

💍 MARITAL STATUS   ☐ Civil Marriage   ☐ Religious Marriage   ☐ Free Union

Date : ....in.. ☐ Marriage contract

Witnesses: ....

👪 ASCENDANCY UP TO XIVth GENERATION

6848 XIII 6849	3424 XII 3425
13698 XIV 13699	3426 XII 3427
13700 XIV 13701	6852 XIII 6853
6850 XIII 6851	6854 XIII 6855
13696 XIV 13697	13710 XIV 13711
13702 XIV 13703	13704 XIV 13705
	13706 XIV 13707
1712 XI 1713	13708 XIV 13709

GX 856 Father

Sosa 428

GX 857 Mother

13714 XIV 13715	13720 XIV 13721
13716 XIV 13717	13726 XIV 13727
13718 XIV 13719	13722 XIV 13723
13712 XIV 13713	13724 XIV 13725
6856 XIII 6857	6860 XIII 6861
6858 XIII 6859	6862 XIII 6863
3428 XII 3429	3430 XII 3431
1714 XI 1715	

428

♀ Surname : ....First name : ....

►Generation IX – maternal ascendant ↓Child page 214 –   □ Implex

Born : ....in...□ baptized

Daughter of : ....and: ....

Occupation(s) : ....

Deceased : ....in..

⚭ CHILDREN ....
....
....

⚸ ASCENDANCY UP TO XIVth GENERATION

6864 XIII 6865	
3432 XII 3433	
13730 XIV 13731	
13732 XIV 13733	
6866 XIII 6867	
1716 XI 1717	
13728 XIV 13729	
13734 XIV 13735	
GX 858 Father	

Sosa 429

GX 859 Mother

| 3434 XII 3435 |
| 6868 XIII 6869 |
| 6870 XIII 6871 |
| 13742 XIV 13743 |
| 13736 XIV 13737 |
| 13738 XIV 13739 |
| 13740 XIV 13741 |

| 13746 XIV 13747 |
| 13748 XIV 13749 |
| 13750 XIV 13751 |
| 13744 XIV 13745 |
| 6872 XIII 6873 |
| 6874 XIII 6875 |
| 3436 XII 3437 |
| 1718 XI 1719 |

| 13752 XIV 13753 |
| 13758 XIV 13759 |
| 6876 XIII 6877 |
| 13754 XIV 13755 |
| 13756 XIV 13757 |
| 6878 XIII 6879 |
| 3438 XII 3439 |

Surname : .... First name : .... ♂

□ Implex

Born : ....in.. □ baptized

Son of : ....and: ....

Occupation(s) : ....

Deceased : ....in..

⚭ MARITAL STATUS   □ Civil Marriage   □ Religious Marriage   □ Free Union

Date : ....in..   □ Marriage contract

Witnesses: ....

👪 ASCENDANCY UP TO XIVth GENERATION

6880 XIII 6881	
3440 XII 3441	3442 XII 3443
13762 XIV 13763	6884 XIII 6885
13764 XIV 13765	6886 XIII 6887
6882 XIII 6883	13774 XIV 13775
	13768 XIV 13769

1720 XI 1721

13760 XIV 13761

13766 XIV 13767

13770 XIV 13771

13772 XIV 13773

GX 860 Father

Sosa 430

GX 861 Mother

13778 XIV 13779

13780 XIV 13781

13784 XIV 13785

13790 XIV 13791

1722 XI 1723

13782 XIV 13783	
13776 XIV 13777	6892 XIII 6893
6888 XIII 6889	13786 XIV 13787
6890 XIII 6891	13788 XIV 13789
3444 XII 3445	6894 XIII 6895
	3446 XII 3447

♀ Surname : .... First name : ....

▶Generation IX – maternal ascendant ↓Child page 215 –

☐ Implex

Born : ....in... ☐ baptized

Daughter of : ....and: ....

Occupation(s) : ....

Deceased : ....in...

⚭ CHILDREN ....

🎎 ASCENDANCY UP TO XIVth GENERATION

6896 XIII 6897	3448 XII 3449
13794 XIV 13795	
13796 XIV 13797	6898 XIII 6899
13792 XIV 13793	
13798 XIV 13799	

1724 XI 1725

GX 862 Father

Sosa 431

GX 863 Mother

3450 XII 3451	
6902 XIII 6903	13806 XIV 13807
	13800 XIV 13801
6900 XIII 6901	
13802 XIV 13803	
13804 XIV 13805	

13810 XIV 13811	
13812 XIV 13813	
13814 XIV 13815	13808 XIV 13809
	6904 XIII 6905
6906 XIII 6907	3452 XII 3453

1726 XI 1727

13816 XIV 13817	
13822 XIV 13823	
6908 XIII 6909	13818 XIV 13819
	13820 XIV 13821
3454 XII 3455	6910 XIII 6911

Surname : .... First name : .... ♂

▶Generation 9 – maternal ascendant ↓Child page 216

□ Implex

Born : .... in... □ baptized

Son of : ....and: ....

Occupation(s) : ....

Deceased : ....in.......................................

⚭ **MARITAL STATUS**   □ *Civil Marriage* □ *Religious Marriage* □ *Free Union*

Date : ....in.. □ Marriage contract

Witnesses: ....

👪 ASCENDANCY UP TO XIVth GENERATION

6912 XIII 6913	
3456 XII 3457	
13826 XIV 13827	
13828 XIV 13829	
6914 XIII 6915	
3458 XII 3459	
6918 XIII 6919	
13838 XIV 13839	
13832 XIV 13833	
6916 XIII 6917	
13824 XIV 13825	
13834 XIV 13835	
13830 XIV 13831	
13836 XIV 13837	

1728 XI 1729

GX 864 Father

Sosa 432

GX 865 Mother

13842 XIV 13843	
13844 XIV 13845	
13848 XIV 13849	
13854 XIV 13855	
13846 XIV 13847	
13840 XIV 13841	
6920 XIII 6921	
6924 XIII 6925	
13850 XIV 13851	
13852 XIV 13853	
6922 XIII 6923	
3460 XII 3461	
3462 XII 3463	
6926 XIII 6927	

1730 XI 1731

♀ Surname : .... First name : ....

▶Generation IX – maternal ascendant ↓Child page 216 – □ Implex

Born : ....in... □ baptized

Daughter of : ....and: ....

Occupation(s) : ....

Deceased : ....in...

⚭ **CHILDREN** ....

....

ASCENDANCY UP TO XIVth GENERATION

6928 XIII 6929	
3464 XII 3465	3466 XII 3467
13858 XIV 13859	13870 XIV 13871
13860 XIV 13861	13864 XIV 13865
6930 XIII 6931	6934 XIII 6935
6932 XIII 6933	

1732 XI 1733

13856 XIV 13857	13866 XIV 13867
13862 XIV 13863	13868 XIV 13869

GX 866 Father

Sosa 433

GX 867 Mother

x

°

†

13874 XIV 13875	13880 XIV 13881
13876 XIV 13877	13886 XIV 13887

1734 XI 1735

13878 XIV 13879	13882 XIV 13883
13872 XIV 13873	13884 XIV 13885
6936 XIII 6937	6940 XIII 6941
6938 XIII 6939	6942 XIII 6943

| 3468 XII 3469 | 3470 XII 3471 |

Surname : .... First name : .... ♂

▶Generation 9 – maternal ascendant ↓Child page 217 ☐ Implex

Born : .... in .... ☐ baptized

Son of : .... and: ....

Occupation(s) : ....

Deceased : .... in ....

⚭ **MARITAL STATUS** ☐ *Civil Marriage* ☐ *Religious Marriage* ☐ *Free Union*

Date : .... in .... ☐ Marriage contract

Witnesses: ....

ASCENDANCY UP TO XIVth GENERATION

3472 XII 3473	3474 XII 3475
6944 XIII 6945	6948 XIII 6949
13890 XIV 13891	13892 XIV 13893	6946 XIII 6947	6950 XIII 6951	13902 XIV 13903	13896 XIV 13897
1736 XI 1737	
13888 XIV 13889	13898 XIV 13899
13894 XIV 13895	13900 XIV 13901

GX 868 Father

Sosa 434

GX 869 Mother

13906 XIV 13907	13912 XIV 13913
13908 XIV 13909	13918 XIV 13919
13910 XIV 13911	13904 XIV 13905	6952 XIII 6953	6956 XIII 6957	13914 XIV 13915	13916 XIV 13917
1738 XI 1739	
6954 XIII 6955	6958 XIII 6959
3476 XII 3477	3478 XII 3479

♀ Surname : ....First name : ....

▶Generation IX – maternal ascendant ↓Child page 217 –
□ Implex

Born : ....in..□ baptized

Daughter of : ....and: ....

Occupation(s) : ....

Deceased : ....in...

◎ **CHILDREN** ....
....
....

👪 ASCENDANCY UP TO XIVth GENERATION

6960 XIII 6961		
13922 XIV 13923	13924 XIV 13925	6962 XIII 6963
		3480 XII 3481
13920 XIV 13921		
13926 XIV 13927		

1740 XI 1741

GX 870 Father

Sosa 435

3482 XII 3483		
6966 XIII 6967	13934 XIV 13935	13928 XIV 13929
		6964 XIII 6965
13930 XIV 13931		
13932 XIV 13933		

GX 871 Mother

x ....
....
....
○ ....
....
† ....

13938 XIV 13939		
13940 XIV 13941	13942 XIV 13943	13936 XIV 13937
		6968 XIII 6969
6970 XIII 6971		3484 XII 3485

1742 XI 1743

13944 XIV 13945		
		13950 XIV 13951
6972 XIII 6973	13946 XIV 13947	13948 XIV 13949
3486 XII 3487		6974 XIII 6975

435

Surname : .... First name : .... ♂

▶Generation 9 – maternal ascendant ↓Child page 218

□ Implex

Born : .... in .... □ baptized

Son of : .... and: ....

Occupation(s) : ....

Deceased : .... in ....

⚭ MARITAL STATUS

□ *Civil Marriage*   □ *Religious Marriage*   □ *Free Union*

Date : .... in ....   □ Marriage contract

Witnesses: ....

👪 ASCENDANCY UP TO XIVth GENERATION

6976 XIII 6977		
13954 XIV 13955	13956 XIV 13957	6978 XIII 6979
		3488 XII 3489
3490 XII 3491		
6982 XIII 6983	13966 XIV 13967	13960 XIV 13961
6980 XIII 6981		

1744 XI 1745

13952 XIV 13953

13958 XIV 13959

13962 XIV 13963

13964 XIV 13965

GX 872 Father

Sosa 436

GX 873 Mother

13970 XIV 13971

13972 XIV 13973

13976 XIV 13977

13982 XIV 13983

1746 XI 1747

13974 XIV 13975

13968 XIV 13969

6984 XIII 6985

6988 XIII 6989

13978 XIV 13979

13980 XIV 13981

6986 XIII 6987

3492 XII 3493

3494 XII 3495

6990 XIII 6991

♀ Surname : .... First name : ....

►Generation IX – maternal ascendant ↓Child page 218 –

☐ Implex

Born : .... in .... ☐ baptized

Daughter of : .... and: ....

Occupation(s) : ....

Deceased : .... in ....

⚭ CHILDREN ....
....
....

🎎 ASCENDANCY UP TO XIVth GENERATION

6992 XIII 6993

3496 XII 3497

13986 XIV 13987

13988 XIV 13989

6994 XIII 6995

3498 XII 3499

6996 XIII 6997

6998 XIII 6999

13998 XIV 13999

13992 XIV 13993

13984 XIV 13985

13990 XIV 13991

1748 XI 1749

GX 874 Father

13994 XIV 13995

13996 XIV 13997

Sosa 437

GX 875 Mother

14002 XIV 14003

14008 XIV 14009

14004 XIV 14005

14014 XIV 14015

14006 XIV 14007

14000 XIV 14001

7000 XIII 7001

1750 XI 1751

7004 XIII 7005

14010 XIV 14011

14012 XIV 14013

7002 XII 7003

3500 XII 3501

3502 XII 3503

7006 XIII 7007

437

438

Surname : .... First name : .... ♂

▶Generation 9 – maternal ascendant ↓Child page 219

☐ Implex

Born : .... in ....☐ baptized

Son of : .... and: ....

Occupation(s) : ....

Deceased : .... in ....

⚭ **MARITAL STATUS**   ☐ *Civil Marriage*   ☐ *Religious Marriage*   ☐ *Free Union*

Date : .... in .... ☐ Marriage contract

Witnesses: ....

👪 **ASCENDANCY UP TO XIVth GENERATION**

7008 XIII 7009	3504 XII 3505
14018 XIV 14019	14020 XIV 14021
7010 XIII 7011	

3506 XII 3507

7014 XIII 7015

14030 XIV 14031

14024 XIV 14025

7012 XIII 7013

1752 XI 1753

14016 XIV 14017

14022 XIV 14023

14026 XIV 14027

14028 XIV 14029

GX 876 Father

Sosa 438

GX 877 Mother

14034 XIV 14035

14040 XIV 14041

14036 XIV 14037

14046 XIV 14047

1754 XI 1755

14038 XIV 14039

14032 XIV 14033

7016 XIII 7017

7020 XIII 7021

14042 XIV 14043

14044 XIV 14045

7022 XIII 7023

7018 XIII 7019

3508 XII 3509

3510 XII 3511

♀ Surname : .... First name : ....

▶Generation IX – maternal ascendant ↓Child page 219 –

☐ Implex

Born : .... in .... ☐ baptized

Daughter of : .... and: ....

Occupation(s) : ....

Deceased : .... in ....

⚭ CHILDREN ....

....

🎋 ASCENDANCY UP TO XIVth GENERATION

7024	XIII	7025
3512	XII	3513
14050	XIV	14051
14052	XIV	14053
7026	XIII	7027
1756	XI	1757
3514	XII	3515
7030	XIII	7031
14062	XIV	14063
14056	XIV	14057
7028	XIII	7029
14048	XIV	14049
14058	XIV	14059
14054	XIV	14055
14060	XIV	14061

GX 878 Father

Sosa 439

GX 879 Mother

X

14066	XIV	14067
14072	XIV	14073
14068	XIV	14069
14078	XIV	14079
1758	XI	1759
14070	XIV	14071
14064	XIV	14065
7032	XIII	7033
7036	XIII	7037
14074	XIV	14075
14076	XIV	14077
7034	XIII	7035
3516	XII	3517
3518	XII	3519
7038	XIII	7039

Sosa
440

Surname : .... First name : .... ♂

►Generation 9 – maternal ascendant ↓Child page 220

☐ Implex

Born : .... in .... ☐ baptized

Son of : .... and: ....

Occupation(s) : ....

Deceased : .... in ....

💍 **MARITAL STATUS**   ☐ *Civil Marriage*   ☐ *Religious Marriage*   ☐ *Free Union*

Date : .... in .... ☐ Marriage contract

Witnesses: ....

👪 **ASCENDANCY UP TO XIVth GENERATION**

7040 XIII 7041	3520 XII 3521
14082 XIV 14083	14084 XIV 14085	7042 XIII 7043
14080 XIV 14081	
14086 XIV 14087	

3522 XII 3523

7046 XIII 7047

14094 XIV 14095 | 14088 XIV 14089

7044 XIII 7045

14090 XIV 14091

14092 XIV 14093

1760 XI 1761

GX 880 Father

Sosa 440

GX 881 Mother

1762 XI 1763

14098 XIV 14099

14100 XIV 14101

14104 XIV 14105

14110 XIV 14111

14102 XIV 14103 | 14096 XIV 14097 | 7048 XIII 7049

7050 XIII 7051 | 3524 XII 3525

7052 XIII 7053

14106 XIV 14107 | 14108 XIV 14109

3526 XII 3527

7054 XIII 7055

440

♀ Surname : .... First name : ....

▶Generation IX – maternal ascendant ↓Child page 220 –

☐ Implex

Born : ....in...................................☐ baptized

Daughter of : ....and: ....

Occupation(s) : ....

Deceased : ....in...................................

⚭ CHILDREN ....

....

....

⚥ ASCENDANCY UP TO XIVth GENERATION

7056 XIII 7057	3528 XII 3529
14114 XIV 14115	14116 XIV 14117
	7058 XIII 7059
	1764 **XI** 1765

3530 XII 3531

7062 XIII 7063

14126 XIV 14127

14120 XIV 14121

7060 XIII 7061

14112 XIV 14113

14118 XIV 14119

GX 882 Father

Sosa 441

GX 883 Mother

14122 XIV 14123

14124 XIV 14125

14130 XIV 14131

14136 XIV 14137

14132 XIV 14133

14142 XIV 14143

1766 **XI** 1767

14134 XIV 14135

14128 XIV 14129

7064 XIII 7065

7068 XIII 7069

14138 XIV 14139

14140 XIV 14141

7066 XIII 7067

3532 XII 3533

3534 XII 3535

7070 XIII 7071

Sosa 442

Surname : .... First name : .... ♂

▶ Generation 9 – maternal ascendant ↓ Child page 221

☐ Implex

Born : .... in .... ☐ baptized

Son of : .... and: ....

Occupation(s) : ....

Deceased : .... in ....

⚭ MARITAL STATUS

☐ Civil Marriage   ☐ Religious Marriage   ☐ Free Union

Date : .... in ....   ☐ Marriage contract

Witnesses: ....

👪 ASCENDANCY UP TO XIVth GENERATION

7072 XIII 7073	
3536 XII 3537	
14146 XIV 14147	
14148 XIV 14149	
7074 XIII 7075	
3538 XII 3539	
14158 XIV 14159	
14152 XIV 14153	
7076 XIII 7077	
7078 XIII 7079	
14144 XIV 14145	
14154 XIV 14155	
14150 XIV 14151	
14156 XIV 14157	

1768 XI 1769

GX 884 Father

Sosa 442

GX 885 Mother

1770 XI 1771

14162 XIV 14163	
14168 XIV 14169	
14164 XIV 14165	
14174 XIV 14175	
14166 XIV 14167	
14160 XIV 14161	
7080 XIII 7081	
7084 XIII 7085	
14170 XIV 14171	
14172 XIV 14173	
7082 XIII 7083	
7086 XIII 7087	
3540 XII 3541	
3542 XII 3543	

♀ Surname : ....First name : ....

▶Generation IX – maternal ascendant ↓Child page 221 –

☐ Implex

Born : ....in...☐ baptized

Daughter of : ....and: ....

Occupation(s) : ....

Deceased : ....in...

👥 CHILDREN ....

....

....

👪 ASCENDANCY UP TO XIVth GENERATION

7088 XIII 7089	3544 XII 3545	3546 XII 3547	7092 XIII 7093

14178 XIV 14179

14180 XIV 14181

7090 XIII 7091

7094 XIII 7095

14190 XIV 14191

14184 XIV 14185

1772 XI 1773

14176 XIV 14177

14186 XIV 14187

14182 XIV 14183

GX 886 Father

14188 XIV 14189

Sosa 443

GX 887 Mother

14194 XIV 14195

14200 XIV 14201

14196 XIV 14197

14206 XIV 14207

14198 XIV 14199

14192 XIV 14193

7096 XIII 7097

1774 XI 1775

7100 XIII 7101

14202 XIV 14203

14204 XIV 14205

7098 XIII 7099

3548 XII 3549

3550 XII 3551

7102 XIII 7103

Sosa
444

Surname : .... First name : .... ♂

▶Generation 9 – maternal ascendant ↓Child page 222   □ Implex

Born : .... in .... □ baptized

Son of : .... and: ....

Occupation(s) : ....

Deceased : .... in ....

⚭ MARITAL STATUS   □ Civil Marriage □ Religious Marriage □ Free Union

Date : .... in .... □ Marriage contract

Witnesses: ....

👪 ASCENDANCY UP TO XIVth GENERATION

7104 XIII 7105	3552 XII 3553	3554 XII 3555	7108 XIII 7109

14210 XIV 14211 | 14212 XIV 14213 | 7106 XIII 7107

7110 XIII 7111 | 14222 XIV 14223 | 14216 XIV 14217

1776 XI 1777

14208 XIV 14209

14218 XIV 14219

14214 XIV 14215

GX 888 Father

14220 XIV 14221

Sosa 444

GX 889 Mother

14226 XIV 14227

14232 XIV 14233

14228 XIV 14229

14238 XIV 14239

1778 XI 1779

14230 XIV 14231 | 14224 XIV 14225 | 7112 XIII 7113

7116 XIII 7117 | 14234 XIV 14235 | 14236 XIV 14237

7114 XIII 7115

3556 XII 3557

3558 XII 3559

7118 XIII 7119

444

♀ Surname : ....First name : ....

►Generation IX – maternal ascendant ↓Child page 222 –   □ Implex

Born : ....in...□ baptized

Daughter of : ....and: ....

Occupation(s) : ....

Deceased : ....in...

⚭ **CHILDREN** ....

....

⚶ ASCENDANCY UP TO XIVth GENERATION

7120 XIII 7121	3560 XII 3561
14242 XIV 14243	14244 XIV 14245
7122 XIII 7123	3562 XII 3563
14240 XIV 14241	7126 XIII 7127
14246 XIV 14247	14254 XIV 14255
	14248 XIV 14249
	7124 XIII 7125

1780 XI 1781

GX 890 Father

Sosa 445

GX 891 Mother

1782 XI 1783

14250 XIV 14251
14252 XIV 14253
14258 XIV 14259
14260 XIV 14261
14264 XIV 14265
14270 XIV 14271
14262 XIV 14263
14256 XIV 14257
7128 XIII 7129
7130 XIII 7131
3564 XII 3565
7132 XIII 7133
14266 XIV 14267
14268 XIV 14269
7134 XIII 7135
3566 XII 3567

445

Sosa
446

Surname : .... First name : .... ♂

▶Generation 9 – maternal ascendant ↓Child page 223 | ☐ Implex

Born : .... in..☐ baptized

Son of : ....and: ....

Occupation(s) : ....

Deceased : ....in...

💍 **MARITAL STATUS** ☐ *Civil Marriage* ☐ *Religious Marriage* ☐ *Free Union*

Date : ....in.. ☐ Marriage contract

Witnesses: ....

👪 ASCENDANCY UP TO XIVth GENERATION

7136 XIII 7137	
3568 XII 3569	3570 XII 3571	7140 XIII 7141
14274 XIV 14275	14276 XIV 14277	7138 XIII 7139	7142 XIII 7143	14286 XIV 14287	14280 XIV 14281
14272 XIV 14273	1784 XI 1785	14282 XIV 14283
14278 XIV 14279	14284 XIV 14285

GX 892 Father

Sosa 446

GX 893 Mother

14290 XIV 14291	14296 XIV 14297
14292 XIV 14293	14302 XIV 14303
14294 XIV 14295	14288 XIV 14289	7144 XIII 7145	1786 XI 1787	7148 XIII 7149	14298 XIV 14299	14300 XIV 14301
7146 XIII 7147	3572 XII 3573	3574 XII 3575	7150 XIII 7151

446

♀ Surname : ....First name : ....

▶Generation IX – maternal ascendant ↓Child page 223 – □ Implex

Born : ....in...□ baptized

Daughter of : ....and: ....

Occupation(s) : ....

Deceased : ....in...

💍 CHILDREN ....

....

....

🏃 ASCENDANCY UP TO XIVth GENERATION

3576 XII 3577	3578 XII 3579
7152 XIII 7153	7156 XIII 7157
14306 XIV 14307	14308 XIV 14309	7154 XIII 7155		7158 XIII 7159	14318 XIV 14319	14312 XIV 14313

1788 XI 1789

14304 XIV 14305

14310 XIV 14311

14316 XIV 14317

14314 XIV 14315

GX 894 Father

Sosa 447

GX 895 Mother

14322 XIV 14323

14324 XIV 14325

14328 XIV 14329

14334 XIV 14335

1790 XI 1791

14326 XIV 14327

14320 XIV 14321

7160 XIII 7161

14330 XIV 14331

14332 XIV 14333

7162 XIII 7163

3580 XII 3581

7164 XIII 7165

3582 XII 3583

7166 XIII 7167

Surname : .... First name : .... ♂

▶Generation 9 – maternal ascendant ↓Child page 224 | □ Implex

Born : .... in .... □ baptized

Son of : .... and: ....

Occupation(s) : ....

Deceased : .... in ....

⚭ **MARITAL STATUS** □ *Civil Marriage* □ *Religious Marriage* □ *Free Union*`

Date : ....in.. □ Marriage contract

Witnesses: ....

👪 **ASCENDANCY UP TO XIVth GENERATION**

7168 XIII 7169	3584 XII 3585
14338 XIV 14339	
14340 XIV 14341	7170 XIII 7171
	1792 XI 1793
14336 XIV 14337	
14342 XIV 14343	GX 896 Father

Sosa 448

GX 897 Mother

3586 XII 3587	7172 XIII 7173
14350 XIV 14351	14344 XIV 14345
7174 XIII 7175	
	14346 XIV 14347
14348 XIV 14349	

14354 XIV 14355	14360 XIV 14361
14356 XIV 14357	
14358 XIV 14359	14366 XIV 14367
14352 XIV 14353	7176 XIII 7177
7178 XIII 7179	3588 XII 3589
	1794 XI 1795
7180 XIII 7181	14362 XIV 14363
	14364 XIV 14365
3590 XII 3591	7182 XIII 7183

♀ Surname : .... First name : ....

▶Generation IX – maternal ascendant ↓Child page 224 – □ Implex

Born : ....in...□ baptized

Daughter of : ....and: ....

Occupation(s) : ....

Deceased : ....in..

⊙⊙ **CHILDREN** ....

....

....

👪 **ASCENDANCY UP TO XIVth GENERATION**

3592 XII 3593		3594 XII 3595
7184 XIII 7185		7188 XIII 7189
14370 XIV 14371	14372 XIV 14373	7186 XIII 7187		7190 XIII 7191	14382 XIV 14383	14376 XIV 14377

1796 XI 1797

14368 XIV 14369

14378 XIV 14379

14374 XIV 14375

GX 898 Father

14380 XIV 14381

Sosa 449

GX 899 Mother

14386 XIV 14387

14392 XIV 14393

14388 XIV 14389

14398 XIV 14399

1798 XI 1799

14390 XIV 14391 | 14384 XIV 14385 | 7192 XIII 7193

7196 XIII 7197 | 14394 XIV 14395 | 14396 XIV 14397

7194 XIII 7195

3596 XII 3597

3598 XII 3599

7198 XIII 7199

Sosa 450

Surname : .... First name : ....♂

▶Generation 9 – maternal ascendant   ↓Child page 225   □ Implex

Born : ....in...□ baptized

Son of : ....and: ....

Occupation(s) : ....

Deceased : ....in...

⚭ MARITAL STATUS   □ Civil Marriage   □ Religious Marriage   □ Free Union

Date : ....in...□ Marriage contract

Witnesses: ....

👪 ASCENDANCY UP TO XIVth GENERATION

7200 XIII **7201**	
3600 XII **3601**	
14402 XIV **14403**	
14404 XIV **14405**	
7202 XIII **7203**	
14400 XIV **14401**	
14406 XIV **14407**	
3602 XII **3603**	
7204 XIII **7205**	
7206 XIII **7207**	
14414 XIV **14415**	
14408 XIV **14409**	
14410 XIV **14411**	
14412 XIV **14413**	

1800 XI 1801

GX 900 Father

Sosa 450

GX 901 Mother

x

14418 XIV **14419**	
14420 XIV **14421**	
7210 XIII **7211**	
14422 XIV **14423**	
14416 XIV **14417**	
7208 XIII **7209**	
3604 XII **3605**	
14424 XIV **14425**	
14430 XIV **14431**	
7212 XIII **7213**	
14426 XIV **14427**	
14428 XIV **14429**	
7214 XIII **7215**	
3606 XII **3607**	

1802 XI 1803

450

♀ Surname : ....First name : ....

▶Generation IX – maternal ascendant ↓Child page 225 – ☐ Implex

Born : ....in...☐ baptized

Daughter of : ....and: ....

Occupation(s) : ....

Deceased : ....in...

💍 **CHILDREN** ....

....

....

👪 ASCENDANCY UP TO XIVth GENERATION

7216 XIII 7217	3608 XII 3609
14434 XIV 14435	14436 XIV 14437	7218 XIII 7219
14432 XIV 14433	
14438 XIV 14439	

1804 XI 1805

3610 XII 3611

7220 XIII 7221

14446 XIV 14447

14440 XIV 14441

7222 XIII 7223

14442 XIV 14443

14444 XIV 14445

GX 902 Father

Sosa 451

GX 903 Mother

14450 XIV 14451

14452 XIV 14453

14456 XIV 14457

14462 XIV 14463

1806 XI 1807

14454 XIV 14455

14448 XIV 14449

7224 XIII 7225

7226 XIII 7227

3612 XII 3613

7228 XIII 7229

14458 XIV 14459

14460 XIV 14461

7230 XIII 7231

3614 XII 3615

Surname : .... First name : .... ♂

▶Generation 9 – maternal ascendant ↓Child page 226 ☐ Implex

Born : ....in.......................................☐ baptized

Son of : ....and: ....

Occupation(s) : ....

Deceased : ....in...

⚭ **MARITAL STATUS** ☐ *Civil Marriage* ☐ *Religious Marriage* ☐ *Free Union*

Date : ....in... ☐ Marriage contract

Witnesses: ....

ASCENDANCY UP TO XIVth GENERATION

7232 XIII 7233	3616 XII 3617	
14466 XIV 14467	14468 XIV 14469	7234 XIII 7235
14464 XIV 14465		
	14470 XIV 14471	

3618 XII 3619

7238 XIII 7239 — 14478 XIV 14479 — 14472 XIV 14473 — 7236 XIII 7237

14474 XIV 14475

14476 XIV 14477

1808 XI 1809

GX 904 Father

Sosa 452

GX 905 Mother

14482 XIV 14483		
14484 XIV 14485		

14488 XIV 14489

14494 XIV 14495

1810 XI 1811

14486 XIV 14487	14480 XIV 14481	7240 XIII 7241
7242 XIII 7243	3620 XII 3621	

7244 XIII 7245 — 14490 XIV 14491 — 14492 XIV 14493 — 7246 XIII 7247

3622 XII 3623

♀ Surname : .... First name : ....

►Generation IX – maternal ascendant ↓Child page 226 –

☐ Implex

Born : ....in...☐ baptized

Daughter of : ....and: ....

Occupation(s) : ....

Deceased : ....in...

⚭ CHILDREN ....

....

....

🏛 ASCENDANCY UP TO XIVth GENERATION

7248 XIII 7249	3624 XII 3625
14498 XIV 14499	
14500 XIV 14501	7250 XIII 7251
14496 XIV 14497	
	14502 XIV 14503

3626 XII 3627

7252 XIII 7253

7254 XIII 7255

14510 XIV 14511

14504 XIV 14505

14506 XIV 14507

14508 XIV 14509

1812 XI 1813

GX 906 Father

Sosa 453

GX 907 Mother

x ....

° ....

† ....

14514 XIV 14515

14516 XIV 14517

14520 XIV 14521

14526 XIV 14527

1814 XI 1815

14518 XIV 14519

14512 XIV 14513

7256 XIII 7257

7258 XIII 7259

3628 XII 3629

7260 XIII 7261

14522 XIV 14523

14524 XIV 14525

7262 XIII 7263

3630 XII 3631

Sosa
454

Surname : .... First name : .... ♂

▶Generation 9 – maternal ascendant ↓Child page 227 □ Implex

Born : ....in..□ baptized

Son of : ....and:..

Occupation(s) : ....

Deceased : ....in.......................................

⚭ MARITAL STATUS □ *Civil Marriage* □ *Religious Marriage* □ *Free Union*

Date : ....in.. □ Marriage contract

Witnesses: ....

👪 ASCENDANCY UP TO XIVth GENERATION

7264 XIII 7265	
3632 XII 3633	3634 XII 3635
14530 XIV 14531	14532 XIV 14533
7266 XIII 7267	7268 XIII 7269
7270 XIII 7271	14542 XIV 14543
14536 XIV 14537	

1816 XI 1817

14528 XIV 14529

14538 XIV 14539

14534 XIV 14535

GX 908 Father

14540 XIV 14541

Sosa 454

GX 909 Mother

14546 XIV 14547

14552 XIV 14553

14548 XIV 14549

14558 XIV 14559

1818 XI 1819

14550 XIV 14551

14544 XIV 14545

7272 XIII 7273

7276 XIII 7277

14554 XIV 14555

14556 XIV 14557

7274 XIII 7275

3636 XII 3637

3638 XII 3639

7278 XIII 7279

♀ Surname : .... First name : ....

□ Implex

Born : .... in... □ baptized

Daughter of : ....and: ....

Occupation(s) : ....

Deceased : .... in...

💍 **CHILDREN** ....

....

....

👪 **ASCENDANCY UP TO XIVth GENERATION**

7280 XIII 7281	3640 XII 3641
14562 XIV 14563	
14564 XIV 14565	7282 XIII 7283
	1820 XI 1821
14560 XIV 14561	
14566 XIV 14567	**GX 910 Father**

Sosa 455

GX 911 Mother

3642 XII 3643	7284 XIII 7285
7286 XIII 7287	14574 XIV 14575
	14568 XIV 14569
	14570 XIV 14571
14572 XIV 14573	

14578 XIV 14579	14584 XIV 14585
14580 XIV 14581	14590 XIV 14591
14582 XIV 14583	
14576 XIV 14577	1822 XI 1823
7288 XIII 7289	7292 XIII 7293
7290 XIII 7291	14586 XIV 14587
3644 XII 3645	14588 XIV 14589
	3646 XII 3647
	7294 XIII 7295

Sosa
456

Surname : .... First name : .... ♂

▶Generation 9 – maternal ascendant ↓Child page 228

☐ Implex

Born : ....in...☐ baptized

Son of : ....and: ....

Occupation(s) : ....

Deceased : ....in...

⚭ MARITAL STATUS

☐ Civil Marriage ☐ Religious Marriage ☐ Free Union

Date : ....in.. ☐ Marriage contract

Witnesses: ....

👪 ASCENDANCY UP TO XIVth GENERATION

3648 XII 3649	
3650 XII 3651	

7296 XIII 7297

14594 XIV 14595

14596 XIV 14597

7298 XIII 7299

7302 XIII 7303

14606 XIV 14607

14600 XIV 14601

7300 XIII 7301

1824 XI 1825

14592 XIV 14593

14598 XIV 14599

14602 XIV 14603

14604 XIV 14605

GX 912 Father

Sosa 456

GX 913 Mother

14610 XIV 14611

14616 XIV 14617

14612 XIV 14613

14622 XIV 14623

14614 XIV 14615

14608 XIV 14609

7304 XIII 7305

7308 XIII 7309

14618 XIV 14619

14620 XIV 14621

1826 XI 1827

7306 XIII 7307

3652 XII 3653

3654 XII 3655

7310 XII 7311

456

♀ Surname : .... First name : ....

▶Generation IX – maternal ascendant ↓Child page 228 –

☐ Implex

Born : .... in ....☐ baptized

Daughter of : ....and: ....

Occupation(s) : ....

Deceased : .... in ....

⚭ CHILDREN ....

....

....

⚜ ASCENDANCY UP TO XIVth GENERATION

7312 XIII 7313	3656 XII 3657
14626 XIV 14627	14628 XIV 14629
7314 XIII 7315	
14624 XIV 14625	
14630 XIV 14631	

1828 XI 1829

GX 914 Father

Sosa 457

GX 915 Mother

3658 XII 3659	7316 XIII 7317
7318 XIII 7319	14638 XIV 14639
14632 XIV 14633	
14634 XIV 14635	
14636 XIV 14637	

14642 XIV 14643	14648 XIV 14649
14644 XIV 14645	14654 XIV 14655
14646 XIV 14647	14640 XIV 14641
7320 XIII 7321	
7322 XIII 7323	
3660 XII 3661	

1830 XI 1831

7324 XIII 7325	
14650 XIV 14651	14652 XIV 14653
3662 XII 3663	7326 XIII 7327

Sosa 458

Surname : .... First name : .... ♂

▶Generation 9 – maternal ascendant ↓Child page 229 □ Implex

Born : .... in .... □ baptized

Son of : .... and: ....

Occupation(s) : ....

Deceased : .... in ....

⚭ MARITAL STATUS
□ Civil Marriage □ Religious Marriage □ Free Union

Date : ....in... □ Marriage contract

Witnesses: ....

👪 ASCENDANCY UP TO XIVth GENERATION

7328 XIII 7329	3664 XII 3665
14658 XIV 14659	14660 XIV 14661
	7330 XIII 7331

3666 XII 3667

7334 XIII 7335

14670 XIV 14671 · 14664 XIV 14665

7332 XIII 7333

1832 XI 1833

14656 XIV 14657

14662 XIV 14663

14666 XIV 14667

14668 XIV 14669

GX 916 Father

Sosa 458

GX 917 Mother

14674 XIV 14675

14676 XIV 14677

14680 XIV 14681

14686 XIV 14687

1834 XI 1835

14678 XIV 14679 · 14672 XIV 14673

7336 XIII 7337

7338 XIII 7339

3668 XII 3669

7340 XIII 7341

14682 XIV 14683 · 14684 XIV 14685

7342 XIII 7343

3670 XII 3671

458

♀ Surname : .... First name : ....

▶Generation IX – maternal ascendant ↓Child page 229 –   □ Implex

Born : ....in...□ baptized

Daughter of : ....and: ....

Occupation(s) : ....

Deceased : ....in...

⊙⊙ **CHILDREN** ....

....

⚶ ASCENDANCY UP TO XIVth GENERATION

7344 XIII 7345	3672 XII 3673
14690 XIV 14691	14692 XIV 14693
	7346 XIII 7347
14688 XIV 14689	
14694 XIV 14695	

1836 XI 1837

GX 918 Father

Sosa 459

GX 919 Mother

3674 XII 3675	7348 XIII 7349
14702 XIV 14703	14696 XIV 14697
7350 XIII 7351	
	14698 XIV 14699
14700 XIV 14701	

14706 XIV 14707	14712 XIV 14713
14708 XIV 14709	14718 XIV 14719
14710 XIV 14711	14704 XIV 14705
7352 XIII 7353	
7354 XIII 7355	3676 XII 3677

1838 XI 1839

7356 XIII 7357	
14714 XIV 14715	14716 XIV 14717
3678 XII 3679	7358 XIII 7359

Sosa
460

Surname : .... First name : .... ♂

▶Generation 9 – maternal ascendant ↓Child page 230

□ Implex

Born : .... in .... □ baptized

Son of : .... and: ....

Occupation(s) : ....

Deceased : .... in ....

⚭ MARITAL STATUS

□ *Civil Marriage*   □ *Religious Marriage*   □ *Free Union*

Date : .... in .... □ Marriage contract

Witnesses: ....

👪 ASCENDANCY UP TO XIVth GENERATION

3680 XII 3681	
7360 XIII 7361	
14722 XIV 14723	14724 XIV 14725
7362 XIII 7363	
	1840 XI 1841
14720 XIV 14721	
14726 XIV 14727	
	GX 920 Father

3682 XII 3683	
7366 XIII 7367	
14734 XIV 14735	14728 XIV 14729
7364 XIII 7365	
14730 XIV 14731	
14732 XIV 14733	

Sosa 460

GX 921 Mother

x.

14738 XIV 14739	
14740 XIV 14741	
14742 XIV 14743	14736 XIV 14737
7368 XIII 7369	
7370 XIII 7371	
3684 XII 3685	
	1842 XI 1843

14744 XIV 14745	
14750 XIV 14751	
14746 XIV 14747	14748 XIV 14749
7372 XIII 7373	
7374 XIII 7375	
3686 XII 3687	

460

♀ Surname : ....First name : ....

▶Generation IX – maternal ascendant ↓Child page 230 –   □ Implex

Born : ....in...□ baptized

Daughter of : ....and: ....

Occupation(s) : ....

Deceased : ....in...

💍 **CHILDREN** ....

....

....

👪 **ASCENDANCY UP TO XIVth GENERATION**

7376 XIII 7377	3688 XII 3689
14754 XIV 14755	14756 XIV 14757	7378 XIII 7379
	1844 XI 1845
14752 XIV 14753	
14758 XIV 14759	
	GX 922 Father
	Sosa 461
	GX 923 Mother
14770 XIV 14771	
14772 XIV 14773	
14774 XIV 14775	14768 XIV 14769	7384 XIII 7385
7386 XIII 7387	3692 XII 3693

3690 XII 3691	7380 XIII 7381
7382 XIII 7383	14766 XIV 14767	14760 XIV 14761
	14762 XIV 14763
14764 XIV 14765	
14776 XIV 14777	
	14782 XIV 14783
1846 XI 1847	
7388 XIII 7389	14778 XIV 14779	14780 XIV 14781
3694 XII 3695	7390 XIII 7391

Sosa
462

Surname : .... First name : .... ♂

▶Generation 9 – maternal ascendant ↓Child page 231

☐ Implex

Born : ....in.................................☐ baptized

Son of : ....and: ....

Occupation(s) : ....

Deceased : ....in..

💍 MARITAL STATUS
☐ Civil Marriage ☐ Religious Marriage ☐ Free Union

Date : ....in..☐ Marriage contract

Witnesses: ....

👫 ASCENDANCY UP TO XIVth GENERATION

7392 XIII 7393	3696 XII 3697	3698 XII 3699
14786 XIV 14787	14788 XIV 14789	7394 XIII 7395
		7398 XIII 7399
14798 XIV 14799	14792 XIV 14793	7396 XIII 7397

1848 XI 1849

14784 XIV 14785

14790 XIV 14791

14794 XIV 14795

14796 XIV 14797

GX 924 Father

Sosa 462

GX 925 Mother

14802 XIV 14803

14808 XIV 14809

14804 XIV 14805

14814 XIV 14815

1850 XI 1851

14806 XIV 14807	14800 XIV 14801	7400 XIII 7401
7402 XIII 7403		

7404 XIII 7405	14810 XIV 14811	14812 XIV 14813
		7406 XIII 7407

3700 XII 3701

3702 XII 3703

462

♀ Surname : .... First name : ....

▶Generation IX – maternal ascendant ↓Child page 231 –
□ Implex

Born : .... in .... □ baptized

Daughter of : .... and: ....

Occupation(s) : ....

Deceased : .... in ....

💍 **CHILDREN** ....

....

....

🏃 ASCENDANCY UP TO XIVth GENERATION

7408 XIII 7409	3704 XII 3705
14818 XIV 14819	14820 XIV 14821	7410 XIII 7411
	1852 XI 1853
14816 XIV 14817	
14822 XIV 14823	GX 926 Father

Sosa 463

3706 XII 3707	7412 XIII 7413
7414 XIII 7415	14830 XIV 14831	14824 XIV 14825
	14826 XIV 14827
14828 XIV 14829	

GX 927 Mother

14834 XIV 14835	14840 XIV 14841
14836 XIV 14837	14846 XIV 14847
14838 XIV 14839	14832 XIV 14833	7416 XIII 7417
1854 XI 1855
7418 XIII 7419	3708 XII 3709
7420 XIII 7421	14842 XIV 14843	14844 XIV 14845
3710 XII 3711	7422 XIII 7423

Sosa
464

Surname : .... First name : .... ♂

▶Generation 9 – maternal ascendant ↓Child page 232

☐ Implex

Born : .... in .... ☐ baptized

Son of : .... and: ....

Occupation(s) : ....

Deceased : .... in ....

⚭ MARITAL STATUS

☐ Civil Marriage ☐ Religious Marriage ☐ Free Union

Date : .... in .... ☐ Marriage contract

Witnesses: ....

👪 ASCENDANCY UP TO XIVth GENERATION

7424 XIII 7425	3712 XII 3713
14850 XIV 14851	14852 XIV 14853
	7426 XIII 7427

3714 XII 3715

7430 XIII 7431

14862 XIV 14863

14856 XIV 14857

7428 XIII 7429

1856 XI 1857

14848 XIV 14849

14854 XIV 14855

14858 XIV 14859

14860 XIV 14861

GX 928 Father

Sosa 464

GX 929 Mother

14866 XIV 14867

14872 XIV 14873

14868 XIV 14869

14878 XIV 14879

1858 XI 1859

14870 XIV 14871

14864 XIV 14865

7432 XIII 7433

7434 XIII 7435

3716 XII 3717

7436 XIII 7437

14874 XIV 14875

14876 XIV 14877

7438 XIII 7439

3718 XII 3719

464

♀ Surname : .... First name : ....

►Generation IX – maternal ascendant ↓Child page 232 –   □ Implex

Born : ....in...□ baptized

Daughter of : ....and: ....

Occupation(s) : ....

Deceased : ....in...

💍 CHILDREN ....

....

....

🧬 ASCENDANCY UP TO XIVth GENERATION

7440 XIII 7441	3720 XII 3721
14882 XIV 14883	14884 XIV 14885	7442 XIII 7443
14880 XIV 14881	
14886 XIV 14887	

1860 XI 1861

GX 930 Father

Sosa 465

GX 931 Mother

3722 XII 3723

7446 XIII 7447

14894 XIV 14895

14888 XIV 14889

7444 XIII 7445

14890 XIV 14891

14892 XIV 14893

14898 XIV 14899

14900 XIV 14901

14904 XIV 14905

14910 XIV 14911

14902 XIV 14903

14896 XIV 14897

7448 XIII 7449

7450 XIII 7451

3724 XII 3725

1862 XI 1863

7452 XIII 7453

14906 XIV 14907

14908 XIV 14909

7454 XIII 7455

3726 XII 3727

Surname : .... First name : .... ♂

▶Generation 9 – maternal ascendant ↓Child page 233   □ Implex

Born : ....in...□ baptized

Son of : ....and: ....

Occupation(s) : ....

Deceased : ....in..

⚭ **MARITAL STATUS**   □ *Civil Marriage* □ *Religious Marriage* □ *Free Union*

Date : ....in..   □ Marriage contract

Witnesses: ....

ASCENDANCY UP TO XIVth GENERATION

7456 XIII 7457	3728 XII 3729
14914 XIV 14915	7458 XIII 7459
14916 XIV 14917	
14912 XIV 14913	
14918 XIV 14919	

1864 XI 1865

GX 932 Father

Sosa 466

GX 933 Mother

1866 XI 1867

3730 XII 3731	7460 XIII 7461
7462 XIII 7463	14926 XIV 14927
	14920 XIV 14921
14922 XIV 14923	
14924 XIV 14925	

14930 XIV 14931	
14932 XIV 14933	
14934 XIV 14935	7464 XIII 7465
14928 XIV 14929	
7466 XIII 7467	3732 XII 3733

14936 XIV 14937	
14942 XIV 14943	
7468 XIII 7469	14938 XIV 14939
	14940 XIV 14941
3734 XII 3735	7470 XIII 7471

Sosa
467

♀ Surname : ....First name : ....

▶Generation IX – maternal ascendant ↓Child page 233 –　　　　　□ Implex

Born : ....in..□ baptized

Daughter of : ....and: ....

Occupation(s) : ....

Deceased : ....in..

💍 CHILDREN ....

🧑‍🧑‍🧒 ASCENDANCY UP TO XIVth GENERATION

7472 XIII 7473	3736 XII 3737
14946 XIV 14947	
14948 XIV 14949	7474 XIII 7475
14944 XIV 14945	
14950 XIV 14951	1868 XI 1869

3738 XII 3739

7478 XIII 7479

14958 XIV 14959

14952 XIV 14953

7476 XIII 7477

14954 XIV 14955

14956 XIV 14957

GX 934 Father

Sosa 467

GX 935 Mother

14962 XIV 14963

14964 XIV 14965

14968 XIV 14969

14974 XIV 14975

14966 XIV 14967

14960 XIV 14961

7480 XIII 7481

1870 XI 1871

7484 XIII 7485

14970 XIV 14971

14972 XIV 14973

7482 XIII 7483

3740 XII 3741

3742 XII 3743

7486 XIII 7487

467

Surname : .... First name : .... ♂

▶Generation 9 – maternal ascendant ↓Child page 234

□ Implex

Born : ....in..□ baptized

Son of : ....and: ....

Occupation(s) : ....

Deceased : ....in..

⚭ **MARITAL STATUS**   □ *Civil Marriage*   □ *Religious Marriage*   □ *Free Union*

Date : ....in.. □ Marriage contract

Witnesses: ....

ASCENDANCY UP TO XIVth GENERATION

7488 XIII 7489	
3744 XII 3745	3746 XII 3747
14978 XIV 14979	7490 XIII 7491	7494 XIII 7495	7492 XIII 7493
14980 XIV 14981	14990 XIV 14991	14984 XIV 14985	
1872 XI 1873	

14976 XIV 14977

14982 XIV 14983

14986 XIV 14987

14988 XIV 14989

GX 936 Father

Sosa 468

GX 937 Mother

x

14994 XIV 14995

15000 XIV 15001

14996 XIV 14997

15006 XIV 15007

1874 XI 1875

14998 XIV 14999

7496 XIII 7497

7500 XIII 7501

14992 XIV 14993

15002 XIV 15003

15004 XIV 15005

7498 XIII 7499

3748 XII 3749

3750 XII 3751

7502 XIII 7503

♀ Surname : .... First name : ....

▶Generation IX – maternal ascendant ↓Child page 234 –

□ Implex

Born : .... in .... □ baptized

Daughter of : .... and: ....

Occupation(s) : ....

Deceased : .... in ....

💍 CHILDREN ....

....

👫 ASCENDANCY UP TO XIVth GENERATION

7504 XIII 7505	3752 XII 3753
15010 XIV 15011	
15012 XIV 15013	7506 XIII 7507
15008 XIV 15009	
15014 XIV 15015	
	1876 XI 1877
	GX 938 Father
	Sosa 469
	GX 939 Mother

3754 XII 3755

7508 XIII 7509

7510 XIII 7511

15022 XIV 15023

15016 XIV 15017

15018 XIV 15019

15020 XIV 15021

15026 XIV 15027

15032 XIV 15033

15028 XIV 15029

15038 XIV 15039

1878 XI 1879

15030 XIV 15031

15024 XIV 15025

7512 XIII 7513

7516 XIII 7517

15034 XIV 15035

15036 XIV 15037

7514 XIII 7515

3756 XII 3757

3758 XII 3759

7518 XIII 7519

Sosa
470

Surname : .... First name : .... ♂

▶Generation 9 – maternal ascendant ↓Child page 235   ☐ Implex

Born : ....in.. ☐ baptized

Son of : ....and:..

Occupation(s) : ....

Deceased : ....in..

⚭ MARITAL STATUS   ☐ *Civil Marriage*   ☐ *Religious Marriage*   ☐ *Free Union*

Date : ....in.. ☐ Marriage contract

Witnesses: ....

👪 ASCENDANCY UP TO XIVth GENERATION

7520 XIII 7521	3760 XII 3761
15042 XIV 15043	15044 XIV 15045
7522 XIII 7523	
15040 XIV 15041	3762 XII 3763
15046 XIV 15047	7526 XIII 7527
	15054 XIV 15055
	15048 XIV 15049
	7524 XIII 7525
1880 XI 1881	15050 XIV 15051
	15052 XIV 15053

GX 940 Father

Sosa 470

GX 941 Mother

15058 XIV 15059	15064 XIV 15065
15060 XIV 15061	15070 XIV 15071
15062 XIV 15063	
15056 XIV 15057	
7528 XIII 7529	
7530 XIII 7531	7532 XIII 7533
3764 XII 3765	15066 XIV 15067
1882 XI 1883	15068 XIV 15069
	7534 XIII 7535
	3766 XII 3767

470

♀ Surname : .... First name : ....

☐ Implex

Born : ....in..☐ baptized

Daughter of : ....and: ....

Occupation(s) : ....

Deceased : ....in...

⚭ **CHILDREN** ....

....

....

👪 **ASCENDANCY UP TO XIVth GENERATION**

7536 XIII 7537	3768 XII 3769	
15074 XIV 15075	15076 XIV 15077	7538 XIII 7539
15072 XIV 15073		
15078 XIV 15079	1884 **XI** 1885	

GX 942 Father

Sosa 471

GX 943 Mother

3770 XII 3771	7540 XIII 7541
7542 XIII 7543	15086 XIV 15087	15080 XIV 15081
15082 XIV 15083
15084 XIV 15085

15090 XIV 15091	15096 XIV 15097	15102 XIV 15103
15092 XIV 15093		
15094 XIV 15095	15088 XIV 15089	7544 XIII 7545
7546 XIII 7547	1886 **XI** 1887	3772 XII 3773

7548 XIII 7549	15098 XIV 15099	15100 XIV 15101
3774 XII 3775	7550 XIII 7551

Surname : .... First name : .... ♂

☐ Implex

Born : ....in.. ☐ baptized

Son of : ....and: ....

Occupation(s) : ....

Deceased : ....in..

⚭ **MARITAL STATUS** ☐ *Civil Marriage* ☐ *Religious Marriage* ☐ *Free Union*

Date : ....in.. ☐ Marriage contract

Witnesses: ....

ASCENDANCY UP TO XIVth GENERATION

7552 XIII 7553	3776 XII 3777
15106 XIV 15107	15108 XIV 15109
7554 XIII 7555	3778 XII 3779
	7558 XIII 7559
	15118 XIV 15119
	15112 XIV 15113
	7556 XIII 7557

1888 XI 1889

15104 XIV 15105

15110 XIV 15111

GX 944 Father

Sosa 472

GX 945 Mother

15114 XIV 15115

15116 XIV 15117

15122 XIV 15123

15124 XIV 15125

15128 XIV 15129

15134 XIV 15135

1890 XI 1891

15126 XIV 15127

15120 XIV 15121

7560 XIII 7561

7562 XIII 7563

3780 XII 3781

7564 XIII 7565

15130 XIV 15131

15132 XIV 15133

3782 XII 3783

7566 XIII 7567

♀ Surname : .... First name : ....

▶Generation IX – maternal ascendant ↓Child page 236 –

☐ Implex

Born : .... in .... ☐ baptized

Daughter of : .... and: ....

Occupation(s) : ....

Deceased : .... in ....

⚭ CHILDREN ....
....
....

👪 ASCENDANCY UP TO XIVth GENERATION

7568 XIII 7569	3784 XII 3785
15138 XIV 15139	
15140 XIV 15141	7570 XIII 7571
15136 XIV 15137	
15142 XIV 15143	

1892 XI 1893

GX 946 Father

Sosa 473

GX 947 Mother

3786 XII 3787	7572 XIII 7573
7574 XIII 7575	15150 XIV 15151
	15144 XIV 15145
	15146 XIV 15147
15148 XIV 15149	

15154 XIV 15155	
15156 XIV 15157	
15158 XIV 15159	
15152 XIV 15153	7576 XIII 7577
7578 XIII 7579	3788 XII 3789

1894 XI 1895

15160 XIV 15161	
15166 XIV 15167	
7580 XIII 7581	
15162 XIV 15163	15164 XIV 15165
3790 XII 3791	7582 XIII 7583

Sosa
474

Surname : .... First name : .... ♂

▶Generation 9 – maternal ascendant ↓Child page 237

☐ Implex

Born : ....in...☐ baptized

Son of : ....and:..

Occupation(s) : ....

Deceased : ....in...

💍 MARITAL STATUS   ☐ Civil Marriage   ☐ Religious Marriage   ☐ Free Union

Date : ....in.. ☐ Marriage contract

Witnesses: ....

👪 ASCENDANCY UP TO XIVth GENERATION

7584 XIII 7585	
3792 XII 3793	
15170 XIV 15171	
15172 XIV 15173	
7586 XIII 7587	
15168 XIV 15169	
15174 XIV 15175	

1896 XI 1897

GX 948 Father

Sosa 474

GX 949 Mother

3794 XII 3795	
7588 XIII 7589	
15182 XIV 15183	
15176 XIV 15177	
7590 XIII 7591	
15178 XIV 15179	
15180 XIV 15181	

15186 XIV 15187	
15188 XIV 15189	
15190 XIV 15191	
15184 XIV 15185	
7592 XIII 7593	
7594 XIII 7595	
3796 XII 3797	

1898 XI 1899

15192 XIV 15193	
15198 XIV 15199	
15194 XIV 15195	
15196 XIV 15197	
7596 XIII 7597	
7598 XIII 7599	
3798 XII 3799	

474

♀ Surname : ....First name : ....

▶Generation IX – maternal ascendant ↓Child page 237 –   □ Implex

Born : ....in...□ baptized

Daughter of : ....and: ....

Occupation(s) : ....

Deceased : ....in..

⚭ **CHILDREN** ....

....

🏃 **ASCENDANCY UP TO XIVth GENERATION**

7600 XIII 7601	3800 XII 3801
15202 XIV 15203	
15204 XIV 15205	7602 XIII 7603
15200 XIV 15201	
15206 XIV 15207	

1900 XI 1901

GX 950 Father

Sosa 475

GX 951 Mother

3802 XII 3803	7604 XIII 7605
7606 XIII 7607	15214 XIV 15215
15208 XIV 15209	
15210 XIV 15211	
15212 XIV 15213	

| 15218 XIV 15219 | 15224 XIV 15225 |
| 15220 XIV 15221 | 15230 XIV 15231 |

1902 XI 1903

15222 XIV 15223	
15216 XIV 15217	7608 XIII 7609
7610 XIII 7611	3804 XII 3805

7612 XIII 7613	
15226 XIV 15227	15228 XIV 15229
3806 XII 3807	7614 XIII 7615

Surname : .... First name : .... ♂

□ Implex

Born : ....in... □ baptized

Son of : ....and: ....

Occupation(s) : ....

Deceased : ....in...

⚭ **MARITAL STATUS**   □ *Civil Marriage*   □ *Religious Marriage*   □ *Free Union*

Date : ....in...   □ Marriage contract

Witnesses: ....

👪 **ASCENDANCY UP TO XIVth GENERATION**

7616 XIII 7617	3808 XII 3809
15234 XIV 15235	15236 XIV 15237
7618 XIII 7619	
15232 XIV 15233	
15238 XIV 15239	

1904 XI 1905

3810 XII 3811

7622 XIII 7623

15246 XIV 15247

15240 XIV 15241

7620 XIII 7621

15242 XIV 15243

15244 XIV 15245

GX 952 Father

Sosa 476

GX 953 Mother

15250 XIV 15251

15252 XIV 15253

15256 XIV 15257

15262 XIV 15263

15254 XIV 15255

15248 XIV 15249

7624 XIII 7625

7626 XIII 7627

3812 XII 3813

1906 XI 1907

7628 XIII 7629

15258 XIV 15259

15260 XIV 15261

7630 XIII 7631

3814 XII 3815

♀ Surname : .... First name : ....

☐ Implex

Born : ....in..☐ baptized

Daughter of : ....and: ....

Occupation(s) : ....

Deceased : ....in...

⊙⊙ CHILDREN ....
....
....

⚶ ASCENDANCY UP TO XIVth GENERATION

7632 XIII 7633	3816 XII 3817
15266 XIV 15267	15268 XIV 15269
	7634 XIII 7635

3818 XII 3819

7636 XIII 7637

7638 XIII 7639

15278 XIV 15279

15272 XIV 15273

15264 XIV 15265

15270 XIV 15271

15274 XIV 15275

15276 XIV 15277

1908 XI 1909

GX 954 Father

Sosa 477

GX 955 Mother

x

15282 XIV 15283

15284 XIV 15285

15288 XIV 15289

15294 XIV 15295

15286 XIV 15287

15280 XIV 15281

7640 XIII 7641

15290 XIV 15291

15292 XIV 15293

7642 XIII 7643

3820 XII 3821

1910 XI 1911

7644 XIII 7645

7646 XIII 7647

3822 XII 3823

Surname : .... First name : .... ♂

▶Generation 9 – maternal ascendant ↓Child page 239   □ Implex

Born : ....in..□ baptized

Son of : ....and: ....

Occupation(s) : ....

Deceased : ....in...

⊙⊙ **MARITAL STATUS**   □ *Civil Marriage*   □ *Religious Marriage*   □ *Free Union*

Date : ....in... □ Marriage contract

Witnesses: ....

ASCENDANCY UP TO XIVth GENERATION

7648 XIII 7649	3824 XII 3825
15298 XIV 15299	
15300 XIV 15301	7650 XIII 7651
15296 XIV 15297	
	15302 XIV 15303

3826 XII 3827

7652 XIII 7653

7654 XIII 7655

15310 XIV 15311

15304 XIV 15305

15306 XIV 15307

15308 XIV 15309

1912 XI 1913

GX 956 Father

Sosa 478

GX 957 Mother

x

°

†

15314 XIV 15315

15316 XIV 15317

15318 XIV 15319

15312 XIV 15313

7656 XIII 7657

7658 XIII 7659

3828 XII 3829

15320 XIV 15321

15326 XIV 15327

1914 XI 1915

7660 XIII 7661

15322 XIV 15323

15324 XIV 15325

7662 XIII 7663

3830 XII 3831

Sosa
479

♀ Surname : .... First name : ....

► Generation IX – maternal ascendant ↓ Child page 239 – ☐ Implex

Born : .... in .... ☐ baptized

Daughter of : .... and: ....

Occupation(s) : ....

Deceased : .... in ....

⚭ CHILDREN ....

....

👪 ASCENDANCY UP TO XIVth GENERATION

7664 XIII 7665	3832 XII 3833
15330 XIV 15331	3834 XII 3835
15332 XIV 15333	7668 XIII 7669
7666 XIII 7667	7670 XIII 7671
15328 XIV 15329	15342 XIV 15343
15334 XIV 15335	15336 XIV 15337

1916 XI 1917

GX 958 Father

Sosa 479

GX 959 Mother

15338 XIV 15339
15340 XIV 15341
15346 XIV 15347
15352 XIV 15353
15348 XIV 15349
15358 XIV 15359

1918 XI 1919

15350 XIV 15351
15344 XIV 15345
7672 XIII 7673
7676 XIII 7677
15354 XIV 15355
15356 XIV 15357
7674 XIII 7675
3836 XII 3837
3838 XII 3839
7678 XIII 7679

479

Sosa
480

Surname : .... First name : .... ♂

☐ Implex

Born : ....in..☐ baptized

Son of : ....and: ....

Occupation(s) : ....

Deceased : ....in...

⚭ MARITAL STATUS

☐ Civil Marriage ☐ Religious Marriage ☐ Free Union

Date : ....in.. ☐ Marriage contract

Witnesses: ....

👪 ASCENDANCY UP TO XIVth GENERATION

7680 XIII 7681	3840 XII 3841
15362 XIV 15363	15364 XIV 15365
	7682 XIII 7683

3842 XII 3843

7686 XIII 7687

15374 XIV 15375

15368 XIV 15369

7684 XIII 7685

15360 XIV 15361

1920 XI 1921

15370 XIV 15371

15366 XIV 15367

15372 XIV 15373

GX 960 Father

Sosa 480

GX 961 Mother

X

○

†

15378 XIV 15379

15384 XIV 15385

15380 XIV 15381

15390 XIV 15391

1922 XI 1923

15382 XIV 15383

15376 XIV 15377

7688 XIII 7689

7692 XIII 7693

15386 XIV 15387

15388 XIV 15389

7690 XIII 7691

3844 XII 3845

3846 XII 3847

7694 XIII 7695

480

♀ Surname : .... First name : ....

▶Generation IX – maternal ascendant ↓Child page 240 –   □ Implex

Born : .... in...□ baptized

Daughter of : ....and: ....

Occupation(s) : ....

Deceased : .... in..

⌗⌗ CHILDREN ....

....

....

⚘ ASCENDANCY UP TO XIVth GENERATION

3848 XII 3849	3850 XII 3851
7696 XIII 7697	7700 XIII 7701
15394 XIV 15395	15406 XIV 15407
15396 XIV 15397	15400 XIV 15401
7698 XIII 7699	7702 XIII 7703

1924 XI 1925

15392 XIV 15393

15398 XIV 15399

15402 XIV 15403

15404 XIV 15405

GX 962 Father

Sosa 481

GX 963 Mother

15410 XIV 15411

15412 XIV 15413

15416 XIV 15417

15422 XIV 15423

15414 XIV 15415

15408 XIV 15409

7704 XIII 7705

7706 XIII 7707

1926 XI 1927

7708 XIII 7709

15418 XIV 15419

15420 XIV 15421

7710 XIII 7711

3852 XII 3853

3854 XII 3855

Sosa
482

Surname : .... First name : .... ♂

☐ Implex

Born : .... in .... ☐ baptized

Son of : .... and: ....

Occupation(s) : ....

Deceased : .... in ....

⚭ MARITAL STATUS

☐ Civil Marriage   ☐ Religious Marriage   ☐ Free Union

Date : .... in .... ☐ Marriage contract

Witnesses: ....

👪 ASCENDANCY UP TO XIVth GENERATION

7712 **XIII** 7713	3856 **XII** 3857
15426 **XIV** 15427	
15428 **XIV** 15429	7714 **XIII** 7715
	1928 **XI** 1929
15424 **XIV** 15425	
15430 **XIV** 15431	
	°
	†
	GX 964 Father

Sosa 482

GX 965 Mother

x

°

†

3858 **XII** 3859

7716 **XIII** 7717

15438 **XIV** 15439

15432 **XIV** 15433

7718 **XIII** 7719

15434 **XIV** 15435

15436 **XIV** 15437

15448 **XIV** 15449

15454 **XIV** 15455

15442 **XIV** 15443

15444 **XIV** 15445

1930 **XI** 1931

15446 **XIV** 15447

15440 **XIV** 15441

7720 **XIII** 7721

7722 **XIII** 7723

3860 **XII** 3861

7724 **XIII** 7725

15450 **XIV** 15451

15452 **XIV** 15453

3862 **XII** 3863

7726 **XIII** 7727

♀ Surname : .... First name : ....

▶Generation IX – maternal ascendant ↓Child page 241 –　　　□ Implex

Born : .... in .... □ baptized

Daughter of : .... and: ....

Occupation(s) : ....

Deceased : .... in ....

⚭ **CHILDREN** ....

....

....

👪 ASCENDANCY UP TO XIVth GENERATION

7728 XIII 7729	3864 XII 3865
15458 XIV 15459	
15460 XIV 15461	7730 XIII 7731
	1932 XI 1933
15456 XIV 15457	
15462 XIV 15463	

3866 XII 3867

7734 XIII 7735

15470 XIV 15471

15464 XIV 15465

7732 XIII 7733

15466 XIV 15467

15468 XIV 15469

GX 966 Father

Sosa 483

GX 967 Mother

x

°

†

15474 XIV 15475

15476 XIV 15477

15480 XIV 15481

15486 XIV 15487

15478 XIV 15479

15472 XIV 15473

7736 XIII 7737

1934 XI 1935

7740 XIII 7741

15482 XIV 15483

15484 XIV 15485

7742 XIII 7743

7738 XIII 7739

3868 XII 3869

3870 XII 3871

Surname : .... First name : .... ♂

☐ Implex

Born : ....in..☐ baptized

Son of : ....and: ....

Occupation(s) : ....

Deceased : ....in..

💍 **MARITAL STATUS**   ☐ *Civil Marriage*   ☐ *Religious Marriage*   ☐ *Free`Union*

Date : ....in.. ☐ Marriage contract

Witnesses: ....

👪 ASCENDANCY UP TO XIVth GENERATION

7744 XIII 7745	
3872 XII 3873	
15490 XIV 15491	15492 XIV 15493
7746 XIII 7747	
3874 XII 3875	
7750 XIII 7751	
15502 XIV 15503	15496 XIV 15497
7748 XIII 7749	

1936 XI 1937

15488 XIV 15489	
15498 XIV 15499	
15494 XIV 15495	
15500 XIV 15501	

GX 968 Father

Sosa 484

GX 969 Mother

x

15506 XIV 15507	
15512 XIV 15513	
15508 XIV 15509	
15518 XIV 15519	

15510 XIV 15511	15504 XIV 15505
7752 XIII 7753	
7756 XIII 7757	
15514 XIV 15515	15516 XIV 15517

1938 XI 1939

7754 XIII 7755	
3876 XII 3877	
3878 XII 3879	
7758 XIII 7759	

♀ Surname : ....First name : ....

☐ Implex

▶Generation IX – maternal ascendant ↓Child page 242 –

Born : ....in................................☐ baptized

Daughter of : ....and: ....

Occupation(s) : ....

Deceased : ....in................................

⚭ **CHILDREN** ....

....

....

👪 **ASCENDANCY UP TO XIVth GENERATION**

7760 XIII 7761	3880 XII 3881
15522 XIV 15523	15524 XIV 15525
	7762 XIII 7763

3882 XII 3883

7764 XIII 7765

7766 XIII 7767

15534 XIV 15535

15528 XIV 15529

1940 XI 1941

15520 XIV 15521

15530 XIV 15531

15526 XIV 15527

15532 XIV 15533

GX 970 Father

Sosa 485

GX 971 Mother

15538 XIV 15539

15544 XIV 15545

15540 XIV 15541

15550 XIV 15551

1942 XI 1943

15542 XIV 15543

15536 XIV 15537

7768 XIII 7769

7772 XIII 7773

15546 XIV 15547

15548 XIV 15549

7770 XIII 7771

3884 XII 3885

3886 XII 3887

7774 XIII 7775

Surname : .... First name : .... ♂

▶Generation 9 – maternal ascendant ↓Child page 243

□ Implex

Born : .... in..□ baptized

Son of : ....and: ....

Occupation(s) : ....

Deceased : ....in...

⚭ **MARITAL STATUS**   □ *Civil Marriage*   □ *Religious Marriage*   □ *Free Union*

Date : ....in.. □ Marriage contract

Witnesses: ....

👪 ASCENDANCY UP TO XIVth GENERATION

♀ Surname : .... First name : ....

Sosa
487

►Generation IX – maternal ascendant ↓Child page 243 –

☐ Implex

Born : ....in...☐ baptized

Daughter of : ....and: ....

Occupation(s) : ....

Deceased : ....in...

⚭ CHILDREN ....

⚛ ASCENDANCY UP TO XIVth GENERATION

7792 XIII 7793	3896 XII 3897
15586 XIV 15587	15588 XIV 15589
	7794 XIII 7795
15584 XIV 15585	
15590 XIV 15591	1948 XI 1949

3898 XII 3899

7796 XIII 7797

7798 XIII 7799

15598 XIV 15599

15592 XIV 15593

15594 XIV 15595

15596 XIV 15597

GX 974 Father

Sosa 487

GX 975 Mother

15602 XIV 15603	
15604 XIV 15605	
7802 XIII 7803	15606 XIV 15607
	15600 XIV 15601
	7800 XIII 7801
	3900 XII 3901

15608 XIV 15609

15614 XIV 15615

1950 XI 1951

7804 XIII 7805

15610 XIV 15611

15612 XIV 15613

7806 XIII 7807

3902 XII 3903

487

Surname : .... First name : .... ♂

▶ Generation 9 – maternal ascendant ↓ Child page 244

□ Implex

Born : .... in .... □ baptized

Son of : .... and: ....

Occupation(s) : ....

Deceased : .... in ....

⚭ **MARITAL STATUS**   □ *Civil Marriage* □ *Religious Marriage* □ *Free Union*

Date : .... in .... □ Marriage contract

Witnesses: ....

👪 **ASCENDANCY UP TO XIVth GENERATION**

7808 XIII 7809	3904 XII 3905
15618 XIV 15619	15620 XIV 15621
7810 XIII 7811	
15616 XIV 15617	3906 XII 3907
15622 XIV 15623	7814 XIII 7815
	15630 XIV 15631
	15624 XIV 15625
	7812 XIII 7813
	15626 XIV 15627
	15628 XIV 15629

1952 XI 1953

GX 976 Father

Sosa 488

GX 977 Mother

1954 XI 1955

15634 XIV 15635	15640 XIV 15641
15636 XIV 15637	15646 XIV 15647
15638 XIV 15639	15642 XIV 15643
15632 XIV 15633	15644 XIV 15645
7816 XIII 7817	7820 XIII 7821
7818 XIII 7819	7822 XIII 7823
3908 XII 3909	3910 XII 3911

Sosa
489

♀ Surname : ....First name : ....

►Generation IX – maternal ascendant ↓Child page 244 –   □ Implex

Born : ....in.. □ baptized

Daughter of : ....and: ....

Occupation(s) : ....

Deceased : ....in...

⚭ CHILDREN ....

....

🗺 ASCENDANCY UP TO XIVth GENERATION

7824 XIII 7825	3912 XII 3913
15650 XIV 15651	
15652 XIV 15653	7826 XIII 7827
	3914 XII 3915
7828 XIII 7829	
15662 XIV 15663	7830 XIII 7831
15656 XIV 15657	

1956 XI 1957

15648 XIV 15649

15654 XIV 15655

15658 XIV 15659

15660 XIV 15661

GX 978 Father

Sosa 489

GX 979 Mother

15666 XIV 15667

15668 XIV 15669

15672 XIV 15673

15678 XIV 15679

1958 XI 1959

15670 XIV 15671

15664 XIV 15665

7832 XIII 7833

7836 XIII 7837

15674 XIV 15675

15676 XIV 15677

7834 XIII 7835

3916 XII 3917

3918 XII 3919

7838 XIII 7839

489

Sosa

490

Surname : .... First name : .... ♂

▶Generation 9 – maternal ascendant ↓Child page 245   □ Implex

Born : ....in.....................................□ baptized

Son of : ....and: ....

Occupation(s) : ....

Deceased : ....in..................................

⊚ MARITAL STATUS   □ Civil Marriage   □ Religious Marriage   □ Free Union

Date : ....in....................................... □ Marriage contract

Witnesses: ....

👪 ASCENDANCY UP TO XIVth GENERATION

3920 XII 3921		3922 XII 3923
7840 XIII 7841		7844 XIII 7845
15682 XIV 15683	15684 XIV 15685	7842 XIII 7843	7846 XIII 7847	15694 XIV 15695	15688 XIV 15689
	1960 XI 1961	
15680 XIV 15681		15690 XIV 15691
15686 XIV 15687		15692 XIV 15693
	GX 980 Father	
	Sosa 490	
	GX 981 Mother	
15698 XIV 15699	15704 XIV 15705	
15700 XIV 15701		15710 XIV 15711
15702 XIV 15703	15696 XIV 15697	7848 XIII 7849	1962 XI 1963	7852 XIII 7853	15706 XIV 15707	15708 XIV 15709
7850 XIII 7851	3924 XII 3925	3926 XII 3927	7854 XIII 7855

490

♀ Surname : .... First name : ....

► Generation IX – maternal ascendant ↓ Child page 245 –

☐ Implex

Born : ....in.. ☐ baptized

Daughter of : ....and: ....

Occupation(s) : ....

Deceased : ....in..

⚭ CHILDREN ....

....

🜚 ASCENDANCY UP TO XIVth GENERATION

7856 XIII 7857	
3928 XII 3929	
15714 XIV 15715	
15716 XIV 15717	
7858 XIII 7859	
1964 XI 1965	
15712 XIV 15713	
15718 XIV 15719	
GX 982 Father	
Sosa 491	
GX 983 Mother	
X	
15730 XIV 15731	
15732 XIV 15733	
1966 XI 1967	
15734 XIV 15735	
15728 XIV 15729	
7864 XIII 7865	
7866 XIII 7867	
3932 XII 3933	
3930 XII 3931	
7860 XIII 7861	
7862 XIII 7863	
15726 XIV 15727	
15720 XIV 15721	
15722 XIV 15723	
15724 XIV 15725	
15736 XIV 15737	
15742 XIV 15743	
7868 XIII 7869	
15738 XIV 15739	
15740 XIV 15741	
7870 XIII 7871	
3934 XII 3935	

Sosa 492

Surname : .... First name : .... ♂

▶Generation 9 – maternal ascendant ↓Child page 246 ☐ Implex

Born : ....in...☐ baptized

Son of : ....and: ....

Occupation(s) : ....

Deceased : ....in...

⚭ MARITAL STATUS   ☐ Civil Marriage   ☐ Religious Marriage   ☐ Free Union

Date : ....in... ☐ Marriage contract

Witnesses: ....

👪 ASCENDANCY UP TO XIVth GENERATION

7872 XIII 7873	
3936 XII 3937	3938 XII 3939
15746 XIV 15747	15748 XIV 15749	7874 XIII 7875
7878 XIII 7879	15758 XIV 15759	15752 XIV 15753
7876 XIII 7877	
15744 XIV 15745	
15754 XIV 15755	
15750 XIV 15751	
15756 XIV 15757	

1968 XI 1969

GX 984 Father

Sosa 492

GX 985 Mother

1970 XI 1971

15762 XIV 15763	
15764 XIV 15765	
15768 XIV 15769	
15774 XIV 15775	
15766 XIV 15767	15760 XIV 15761	7880 XIII 7881
7884 XIII 7885	15770 XIV 15771	15772 XIV 15773
7882 XIII 7883	
7886 XIII 7887	
3940 XII 3941	3942 XII 3943

♀ Surname : ....First name : ....

▶Generation IX – maternal ascendant ↓Child page 246 –

□ Implex

Born : ....in..□ baptized

Daughter of : ....and: ....

Occupation(s) : ....

Deceased : ....in..

⚭ **CHILDREN** ....

....

....

⚶ ASCENDANCY UP TO XIVth GENERATION

7888 XIII 7889	3944 XII 3945	
15778 XIV 15779		
15780 XIV 15781	7890 XIII 7891	
		1972 XI 1973
15776 XIV 15777		
15782 XIV 15783		GX 986 Father

Sosa 493

GX 987 Mother

3946 XII 3947	
7894 XIII 7895	
15790 XIV 15791	
15784 XIV 15785	
7892 XIII 7893	
15786 XIV 15787	
15788 XIV 15789	

15794 XIV 15795	
15796 XIV 15797	
15798 XIV 15799	
15792 XIV 15793	7896 XIII 7897
7898 XIII 7899	3948 XII 3949
	1974 XI 1975

15800 XIV 15801	
15806 XIV 15807	
7900 XIII 7901	
15802 XIV 15803	
15804 XIV 15805	
7902 XIII 7903	
3950 XII 3951	

Surname : .... First name : .... ♂

▶Generation 9 – maternal ascendant ↓Child page 247

☐ Implex

Born : ....in...................................☐ baptized

Son of : ....and: ....

Occupation(s) : ....

Deceased : ....in...................................

⚭ MARITAL STATUS

☐ Civil Marriage   ☐ Religious Marriage   ☐ Free Union

Date : ....in...................................

☐ Marriage contract

Witnesses: ....

👪 ASCENDANCY UP TO XIVth GENERATION

| 3952 XII 3953 |
| 3954 XII 3955 |

7904 XIII 7905

15810 XIV 15811

15812 XIV 15813

7906 XIII 7907

7910 XIII 7911

15822 XIV 15823

15816 XIV 15817

7908 XIII 7909

1976 XI 1977

15808 XIV 15809

15814 XIV 15815

15818 XIV 15819

15820 XIV 15821

GX 988 Father

Sosa 494

GX 989 Mother

15826 XIV 15827

15828 XIV 15829

15832 XIV 15833

15838 XIV 15839

1978 XI 1979

15830 XIV 15831

15824 XIV 15825

7912 XIII 7913

7916 XIII 7917

15834 XIV 15835

15836 XIV 15837

7914 XIII 7915

7918 XIII 7919

3956 XII 3957

3958 XII 3959

♀ Surname : ....First name : ....

▶Generation IX – maternal ascendant ↓Child page 247 –

□ Implex

Born : ....in..□ baptized

Daughter of : ....and: ....

Occupation(s) : ....

Deceased : ....in...

⚭ CHILDREN ....

....

....

⚥ ASCENDANCY UP TO XIVth GENERATION

7920 **XIII** 7921	3960 **XII** 3961
15842 **XIV** 15843	
15844 **XIV** 15845	7922 **XIII** 7923
15840 **XIV** 15841	
15846 **XIV** 15847	

1980 XI 1981

GX 990 Father

Sosa 495

GX 991 Mother

3962 **XII** 3963	7924 **XIII** 7925
15854 **XIV** 15855	15848 **XIV** 15849
7926 **XIII** 7927	
15850 **XIV** 15851	
15852 **XIV** 15853	

15858 **XIV** 15859	15864 **XIV** 15865
15860 **XIV** 15861	15870 **XIV** 15871
7930 **XIII** 7931	
15862 **XIV** 15863	
15856 **XIV** 15857	7928 **XIII** 7929
	7932 **XIII** 7933
	15866 **XIV** 15867
	15868 **XIV** 15869
3964 **XII** 3965	3966 **XII** 3967
	7934 **XIII** 7935

1982 XI 1983

Surname : .... First name : .... ♂

▶Generation 9 – maternal ascendant   ↓Child page 248

□ Implex

Born : .... in .... □ baptized

Son of : .... and: ....

Occupation(s) : ....

Deceased : .... in ....

💍 MARITAL STATUS

□ *Civil Marriage*   □ *Religious Marriage*   □ *Free Union*

Date : .... in ....   □ Marriage contract

Witnesses: ....

👪 ASCENDANCY UP TO XIVth GENERATION

7936 XIII 7937	3968 XII 3969
15874 XIV 15875	15876 XIV 15877	7938 XIII 7939
15872 XIV 15873	
15878 XIV 15879	

1984 XI 1985

GX 992 Father

Sosa 496

GX 993 Mother

1986 XI 1987

| 3970 XII 3971 | |
| 7942 XIII 7943 | 15886 XIV 15887 | 15880 XIV 15881 | 7940 XIII 7941 |
| 15882 XIV 15883 |
| 15884 XIV 15885 |

15890 XIV 15891	
15892 XIV 15893	
15894 XIV 15895	15888 XIV 15889	7944 XIII 7945
7946 XIII 7947	3972 XII 3973

15896 XIV 15897	
15902 XIV 15903	
7948 XIII 7949	15898 XIV 15899	15900 XIV 15901	7950 XIII 7951
3974 XII 3975	

♀ Surname : .... First name : ....

▶Generation IX – maternal ascendant ↓Child page 248 –

☐ Implex

Born : .... in .... ☐ baptized

Daughter of : ....and: ....

Occupation(s) : ....

Deceased : .... in ....

💍 **CHILDREN** ....
....
....

👪 **ASCENDANCY UP TO XIVth GENERATION**

7952 XIII 7953	3976 XII 3977	3978 XII 3979
15906 XIV 15907	7954 XIII 7955	7958 XIII 7959
15908 XIV 15909		15918 XIV 15919

1988 XI 1989

GX 994 Father

15904 XIV 15905

15910 XIV 15911

7956 XIII 7957

15912 XIV 15913

15914 XIV 15915

15916 XIV 15917

Sosa 497

GX 995 Mother
x...
°...
†...

15922 XIV 15923

15928 XIV 15929

15924 XIV 15925

15934 XIV 15935

1990 XI 1991

15926 XIV 15927

15920 XIV 15921

7960 XIII 7961

7964 XIII 7965

15930 XIV 15931

15932 XIV 15933

7962 XIII 7963

3980 XII 3981

3982 XII 3983

7966 XII 7967

Sosa
498

Surname : .... First name : .... ♂

▶Generation 9 – maternal ascendant ↓Child page 249

☐ Implex

Born : .... in .... ☐ baptized

Son of : .... and: ....

Occupation(s) : ....

Deceased : .... in ....

⚭ MARITAL STATUS

☐ *Civil Marriage*   ☐ *Religious Marriage*   ☐ *Free Union*

Date : .... in ....

☐ Marriage contract

Witnesses: ....

ASCENDANCY UP TO XIVth GENERATION

7968 XIII 7969	3984 XII 3985
15938 XIV 15939	
15940 XIV 15941	7970 XIII 7971
15936 XIV 15937	
15942 XIV 15943	

1992 XI 1993

3986 XII 3987

7974 XIII 7975	7972 XIII 7973
15950 XIV 15951	15944 XIV 15945
	15946 XIV 15947
15948 XIV 15949	

GX 996 Father

Sosa 498

GX 997 Mother

15954 XIV 15955	
15956 XIV 15957	
	15958 XIV 15959
	15952 XIV 15953
7978 XIII 7979	7976 XIII 7977

15960 XIV 15961	
	15966 XIV 15967
7980 XIII 7981	
15962 XIV 15963	15964 XIV 15965
	7982 XIII 7983

1994 XI 1995

3988 XII 3989

3990 XII 3991

498

♀ Surname : .... First name : ....

▶Generation IX – maternal ascendant ↓Child page 249 –   □ Implex

Born : ....in...□ baptized

Daughter of : ....and:..............................

Occupation(s) : ....

Deceased : ....in.....................................

💍 CHILDREN ....

....

🎎 ASCENDANCY UP TO XIVth GENERATION

Sosa	Gen
7984	XIII
7985	
3992	XII
3993	
3994	XII
3995	
7988	XIII
7989	
15970	XIV
15971	
15972	XIV
15973	
7986	XIII
7987	
7990	XIII
7991	
15982	XIV
15983	
15976	XIV
15977	

1996 XI 1997

15968 XIV 15969

15974 XIV 15975

15978 XIV 15979

15980 XIV 15981

GX 998 Father

Sosa 499

GX 999 Mother
x

15986 XIV 15987

15992 XIV 15993

15988 XIV 15989

15998 XIV 15999

1998 XI 1999

15990 XIV 15991

15984 XIV 15985

7992 XIII 7993

7996 XIII 7997

15994 XIV 15995

15996 XIV 15997

7994 XIII 7995

3996 XII 3997

3998 XII 3999

7998 XIII 7999

Surname : .... First name : .... ♂

▶Generation 9 – maternal ascendant ↓Child page 250

□ Implex

Born : .... in..□ baptized

Son of : ....and: ....

Occupation(s) : ....

Deceased : ....in...

⚭ **MARITAL STATUS**   □ *Civil Marriage*   □ *Religious Marriage*   □ *Free Union*

Date : ....in.. □ Marriage contract

Witnesses: ....

ASCENDANCY UP TO XIVth GENERATION

8000 XIII 8001	4000 XII 4001
16002 XIV 16003	8002 XIII 8003
16004 XIV 16005	
16000 XIV 16001	2000 XI 2001
16006 XIV 16007	

4002 XII 4003

8006 XIII 8007

16014 XIV 16015

16008 XIV 16009

8004 XIII 8005

16010 XIV 16011

16012 XIV 16013

GX 1000 Father

Sosa 500

GX 1001 Mother

16018 XIV 16019

16020 XIV 16021

16024 XIV 16025

16030 XIV 16031

16022 XIV 16023

16016 XIV 16017

8008 XIII 8009

2002 XI 2003

8012 XIII 8013

16026 XIV 16027

16028 XIV 16029

8010 XIII 8011

4004 XII 4005

4006 XII 4007

8014 XIII 8015

♀ Surname : ....First name : ....

▶Generation IX – maternal ascendant ↓Child page 250 –   □ Implex

Born : ....in...□ baptized

Daughter of : ....and: ....

Occupation(s) : ....

Deceased : ....in..

⚭ **CHILDREN** ....
....
....

⚶ ASCENDANCY UP TO XIVth GENERATION

8016 XIII 8017	4008 XII 4009
16034 XIV 16035	8018 XIII 8019
16036 XIV 16037	
16032 XIV 16033	
16038 XIV 16039	2004 XI 2005

GX 1002 Father

Sosa 501

GX 1003 Mother

4010 XII 4011	8020 XIII 8021
8022 XIII 8023	16046 XIV 16047
	16040 XIV 16041
	16042 XIV 16043
16044 XIV 16045	

16050 XIV 16051	
16052 XIV 16053	
16054 XIV 16055	
16048 XIV 16049	8024 XIII 8025
8026 XIII 8027	4012 XII 4013

2006 XI 2007

16056 XIV 16057	
16062 XIV 16063	
4014 XII 4015	8028 XIII 8029
	16058 XIV 16059
	16060 XIV 16061
	8030 XIII 8031

Sosa
502

Surname : ....First name : ....♂

▶Generation 9 – maternal ascendant ↓Child page 251 □ Implex

Born : ....in...□ baptized

Son of : ....and: ....

Occupation(s) : ....

Deceased : ....in...

⊙ MARITAL STATUS

□ *Civil Marriage*   □ *Religious Marriage*   □ *Free Union*

Date : ....in... □ Marriage contract

Witnesses: ....

ASCENDANCY UP TO XIVth GENERATION

8032 XIII 8033	4016 XII 4017
16066 XIV 16067	16068 XIV 16069	8034 XIII 8035
16064 XIV 16065	
16070 XIV 16071	GX 1004 Father

Sosa 502

GX 1005 Mother

| 4018 XII 4019 | 8036 XIII 8037 |
| 8038 XIII 8039 | 16078 XIV 16079 | 16072 XIV 16073 |
| 16074 XIV 16075 |
| 16076 XIV 16077 |

2008 XI 2009

16082 XIV 16083	16088 XIV 16089
16084 XIV 16085	16094 XIV 16095
8042 XIII 8043	16086 XIV 16087	16080 XIV 16081	8040 XIII 8041
4020 XII 4021

2010 XI 2011

| 8044 XIII 8045 | 16090 XIV 16091 | 16092 XIV 16093 |
| 4022 XII 4023 | 8046 XIII 8047 |

502

♀ Surname : .... First name : ....

□ Implex

▶Generation IX – maternal ascendant ↓Child page 251 –

Born : ....in..□ baptized

Daughter of : ....and: ....

Occupation(s) : ....

Deceased : ....in...

⚭ CHILDREN ....
....
....

👪 ASCENDANCY UP TO XIVth GENERATION

8048 XIII 8049	4024 XII 4025
16098 XIV 16099	
16100 XIV 16101	8050 XIII 8051
	2012 XI 2013
16096 XIV 16097	
16102 XIV 16103	GX 1006 Father

Sosa 503

GX 1007 Mother

4026 XII 4027	8052 XIII 8053
8054 XIII 8055	16110 XIV 16111
	16104 XIV 16105
16106 XIV 16107	
16108 XIV 16109	

16114 XIV 16115	16120 XIV 16121
16116 XIV 16117	16126 XIV 16127
16118 XIV 16119	
16112 XIV 16113	8056 XIII 8057
8058 XIII 8059	4028 XII 4029
	2014 XI 2015
8060 XIII 8061	16122 XIV 16123
	16124 XIV 16125
4030 XII 4031	8062 XIII 8063

Sosa

504

Surname : .... First name : .... ♂

□ Implex

Born : ....in...□ baptized

Son of : ....and: ....

Occupation(s) : ....

Deceased : ....in..

⚭ MARITAL STATUS   □ Civil Marriage   □ Religious Marriage   □ Free Union

Date : ....in.. □ Marriage contract

Witnesses: ....

👪 ASCENDANCY UP TO XIVth GENERATION

504

♀ Surname : .... First name : ....

▶Generation IX – maternal ascendant ↓Child page 252 –

☐ Implex

Born : .... in .... ☐ baptized

Daughter of : .... and: ....

Occupation(s) : ....

Deceased : .... in ....

💍 **CHILDREN** ....

....

....

👪 **ASCENDANCY UP TO XIVth GENERATION**

8080 XIII 8081	
4040 XII 4041	
16162 XIV 16163	
16164 XIV 16165	
8082 XIII 8083	
4042 XII 4043	
8084 XIII 8085	
8086 XIII 8087	
16174 XIV 16175	
16168 XIV 16169	

2020 XI 2021

GX 1010 Father

Sosa 505

GX 1011 Mother

x..............................

16160 XIV 16161	
16166 XIV 16167	
16172 XIV 16173	
16170 XIV 16171	
16178 XIV 16179	
16184 XIV 16185	
16180 XIV 16181	
16190 XIV 16191	

2022 XI 2023

16182 XIV 16183	
16176 XIV 16177	
8088 XIII 8089	
8090 XIII 8091	
4044 XII 4045	
8092 XIII 8093	
16186 XIV 16187	
16188 XIV 16189	
8094 XIII 8095	
4046 XII 4047	

Sosa
506

Surname : .... First name : .... ♂

▶Generation 9 – maternal ascendant ↓Child page 253

☐ Implex

Born : .... in .... ☐ baptized

Son of : .... and: ....

Occupation(s) : ....

Deceased : .... in ....

⚭ MARITAL STATUS

☐ Civil Marriage   ☐ Religious Marriage   ☐ Free Union

Date : .... in .... ☐ Marriage contract

Witnesses: ....

👪 ASCENDANCY UP TO XIVth GENERATION

8096 XIII 8097	
16194 XIV 16195	16196 XIV 16197
4048 XII 4049	4050 XII 4051
8098 XIII 8099	8100 XIII 8101
8102 XIII 8103	16206 XIV 16207	16200 XIV 16201

2024 XI 2025

16192 XIV 16193

16198 XIV 16199

16202 XIV 16203

16204 XIV 16205

GX 1012 Father

Sosa 506

GX 1013 Mother

x..............
°
†

16210 XIV 16211

16212 XIV 16213

16216 XIV 16217

16222 XIV 16223

2026 XI 2027

16214 XIV 16215

16208 XIV 16209

8104 XIII 8105

8106 XIII 8107

4052 XII 4053

8108 XIII 8109

16218 XIV 16219

16220 XIV 16221

8110 XIII 8111

4054 XII 4055

506

♀ Surname : .... First name : ....

☐ Implex

Born : .... in .... ☐ baptized

Daughter of : .... and: ....

Occupation(s) : ....

Deceased : .... in ....

⚭ **CHILDREN** ....

....

....

👪 ASCENDANCY UP TO XIVth GENERATION

8112 XIII 8113	4056 XII 4057
16226 XIV 16227	4058 XII 4059
16228 XIV 16229	8114 XIII 8115
	8116 XIII 8117
8118 XIII 8119	16238 XIV 16239
	16232 XIV 16233

2028 XI 2029

16224 XIV 16225

16230 XIV 16231

16234 XIV 16235

16236 XIV 16237

GX 1014 Father

Sosa 507

GX 1015 Mother

16242 XIV 16243

16248 XIV 16249

16244 XIV 16245

16254 XIV 16255

2030 XI 2031

16246 XIV 16247

16240 XIV 16241

8120 XIII 8121

8124 XIII 8125

16250 XIV 16251

16252 XIV 16253

8122 XIII 8123

4060 XII 4061

4062 XII 4063

8126 XIII 8127

Sosa
508

Surname : .... First name : .... ♂

▶Generation 9 – maternal ascendant ↓Child page 254

☐ Implex

Born : .... in .... ☐ baptized

Son of : .... and: ....

Occupation(s) : ....

Deceased : .... in ....

⚭ MARITAL STATUS

☐ *Civil Marriage*   ☐ *Religious Marriage*   ☐ *Free Union*

Date : .... in ....

☐ Marriage contract

Witnesses: ....

👪 ASCENDANCY UP TO XIVth GENERATION

8128 XIII 8129	
4064 XII 4065	
16258 XIV 16259	16260 XIV 16261
8130 XIII 8131	
16256 XIV 16257	
16262 XIV 16263	

2032 XI 2033

GX 1016 Father

Sosa 508

GX 1017 Mother

4066 XII 4067

8132 XIII 8133

8134 XIII 8135

16270 XIV 16271

16264 XIV 16265

16266 XIV 16267

16268 XIV 16269

16274 XIV 16275

16276 XIV 16277

16278 XIV 16279

16272 XIV 16273

8136 XIII 8137

8138 XIII 8139

4068 XII 4069

2034 XI 2035

16280 XIV 16281

16286 XIV 16287

8140 XIII 8141

16282 XIV 16283

16284 XIV 16285

8142 XIII 8143

4070 XII 4071

508

♀ Surname : ....First name : ....

□ Implex

Born : ....in..□ baptized

Daughter of : ....and: ....

Occupation(s) : ....

Deceased : ....in...

⚭ CHILDREN ....

....
....

👪 ASCENDANCY UP TO XIVth GENERATION

8144 XIII 8145	4072 XII 4073
16290 XIV 16291	16292 XIV 16293
8146 XIII 8147	

2036 XI 2037

4074 XII 4075

8150 XIII 8151

16302 XIV 16303

16296 XIV 16297

8148 XIII 8149

16288 XIV 16289

16294 XIV 16295

16298 XIV 16299

16300 XIV 16301

GX 1018 Father

Sosa 509

GX 1019 Mother

16306 XIV 16307

16312 XIV 16313

16308 XIV 16309

16318 XIV 16319

2038 XI 2039

16310 XIV 16311

16304 XIV 16305

8152 XIII 8153

8156 XIII 8157

16314 XIV 16315

16316 XIV 16317

8154 XIII 8155

4076 XII 4077

4078 XII 4079

8158 XIII 8159

Surname : .... First name : .... ♂

▶Generation 9 – maternal ascendant ↓Child page 255

□ Implex

Born : .... in ....□ baptized

Son of : .... and: ....

Occupation(s) : ....

Deceased : .... in ....

○ **MARITAL STATUS**   □ *Civil Marriage*   □ *Religious Marriage*   □ *Free Union*

Date : ....in.. □ Marriage contract

Witnesses: ....

ASCENDANCY UP TO XIVth GENERATION

8160 / XIII / 8161	
4080 / XII / 4081	
16322 / XIV / 16323	
16324 / XIV / 16325	
8162 / XIII / 8163	
2040 / XI / 2041	
4082 / XII / 4083	
8166 / XIII / 8167	
16334 / XIV / 16335	
16328 / XIV / 16329	
8164 / XIII / 8165	
16320 / XIV / 16321	
16326 / XIV / 16327	
16330 / XIV / 16331	
16332 / XIV / 16333	

GX 1020 Father

Sosa 510

GX 1021 Mother

16338 / XIV / 16339	
16340 / XIV / 16341	
16342 / XIV / 16343	
16336 / XIV / 16337	
8168 / XIII / 8169	
2042 / XI / 2043	
16344 / XIV / 16345	
16350 / XIV / 16351	
8172 / XIII / 8173	
16346 / XIV / 16347	
16348 / XIV / 16349	
8174 / XIII / 8175	
8170 / XIII / 8171	
4084 / XII / 4085	
4086 / XII / 4087	

♀ Surname : .... First name : ....

▶Generation IX – maternal ascendant ↓Child page 255 –   ☐ Implex

Born : ....in.. ☐ baptized

Daughter of : ....and:.................................

Occupation(s) : ....

Deceased : ....in..

⚭ CHILDREN ....

....

....

🎎 ASCENDANCY UP TO XIVth GENERATION

| 8176 XIII 8177 | | 4088 XII 4089 | | | 4090 XII 4091 | | 8180 XIII 8181 |

| 16354 XIV 16355 | 16356 XIV 16357 | 8178 XIII 8179 | | 8182 XIII 8183 | 16366 XIV 16367 | 16360 XIV 16361 | |

2044 XI 2045

| 16352 XIV 16353 | | | | | | 16362 XIV 16363 |

| 16358 XIV 16359 | | | | 16364 XIV 16365 |

GX 1022 Father

Sosa 511

GX 1023 Mother

| 16370 XIV 16371 | | | | 16376 XIV 16377 |

| 16372 XIV 16373 | | | | | | 16382 XIV 16383 |

2046 XI 2047

| 16374 XIV 16375 | 16368 XIV 16369 | 8184 XIII 8185 | | 8188 XIII 8189 | 16378 XIV 16379 | 16380 XIV 16381 | |

| 8186 XIII 8187 | | 4092 XII 4093 | | 4094 XII | | 8190 XIII 8191 |

📍 Location name: ....

Type of location : ....

Latitude : ....

Longitude : ....

Concerned sosas

....

....

....

....

....

....

Notes: ....
....
....

📍 Location name: ....

Type of location : ....

Latitude : ....

Longitude : ....

Concerned sosas

....

....

....

....

....

....

Notes: ....
....
....

Location name: ....

Type of location : ....

Latitude : ....

Longitude : ....

Concerned sosas

....
....
....
....
....
....

Notes: ....
....
....

Location name: ....

Type of location : ....

Latitude : ....

Longitude : ....

Concerned sosas

....
....
....
....
....
....

Notes: ....
....
....

📍 Location name: ....

Type of location :

....

Latitude :

....

Longitude :

....

Concerned sosas

....

....

....

....

....

....

Notes: ....
....
....

📍 Location name: ....

Type of location :

....

Latitude :

....

Longitude :

....

Concerned sosas

....

....

....

....

....

....

Notes: ....
....
....

Location name: ....

Type of location :

....

Latitude :

....

Longitude :

....

Concerned sosas

....

....

....

....

....

....

Notes: ....
....
....

Location name: ....

Type of location :

....

Latitude :

....

Longitude :

....

Concerned sosas

....

....

....

....

....

....

Notes: ....
....
....

📍 Location name: ....

Type of location :

....

Latitude :

....

Longitude :

....

Concerned sosas

....

....

....

....

....

....

Notes: ....

....

....

📍 Location name: ....

Type of location :

....

Latitude :

....

Longitude :

....

Concerned sosas

....

....

....

....

....

....

Notes: ....

....

....

Location name: ....

Type of location : ....

Latitude : ....

Longitude : ....

Concerned sosas

....

....

....

....

....

....

Notes: ....
....
....

Location name: ....

Type of location : ....

Latitude : ....

Longitude : ....

Concerned sosas

....

....

....

....

....

....

Notes: ....
....
....

📍 Location name: ....

Type of location : ....

Latitude : ....

Longitude : ....

Concerned sosas

....

....

....

....

....

....

Notes: ....
....
....

📍 Location name: ....

Type of location : ....

Latitude : ....

Longitude : ....

Concerned sosas

....

....

....

....

....

....

Notes: ....
....
....

Location name: ....

Type of location :

....

Latitude :

....

Longitude :

....

Concerned sosas

....

....

....

....

....

....

Notes: ....
....
....

Location name: ....

Type of location :

....

Latitude :

....

Longitude :

....

Concerned sosas

....

....

....

....

....

....

Notes: ....
....
....

Location name: ....

Type of location : ....

Latitude : ....

Longitude : ....

Concerned sosas
....
....
....
....
....
....

Notes: ....
....
....

Location name: ....

Type of location : ....

Latitude : ....

Longitude : ....

Concerned sosas
....
....
....
....
....
....

Notes: ....
....
....

📍 Location name: ....

Type of location :

....

Latitude :

....

Longitude :

....

Concerned sosas

....

....

....

....

....

....

Notes: ....
....
....

📍 Location name: ....

Type of location :

....

Latitude :

....

Longitude :

....

Concerned sosas

....

....

....

....

....

....

Notes: ....
....
....

📍 Location name: ....

Type of location :

....

Latitude :

....

Longitude :

....

Concerned sosas

....

....

....

....

....

....

Notes: ....
....
....

📍 Location name: ....

Type of location :

....

Latitude :

....

Longitude :

....

Concerned sosas

....

....

....

....

....

....

Notes: ....
....
....

Location name: ....

Type of location :

....

Latitude :

....

Longitude :

....

Concerned sosas

....
....
....
....
....
....

Notes: ....
....
....

Location name: ....

Type of location :

....

Latitude :

....

Longitude :

....

Concerned sosas

....
....
....
....
....
....

Notes: ....
....
....

Location name: ....

Type of location : ....

Latitude : ....

Longitude : ....

Concerned sosas

....

....

....

....

....

....

Notes: ....
....
....

Location name: ....

Type of location : ....

Latitude : ....

Longitude : ....

Concerned sosas

....

....

....

....

....

....

Notes: ....
....
....

Location name: ....

Type of location :

....

Latitude :

....

Longitude :

....

Concerned sosas

....
....
....
....
....
....
....

Notes: ....
....
....

Location name: ....

Type of location :

....

Latitude :

....

Longitude :

....

Concerned sosas

....
....
....
....
....
....

Notes: ....
....
....

525

Location name: ....

Type of location : ....

Latitude : ....

Longitude : ....

Concerned sosas

....

....

....

....

....

....

Notes: ....
....
....

Location name: ....

Type of location : ....

Latitude : ....

Longitude : ....

Concerned sosas

....

....

....

....

....

....

Notes: ....
....
....

📍 Location name: ....

Type of location : ....

Latitude : ....

Longitude : ....

Concerned sosas
....
....
....
....
....
....

Notes: ....
....
....

📍 Location name: ....

Type of location : ....

Latitude : ....

Longitude : ....

Concerned sosas
....
....
....
....
....
....

Notes: ....
....
....

📍 Location name: ....

Type of location : ....

Latitude : ....

Longitude : ....

Concerned sosas

....

....

....

....

....

....

Notes: ....
....
....

📍 Location name: ....

Type of location : ....

Latitude : ....

Longitude : ....

Concerned sosas

....

....

....

....

....

....

Notes: ....
....
....

Location name: ....

Type of location :

....

Latitude :

....

Longitude :

....

Concerned sosas

....

....

....

....

....

....

Notes: ....

....

....

Location name: ....

Type of location :

....

Latitude :

....

Longitude :

....

Concerned sosas

....

....

....

....

....

....

Notes: ....

....

....

📍 Location name: ....

Type of location :

....

Latitude :

....

Longitude :

....

Concerned sosas

....

....

....

....

....

....

Notes: ....

....

....

📍 Location name: ....

Type of location :

....

Latitude :

....

Longitude :

....

Concerned sosas

....

....

....

....

....

....

Notes: ....

....

....

Location name: ....

Type of location : ....

Latitude : ....

Longitude : ....

Concerned sosas
....
....
....
....
....
....

Notes: ....
....
....

Location name: ....

Type of location : ....

Latitude : ....

Longitude : ....

Concerned sosas
....
....
....
....
....
....

Notes: ....
....
....

Location name: ....

Type of location : ....

Latitude : ....

Longitude : ....

Concerned sosas

....
....
....
....
....
....

Notes: ....
....
....

Location name: ....

Type of location : ....

Latitude : ....

Longitude : ....

Concerned sosas

....
....
....
....
....

Notes: ....
....
....

📍 Location name: ....

Type of location : ....

Latitude : ....

Longitude : ....

Concerned sosas

....
....
....
....
....
....

Notes: ....
....
....

📍 Location name: ....

Type of location : ....

Latitude : ....

Longitude : ....

Concerned sosas

....
....
....
....
....
....

Notes: ....
....
....

Type of location : ....

Location name: ....

Type of location : ....

Latitude : ....

Longitude : ....

Concerned sosas

....
....
....
....
....
....

Notes: ....
....
....

Location name: ....

Type of location : ....

Latitude : ....

Longitude : ....

Concerned sosas

....
....
....
....
....
....

Notes: ....
....
....

📍 Location name: ....

Type of location :

....

Latitude :

....

Longitude :

....

Concerned sosas

....

....

....

....

....

....

Notes: ....
....
....

📍 Location name: ....

Type of location :

....

Latitude :

....

Longitude :

....

Concerned sosas

....

....

....

....

....

....

Notes: ....
....
....

Location name: ....

Type of location :

....

Latitude :

....

Longitude :

....

Concerned sosas

....

....

....

....

....

....

Notes: ....
....
....

Location name: ....

Type of location :

....

Latitude :

....

Longitude :

....

Concerned sosas

....

....

....

....

....

....

Notes: ....
....
....

Location name: ....

Type of location : ....

Latitude : ....

Longitude : ....

Concerned sosas

....
....
....
....
....
....

Notes: ....
....
....

Location name: ....

Type of location : ....

Latitude : ....

Longitude : ....

Concerned sosas

....
....
....
....
....
....

Notes: ....
....
....

📍 Location name: ....

Type of location :
....

Latitude :
....

Longitude :
....

Concerned sosas
....
....
....
....
....
....

Notes: ....
....
....

📍 Location name: ....

Type of location :
....

Latitude :
....

Longitude :
....

Concerned sosas
....
....
....
....
....
....

Notes: ....
....
....

Location name: ....

Type of location :
....

Latitude :
....

Longitude :
....

Concerned sosas
....
....
....
....
....
....

Notes: ....
....
....

Location name: ....

Type of location :
....

Latitude :
....

Longitude :
....

Concerned sosas
....
....
....
....
....
....

Notes: ....
....
....

Location name: ....

Type of location : ....

Latitude : ....

Longitude : ....

Concerned sosas ....
....
....
....
....
....

Notes: ....
....
....

Location name: ....

Type of location : ....

Latitude : ....

Longitude : ....

Concerned sosas ....
....
....
....
....
....

Notes: ....
....
....

📍 Location name: ....

Type of location : ....

Latitude : ....

Longitude : ....

Concerned sosas

....
....
....
....
....
....

Notes: ....
....
....

📍 Location name: ....

Type of location : ....

Latitude : ....

Longitude : ....

Concerned sosas

....
....
....
....
....
....

Notes: ....
....
....

📍 Location name: ....

Type of location : ....

Latitude : ....

Longitude : ....

Concerned sosas

....

....

....

....

....

....

Notes: ....
....
....

📍 Location name: ....

Type of location : ....

Latitude : ....

Longitude : ....

Concerned sosas

....

....

....

....

....

....

Notes: ....
....
....

Location name: ....

Type of location :

....

Latitude :

....

Longitude :

....

Concerned sosas

....
....
....
....
....
....

Notes: ....
....
....

Location name: ....

Type of location :

....

Latitude :

....

Longitude :

....

Concerned sosas

....
....
....
....
....
....

Notes: ....
....
....

📍 Location name: ....

Type of location : ....

Latitude : ....

Longitude : ....

Concerned sosas

....

....

....

....

....

....

Notes: ....
....
....

📍 Location name: ....

Type of location : ....

Latitude : ....

Longitude : ....

Concerned sosas

....

....

....

....

....

....

Notes: ....
....
....

Location name: ....

Type of location :

....

Latitude :

....

Longitude :

....

Concerned sosas

....

....

....

....

....

....

Notes: ....
....
....

Location name: ....

Type of location :

....

Latitude :

....

Longitude :

....

Concerned sosas

....

....

....

....

....

....

Notes: ....
....
....

545

📍 Location name: ....

Type of location : ....

Latitude : ....

Longitude : ....

Concerned sosas

....

....

....

....

....

....

Notes: ....
....
....

📍 Location name: ....

Type of location : ....

Latitude : ....

Longitude : ....

Concerned sosas

....

....

....

....

....

....

Notes: ....
....
....

📍 Location name: ....

Type of location :

....

Latitude :

....

Longitude :

....

Concerned sosas

....

....

....

....

....

Notes: ....
....
....

📍 Location name: ....

Type of location :

....

Latitude :

....

Longitude :

....

Concerned sosas

....

....

....

....

....

....

Notes: ....
....
....

Location name: ....

Type of location :

....

Latitude :

....

Longitude :

....

Concerned sosas

....

....

....

....

....

....

Notes: ....
....
....

Location name: ....

Type of location :

....

Latitude :

....

Longitude :

....

Concerned sosas

....

....

....

....

....

....

Notes: ....
....
....

Location name: ....

Type of location :

....

Latitude :

....

Longitude :

....

Concerned sosas

....
....
....
....
....
....

Notes: ....
....
....

Location name: ....

Type of location :

....

Latitude :

....

Longitude :

....

Concerned sosas

....
....
....
....
....
....

Notes: ....
....
....

📍 Location name: ....

Type of location : ....

Latitude : ....

Longitude : ....

Concerned sosas

....
....
....
....
....
....

Notes: ....
....
....

📍 Location name: ....

Type of location : ....

Latitude : ....

Longitude : ....

Concerned sosas

....
....
....
....
....
....

Notes: ....
....
....

Location name: ....

Type of location :

....

Latitude :

....

Longitude :

....

Concerned sosas

....

....

....

....

....

....

Notes: ....

....

....

Location name: ....

Type of location :

....

Latitude :

....

Longitude :

....

Concerned sosas

....

....

....

....

....

....

Notes: ....

....

....

📍 Location name: ....

Type of location : ....

Latitude : ....

Longitude : ....

Concerned sosas

....
....
....
....
....
....

Notes: ....
....
....

📍 Location name: ....

Type of location : ....

Latitude : ....

Longitude : ....

Concerned sosas

....
....
....
....
....

Notes: ....
....
....

Location name: ....

Type of location :

....

Latitude :

....

Longitude :

....

Concerned sosas

....

....

....

....

....

....

Notes: ....
....
....

Location name: ....

Type of location :

....

Latitude :

....

Longitude :

....

Concerned sosas

....

....

....

....

....

....

Notes: ....
....
....

Location name: ....

Type of location :

....

Latitude :

....

Longitude :

....

Concerned sosas

....

....

....

....

....

Notes: ....
....
....

Location name: ....

Type of location :

....

Latitude :

....

Longitude :

....

Concerned sosas

....

....

....

....

....

Notes: ....
....
....

Location name: ....

Type of location :

....

Latitude :

....

Longitude :

....

Concerned sosas

....

....

....

....

....

....

Notes: ....
....
....

Location name: ....

Type of location :

....

Latitude :

....

Longitude :

....

Concerned sosas

....

....

....

....

....

....

Notes: ....
....
....

📍 Location name: ....

Type of location :

....

Latitude :

....

Longitude :

....

Concerned sosas

....
....
....
....
....
....

Notes: ....
....
....

📍 Location name: ....

Type of location :

....

Latitude :

....

Longitude :

....

Concerned sosas

....
....
....
....
....
....

Notes: ....
....
....

Location name: ....

Type of location : ....

Latitude : ....

Longitude : ....

Concerned sosas

....
....
....
....
....
....

Notes: ....
....
....

Location name: ....

Type of location : ....

Latitude : ....

Longitude : ....

Concerned sosas

....
....
....
....
....
....

Notes: ....
....
....

📍 Location name: ....

Type of location :

....

Latitude :

....

Longitude :

....

Concerned sosas

....

....

....

....

....

....

Notes: ....

....

....

📍 Location name: ....

Type of location :

....

Latitude :

....

Longitude :

....

Concerned sosas

....

....

....

....

....

....

Notes: ....

....

....

📍 Location name: ....

	Type of location :
	....
	Latitude :
	....
	Longitude :
	....
	Concerned sosas
	....
	....
	....
	....
	....
	....

Notes: ....
....
....

📍 Location name: ....

	Type of location :
	....
	Latitude :
	....
	Longitude :
	....
	Concerned sosas
	....
	....
	....
	....
	....
	....

Notes: ....
....
....

📍 Location name: ....

Type of location : ....

Latitude : ....

Longitude : ....

Concerned sosas

....

....

....

....

....

....

Notes: ....
....
....

📍 Location name: ....

Type of location : ....

Latitude : ....

Longitude : ....

Concerned sosas

....

....

....

....

....

....

Notes: ....
....
....

Location name: ....

Type of location :

....

Latitude :

....

Longitude :

....

Concerned sosas

....

....

....

....

....

....

Notes: ....
....
....

Location name: ....

Type of location :

....

Latitude :

....

Longitude :

....

Concerned sosas

....

....

....

....

....

....

Notes: ....
....
....

👤 Surname : ....First name : ....

□ *Male* □ *Female* Individual related with sosa(s) : ....
Type of link:...
Born : ....in...
Son/Daughter of : ....and:.......................................
Occupation(s) : ....
Deceased : ....in...................................Cause:..........................
Notes : ....
....

👤 Surname : ....First name : ....

□ *Male* □ *Female* Individual related with sosa(s) : ....
Type of link:...
Born : ....in...
Son/Daughter of : ....and:.......................................
Occupation(s) : ....
Deceased : ....in...................................Cause:..........................
Notes : ....
....

👤 Surname : ....First name : ....

□ *Male* □ *Female* Individual related with sosa(s) : ....
Type of link:...
Born : ....in...
Son/Daughter of : ....and:.......................................
Occupation(s) : ....
Deceased : ....in...................................Cause:..........................
Notes : ....
....

👤 Surname : ....First name : ....

□ *Male* □ *Female* Individual related with sosa(s) : ....
Type of link:...
Born : ....in...
Son/Daughter of : ....and:.......................................
Occupation(s) : ....
Deceased : ....in...................................Cause:..........................
Notes : ....
....

👤 Surname : .... First name : ....

☐ *Male* ☐ *Female* Individual related with sosa(s) : ....
Type of link:..
Born : ....in..
Son/Daughter of : ....and:.................................
Occupation(s) : ....
Deceased : ....in..............................Cause:..........................
Notes : ....
....
....

👤 Surname : .... First name : ....

☐ *Male* ☐ *Female* Individual related with sosa(s) : ....
Type of link:..
Born : ....in..
Son/Daughter of : ....and:.................................
Occupation(s) : ....
Deceased : ....in..............................Cause:..........................
Notes : ....
....
....

👤 Surname : .... First name : ....

☐ *Male* ☐ *Female* Individual related with sosa(s) : ....
Type of link:..
Born : ....in..
Son/Daughter of : ....and:.................................
Occupation(s) : ....
Deceased : ....in..............................Cause:..........................
Notes : ....
....
....

👤 Surname : .... First name : ....

☐ *Male* ☐ *Female* Individual related with sosa(s) : ....
Type of link:..
Born : ....in..
Son/Daughter of : ....and:.................................
Occupation(s) : ....
Deceased : ....in..............................Cause:..........................
Notes : ....
....
....

Surname : ....First name : ....

☐ *Male* ☐ *Female*   Individual related with sosa(s) : ....

Type of link:...

Born : ....in...

Son/Daughter of : ....and: ....

Occupation(s) : ....

Deceased : ....in..............................Cause:.........................

Notes : ....

....

....

Surname : ....First name : ....

☐ *Male* ☐ *Female*   Individual related with sosa(s) : ....

Type of link:...

Born : ....in...

Son/Daughter of : ....and: ....

Occupation(s) : ....

Deceased : ....in..............................Cause:.........................

Notes : ....

....

....

Surname : ....First name : ....

☐ *Male* ☐ *Female*   Individual related with sosa(s) : ....

Type of link:...

Born : ....in...

Son/Daughter of : ....and: ....

Occupation(s) : ....

Deceased : ....in..............................Cause:.........................

Notes : ....

....

....

Surname : ....First name : ....

☐ *Male* ☐ *Female*   Individual related with sosa(s) : ....

Type of link:...

Born : ....in...

Son/Daughter of : ....and: ....

Occupation(s) : ....

Deceased : ....in..............................Cause:.........................

Notes : ....

....

....

Surname : ....First name : ....

□ *Male* □ *Female* Individual related with sosa(s) : ....
Type of link:...
Born : ....in..
Son/Daughter of : ....and: ....
Occupation(s) : ....
Deceased : ....in...........................Cause:...................................
Notes : ....
....
....

Surname : ....First name : ....

□ *Male* □ *Female* Individual related with sosa(s) : ....
Type of link:...
Born : ....in..
Son/Daughter of : ....and: ....
Occupation(s) : ....
Deceased : ....in...........................Cause:...................................
Notes : ....
....
....

Surname : ....First name : ....

□ *Male* □ *Female* Individual related with sosa(s) : ....
Type of link:...
Born : ....in..
Son/Daughter of : ....and: ....
Occupation(s) : ....
Deceased : ....in...........................Cause:...................................
Notes : ....
....
....

Surname : ....First name : ....

□ *Male* □ *Female* Individual related with sosa(s) : ....
Type of link:...
Born : ....in..
Son/Daughter of : ....and: ....
Occupation(s) : ....
Deceased : ....in...........................Cause:...................................
Notes : ....
....
....

👤 Surname : ....First name : ....

☐ *Male* ☐ *Female*   Individual related with sosa(s) : ....
Type of link:..
Born : ....in..
Son/Daughter of : ....and: ....
Occupation(s) : ....
Deceased : ....in...............................Cause:.................................
Notes : ....
....
....

👤 Surname : ....First name : ....

☐ *Male* ☐ *Female*   Individual related with sosa(s) : ....
Type of link:..
Born : ....in..
Son/Daughter of : ....and: ....
Occupation(s) : ....
Deceased : ....in...............................Cause:.................................
Notes : ....
....
....

👤 Surname : ....First name : ....

☐ *Male* ☐ *Female*   Individual related with sosa(s) : ....
Type of link:..
Born : ....in..
Son/Daughter of : ....and: ....
Occupation(s) : ....
Deceased : ....in...............................Cause:.................................
Notes : ....
....
....

👤 Surname : ....First name : ....

☐ *Male* ☐ *Female*   Individual related with sosa(s) : ....
Type of link:..
Born : ....in..
Son/Daughter of : ....and: ....
Occupation(s) : ....
Deceased : ....in...............................Cause:.................................
Notes : ....
....
....

👤 Surname : ....First name : ....

☐ *Male* ☐ *Female* Individual related with sosa(s) : ....

Type of link:...

Born : ....in...

Son/Daughter of : ....and:............................

Occupation(s) : ....

Deceased : ....in.............................Cause:............................

Notes : ....

....

👤 Surname : ....First name : ....

☐ *Male* ☐ *Female* Individual related with sosa(s) : ....

Type of link:...

Born : ....in...

Son/Daughter of : ....and:............................

Occupation(s) : ....

Deceased : ....in.............................Cause:............................

Notes : ....

....

👤 Surname : ....First name : ....

☐ *Male* ☐ *Female* Individual related with sosa(s) : ....

Type of link:...

Born : ....in...

Son/Daughter of : ....and:............................

Occupation(s) : ....

Deceased : ....in.............................Cause:............................

Notes : ....

....

👤 Surname : ....First name : ....

☐ *Male* ☐ *Female* Individual related with sosa(s) : ....

Type of link:...

Born : ....in...

Son/Daughter of : ....and:............................

Occupation(s) : ....

Deceased : ....in.............................Cause:............................

Notes : ....

....

567

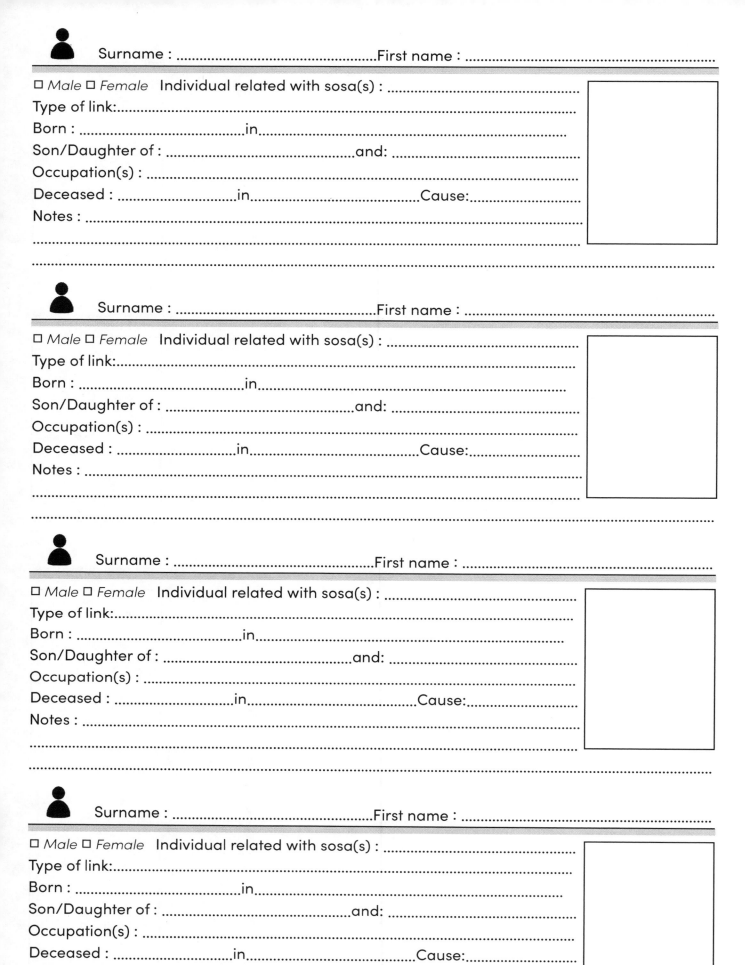

Surname : ....First name : ....

□ *Male* □ *Female* Individual related with sosa(s) : ....

Type of link:...

Born : ....in...

Son/Daughter of : ....and: ....

Occupation(s) : ....

Deceased : ....in.............................Cause:.............................

Notes : ....

....

....

Surname : ....First name : ....

□ *Male* □ *Female* Individual related with sosa(s) : ....

Type of link:...

Born : ....in...

Son/Daughter of : ....and: ....

Occupation(s) : ....

Deceased : ....in.............................Cause:.............................

Notes : ....

....

....

Surname : ....First name : ....

□ *Male* □ *Female* Individual related with sosa(s) : ....

Type of link:...

Born : ....in...

Son/Daughter of : ....and: ....

Occupation(s) : ....

Deceased : ....in.............................Cause:.............................

Notes : ....

....

....

Surname : ....First name : ....

□ *Male* □ *Female* Individual related with sosa(s) : ....

Type of link:...

Born : ....in...

Son/Daughter of : ....and: ....

Occupation(s) : ....

Deceased : ....in.............................Cause:.............................

Notes : ....

....

....

Surname : ....First name : ....

□ *Male* □ *Female* Individual related with sosa(s) : ....

Type of link:...

Born : ....in...

Son/Daughter of : ....and: ....

Occupation(s) : ....

Deceased : ....in...............................Cause:.............................

Notes : ....

....

Surname : ....First name : ....

□ *Male* □ *Female* Individual related with sosa(s) : ....

Type of link:...

Born : ....in...

Son/Daughter of : ....and: ....

Occupation(s) : ....

Deceased : ....in...............................Cause:.............................

Notes : ....

....

Surname : ....First name : ....

□ *Male* □ *Female* Individual related with sosa(s) : ....

Type of link:...

Born : ....in...

Son/Daughter of : ....and: ....

Occupation(s) : ....

Deceased : ....in...............................Cause:.............................

Notes : ....

....

Surname : ....First name : ....

□ *Male* □ *Female* Individual related with sosa(s) : ....

Type of link:...

Born : ....in...

Son/Daughter of : ....and: ....

Occupation(s) : ....

Deceased : ....in...............................Cause:.............................

Notes : ....

....

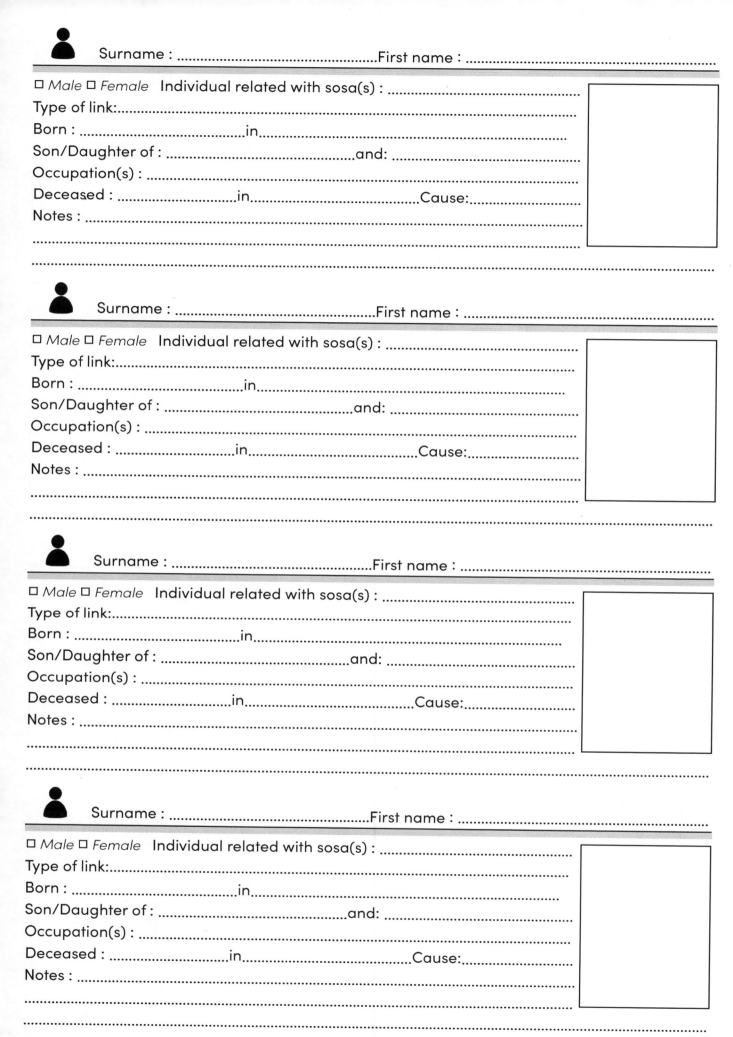

Surname : ....First name : ....

□ *Male* □ *Female*   Individual related with sosa(s) : ....
Type of link:..
Born : ....in...
Son/Daughter of : ....and:..
Occupation(s) : ....
Deceased : ....in...Cause:................................
Notes : ....
....
....

Surname : ....First name : ....

□ *Male* □ *Female*   Individual related with sosa(s) : ....
Type of link:..
Born : ....in...
Son/Daughter of : ....and:..
Occupation(s) : ....
Deceased : ....in...Cause:................................
Notes : ....
....
....

Surname : ....First name : ....

□ *Male* □ *Female*   Individual related with sosa(s) : ....
Type of link:..
Born : ....in...
Son/Daughter of : ....and:..
Occupation(s) : ....
Deceased : ....in...Cause:................................
Notes : ....
....
....

Surname : ....First name : ....

□ *Male* □ *Female*   Individual related with sosa(s) : ....
Type of link:..
Born : ....in...
Son/Daughter of : ....and:..
Occupation(s) : ....
Deceased : ....in...Cause:................................
Notes : ....
....
....

👤 Surname : ....First name : ....

☐ *Male* ☐ *Female* Individual related with sosa(s) : ....
Type of link:...
Born : ....in...
Son/Daughter of : ....and: ....
Occupation(s) : ....
Deceased : ....in...Cause:...........................
Notes : ....

....

👤 Surname : ....First name : ....

☐ *Male* ☐ *Female* Individual related with sosa(s) : ....
Type of link:...
Born : ....in...
Son/Daughter of : ....and: ....
Occupation(s) : ....
Deceased : ....in...Cause:...........................
Notes : ....

....

👤 Surname : ....First name : ....

☐ *Male* ☐ *Female* Individual related with sosa(s) : ....
Type of link:...
Born : ....in...
Son/Daughter of : ....and: ....
Occupation(s) : ....
Deceased : ....in...Cause:...........................
Notes : ....

....

👤 Surname : ....First name : ....

☐ *Male* ☐ *Female* Individual related with sosa(s) : ....
Type of link:...
Born : ....in...
Son/Daughter of : ....and: ....
Occupation(s) : ....
Deceased : ....in...Cause:...........................
Notes : ....

....

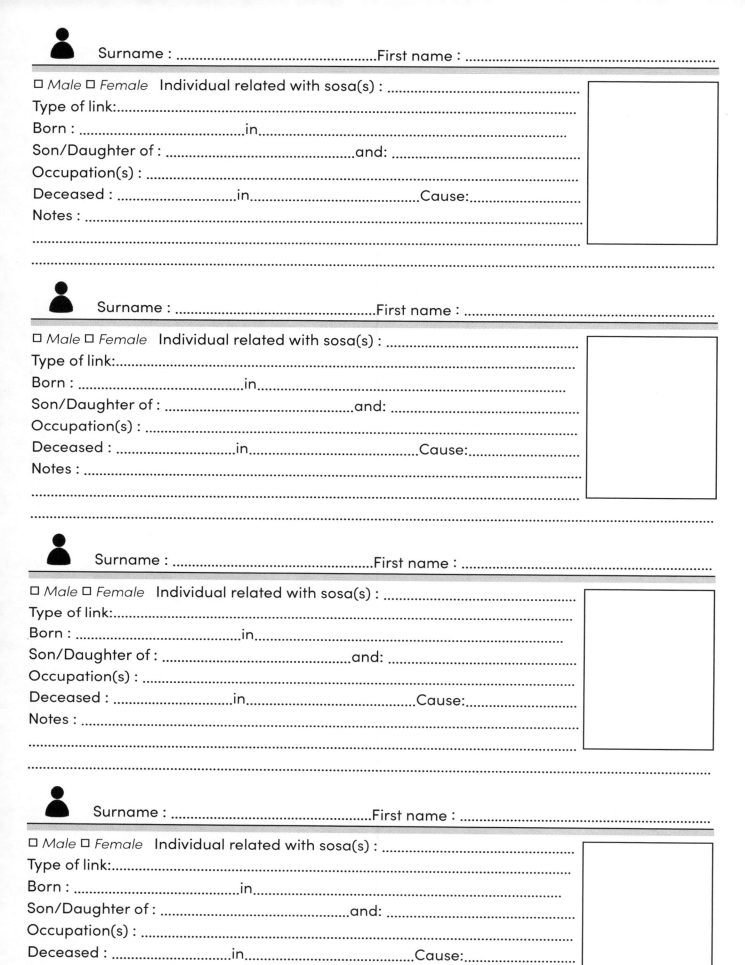

Surname : ....**First name :** ....

☐ *Male* ☐ *Female*   Individual related with sosa(s) : ....

Type of link:..

Born : ....in..

Son/Daughter of : ....and: ....

Occupation(s) : ....

Deceased : ....in..............................Cause:....................................

Notes : ....

....

....

Surname : ....**First name :** ....

☐ *Male* ☐ *Female*   Individual related with sosa(s) : ....

Type of link:..

Born : ....in..

Son/Daughter of : ....and: ....

Occupation(s) : ....

Deceased : ....in..............................Cause:....................................

Notes : ....

....

....

Surname : ....**First name :** ....

☐ *Male* ☐ *Female*   Individual related with sosa(s) : ....

Type of link:..

Born : ....in..

Son/Daughter of : ....and: ....

Occupation(s) : ....

Deceased : ....in..............................Cause:....................................

Notes : ....

....

....

Surname : ....**First name :** ....

☐ *Male* ☐ *Female*   Individual related with sosa(s) : ....

Type of link:..

Born : ....in..

Son/Daughter of : ....and: ....

Occupation(s) : ....

Deceased : ....in..............................Cause:....................................

Notes : ....

....

....

Surname : ....First name : ....

□ *Male* □ *Female* Individual related with sosa(s) : ....

Type of link:...

Born : ....in...

Son/Daughter of : ....and:..

Occupation(s) : ....

Deceased : ....in...Cause:.............................

Notes : ....

....

....

Surname : ....First name : ....

□ *Male* □ *Female* Individual related with sosa(s) : ....

Type of link:...

Born : ....in...

Son/Daughter of : ....and:..

Occupation(s) : ....

Deceased : ....in...Cause:.............................

Notes : ....

....

....

Surname : ....First name : ....

□ *Male* □ *Female* Individual related with sosa(s) : ....

Type of link:...

Born : ....in...

Son/Daughter of : ....and:..

Occupation(s) : ....

Deceased : ....in...Cause:.............................

Notes : ....

....

....

Surname : ....First name : ....

□ *Male* □ *Female* Individual related with sosa(s) : ....

Type of link:...

Born : ....in...

Son/Daughter of : ....and:..

Occupation(s) : ....

Deceased : ....in...Cause:.............................

Notes : ....

....

....

Surname : ....First name : ....

□ *Male* □ *Female*   Individual related with sosa(s) : ....

Type of link:..

Born : ....in...

Son/Daughter of : ....and: ....

Occupation(s) : ....

Deceased : ....in...Cause:.................

Notes : ....

....

Surname : ....First name : ....

□ *Male* □ *Female*   Individual related with sosa(s) : ....

Type of link:..

Born : ....in...

Son/Daughter of : ....and: ....

Occupation(s) : ....

Deceased : ....in...Cause:.................

Notes : ....

....

Surname : ....First name : ....

□ *Male* □ *Female*   Individual related with sosa(s) : ....

Type of link:..

Born : ....in...

Son/Daughter of : ....and: ....

Occupation(s) : ....

Deceased : ....in...Cause:.................

Notes : ....

....

Surname : ....First name : ....

□ *Male* □ *Female*   Individual related with sosa(s) : ....

Type of link:..

Born : ....in...

Son/Daughter of : ....and: ....

Occupation(s) : ....

Deceased : ....in...Cause:.................

Notes : ....

....

👤 Surname : ....First name : ....

□ *Male* □ *Female* Individual related with sosa(s) : ....
Type of link: ....
Born : ....in...
Son/Daughter of : ....and: ....
Occupation(s) : ....
Deceased : ....in...Cause: ....
Notes : ....
....
....

👤 Surname : ....First name : ....

□ *Male* □ *Female* Individual related with sosa(s) : ....
Type of link: ....
Born : ....in...
Son/Daughter of : ....and: ....
Occupation(s) : ....
Deceased : ....in...Cause: ....
Notes : ....
....
....

👤 Surname : ....First name : ....

□ *Male* □ *Female* Individual related with sosa(s) : ....
Type of link: ....
Born : ....in...
Son/Daughter of : ....and: ....
Occupation(s) : ....
Deceased : ....in...Cause: ....
Notes : ....
....
....

👤 Surname : ....First name : ....

□ *Male* □ *Female* Individual related with sosa(s) : ....
Type of link: ....
Born : ....in...
Son/Daughter of : ....and: ....
Occupation(s) : ....
Deceased : ....in...Cause: ....
Notes : ....
....
....

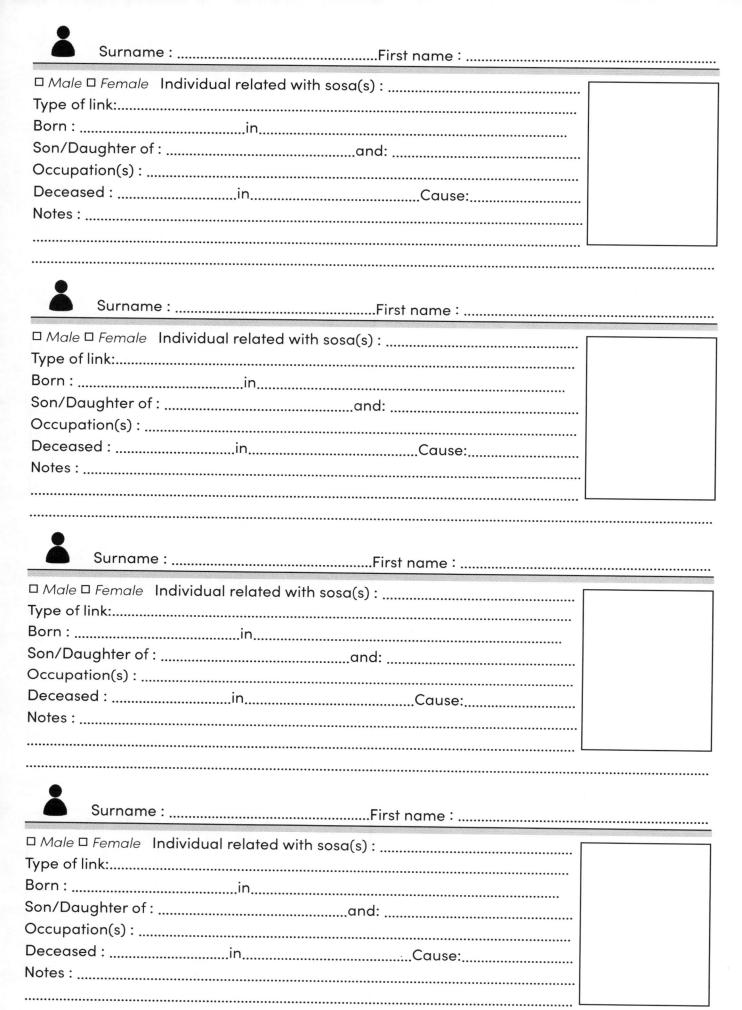

👤 Surname : ....First name : ....

☐ *Male* ☐ *Female*   Individual related with sosa(s) : ....
Type of link:..
Born : ....in..
Son/Daughter of : ....and: ....
Occupation(s) : ....
Deceased : ....in..............................Cause: ....
Notes : ....
....
....

👤 Surname : ....First name : ....

☐ *Male* ☐ *Female*   Individual related with sosa(s) : ....
Type of link:..
Born : ....in..
Son/Daughter of : ....and: ....
Occupation(s) : ....
Deceased : ....in..............................Cause: ....
Notes : ....
....
....

👤 Surname : ....First name : ....

☐ *Male* ☐ *Female*   Individual related with sosa(s) : ....
Type of link:..
Born : ....in..
Son/Daughter of : ....and: ....
Occupation(s) : ....
Deceased : ....in..............................Cause: ....
Notes : ....
....
....

👤 Surname : ....First name : ....

☐ *Male* ☐ *Female*   Individual related with sosa(s) : ....
Type of link:..
Born : ....in..
Son/Daughter of : ....and: ....
Occupation(s) : ....
Deceased : ....in..............................Cause: ....
Notes : ....
....
....

Surname : ....**First name :** ....

□ *Male* □ *Female* Individual related with sosa(s) : ....
Type of link:..
Born : ....in..
Son/Daughter of : ....and: ....
Occupation(s) : ....
Deceased : ....in..Cause:..
Notes : ....
....
....

Surname : ....**First name :** ....

□ *Male* □ *Female* Individual related with sosa(s) : ....
Type of link:..
Born : ....in..
Son/Daughter of : ....and: ....
Occupation(s) : ....
Deceased : ....in..Cause:..
Notes : ....
....
....

Surname : ....**First name :** ....

□ *Male* □ *Female* Individual related with sosa(s) : ....
Type of link:..
Born : ....in..
Son/Daughter of : ....and: ....
Occupation(s) : ....
Deceased : ....in..Cause:..
Notes : ....
....
....

Surname : ....**First name :** ....

□ *Male* □ *Female* Individual related with sosa(s) : ....
Type of link:..
Born : ....in..
Son/Daughter of : ....and: ....
Occupation(s) : ....
Deceased : ....in..Cause:..
Notes : ....
....
....

👤 Surname : ....First name : ....

☐ *Male* ☐ *Female* Individual related with sosa(s) : ....
Type of link:...
Born : ....in...
Son/Daughter of : ....and: ....
Occupation(s) : ....
Deceased : ....in...........................Cause:.....................................
Notes : ....
....
....

👤 Surname : ....First name : ....

☐ *Male* ☐ *Female* Individual related with sosa(s) : ....
Type of link:...
Born : ....in...
Son/Daughter of : ....and: ....
Occupation(s) : ....
Deceased : ....in...........................Cause:.....................................
Notes : ....
....
....

👤 Surname : ....First name : ....

☐ *Male* ☐ *Female* Individual related with sosa(s) : ....
Type of link:...
Born : ....in...
Son/Daughter of : ....and: ....
Occupation(s) : ....
Deceased : ....in...........................Cause:.....................................
Notes : ....
....
....

👤 Surname : ....First name : ....

☐ *Male* ☐ *Female* Individual related with sosa(s) : ....
Type of link:...
Born : ....in...
Son/Daughter of : ....and: ....
Occupation(s) : ....
Deceased : ....in...........................Cause:.....................................
Notes : ....
....

Surname : ....First name : ....

□ *Male* □ *Female* Individual related with sosa(s) : ....

Type of link:...

Born : ....in..

Son/Daughter of : ....and: ....

Occupation(s) : ....

Deceased : ....in.............................Cause:.....................

Notes : ....

....

Surname : ....First name : ....

□ *Male* □ *Female* Individual related with sosa(s) : ....

Type of link:...

Born : ....in..

Son/Daughter of : ....and: ....

Occupation(s) : ....

Deceased : ....in.............................Cause:.....................

Notes : ....

....

Surname : ....First name : ....

□ *Male* □ *Female* Individual related with sosa(s) : ....

Type of link:...

Born : ....in..

Son/Daughter of : ....and: ....

Occupation(s) : ....

Deceased : ....in.............................Cause:.....................

Notes : ....

....

Surname : ....First name : ....

□ *Male* □ *Female* Individual related with sosa(s) : ....

Type of link:...

Born : ....in..

Son/Daughter of : ....and: ....

Occupation(s) : ....

Deceased : ....in.............................Cause:.....................

Notes : ....

....

👤 Surname : ....First name : ....

☐ *Male* ☐ *Female*   Individual related with sosa(s) : ....

Type of link:..

Born : ....in..

Son/Daughter of : ....and: ....

Occupation(s) : ....

Deceased : ....in................................Cause:..............................

Notes : ....

....

👤 Surname : ....First name : ....

☐ *Male* ☐ *Female*   Individual related with sosa(s) : ....

Type of link:..

Born : ....in..

Son/Daughter of : ....and: ....

Occupation(s) : ....

Deceased : ....in................................Cause:..............................

Notes : ....

....

👤 Surname : ....First name : ....

☐ *Male* ☐ *Female*   Individual related with sosa(s) : ....

Type of link:..

Born : ....in..

Son/Daughter of : ....and: ....

Occupation(s) : ....

Deceased : ....in................................Cause:..............................

Notes : ....

....

👤 Surname : ....First name : ....

☐ *Male* ☐ *Female*   Individual related with sosa(s) : ....

Type of link:..

Born : ....in..

Son/Daughter of : ....and: ....

Occupation(s) : ....

Deceased : ....in................................Cause:..............................

Notes : ....

....

👤 Surname : ....First name : ....

☐ *Male* ☐ *Female* Individual related with sosa(s) : ....

Type of link:...

Born : ....in..

Son/Daughter of : ....and:...

Occupation(s) : ....

Deceased : ....in...Cause:...............................

Notes : ....

....

....

👤 Surname : ....First name : ....

☐ *Male* ☐ *Female* Individual related with sosa(s) : ....

Type of link:...

Born : ....in..

Son/Daughter of : ....and:...

Occupation(s) : ....

Deceased : ....in...Cause:...............................

Notes : ....

....

....

👤 Surname : ....First name : ....

☐ *Male* ☐ *Female* Individual related with sosa(s) : ....

Type of link:...

Born : ....in..

Son/Daughter of : ....and:...

Occupation(s) : ....

Deceased : ....in...Cause:...............................

Notes : ....

....

....

👤 Surname : ....First name : ....

☐ *Male* ☐ *Female* Individual related with sosa(s) : ....

Type of link:...

Born : ....in..

Son/Daughter of : ....and:...

Occupation(s) : ....

Deceased : ....in...Cause:...............................

Notes : ....

....

....

Surname : ....**First name :** ....

☐ *Male* ☐ *Female* Individual related with sosa(s) : ....
Type of link:..
Born : ....in...
Son/Daughter of : ....and: ....
Occupation(s) : ....
Deceased : ....in...Cause: ....
Notes : ....
....
....

Surname : ....**First name :** ....

☐ *Male* ☐ *Female* Individual related with sosa(s) : ....
Type of link:..
Born : ....in...
Son/Daughter of : ....and: ....
Occupation(s) : ....
Deceased : ....in...Cause: ....
Notes : ....
....
....

Surname : ....**First name :** ....

☐ *Male* ☐ *Female* Individual related with sosa(s) : ....
Type of link:..
Born : ....in...
Son/Daughter of : ....and: ....
Occupation(s) : ....
Deceased : ....in...Cause: ....
Notes : ....
....
....

Surname : ....**First name :** ....

☐ *Male* ☐ *Female* Individual related with sosa(s) : ....
Type of link:..
Born : ....in...
Son/Daughter of : ....and: ....
Occupation(s) : ....
Deceased : ....in...Cause: ....
Notes : ....
....
....

👤 Surname : ....First name : ....

☐ *Male* ☐ *Female* Individual related with sosa(s) : ....
Type of link:...
Born : ....in...
Son/Daughter of : ....and:..
Occupation(s) : ....
Deceased : ....in..Cause:............................
Notes : ....
....
....

👤 Surname : ....First name : ....

☐ *Male* ☐ *Female* Individual related with sosa(s) : ....
Type of link:...
Born : ....in...
Son/Daughter of : ....and:..
Occupation(s) : ....
Deceased : ....in..Cause:............................
Notes : ....
....
....

👤 Surname : ....First name : ....

☐ *Male* ☐ *Female* Individual related with sosa(s) : ....
Type of link:...
Born : ....in...
Son/Daughter of : ....and:..
Occupation(s) : ....
Deceased : ....in..Cause:............................
Notes : ....
....
....

👤 Surname : ....First name : ....

☐ *Male* ☐ *Female* Individual related with sosa(s) : ....
Type of link:...
Born : ....in...
Son/Daughter of : ....and:..
Occupation(s) : ....
Deceased : ....in..Cause:............................
Notes : ....
....
....

Surname : .... **First name :** ....

☐ *Male* ☐ *Female* Individual related with sosa(s) : ....
Type of link:..
Born : ....in..
Son/Daughter of : ....and:..
Occupation(s) : ....
Deceased : ....in......................................Cause:......................................
Notes : ....
....
....

Surname : .... **First name :** ....

☐ *Male* ☐ *Female* Individual related with sosa(s) : ....
Type of link:..
Born : ....in..
Son/Daughter of : ....and:..
Occupation(s) : ....
Deceased : ....in......................................Cause:......................................
Notes : ....
....
....

Surname : .... **First name :** ....

☐ *Male* ☐ *Female* Individual related with sosa(s) : ....
Type of link:..
Born : ....in..
Son/Daughter of : ....and:..
Occupation(s) : ....
Deceased : ....in......................................Cause:......................................
Notes : ....
....
....

Surname : .... **First name :** ....

☐ *Male* ☐ *Female* Individual related with sosa(s) : ....
Type of link:..
Born : ....in..
Son/Daughter of : ....and:..
Occupation(s) : ....
Deceased : ....in......................................Cause:......................................
Notes : ....
....
....

👤 Surname : ....First name : ....

☐ *Male* ☐ *Female* Individual related with sosa(s) : ....

Type of link:...

Born : ....in...............................

Son/Daughter of : ....and:...............................

Occupation(s) : ....

Deceased : ....in...............................Cause:...............................

Notes : ....

....

....

👤 Surname : ....First name : ....

☐ *Male* ☐ *Female* Individual related with sosa(s) : ....

Type of link:...

Born : ....in...............................

Son/Daughter of : ....and:...............................

Occupation(s) : ....

Deceased : ....in...............................Cause:...............................

Notes : ....

....

....

👤 Surname : ....First name : ....

☐ *Male* ☐ *Female* Individual related with sosa(s) : ....

Type of link:...

Born : ....in...............................

Son/Daughter of : ....and:...............................

Occupation(s) : ....

Deceased : ....in...............................Cause:...............................

Notes : ....

....

....

👤 Surname : ....First name : ....

☐ *Male* ☐ *Female* Individual related with sosa(s) : ....

Type of link:...

Born : ....in...............................

Son/Daughter of : ....and:...............................

Occupation(s) : ....

Deceased : ....in...............................Cause:...............................

Notes : ....

....

....

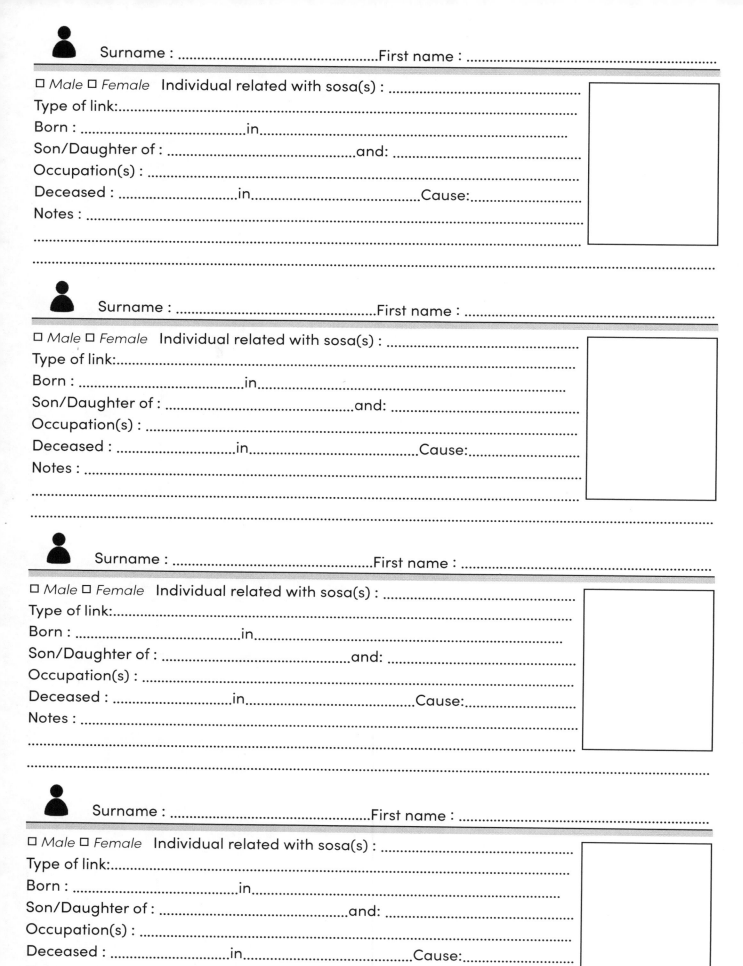

Surname : .... **First name :** ....

☐ *Male* ☐ *Female* Individual related with sosa(s) : ....

Type of link: ....

Born : .... in ....

Son/Daughter of : .... and: ....

Occupation(s) : ....

Deceased : .... in .... Cause: ....

Notes : ....

....

....

Surname : .... **First name :** ....

☐ *Male* ☐ *Female* Individual related with sosa(s) : ....

Type of link: ....

Born : .... in ....

Son/Daughter of : .... and: ....

Occupation(s) : ....

Deceased : .... in .... Cause: ....

Notes : ....

....

....

Surname : .... **First name :** ....

☐ *Male* ☐ *Female* Individual related with sosa(s) : ....

Type of link: ....

Born : .... in ....

Son/Daughter of : .... and: ....

Occupation(s) : ....

Deceased : .... in .... Cause: ....

Notes : ....

....

....

Surname : .... **First name :** ....

☐ *Male* ☐ *Female* Individual related with sosa(s) : ....

Type of link: ....

Born : .... in ....

Son/Daughter of : .... and: ....

Occupation(s) : ....

Deceased : .... in .... Cause: ....

Notes : ....

....

....

👤 Surname : ....First name : ....

☐ *Male* ☐ *Female* Individual related with sosa(s) : ....
Type of link:...
Born : ....in...
Son/Daughter of : ....and:...
Occupation(s) : ....
Deceased : ....in...Cause:...
Notes : ....
....
....

👤 Surname : ....First name : ....

☐ *Male* ☐ *Female* Individual related with sosa(s) : ....
Type of link:...
Born : ....in...
Son/Daughter of : ....and:...
Occupation(s) : ....
Deceased : ....in...Cause:...
Notes : ....
....
....

👤 Surname : ....First name : ....

☐ *Male* ☐ *Female* Individual related with sosa(s) : ....
Type of link:...
Born : ....in...
Son/Daughter of : ....and:...
Occupation(s) : ....
Deceased : ....in...Cause:...
Notes : ....
....
....

👤 Surname : ....First name : ....

☐ *Male* ☐ *Female* Individual related with sosa(s) : ....
Type of link:...
Born : ....in...
Son/Daughter of : ....and:...
Occupation(s) : ....
Deceased : ....in...Cause:...
Notes : ....
....
....

Surname : ....First name : ....

☐ *Male* ☐ *Female* Individual related with sosa(s) : ....

Type of link:...

Born : ....in..

Son/Daughter of : ....and: ....

Occupation(s) : ....

Deceased : ....in.......................................Cause:..........................

Notes : ....

....

....

Surname : ....First name : ....

☐ *Male* ☐ *Female* Individual related with sosa(s) : ....

Type of link:...

Born : ....in..

Son/Daughter of : ....and: ....

Occupation(s) : ....

Deceased : ....in.......................................Cause:..........................

Notes : ....

....

....

Surname : ....First name : ....

☐ *Male* ☐ *Female* Individual related with sosa(s) : ....

Type of link:...

Born : ....in..

Son/Daughter of : ....and: ....

Occupation(s) : ....

Deceased : ....in.......................................Cause:..........................

Notes : ....

....

....

Surname : ....First name : ....

☐ *Male* ☐ *Female* Individual related with sosa(s) : ....

Type of link:...

Born : ....in..

Son/Daughter of : ....and: ....

Occupation(s) : ....

Deceased : ....in.......................................Cause:..........................

Notes : ....

....

....

👤 Surname : ....First name : ....

□ *Male* □ *Female* Individual related with sosa(s) : ....
Type of link:...
Born : ....in...
Son/Daughter of : ....and: ....
Occupation(s) : ....
Deceased : ....in...Cause:.............................
Notes : ....
....
....

👤 Surname : ....First name : ....

□ *Male* □ *Female* Individual related with sosa(s) : ....
Type of link:...
Born : ....in...
Son/Daughter of : ....and: ....
Occupation(s) : ....
Deceased : ....in...Cause:.............................
Notes : ....
....
....

👤 Surname : ....First name : ....

□ *Male* □ *Female* Individual related with sosa(s) : ....
Type of link:...
Born : ....in...
Son/Daughter of : ....and: ....
Occupation(s) : ....
Deceased : ....in...Cause:.............................
Notes : ....
....
....

👤 Surname : ....First name : ....

□ *Male* □ *Female* Individual related with sosa(s) : ....
Type of link:...
Born : ....in...
Son/Daughter of : ....and: ....
Occupation(s) : ....
Deceased : ....in...Cause:.............................
Notes : ....
....

👤 Surname : ....First name : ....

☐ *Male* ☐ *Female* Individual related with sosa(s) : ....
Type of link:...
Born : ....in...
Son/Daughter of : ....and: ....
Occupation(s) : ....
Deceased : ....in...............................Cause:...............................
Notes : ....
....
....

👤 Surname : ....First name : ....

☐ *Male* ☐ *Female* Individual related with sosa(s) : ....
Type of link:...
Born : ....in...
Son/Daughter of : ....and: ....
Occupation(s) : ....
Deceased : ....in...............................Cause:...............................
Notes : ....
....
....

👤 Surname : ....First name : ....

☐ *Male* ☐ *Female* Individual related with sosa(s) : ....
Type of link:...
Born : ....in...
Son/Daughter of : ....and: ....
Occupation(s) : ....
Deceased : ....in...............................Cause:...............................
Notes : ....
....
....

👤 Surname : ....First name : ....

☐ *Male* ☐ *Female* Individual related with sosa(s) : ....
Type of link:...
Born : ....in...
Son/Daughter of : ....and: ....
Occupation(s) : ....
Deceased : ....in...............................Cause:...............................
Notes : ....
....
....

● Surname : ....First name : ....

☐ *Male* ☐ *Female*   Individual related with sosa(s) : ....
Type of link:..
Born : ....in...
Son/Daughter of : ....and: ....
Occupation(s) : ....
Deceased : ....in.......................Cause:...............................
Notes : ....
....

● Surname : ....First name : ....

☐ *Male* ☐ *Female*   Individual related with sosa(s) : ....
Type of link:..
Born : ....in...
Son/Daughter of : ....and: ....
Occupation(s) : ....
Deceased : ....in.......................Cause:...............................
Notes : ....
....

● Surname : ....First name : ....

☐ *Male* ☐ *Female*   Individual related with sosa(s) : ....
Type of link:..
Born : ....in...
Son/Daughter of : ....and: ....
Occupation(s) : ....
Deceased : ....in.......................Cause:...............................
Notes : ....
....

● Surname : ....First name : ....

☐ *Male* ☐ *Female*   Individual related with sosa(s) : ....
Type of link:..
Born : ....in...
Son/Daughter of : ....and: ....
Occupation(s) : ....
Deceased : ....in.......................Cause:...............................
Notes : ....
....

👤 Surname : ....First name : ....

☐ *Male* ☐ *Female* Individual related with sosa(s) : ....

Type of link:..

Born : ....in...

Son/Daughter of : ....and: ....

Occupation(s) : ....

Deceased : ....in..................................Cause:........................

Notes : ....

....

....

👤 Surname : ....First name : ....

☐ *Male* ☐ *Female* Individual related with sosa(s) : ....

Type of link:..

Born : ....in...

Son/Daughter of : ....and: ....

Occupation(s) : ....

Deceased : ....in..................................Cause:........................

Notes : ....

....

....

👤 Surname : ....First name : ....

☐ *Male* ☐ *Female* Individual related with sosa(s) : ....

Type of link:..

Born : ....in...

Son/Daughter of : ....and: ....

Occupation(s) : ....

Deceased : ....in..................................Cause:........................

Notes : ....

....

....

👤 Surname : ....First name : ....

☐ *Male* ☐ *Female* Individual related with sosa(s) : ....

Type of link:..

Born : ....in...

Son/Daughter of : ....and: ....

Occupation(s) : ....

Deceased : ....in..................................Cause:........................

Notes : ....

....

....

Surname : .... **First name :** ....

☐ *Male* ☐ *Female* Individual related with sosa(s) : ....
Type of link: ....
Born : .... in ....
Son/Daughter of : .... and: ....
Occupation(s) : ....
Deceased : .... in .... Cause: ....
Notes : ....
....
....

Surname : .... **First name :** ....

☐ *Male* ☐ *Female* Individual related with sosa(s) : ....
Type of link: ....
Born : .... in ....
Son/Daughter of : .... and: ....
Occupation(s) : ....
Deceased : .... in .... Cause: ....
Notes : ....
....
....

Surname : .... **First name :** ....

☐ *Male* ☐ *Female* Individual related with sosa(s) : ....
Type of link: ....
Born : .... in ....
Son/Daughter of : .... and: ....
Occupation(s) : ....
Deceased : .... in .... Cause: ....
Notes : ....
....
....

Surname : .... **First name :** ....

☐ *Male* ☐ *Female* Individual related with sosa(s) : ....
Type of link: ....
Born : .... in ....
Son/Daughter of : .... and: ....
Occupation(s) : ....
Deceased : .... in .... Cause: ....
Notes : ....
....
....

Surname : ....First name : ....

□ *Male* □ *Female* Individual related with sosa(s) : ....
Type of link:...
Born : ....in...
Son/Daughter of : ....and:.................................
Occupation(s) : ....
Deceased : ....in...........................Cause:...............
Notes : ....
....
....

Surname : ....First name : ....

□ *Male* □ *Female* Individual related with sosa(s) : ....
Type of link:...
Born : ....in...
Son/Daughter of : ....and:.................................
Occupation(s) : ....
Deceased : ....in...........................Cause:...............
Notes : ....
....
....

Surname : ....First name : ....

□ *Male* □ *Female* Individual related with sosa(s) : ....
Type of link:...
Born : ....in...
Son/Daughter of : ....and:.................................
Occupation(s) : ....
Deceased : ....in...........................Cause:...............
Notes : ....
....
....

Surname : ....First name : ....

□ *Male* □ *Female* Individual related with sosa(s) : ....
Type of link:...
Born : ....in...
Son/Daughter of : ....and:.................................
Occupation(s) : ....
Deceased : ....in...........................Cause:...............
Notes : ....
....

Surname : ....First name : ....

☐ *Male* ☐ *Female* Individual related with sosa(s) : ....
Type of link:...
Born : ....in...
Son/Daughter of : ....and:.......................................
Occupation(s) : ....
Deceased : ....in...Cause:.....................
Notes : ....
....

Surname : ....First name : ....

☐ *Male* ☐ *Female* Individual related with sosa(s) : ....
Type of link:...
Born : ....in...
Son/Daughter of : ....and:.......................................
Occupation(s) : ....
Deceased : ....in...Cause:.....................
Notes : ....
....

Surname : ....First name : ....

☐ *Male* ☐ *Female* Individual related with sosa(s) : ....
Type of link:...
Born : ....in...
Son/Daughter of : ....and:.......................................
Occupation(s) : ....
Deceased : ....in...Cause:.....................
Notes : ....
....

Surname : ....First name : ....

☐ *Male* ☐ *Female* Individual related with sosa(s) : ....
Type of link:...
Born : ....in...
Son/Daughter of : ....and:.......................................
Occupation(s) : ....
Deceased : ....in...Cause:.....................
Notes : ....
....

👤 Surname : ....First name : ....

☐ *Male* ☐ *Female*   Individual related with sosa(s) : ....
Type of link:...
Born : ....in...
Son/Daughter of : ....and: ....
Occupation(s) : ....
Deceased : ....in...........................Cause:....................................
Notes : ....
....
....

👤 Surname : ....First name : ....

☐ *Male* ☐ *Female*   Individual related with sosa(s) : ....
Type of link:...
Born : ....in...
Son/Daughter of : ....and: ....
Occupation(s) : ....
Deceased : ....in...........................Cause:....................................
Notes : ....
....
....

👤 Surname : ....First name : ....

☐ *Male* ☐ *Female*   Individual related with sosa(s) : ....
Type of link:...
Born : ....in...
Son/Daughter of : ....and: ....
Occupation(s) : ....
Deceased : ....in...........................Cause:....................................
Notes : ....
....
....

👤 Surname : ....First name : ....

☐ *Male* ☐ *Female*   Individual related with sosa(s) : ....
Type of link:...
Born : ....in...
Son/Daughter of : ....and: ....
Occupation(s) : ....
Deceased : ....in...........................Cause:....................................
Notes : ....
....
....

Surname : ....First name : ....

□ *Male* □ *Female* Individual related with sosa(s) : ....
Type of link:...
Born : ....in...
Son/Daughter of : ....and: ....
Occupation(s) : ....
Deceased : ....in...Cause:...
Notes : ....
....
....

Surname : ....First name : ....

□ *Male* □ *Female* Individual related with sosa(s) : ....
Type of link:...
Born : ....in...
Son/Daughter of : ....and: ....
Occupation(s) : ....
Deceased : ....in...Cause:...
Notes : ....
....
....

Surname : ....First name : ....

□ *Male* □ *Female* Individual related with sosa(s) : ....
Type of link:...
Born : ....in...
Son/Daughter of : ....and: ....
Occupation(s) : ....
Deceased : ....in...Cause:...
Notes : ....
....
....

Surname : ....First name : ....

□ *Male* □ *Female* Individual related with sosa(s) : ....
Type of link:...
Born : ....in...
Son/Daughter of : ....and: ....
Occupation(s) : ....
Deceased : ....in...Cause:...
Notes : ....
....
....

👤 Surname : ....First name : ....

☐ *Male* ☐ *Female* Individual related with sosa(s) : ....
Type of link:..
Born : ....in...
Son/Daughter of : ....and:...
Occupation(s) : ....
Deceased : ....in...............................Cause:.................................
Notes : ....
....
....

👤 Surname : ....First name : ....

☐ *Male* ☐ *Female* Individual related with sosa(s) : ....
Type of link:..
Born : ....in...
Son/Daughter of : ....and:...
Occupation(s) : ....
Deceased : ....in...............................Cause:.................................
Notes : ....
....
....

👤 Surname : ....First name : ....

☐ *Male* ☐ *Female* Individual related with sosa(s) : ....
Type of link:..
Born : ....in...
Son/Daughter of : ....and:...
Occupation(s) : ....
Deceased : ....in...............................Cause:.................................
Notes : ....
....
....

👤 Surname : ....First name : ....

☐ *Male* ☐ *Female* Individual related with sosa(s) : ....
Type of link:..
Born : ....in...
Son/Daughter of : ....and:...
Occupation(s) : ....
Deceased : ....in...............................Cause:.................................
Notes : ....
....
....

👤 Surname : ....First name : ....

☐ *Male* ☐ *Female* Individual related with sosa(s) : ....
Type of link:...
Born : ....in...
Son/Daughter of : ....and: ....
Occupation(s) : ....
Deceased : ....in...........................Cause:...............................
Notes : ....
....

👤 Surname : ....First name : ....

☐ *Male* ☐ *Female* Individual related with sosa(s) : ....
Type of link:...
Born : ....in...
Son/Daughter of : ....and: ....
Occupation(s) : ....
Deceased : ....in...........................Cause:...............................
Notes : ....
....

👤 Surname : ....First name : ....

☐ *Male* ☐ *Female* Individual related with sosa(s) : ....
Type of link:...
Born : ....in...
Son/Daughter of : ....and: ....
Occupation(s) : ....
Deceased : ....in...........................Cause:...............................
Notes : ....
....

👤 Surname : ....First name : ....

☐ *Male* ☐ *Female* Individual related with sosa(s) : ....
Type of link:...
Born : ....in...
Son/Daughter of : ....and: ....
Occupation(s) : ....
Deceased : ....in...........................Cause:...............................
Notes : ....
....

👤 Surname : ....First name : ....

☐ *Male* ☐ *Female*   Individual related with sosa(s) : ....
Type of link:..
Born : ....in..
Son/Daughter of : ....and:..
Occupation(s) : ....
Deceased : ....in..Cause:..................................
Notes : ....
....
....

👤 Surname : ....First name : ....

☐ *Male* ☐ *Female*   Individual related with sosa(s) : ....
Type of link:..
Born : ....in..
Son/Daughter of : ....and:..
Occupation(s) : ....
Deceased : ....in..Cause:..................................
Notes : ....
....
....

👤 Surname : ....First name : ....

☐ *Male* ☐ *Female*   Individual related with sosa(s) : ....
Type of link:..
Born : ....in..
Son/Daughter of : ....and:..
Occupation(s) : ....
Deceased : ....in..Cause:..................................
Notes : ....
....
....

👤 Surname : ....First name : ....

☐ *Male* ☐ *Female*   Individual related with sosa(s) : ....
Type of link:..
Born : ....in..
Son/Daughter of : ....and:..
Occupation(s) : ....
Deceased : ....in..Cause:..................................
Notes : ....
....
....

👤   Surname : ....First name : ....

☐ *Male* ☐ *Female*   Individual related with sosa(s) : ....

Type of link:..

Born : ....in...

Son/Daughter of : ....and:.................................

Occupation(s) : ....

Deceased : ....in..Cause:................................

Notes : ....

....

....

👤   Surname : ....First name : ....

☐ *Male* ☐ *Female*   Individual related with sosa(s) : ....

Type of link:..

Born : ....in...

Son/Daughter of : ....and:.................................

Occupation(s) : ....

Deceased : ....in..Cause:................................

Notes : ....

....

....

👤   Surname : ....First name : ....

☐ *Male* ☐ *Female*   Individual related with sosa(s) : ....

Type of link:..

Born : ....in...

Son/Daughter of : ....and:.................................

Occupation(s) : ....

Deceased : ....in..Cause:................................

Notes : ....

....

....

👤   Surname : ....First name : ....

☐ *Male* ☐ *Female*   Individual related with sosa(s) : ....

Type of link:..

Born : ....in...

Son/Daughter of : ....and:.................................

Occupation(s) : ....

Deceased : ....in..Cause:................................

Notes : ....

....

☻ Surname : ....First name : ....

□ *Male* □ *Female*   Individual related with sosa(s) : ....
Type of link:..
Born : ....in...
Son/Daughter of : ....and: ....
Occupation(s) : ....
Deceased : ....in.............................Cause:.............................
Notes : ....
....
....

☻ Surname : ....First name : ....

□ *Male* □ *Female*   Individual related with sosa(s) : ....
Type of link:..
Born : ....in...
Son/Daughter of : ....and: ....
Occupation(s) : ....
Deceased : ....in.............................Cause:.............................
Notes : ....
....
....

☻ Surname : ....First name : ....

□ *Male* □ *Female*   Individual related with sosa(s) : ....
Type of link:..
Born : ....in...
Son/Daughter of : ....and: ....
Occupation(s) : ....
Deceased : ....in.............................Cause:.............................
Notes : ....
....
....

☻ Surname : ....First name : ....

□ *Male* □ *Female*   Individual related with sosa(s) : ....
Type of link:..
Born : ....in...
Son/Daughter of : ....and: ....
Occupation(s) : ....
Deceased : ....in.............................Cause:.............................
Notes : ....
....
....

👤 Surname : ....First name : ....

☐ *Male* ☐ *Female* Individual related with sosa(s) : ....

Type of link:...

Born : ....in...

Son/Daughter of : ....and:...

Occupation(s) : ....

Deceased : ....in..Cause:................................

Notes : ....

....

....

👤 Surname : ....First name : ....

☐ *Male* ☐ *Female* Individual related with sosa(s) : ....

Type of link:...

Born : ....in...

Son/Daughter of : ....and:...

Occupation(s) : ....

Deceased : ....in..Cause:................................

Notes : ....

....

....

👤 Surname : ....First name : ....

☐ *Male* ☐ *Female* Individual related with sosa(s) : ....

Type of link:...

Born : ....in...

Son/Daughter of : ....and:...

Occupation(s) : ....

Deceased : ....in..Cause:................................

Notes : ....

....

....

👤 Surname : ....First name : ....

☐ *Male* ☐ *Female* Individual related with sosa(s) : ....

Type of link:...

Born : ....in...

Son/Daughter of : ....and:...

Occupation(s) : ....

Deceased : ....in..Cause:................................

Notes : ....

....

👤 Surname : ....First name : ....

☐ *Male* ☐ *Female* Individual related with sosa(s) : ....
Type of link:..
Born : ....in...
Son/Daughter of : ....and: ....
Occupation(s) : ....
Deceased : ....in...........................Cause:.................................
Notes : ....
....
....

👤 Surname : ....First name : ....

☐ *Male* ☐ *Female* Individual related with sosa(s) : ....
Type of link:..
Born : ....in...
Son/Daughter of : ....and: ....
Occupation(s) : ....
Deceased : ....in...........................Cause:.................................
Notes : ....
....
....

👤 Surname : ....First name : ....

☐ *Male* ☐ *Female* Individual related with sosa(s) : ....
Type of link:..
Born : ....in...
Son/Daughter of : ....and: ....
Occupation(s) : ....
Deceased : ....in...........................Cause:.................................
Notes : ....
....
....

👤 Surname : ....First name : ....

☐ *Male* ☐ *Female* Individual related with sosa(s) : ....
Type of link:..
Born : ....in...
Son/Daughter of : ....and: ....
Occupation(s) : ....
Deceased : ....in...........................Cause:.................................
Notes : ....
....
....

👤 Surname : ....First name : ....

☐ *Male* ☐ *Female* Individual related with sosa(s) : ....
Type of link:...
Born : ....in...
Son/Daughter of : ....and:...
Occupation(s) : ....
Deceased : ....in...........................Cause:..................................
Notes : ....
....
....

👤 Surname : ....First name : ....

☐ *Male* ☐ *Female* Individual related with sosa(s) : ....
Type of link:...
Born : ....in...
Son/Daughter of : ....and:...
Occupation(s) : ....
Deceased : ....in...........................Cause:..................................
Notes : ....
....
....

👤 Surname : ....First name : ....

☐ *Male* ☐ *Female* Individual related with sosa(s) : ....
Type of link:...
Born : ....in...
Son/Daughter of : ....and:...
Occupation(s) : ....
Deceased : ....in...........................Cause:..................................
Notes : ....
....
....

👤 Surname : ....First name : ....

☐ *Male* ☐ *Female* Individual related with sosa(s) : ....
Type of link:...
Born : ....in...
Son/Daughter of : ....and:...
Occupation(s) : ....
Deceased : ....in...........................Cause:..................................
Notes : ....
....
....

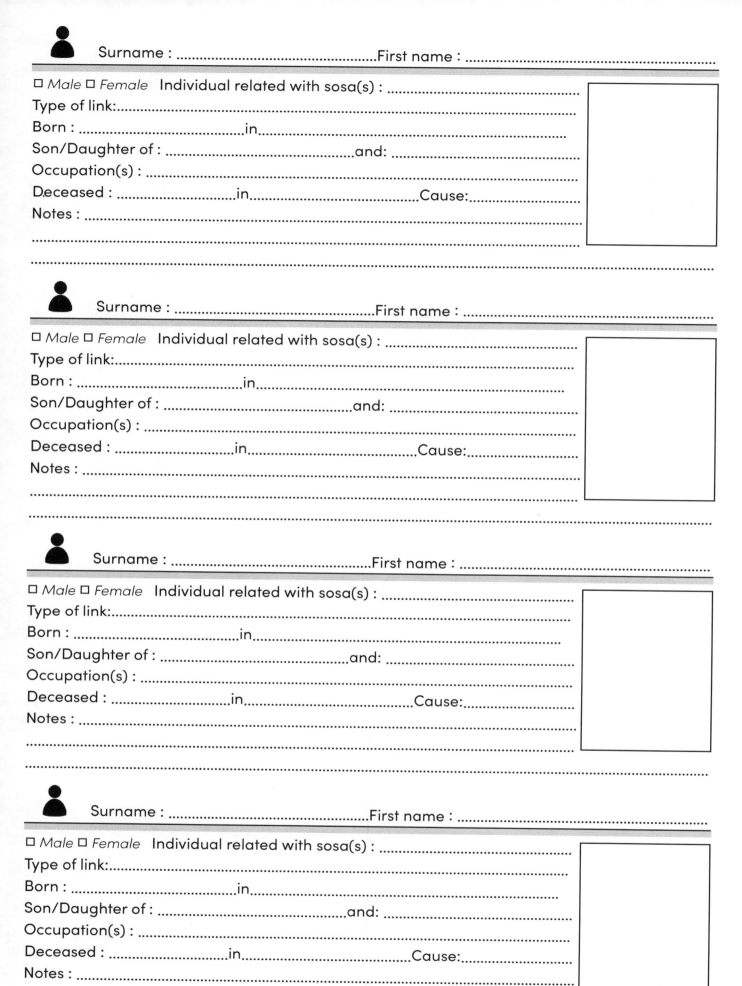

👤 Surname : ....First name : ....

☐ *Male* ☐ *Female* Individual related with sosa(s) : ....
Type of link:..
Born : ....in...
Son/Daughter of : ....and: ....
Occupation(s) : ....
Deceased : ....in.............................Cause:.........................
Notes : ....
....
....

👤 Surname : ....First name : ....

☐ *Male* ☐ *Female* Individual related with sosa(s) : ....
Type of link:..
Born : ....in...
Son/Daughter of : ....and: ....
Occupation(s) : ....
Deceased : ....in.............................Cause:.........................
Notes : ....
....
....

👤 Surname : ....First name : ....

☐ *Male* ☐ *Female* Individual related with sosa(s) : ....
Type of link:..
Born : ....in...
Son/Daughter of : ....and: ....
Occupation(s) : ....
Deceased : ....in.............................Cause:.........................
Notes : ....
....
....

👤 Surname : ....First name : ....

☐ *Male* ☐ *Female* Individual related with sosa(s) : ....
Type of link:..
Born : ....in...
Son/Daughter of : ....and: ....
Occupation(s) : ....
Deceased : ....in.............................Cause:.........................
Notes : ....
....
....

Surname : .... **First name :** ....

□ *Male* □ *Female*   Individual related with sosa(s) : ....
Type of link:..
Born : ....in..
Son/Daughter of : ....and: ....
Occupation(s) : ....
Deceased : ....in..Cause:..
Notes : ....
....
....

Surname : .... **First name :** ....

□ *Male* □ *Female*   Individual related with sosa(s) : ....
Type of link:..
Born : ....in..
Son/Daughter of : ....and: ....
Occupation(s) : ....
Deceased : ....in..Cause:..
Notes : ....
....
....

Surname : .... **First name :** ....

□ *Male* □ *Female*   Individual related with sosa(s) : ....
Type of link:..
Born : ....in..
Son/Daughter of : ....and: ....
Occupation(s) : ....
Deceased : ....in..Cause:..
Notes : ....
....
....

Surname : .... **First name :** ....

□ *Male* □ *Female*   Individual related with sosa(s) : ....
Type of link:..
Born : ....in..
Son/Daughter of : ....and: ....
Occupation(s) : ....
Deceased : ....in..Cause:..
Notes : ....
....

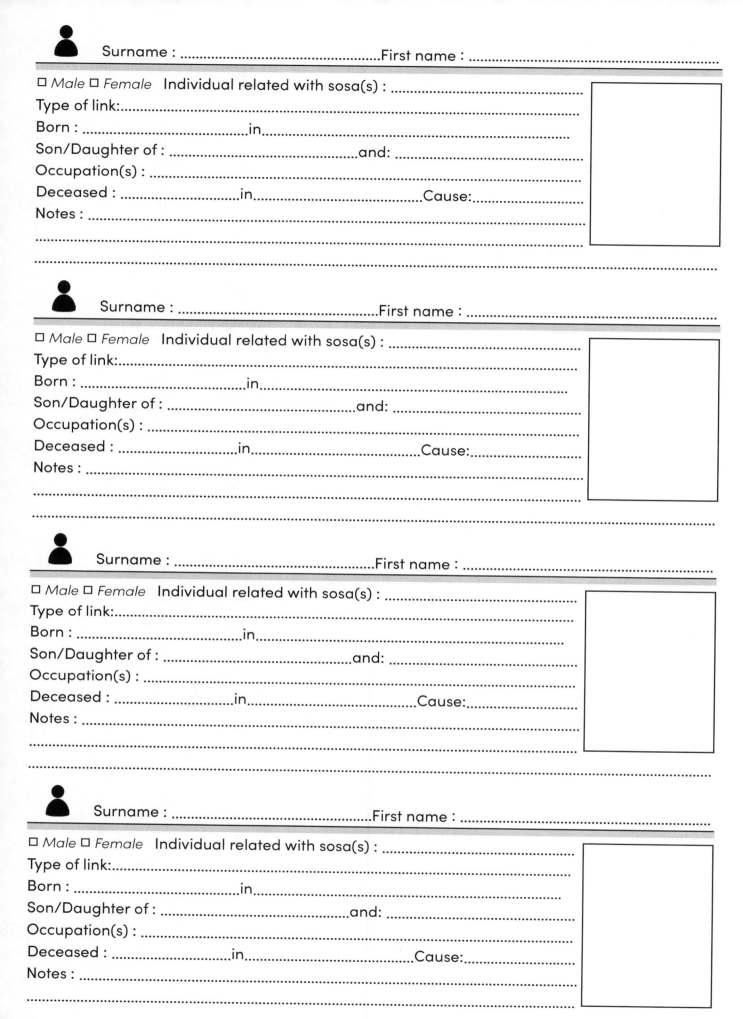

Surname : ....First name : ....

☐ *Male* ☐ *Female*   Individual related with sosa(s) : ....
Type of link:...
Born : ....in...
Son/Daughter of : ....and: ....
Occupation(s) : ....
Deceased : ....in.................................Cause:..................................
Notes : ....
....
....

Surname : ....First name : ....

☐ *Male* ☐ *Female*   Individual related with sosa(s) : ....
Type of link:...
Born : ....in...
Son/Daughter of : ....and: ....
Occupation(s) : ....
Deceased : ....in.................................Cause:..................................
Notes : ....
....
....

Surname : ....First name : ....

☐ *Male* ☐ *Female*   Individual related with sosa(s) : ....
Type of link:...
Born : ....in...
Son/Daughter of : ....and: ....
Occupation(s) : ....
Deceased : ....in.................................Cause:..................................
Notes : ....
....
....

Surname : ....First name : ....

☐ *Male* ☐ *Female*   Individual related with sosa(s) : ....
Type of link:...
Born : ....in...
Son/Daughter of : ....and: ....
Occupation(s) : ....
Deceased : ....in.................................Cause:..................................
Notes : ....
....
....

Surname : .... **First name :** ....

☐ *Male* ☐ *Female* Individual related with sosa(s) : ....
Type of link: ....
Born : ....in..
Son/Daughter of : ....and: ....
Occupation(s) : ....
Deceased : ....in....................................Cause: ....
Notes : ....
....

Surname : .... **First name :** ....

☐ *Male* ☐ *Female* Individual related with sosa(s) : ....
Type of link: ....
Born : ....in..
Son/Daughter of : ....and: ....
Occupation(s) : ....
Deceased : ....in....................................Cause: ....
Notes : ....
....

Surname : .... **First name :** ....

☐ *Male* ☐ *Female* Individual related with sosa(s) : ....
Type of link: ....
Born : ....in..
Son/Daughter of : ....and: ....
Occupation(s) : ....
Deceased : ....in....................................Cause: ....
Notes : ....
....

Surname : .... **First name :** ....

☐ *Male* ☐ *Female* Individual related with sosa(s) : ....
Type of link: ....
Born : ....in..
Son/Daughter of : ....and: ....
Occupation(s) : ....
Deceased : ....in....................................Cause: ....
Notes : ....
....

Surname : ....**First name :** ....

☐ *Male* ☐ *Female*   Individual related with sosa(s) : ....
Type of link:...
Born : ....in...
Son/Daughter of : ....and:...
Occupation(s) : ....
Deceased : ....in...Cause:.............................
Notes : ....
....
....

Surname : ....**First name :** ....

☐ *Male* ☐ *Female*   Individual related with sosa(s) : ....
Type of link:...
Born : ....in...
Son/Daughter of : ....and:...
Occupation(s) : ....
Deceased : ....in...Cause:.............................
Notes : ....
....
....

Surname : ....**First name :** ....

☐ *Male* ☐ *Female*   Individual related with sosa(s) : ....
Type of link:...
Born : ....in...
Son/Daughter of : ....and:...
Occupation(s) : ....
Deceased : ....in...Cause:.............................
Notes : ....
....
....

Surname : ....**First name :** ....

☐ *Male* ☐ *Female*   Individual related with sosa(s) : ....
Type of link:...
Born : ....in...
Son/Daughter of : ....and:...
Occupation(s) : ....
Deceased : ....in...Cause:.............................
Notes : ....
....
....

Surname : ....**First name :** ....

□ *Male* □ *Female* Individual related with sosa(s) : ....

Type of link:..

Born : ....in...

Son/Daughter of : ....and: ....

Occupation(s) : ....

Deceased : ....in.............................Cause:..................................

Notes : ....

....

....

Surname : ....**First name :** ....

□ *Male* □ *Female* Individual related with sosa(s) : ....

Type of link:..

Born : ....in...

Son/Daughter of : ....and: ....

Occupation(s) : ....

Deceased : ....in.............................Cause:..................................

Notes : ....

....

....

Surname : ....**First name :** ....

□ *Male* □ *Female* Individual related with sosa(s) : ....

Type of link:..

Born : ....in...

Son/Daughter of : ....and: ....

Occupation(s) : ....

Deceased : ....in.............................Cause:..................................

Notes : ....

....

....

Surname : ....**First name :** ....

□ *Male* □ *Female* Individual related with sosa(s) : ....

Type of link:..

Born : ....in...

Son/Daughter of : ....and: ....

Occupation(s) : ....

Deceased : ....in.............................Cause:..................................

Notes : ....

....

....

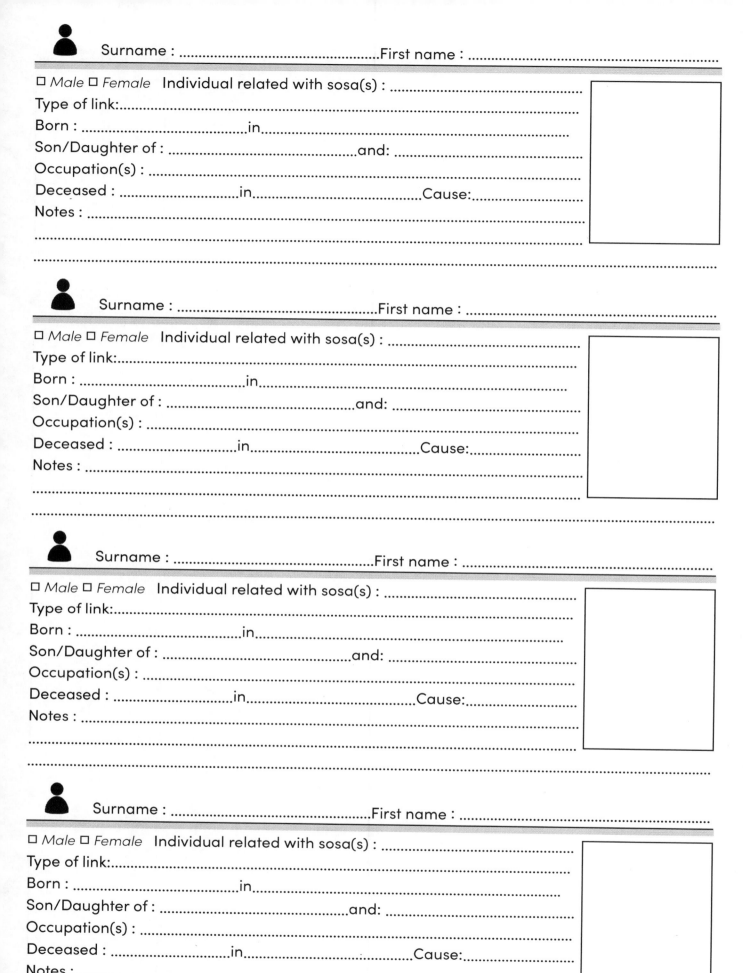

Surname : ....First name : ....

□ *Male* □ *Female*　Individual related with sosa(s) : ....
Type of link:..
Born : ....in...
Son/Daughter of : ....and: ....
Occupation(s) : ....
Deceased : ....in....................................Cause:..............................
Notes : ....
....
....

Surname : ....First name : ....

□ *Male* □ *Female*　Individual related with sosa(s) : ....
Type of link:..
Born : ....in...
Son/Daughter of : ....and: ....
Occupation(s) : ....
Deceased : ....in....................................Cause:..............................
Notes : ....
....
....

Surname : ....First name : ....

□ *Male* □ *Female*　Individual related with sosa(s) : ....
Type of link:..
Born : ....in...
Son/Daughter of : ....and: ....
Occupation(s) : ....
Deceased : ....in....................................Cause:..............................
Notes : ....
....
....

Surname : ....First name : ....

□ *Male* □ *Female*　Individual related with sosa(s) : ....
Type of link:..
Born : ....in...
Son/Daughter of : ....and: ....
Occupation(s) : ....
Deceased : ....in....................................Cause:..............................
Notes : ....
....

👤 Surname : ....First name : ....

☐ *Male* ☐ *Female* Individual related with sosa(s) : ....
Type of link:...
Born : ....in...
Son/Daughter of : ....and: ....
Occupation(s) : ....
Deceased : ....in...Cause: ....
Notes : ....
....
....

👤 Surname : ....First name : ....

☐ *Male* ☐ *Female* Individual related with sosa(s) : ....
Type of link:...
Born : ....in...
Son/Daughter of : ....and: ....
Occupation(s) : ....
Deceased : ....in...Cause: ....
Notes : ....
....
....

👤 Surname : ....First name : ....

☐ *Male* ☐ *Female* Individual related with sosa(s) : ....
Type of link:...
Born : ....in...
Son/Daughter of : ....and: ....
Occupation(s) : ....
Deceased : ....in...Cause: ....
Notes : ....
....
....

👤 Surname : ....First name : ....

☐ *Male* ☐ *Female* Individual related with sosa(s) : ....
Type of link:...
Born : ....in...
Son/Daughter of : ....and: ....
Occupation(s) : ....
Deceased : ....in...Cause: ....
Notes : ....
....
....

Migrations in USA

N°	Surnames	Years	Origins	Arrivals

N°	Surnames	Years	Origins	Arrivals
N°	Surnames	Years	Origins	Arrivals

Migrations in USA

N°	Surnames	Years	Origins	Arrivals

N°	Surnames	Years	Origins	Arrivals
N°	Surnames	Years	Origins	Arrivals

Migrations in USA

N°	Surnames	Years	Origins	Arrivals

N°	Surnames	Years	Origins	Arrivals
N°	Surnames	Years	Origins	Arrivals

Migrations in USA

N°	Surnames	Years	Origins	Arrivals

N°	Surnames	Years	Origins	Arrivals
N°	Surnames	Years	Origins	Arrivals

Migrations in Canada

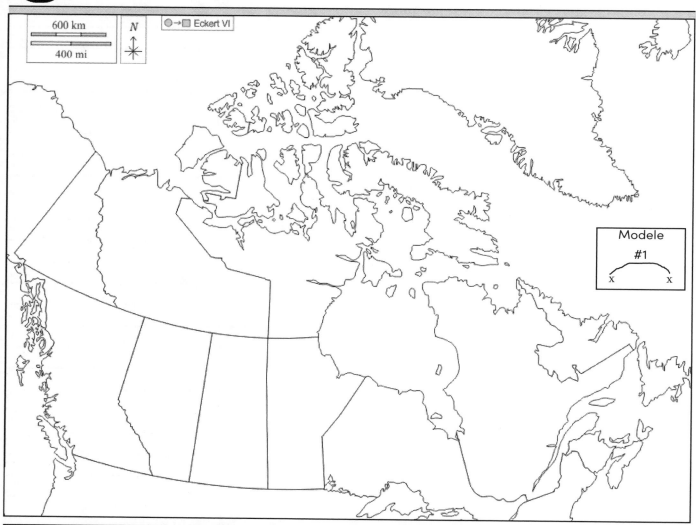

N°	Surnames	Years	Origins	Arrivals

N°	Surnames	Years	Origins	Arrivals
N°	Surnames	Years	Origins	Arrivals

Migrations in Canada

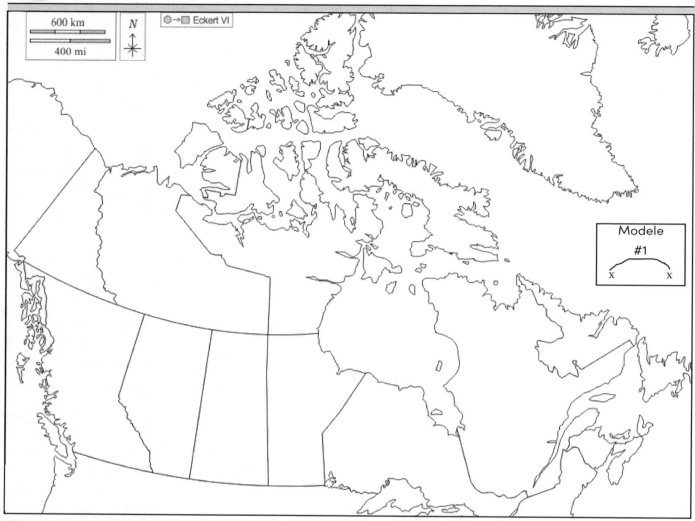

N°	Surnames	Years	Origins	Arrivals

N°	Surnames	Years	Origins	Arrivals
N°	Surnames	Years	Origins	Arrivals

Migrations in Canada

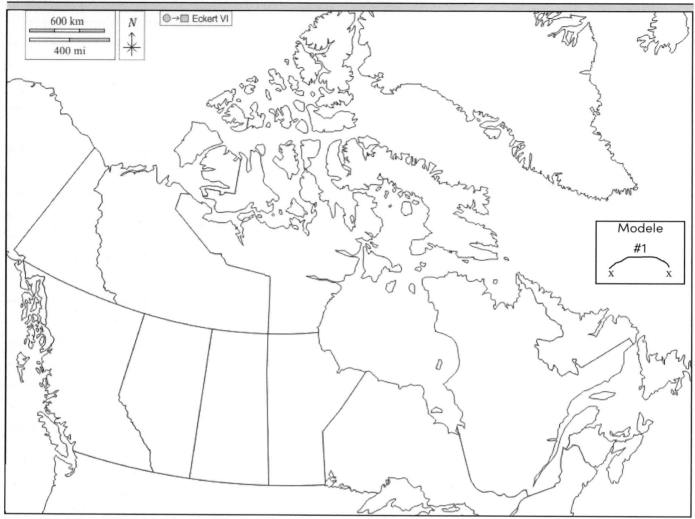

N°	Surnames	Years	Origins	Arrivals

N°	Surnames	Years	Origins	Arrivals
N°	Surnames	Years	Origins	Arrivals

Migrations in Canada

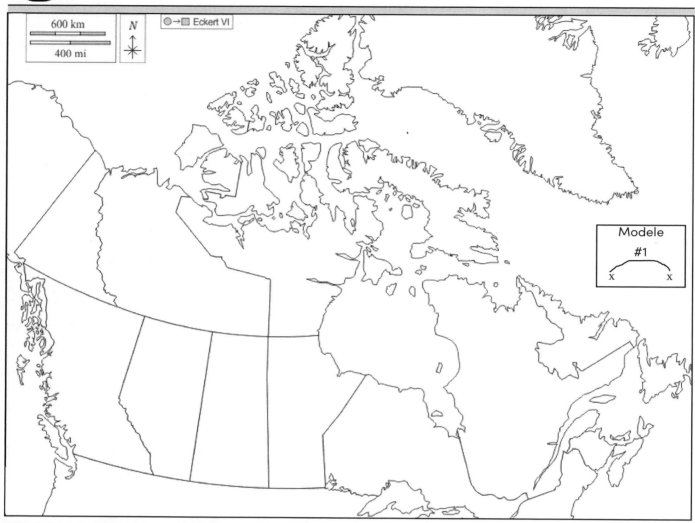

N°	Surnames	Years	Origins	Arrivals

N°	Surnames	Years	Origins	Arrivals
N°	Surnames	Years	Origins	Arrivals

Migrations in North America

Modele
#1

1000 km
600 mi

N

⊙→▨ Eckert VI modified

N°	Surnames	Years	Origins	Arrivals

630

N°	Surnames	Years	Origins	Arrivals
N°	Surnames	Years	Origins	Arrivals

Modele
#1
X   X

1000 km

600 mi

N

⊙→▦ Eckert VI modified

N°	Surnames	Years	Origins	Arrivals

N°	Surnames	Years	Origins	Arrivals
N°	Surnames	Years	Origins	Arrivals

Migrations in South America

Modele

#1

x   x

1000 km

600 mi

Eckert VI modified

N

N°	Surnames	Years	Origins	Arrivals

N°	Surnames	Years	Origins	Arrivals
N°	Surnames	Years	Origins	Arrivals

Migrations in United Kingdom

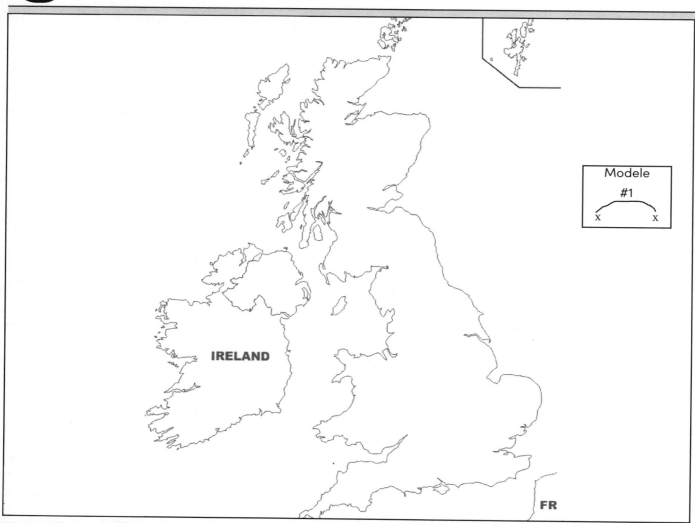

N°	Surnames	Years	Origins	Arrivals

N°	Surnames	Years	Origins	Arrivals
N°	Surnames	Years	Origins	Arrivals

Migrations in United Kingdom

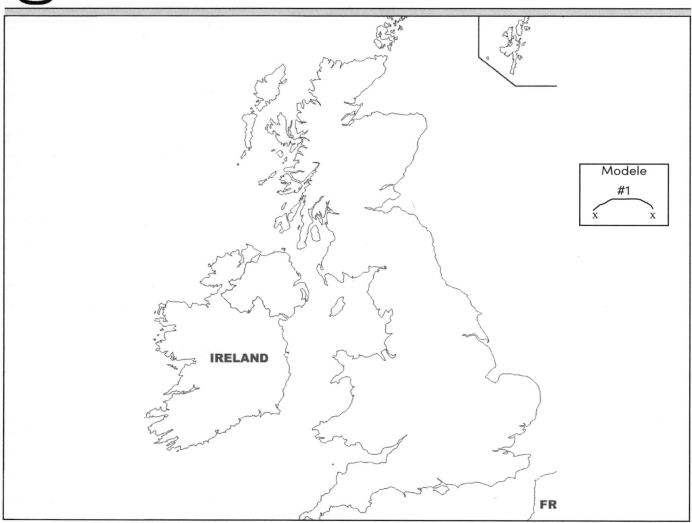

N°	Surnames	Years	Origins	Arrivals

N°	Surnames	Years	Origins	Arrivals
N°	Surnames	Years	Origins	Arrivals

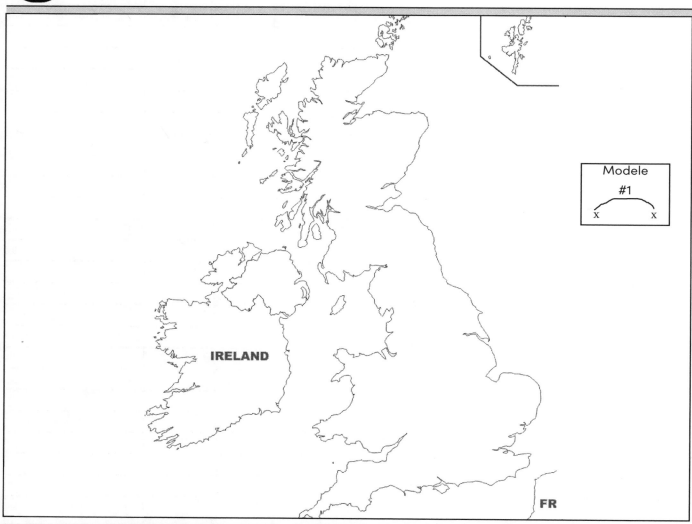

Modele
#1
x   x

IRELAND

FR

N°	Surnames	Years	Origins	Arrivals

N°	Surnames	Years	Origins	Arrivals
N°	Surnames	Years	Origins	Arrivals

Migrations in United Kingdom

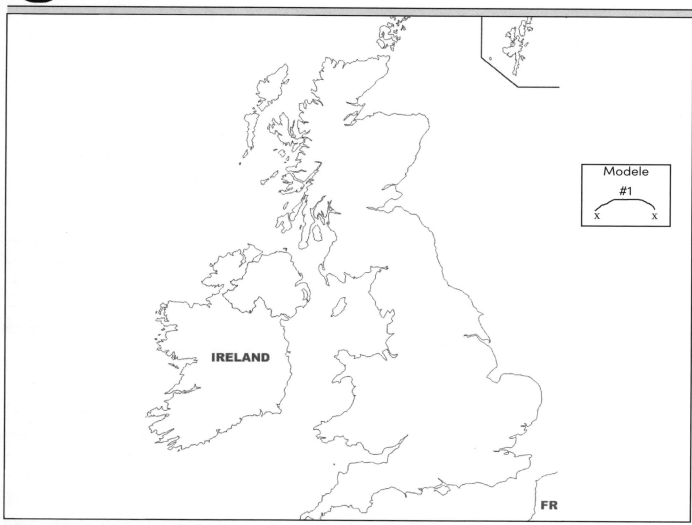

N°	Surnames	Years	Origins	Arrivals

N°	Surnames	Years	Origins	Arrivals
N°	Surnames	Years	Origins	Arrivals

Migrations in Scotland

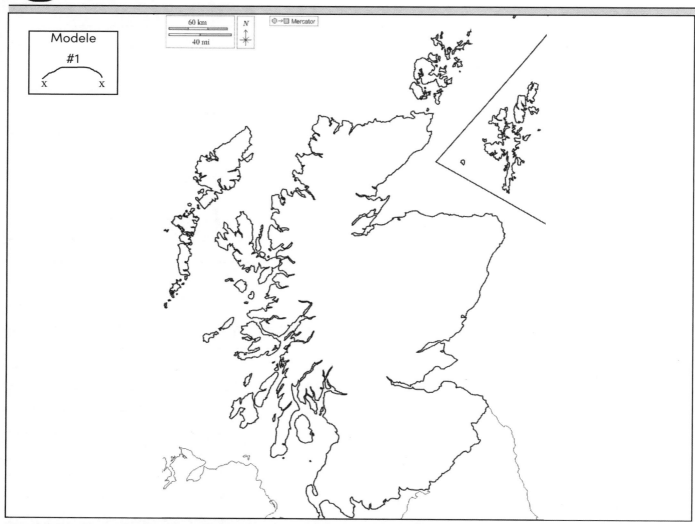

N°	Surnames	Years	Origins	Arrivals

N°	Surnames	Years	Origins	Arrivals
N°	Surnames	Years	Origins	Arrivals

Migrations in Scotland

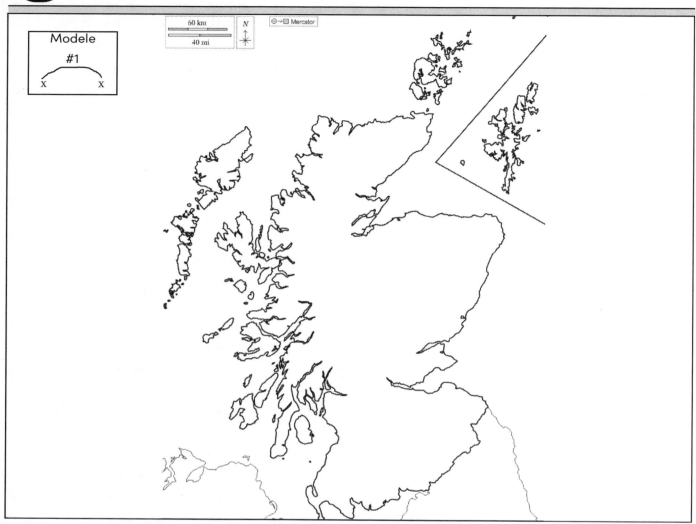

N°	Surnames	Years	Origins	Arrivals

N°	Surnames	Years	Origins	Arrivals
	Surnames	Years	Origins	Arrivals

Migrations in Northern Ireland

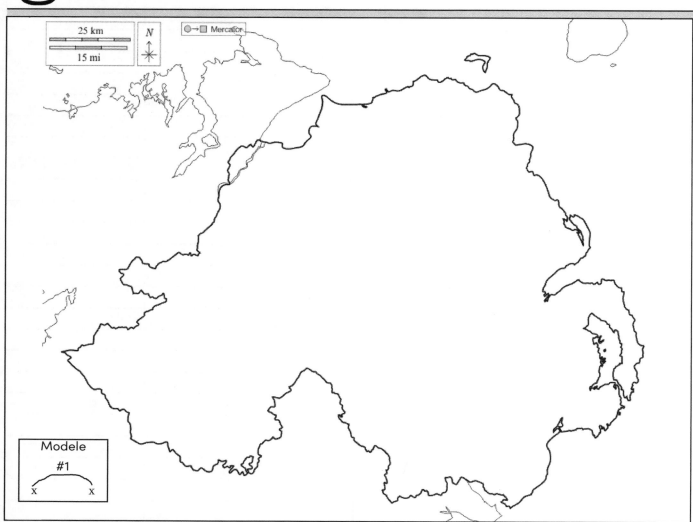

N°	Surnames	Years	Origins	Arrivals

N°	Surnames	Years	Origins	Arrivals
N°	Surnames	Years	Origins	Arrivals

Migrations in Northern Ireland

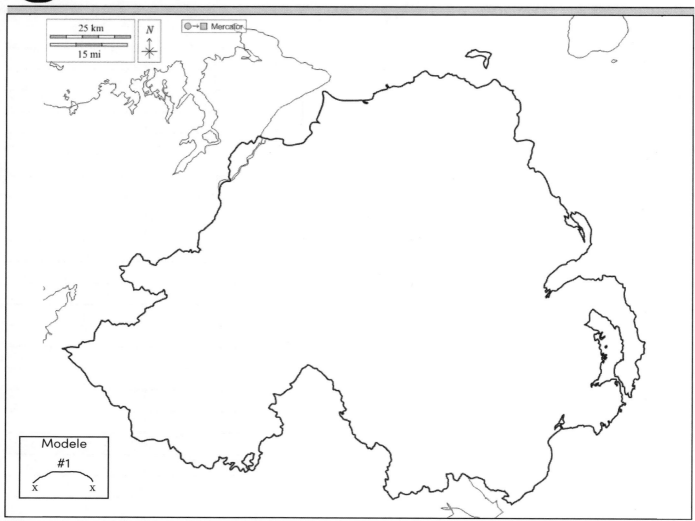

N°	Surnames	Years	Origins	Arrivals

N°	Surnames	Years	Origins	Arrivals
N°	Surnames	Years	Origins	Arrivals

Migrations in Europa

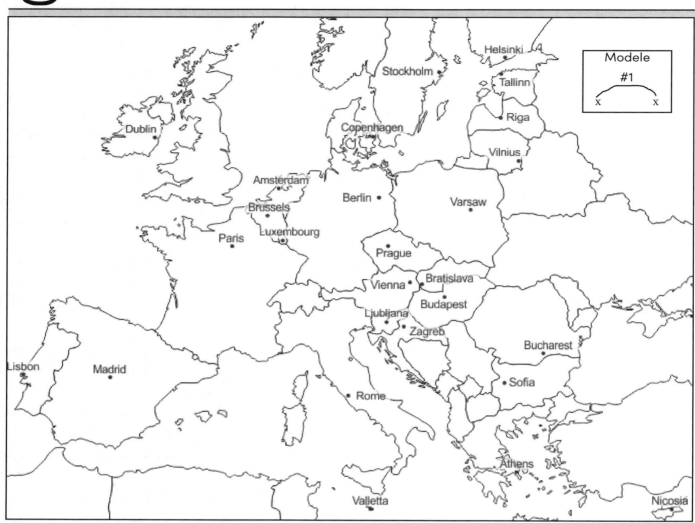

N°	Surnames	Years	Origins	Arrivals

N°	Surnames	Years	Origins	Arrivals
N°	Surnames	Years	Origins	Arrivals

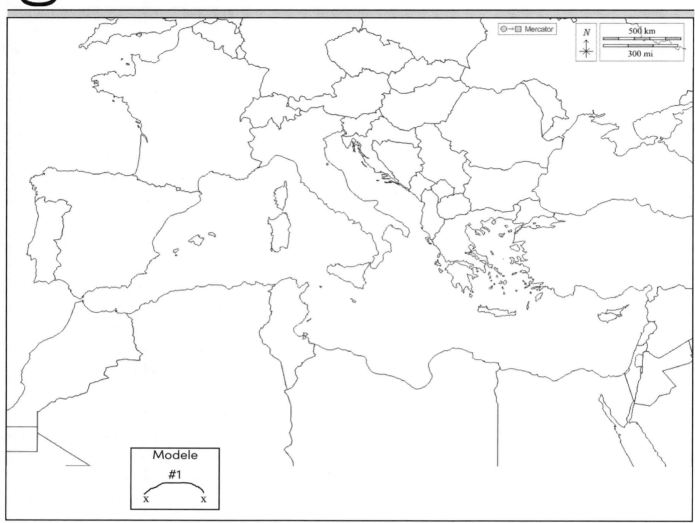

Modele
#1
x   x

N°	Surnames	Years	Origins	Arrivals

N°	Surnames	Years	Origins	Arrivals
N°	Surnames	Years	Origins	Arrivals

Migrations in Africa

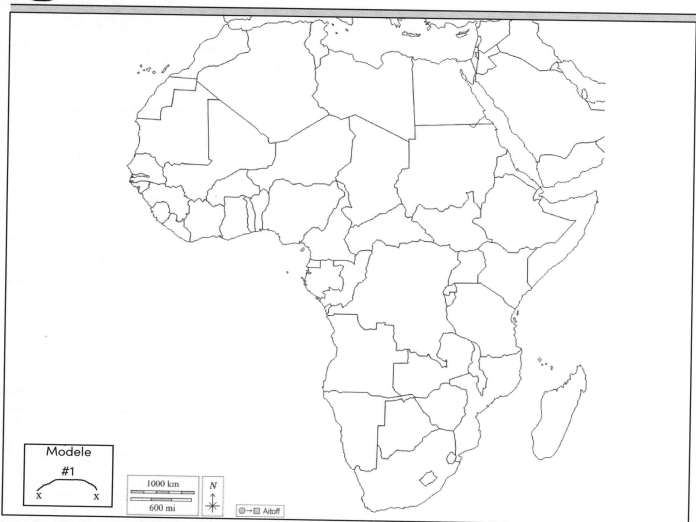

Modele
#1

1000 km
600 mi

N

⊙→▢ Aitoff

N°	Surnames	Years	Origins	Arrivals

N°	Surnames	Years	Origins	Arrivals
N°	Surnames	Years	Origins	Arrivals

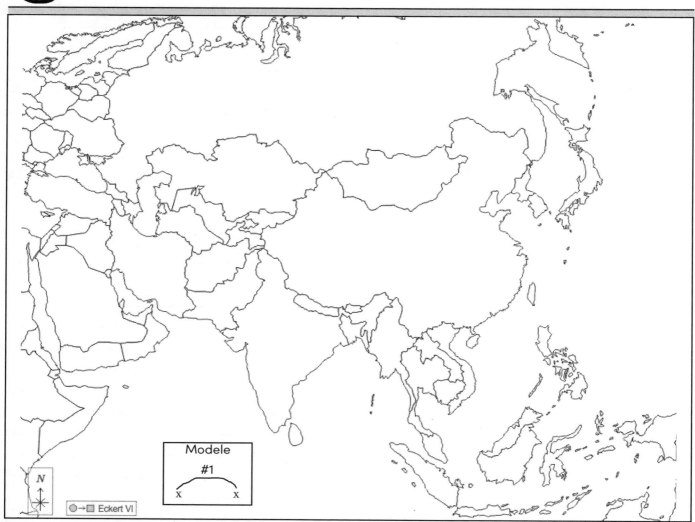

Modele
#1
x   x

N

●→☐ Eckert VI

N°	Surnames	Years	Origins	Arrivals

N°	Surnames	Years	Origins	Arrivals
N°	Surnames	Years	Origins	Arrivals

Migrations in Oceania

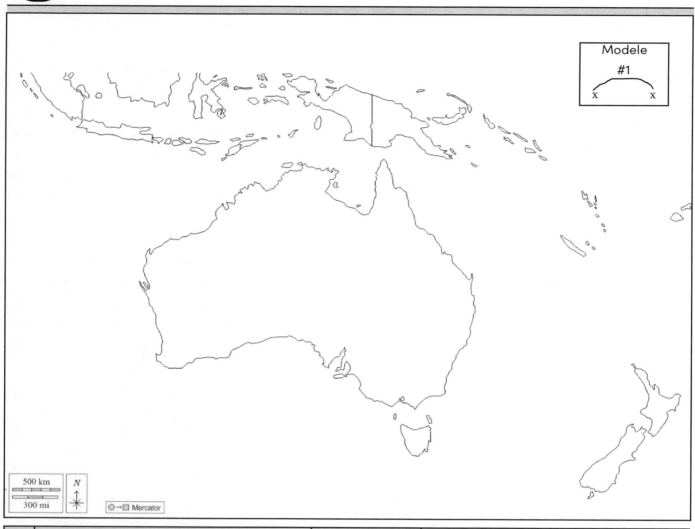

Modele #1
x   x

500 km
300 mi

N

◎→▣ Mercator

N°	Surnames	Years	Origins	Arrivals

N°	Surnames	Years	Origins	Arrivals
N°	Surnames	Years	Origins	Arrivals

Migrations in Australia

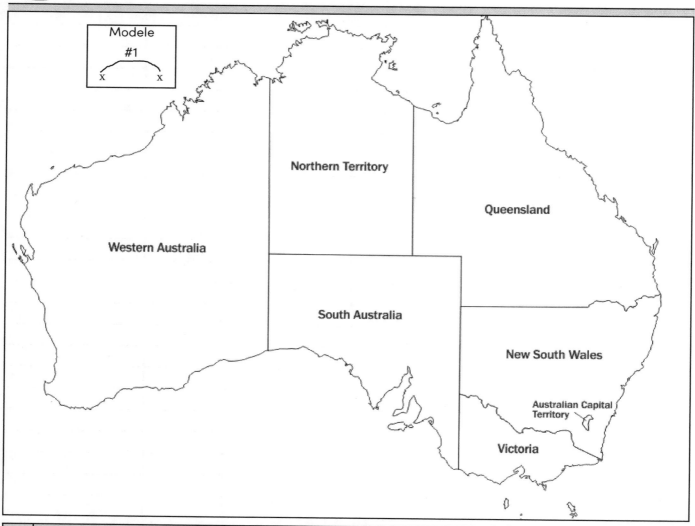

N°	Surnames	Years	Origins	Arrivals

N°	Surnames	Years	Origins	Arrivals
N°	Surnames	Years	Origins	Arrivals

Migrations in Tasmania

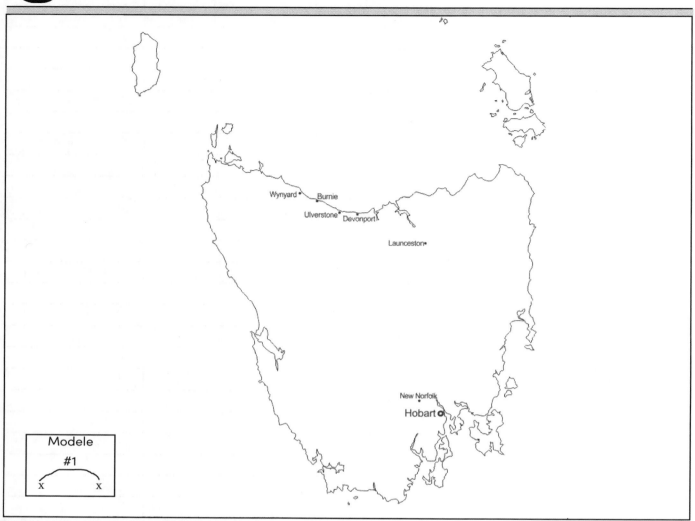

N°	Surnames	Years	Origins	Arrivals

N°	Surnames	Years	Origins	Arrivals
N°	Surnames	Years	Origins	Arrivals

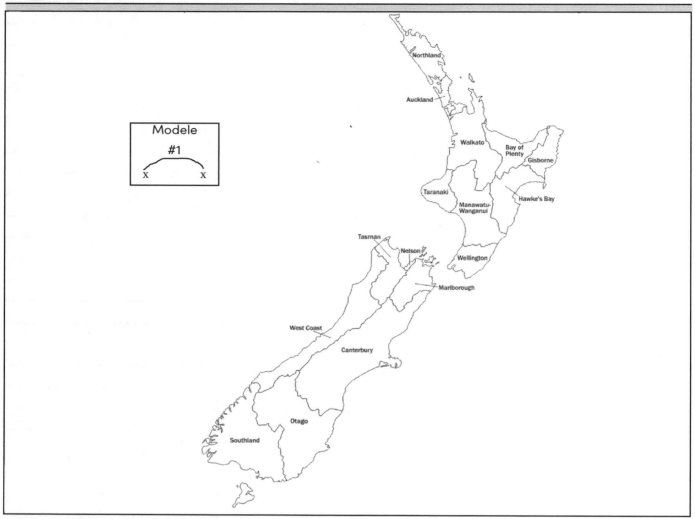

Modele
#1
X   X

N°	Surnames	Years	Origins	Arrivals

N°	Surnames	Years	Origins	Arrivals
N°	Surnames	Years	Origins	Arrivals

🕐 Time lines

Title: ....Years : ....

....
....
....

```
┌─────────────────────────────────────────────────────────────┐
│                                                               │
└─────────────────────────────────────────────────────────────┘
```

....
....
....

Title: ....Years : ....

....
....
....

```
┌─────────────────────────────────────────────────────────────┐
│                                                               │
└─────────────────────────────────────────────────────────────┘
```

....
....
....

Title: ....Years : ....

....
....
....

```
┌─────────────────────────────────────────────────────────────┐
│                                                               │
└─────────────────────────────────────────────────────────────┘
```

....
....
....

Title: ....Years : ....

....
....
....

```
┌─────────────────────────────────────────────────────────────┐
│                                                               │
└─────────────────────────────────────────────────────────────┘
```

....
....
....

Time lines

Title: ....Years : ....
....
....
....

....
....
....

Title: ....Years : ....
....
....
....

....
....
....

Title: ....Years : ....
....
....
....

....
....
....

Title: ....Years : ....
....
....
....

....
....
....

Title: ....Years : ....
....
....
....

....
....
....

Title: ....Years : ....
....
....
....

....
....
....

Title: ....Years : ....
....
....
....

....
....
....

Title: ....Years : ....
....
....
....

....
....
....

Title: ....Years : ....

....
....
....

```
|__|__|__|__|__|__|__|__|__|__|__|__|__|__|__|__|__|__|__|__|__|__|__|__|__|__|__|__|__|__|
```

....
....
....

Title: ....Years : ....

....
....
....

```
|__|__|__|__|__|__|__|__|__|__|__|__|__|__|__|__|__|__|__|__|__|__|__|__|__|__|__|__|__|__|
```

....
....
....

Title: ....Years : ....

....
....
....

```
|__|__|__|__|__|__|__|__|__|__|__|__|__|__|__|__|__|__|__|__|__|__|__|__|__|__|__|__|__|__|
```

....
....
....

Title: ....Years : ....

....
....
....

```
|__|__|__|__|__|__|__|__|__|__|__|__|__|__|__|__|__|__|__|__|__|__|__|__|__|__|__|__|__|__|
```

....
....
....

⏰ Time lines

Title: ....Years : ....
....
....
....

....
....
....

Title: ....Years : ....
....
....
....

....
....
....

Title: ....Years : ....
....
....
....

....
....
....

Title: ....Years : ....
....
....
....

....
....
....

⏰ Time lines

Title: ....Years : ....
....
....
....

....
....
....

Title: ....Years : ....
....
....
....

....
....
....

Title: ....Years : ....
....
....
....

....
....
....

Title: ....Years : ....
....
....
....

....
....
....

🕐 Time lines

Title: ....Years : ....
....
....
....

```
┌────────────────────────────────────────────────────────────────┐
│                                                                  │
└────────────────────────────────────────────────────────────────┘
```

....
....
....

Title: ....Years : ....
....
....
....

```
┌────────────────────────────────────────────────────────────────┐
│                                                                  │
└────────────────────────────────────────────────────────────────┘
```

....
....
....

Title: ....Years : ....
....
....
....

```
┌────────────────────────────────────────────────────────────────┐
│                                                                  │
└────────────────────────────────────────────────────────────────┘
```

....
....
....

Title: ....Years : ....
....
....
....

```
┌────────────────────────────────────────────────────────────────┐
│                                                                  │
└────────────────────────────────────────────────────────────────┘
```

....
....
....

⏰ Time lines

Title: .... Years : ....

....
....
....

....
....
....

Title: .... Years : ....

....
....
....

....
....
....

Title: .... Years : ....

....
....
....

....
....
....

Title: .... Years : ....

....
....
....

....
....
....

🕐 Time lines

Title: .... Years : ....

....
....
....

```
┌─────────────────────────────────────────────────────────────────────┐
│ ┬ ┬ ┬ ┬ ┬ ┬ ┬ ┬ ┬ ┬ ┬ ┬ ┬ ┬ ┬ ┬ ┬ ┬ ┬ ┬ ┬ ┬ ┬ ┬ ┬ ┬ ┬ ┬ ┬ ┬ ┬ ┬ ┬ │
└─────────────────────────────────────────────────────────────────────┘
```

....
....
....

Title: .... Years : ....

....
....
....

```
┌─────────────────────────────────────────────────────────────────────┐
│ ┬ ┬ ┬ ┬ ┬ ┬ ┬ ┬ ┬ ┬ ┬ ┬ ┬ ┬ ┬ ┬ ┬ ┬ ┬ ┬ ┬ ┬ ┬ ┬ ┬ ┬ ┬ ┬ ┬ ┬ ┬ ┬ ┬ │
└─────────────────────────────────────────────────────────────────────┘
```

....
....
....

Title: .... Years : ....

....
....
....

```
┌─────────────────────────────────────────────────────────────────────┐
│ ┬ ┬ ┬ ┬ ┬ ┬ ┬ ┬ ┬ ┬ ┬ ┬ ┬ ┬ ┬ ┬ ┬ ┬ ┬ ┬ ┬ ┬ ┬ ┬ ┬ ┬ ┬ ┬ ┬ ┬ ┬ ┬ ┬ │
└─────────────────────────────────────────────────────────────────────┘
```

....
....
....

Title: .... Years : ....

....
....
....

```
┌─────────────────────────────────────────────────────────────────────┐
│ ┬ ┬ ┬ ┬ ┬ ┬ ┬ ┬ ┬ ┬ ┬ ┬ ┬ ┬ ┬ ┬ ┬ ┬ ┬ ┬ ┬ ┬ ┬ ┬ ┬ ┬ ┬ ┬ ┬ ┬ ┬ ┬ ┬ │
└─────────────────────────────────────────────────────────────────────┘
```

....
....
....

⏰ Time lines

Title: ....Years : ....
....
....
....

....
....
....

Title: ....Years : ....
....
....
....

....
....
....

Title: ....Years : ....
....
....
....

....
....
....

Title: ....Years : ....
....
....
....

....
....
....

677

 Sources

N°	Source name	Url/Contact	Comments
		678	
N°	Source name	Url/Contact	Comments

📄 Sources

N°	Source name	Url/Contact	Comments
		679	
N°	Source name	Url/Contact	Comments

 Sources

N°	Source name	Url/Contact	Comments
		680	
N°	Source name	Url/Contact	Comments

 Sources

N°	Source name	Url/Contact	Comments
N°	Source name	Url/Contact	Comments

 Sources

N°	Source name	Url/Contact	Comments
		682	
N°	Source name	Url/Contact	Comments

Sources

N°	Source name	Url/Contact	Comments
N°		Url/Contact	Comments

Sources

N°	Source name	Url/Contact	Comments
		684	
	N°	Source name	Url/Contact	Comments

 Sources

N°	Source name	Url/Contact	Comments
N°	Source name	Url/Contact	Comments

 Notes

 Notes

Notes

Notes

Notes

692

Notes

Notes

Notes

Notes

Notes

 Notes

Notes

Notes

Notes

 Notes

Notes

 Notes

Notes

Notes

Notes

Notes

Made in the USA
Monee, IL
05 December 2024